THE RELIGIONS OF TIBET

Tibetology has progressed from Tucci's days, and Tibet has also undergone a deep cultural transformation. This book is actually a university text written by one of the foremost Tibetologists of all times.

Giuseppe Tucci

THE RELIGIONS OF TIBET

Translated from the German and Italian by
GEOFFREY SAMUEL

New Age Books

The Religions of Tibet

ISBN: 978-81-7822-360-5

First Indian Edition: 2011

First Published as *Die Religionen Tibets* in *Die Religionen Tibets und der Mongolei* by Giuseppe Tucci and Walther Heissig

This translation first published in 1980 by
Routledge & Kegan Paul Ltd.
London, Boston and Henley

Published by
NEW AGE BOOKS
A-44 Naraina Industrial Area, Phase-I
New Delhi (India)-110 028
Email: nab@vsnl.in
Website: www.newagebooksindia.com

Printed in India
at Shri Jainendra Press
A-45 Naraina Indl. Area, Phase-I, New Delhi-110 028

CONTENTS

PREFACE

At the beginning of 1958, when Dr C. M. Schröder asked me to write the volume on Tibetan religion for the collection edited by him, 'Die Religionen der Menschheit', which in its totality constitutes a remarkable body of material on the history of religion, I hesitated before I accepted. The writing of a book on the subject of Tibetan religion is not a task to be taken on light-heartedly. The main reason for this is that we still know little about Tibetan religion in comparison with other religions; the vast literature which it has produced, and which illuminates its history, is still far from having been made fully accessible or edited, and is in any case so enormous that a single human life is not enough to master it. In addition there is a deep division between monastic Lamaism and religion as it is lived by the people; the former, too, is fragmented into many schools, while the latter shows numerous variations from place to place.

While I was writing it became progressively clearer to me that an account of Lamaism presupposed a presentation of its theoretical foundations; for these, as always in Buddhism, condition the actual religious experience, and give the individual schools their particular character. This however makes it necessary to refer continually to the theory of Indian Buddhism. On the other hand my task was precisely to uncover and ascertain what in Tibetan Buddhism had been created in the meeting between old forms of religious experience and new ideas and motives that was new and individual. A further difficulty, perhaps the greatest of all, has still to be mentioned; no agreement has yet been reached on the precise translation of the religious terminology, of the technical terms, that is, which are used in Tibetan religion and gnosis. One wavers between the two extremes of a comparatively literal rendition, as has mostly been used for Indian Buddhism (although there too there has been a similar lack of unanimity), and the recent fashion of adopting the vocabulary of the more modern philosophical schools of the West as a terminological basis for this area, which is so different in its nature. This latter procedure is certainly the more dangerous of the two, for it misrepresents or even falsifies Tibetan modes of thought. I became convinced of this when I showed Tibetans who knew English well certain translations which had recently appeared of particular works or of commentaries on the doctrines they contained. The Tibetan scholars found it difficult to make any sense of these translations, since Buddhist thought was expressed in them in a mode other than that in which they were used to understanding it. Besides this, many Tibetan concepts and doctrines refer to interior and mystical experiences, and their transposition into rational concepts and expressions is extremely problematic. The corresponding Tibetan words are symbols, which can evoke living experiences which the word as such can only suggest but not define. We are faced here with an extremely difficult, almost impossible task: to coin equivalent technical terms for experiences which take place within the spiritual realm, and which can radically modify our psychic and spiritual reality. I have tried to translate Tibetan expressions in such a way as to avoid both of the extremes mentioned above, those of over-literalness and of arbitrariness, and have struggled throughout to render the Tibetan *termini technici* with words of meaning close to that which the Tibetan masters appear to give to them. I am not sure that I have always succeeded, but I believe that I have done my best to make accessible to Western readers the complex speculative structure which constitutes the foundation of Tibetan religion. At the same time I recognize that in this field there are real limiting cases. To give an example: the word *sems*, a pillar of the Lamaist doctrinal edifice, is sometimes translated in English as 'mind', 'mind-stuff' and so on; in the German edition of this book it was rendered as *Geist*.* All the same it is evident that the terms *Geist* and *sems* do not entirely coincide. The meaning of the term *sems* will only become clearer to the reader when he has attained an overview of the whole region of signification which this word has, after acquainting himself with the entire contents of the book. For this reason I have, to avoid misunderstanding, almost always retained the Tibetan form *sems*, so as to lead the reader gradually to connect the word with the corresponding concept or range of concepts.

In the writing of this book I was able to call upon both my personal

* Some writers have used 'spirit' and related terms in English; thus W. Rahula renders the Sanskrit word *citta* (= Tib. *sems*) as *esprit* in his translation of the *Abhidharmasamuccaya*, and in T. C. Dhongthog's recent *The New Light English-Tibetan Dictionary* the English word 'spirit' is translated by *sems*. (G.T.) 'Spirit' in English however (unlike *Geist*, and *esprit* and *spirito*, used in the French and Italian translations) nowadays refers almost exclusively to the transcendent and external, and I have generally felt it less confusing to use 'mind' and 'mental'. Wherever possible, however, the Tibetan form itself is used. (G.B.S.)

experiences and a critical review which I had recently carried out of the literature, both that which was known and which was previously unfamiliar to me. The reader will find many of these texts in the bibliography at the end of the work, which however makes no claim to be comprehensive. I have only included those works which have become familiar to me through constant usage. In the text references are given only where it has appeared necessary to indicate the sources and explanatory material concerned. Considering that my intention was to give in this work an overview of the Tibetan religious world, such indications had to be kept to a minimum, in other words primarily to isolated facts and references to sources. Taken all in all my presentation may serve as a summary of past researches, and at the same time as an anticipation of future, more conclusive studies; it is in short an attempt at a bringing to account of the results of an involvement with Tibetan Buddhism which has lasted many years.

What is said above will scarcely seem surprising if it is remembered that we have not yet succeeded in completing a comprehensive and convincing account of the Indian world of thought, and particularly of the religious conceptions of India, although today the sources are more easily accessible than in the past, and for many years now accounts of the individual philosophical and religious schools have constantly been appearing. I myself have attempted such a synthesis in my *Storia della filosofia indiana* (Bari, 1957), although I did it more with the aim of clarifying my own ideas in this field than to present those of others.

In my work I have been greatly aided by the counsel, always freely given, of Geshe (*Lha ram pa*) Jampel Sanghie, a scholar initiated into all the doctrinal problems and details of the reformed school of *Tsong kha pa* and of its offshoots, and also by the assistance of Professor Namkhai Norbu, formerly a *sprul sku* of Gönchen monastery, who is closely familiar with all the philosophical doctrines of the *rNying ma pa* school, and also served as a pre-eminent source of information on the folk traditions. Both these two Tibetan religious scholars have lived in Rome for ten years as collaborators of the Istituto Italiano per il Medio ed Estremo Oriente (IsMEO). Professor Norbu teaches Tibetan language at the Istituto Universitario Oriental in Naples. He is also responsible for the drawings which accompany the book, which were prepared in a form suitable for publication by Mr Fiorentini of IsMEO. I am deeply indebted to both gentlemen for this valuable co-operation.

I owe much gratitude also to Dr Giovanna Vallauri Galluppi of Rome, who during my absence of a year (in connection with the archaeological excavations entrusted to me in the Orient) maintained contact with Dr C. M. Schröder, assisted me with valuable advice, and also helped untiringly with the correction of the proofs.

This English version includes certain modifications and additions made in the Italian translation. These include two summaries which clarify the meditative stages of the two processes which are open to the neophyte; (a) the gradual method of the Prajnaparamita, as systematized by Nagarjuna and his followers, and presented in the *Abhisamayalamkara*; and (b) the method of the Tantra (*rgyud*) which naturally starts off from the previous method, which forms an indispensable preliminary training, but is more complex, in particular in that it proposes experiencing in this very life the concatenation of the three phases of the path (*lam*) of salvation: (i) the initial phase, (ii) the path itself, (iii) the phase of the result or effect.

The English translation, as the most recent, has the advantage of some further additions or reconsiderations which I think should facilitate the reading of a book which is certainly not easy. Since Dr Samuel is a Tibetanist himself his work in several places has been not merely that of a translator but also of a knowledgeable advisor. Thus the arrangement of chapters and of some appendices has been altered from that in the other editions at his suggestion, with the intention of making the flow of the argument easier to follow. I am particularly grateful for his many suggestions and for the careful corrections of some errors which had escaped me, the worst corrector of proofs. Thus this English edition has the advantage of being the most readable. Naturally I am already thinking of adding some further chapters and of changing some sections if further editions are made; I certainly do not have the presumption to believe that the first version of a work can be perfect; but it may get there if it is chiselled and filed with revisions and modesty. In short I have no great dislike for being my own *zhu chen*, especially if in the course of the years I can avail myself of the good advice of a *kalyanamitra*.

During the preparation of the book I was continually aware of a difficulty which I was not in a position to deal with consistently; in describing Tibetan religion I sometimes use the present tense, sometimes the past. This inconsistency of verbal forms is brought about by the singular situation in which Tibet is placed today; it is hardly necessary to say that Tibet is today no longer the same country, from an economic, social and religious point of view, as before becoming an 'autonomous region' of the Chinese People's Republic. Many things have been radically changed. Along with the conditions of life in general, religion too has undergone a violent upheaval. The lamas, like all the other Tibetans who fled to India and other countries, have been able to preserve their beliefs, but their new environment is not like that in which almost their entire previous existence took place. They have been forced to put down new roots in a completely different milieu; but above all the natural links have been broken which until then had bound together men of the same thoughts and concepts, of the same heritage of religious fears and hopes. Tibetan Buddhism as it lives in the sacred scriptures and in ancient traditions–and with it the spiritual world in which these refugees have grown up and been educated–has found its last homeland, beyond all worldly change, in their souls. Their country of origin has meanwhile become the scene of profound upheavals, as a consequence of which much contained in the present pages may seem to belong to the past.

The present crisis of Tibet is not only political; it is also religious. A centuries-old total social structure has been overthrown, to give place to a completely different one. This is the reason for the 'duplicity' of my mode of expression, which now slips from past to present, now falls back from present into past. If I were required to renounce the ambiguity I would rather use the past tense exclusively; although the ideological and theoretical premises, thanks to their universality, remain the same, their echo in the soul is different today, and will be different again in the future. Along with it the basic religious situation will also alter more and more. Such transformations are taking place before our eyes also in all the other religions, progressively exposed to new ways of thinking and of conceiving; throughout the whole world their strength and their powers of resistance will be put to a hard test.

Giuseppe Tucci

Rome, August 1969–February 1978

NOTE ON TRANSCRIPTION AND PRONUNCIATION

In the text diacritical marks on Sanskrit words have been omitted. They can be found in the index. Tibetan words are transliterated, following the Tibetan spelling, according to the Wylie system (T. V. Wylie, 1959, 'A standard system of Tibetan transcription', *Harvard Journal of Asiatic Studies*, vol.22, pp.261-7). This system uses no diacritical marks, so the forms in the text are complete. (Some letters only used in words borrowed from Sanskrit form an exception; the only one of these letters to occur at all frequently here is ṇ, in *paṇ chen* and *maṇi*.) It should be noted that ' is a letter in the Wylie transcription, and that *g.y* (as in *g.yag*) and *gy* (as in *rgyal*) are two distinct combinations of Tibetan consonants. The complete alphabet is as follows: *k kh g ng c ch j ny t th d n p ph b m ts tsh dz w zh z 'y r l sh s h a*.

The clusters of initial consonants in Tibetan words are generally much simplified in actual pronunciation. *bKa' brgyud pa* becomes Kagyüpa or Kajüpa; *khri srong lde'u brtsan* is pronounced as Trisong Detsen. The rules governing such transformations are quite regular, though they vary somewhat between dialects. They are, however, too complicated to be summarized here. A brief account may be found in Anagarika Govinda's *Foundations of Tibetan Mysticism* (pp.286-92 of the paperback edition, London, 1969). Approximate pronunciations for proper names and for the main technical terms used in this book are given in the index (following the system used in R. A. Stein's *Tibetan Civilization*, London, 1972).

Readers who do not know the Tibetan language should perhaps be warned also that it employs a large number of short particles (e.g. *kyi*, *kyis*, *gi*, *pa*, *po*, *du*) which are frequently omitted in literary compounds and abbreviations. Thus *rnam par shes pa* (= Skt. *vijnana*) can be reduced to *rnam shes*, and *shes rab kyi pha rol tu phyin pa* (Skt. Prajnaparamita) can become *shes rab phar phyin*, or be abbreviated even further to *sher phyin*. Several terms occur in the text in both extended and abbreviated forms.

G.B.S.

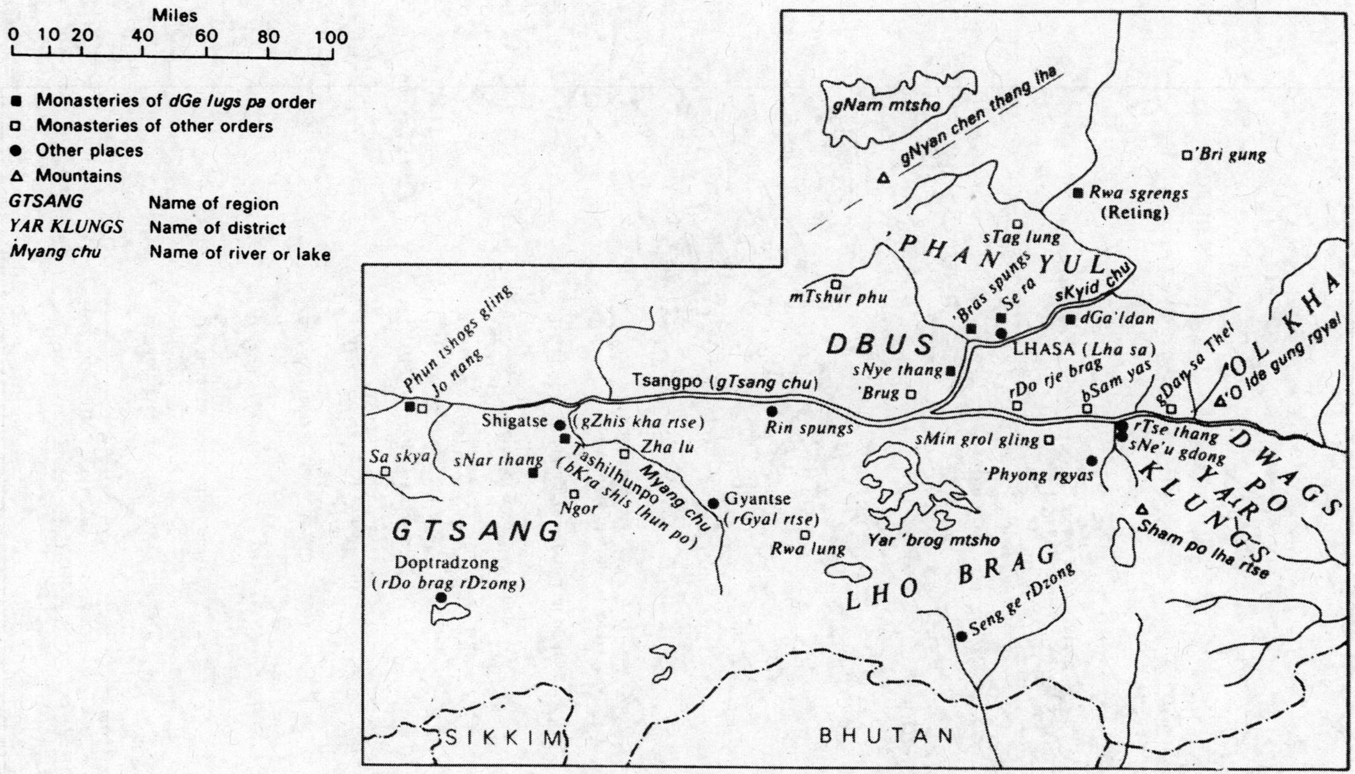
Miles
0 10 20 40 60 80 100
Monasteries of dGe lugs pa order
Monasteries of other orders
Other places
Mountains
GTSANG Name of region
YAR KLUNGS Name of district
Myang chu Name of river or lake
gNam mtsho
gNyan chen thang lha
'Bri gung
Rwa sgrengs
(Reting)
sTag lung
'PHAN YUL
mTshur phu
'Bras spungs
Se ra
sKyid chu
dGa' ldan
DBUS
LHASA (Lha sa)
sNye thang
'Brug
Tsangpo (gTsang chu)
rDo rje brag
bSam yas
gDan sa Thel
OL KHA
'O lde gung rgyal
Phun tshogs gling
Jo nang
Shigatse
(gZhis kha rtse)
Zha lu
Rin spungs
sMin grol gling
rTse thang
sNe'u gdong
DWAGS PO
YAR KLUNGS
'Phyong rgyas
Sa skya
sNar thang
Tashilhunpo
(bKra shis lhun po)
Myang chu
Ngor
Gyantse
(rGyal rtse)
Rwa lung
Yar 'brog mtsho
Sham po lha rtse
GTSANG
Doptradzong
(rDo brag rDzong)
LHO BRAG
Seng ge rDzong
SIKKIM
BHUTAN

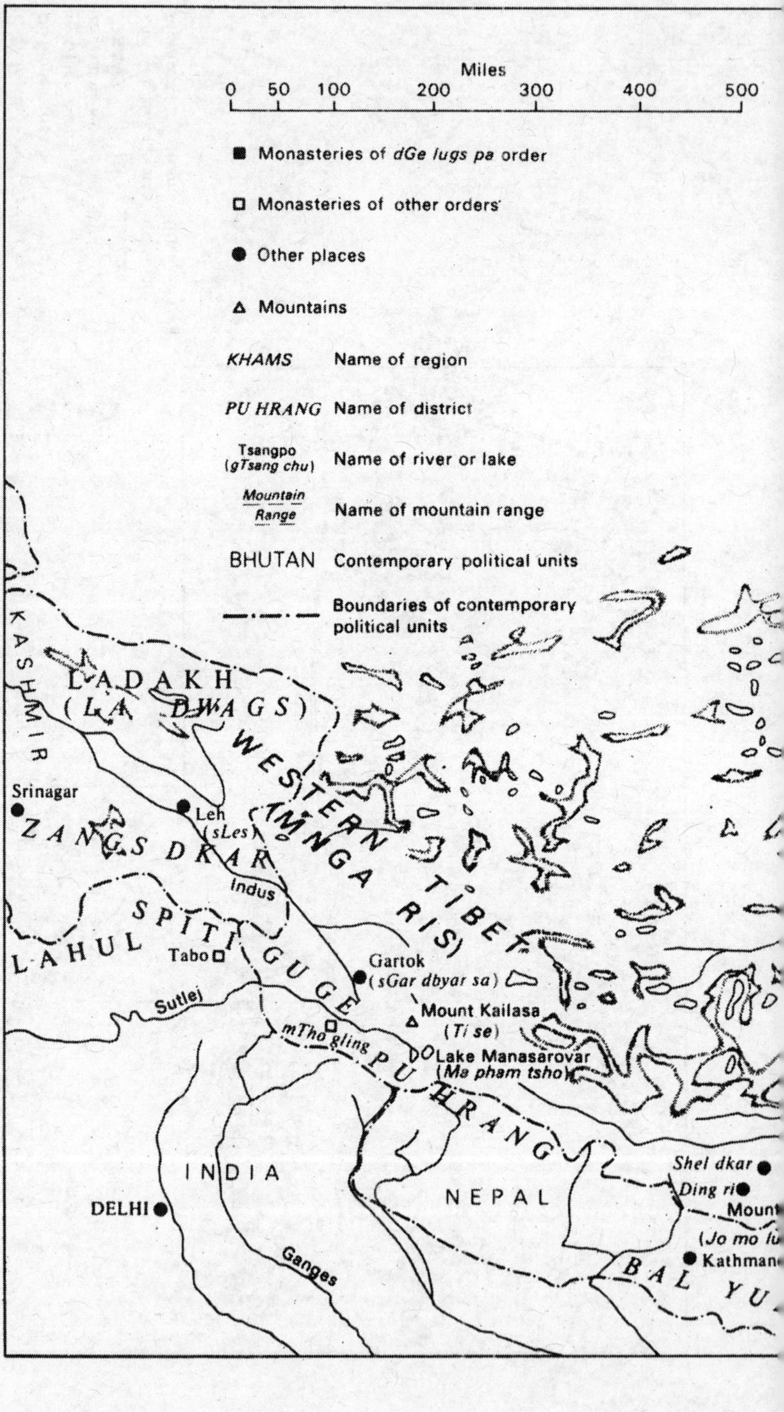

Miles
0 50 100 200 300 400 500
Monasteries of dGe lugs pa order
Monasteries of other orders
Other places
Mountains
KHAMS Name of region
PU HRANG Name of district
Tsangpo (gTsang chu) Name of river or lake
Mountain Range Name of mountain range
BHUTAN Contemporary political units
Boundaries of contemporary political units
KASHMIR
LADAKH (LA DWAGS)
WESTERN TIBET (MNGA RIS)
Srinagar
Leh (sLes)
ZANGS DKAR
Indus
SPITI
LAHUL
Tabo
GUGE
Gartok (sGar dbyar sa)
Sutlej
Mount Kailasa (Ti se)
mTho gling
Lake Manasarovar (Ma pham tsho)
PU HRANG
INDIA
DELHI
NEPAL
Ganges
Shel dkar
Ding ri
Kathman
BAL YU

TSONG KHA
Lake Kokonor
(mTsho sngon po)
Sining
Huang Ho
Kumbum
(sKu 'bum)
Labrang
(bLa brang)
NORTH-EASTERN TIBET (A MDO)
sPom A myes rma chen
rMa chu
EASTERN TIBET (KHAMS)
Jyekundo
(Khyer dgun mdo)
'Bri chu
rDza chu
Derge
(sDe dge)
Be ri
Chab mdo
Nag chu
Area covered by map of central Tibet
Li thang
Tatsienlu
(Dar rtse mdo)
dNgul chu
CENTRAL TIBET (DBUS)
LHASA
RKONG PO
SPO BO
Tsangpo
(gTsang chu)
CENTRAL
(GTSANG)
Punakha
BRUG YUL
HUTAN
Brahmaputra
BURMA
INDIA
Salween
Mekong
Yangtse

ONE

THE FIRST DIFFUSION OF BUDDHISM IN TIBET

1 The beginnings

The dates of the first penetration of Buddhism into Tibet, and of the commencement of large-scale conversion, have already been discussed many times, as have the accompanying events. Of course there is no problem for the Tibetans themselves. For them only the traditional account is valid, and it is believed as an act of faith. According to this traditional account, Buddhism was introduced into Tibet during the lifetime of *Srong btsan sgam po*, who died in 649, and is held by all schools to be the founder of the Tibetan royal dynasty. Occasional voices, admittedly, go back in time beyond this legend. With the aim of giving their native country a stronger claim to religious pre-eminence, they assert that there was a first encounter with the Buddhist teachings during the time of *Lha tho tho ri*, a distant ancestor of *Srong btsan sgam po*. At that period Buddhist scriptures and symbols fell from the sky for the first time. Other commentators, wishing to give a rational foundation to the legend, point to the arrival of certain religious teachers from Central Asia and from India at that time. In any case, the adoption and first diffusion of Buddhism is attributed to *Srong btsan sgam po*.[1] His conversion was said to result from the influence of his two wives, a Nepalese princess and a Chinese princess. While there are doubts, in my opinion well-founded,[2] concerning the first marriage, the second marriage is confirmed by the chronicles. Whatever the truth may have been, the Chinese wife (*rgya bza'*) was said to have brought with her the image of *Śākyamuni* known as the *Jo bo* and to have installed it in the temple of *Ra mo che*[3] which she founded. To the Nepalese wife, on the other hand, is attributed the merit of having brought in her dowry the image of *Mi bskyod rdo rje* and of having erected the temple of *'Phrul snang*.

Certainly one cannot deny the possibility of an earlier, sporadic penetration of Buddhist teachings into Tibet by various routes, from Central Asia, from China or from Nepal, before the reign of *Srong btsan sgam po*. However, the question of the 'prehistory' of Tibetan Buddhism needs to be understood correctly. The orthodox tradition cannot be taken as literally true. There can be no question of a conversion of King *Srong btsan sgam po*, or of an extensive diffusion of the faith carried out by him. Even the edicts of the later kings *Khri srong lde brtsan* and *Khri lde srong btsan*, as preserved in the history of *dPa'o gtsug lag* (provided always that we are not dealing here with later interpolations), speak of King *Srong btsan sgam po* only in very obscure terms. They confine themselves to attributing to him, in the first edict, the foundation of the temple of *'Phrul snang*, without mentioning the Nepalese princess, while the Chinese princess is mentioned as founding the *Ra mo che* temple. The second edict ascribes to *Srong btsan sgam po* the second temple of *Pe har* in *Ra sa*.[4] Certainly, in view of the links between Tibet and China, the existence of cult centres on a small scale is perhaps already possible at that time. The Tibetans would have tolerated them with that respect, mixed with fear of invisible, mysterious powers of whatever kind they might be, which is natural to them. However, the chronicles do not appear to offer proof of a real conversion of King *Srong btsan sgam po* to Buddhism, or even of his profession of faith in it or active support for it, such as the orthodox tradition maintains. Events of this kind first happen in the time of *Khri srong lde brtsan* (756-97?), well after the period of *Srong btsan sgam po*, and culminate in the founding of the monastery of *bSam yas*.

At the same time, one can hardly imagine that king *Khri srong lde brtsan*'s pro-Buddhist policy was the result of a spur-of-the-moment decision. It must have been the fruit of a gradual process of maturation. Despite the uncertain and contradictory character of our sources, the assumption of earlier occasional infiltrations of Buddhist elements into Tibet is an obvious one to make. We are perhaps concerned here more with Chinese and Central Asian influences than with those from India. Such influences must have become steadily stronger after the arrival of Princess Wen-ch'eng (Tibetan *Kong chu, Kong jo*). The fact also cannot be ignored that *Khri srong lde brtsan* was not the first Tibetan king to show an interest in Buddhism. His father, King *Khri lde gtsug brtsan* (704-55), had already made efforts in this direction, as *Khri lde srong brtsan*'s edict at Karchung reports, but he was frustrated through the forceful and decisive opposition of some ministers. The hostility of these ministers towards Buddhism persisted during the time of *Khri lde gtsug brtsan*. In addition, even after the acceptance of Buddhism, there are signs of indecision between the Chinese and Indian traditions. This indecision can only be explained on the assumption that two currents of thought had already come into conflict, one proposing adherence to China and the other inclining towards Indian Buddhism. Two personalities played an outstanding role at this point in time; *gSal snang* of *sBa*, and a Chinese, called *Sang shi* in the chronicles, who according to the tradition had been a playing-companion of the young *Khri srong lde brtsan*.[5] In this case too we have in the sources both the echo of real events and, simultaneously, a fantastic overgrowth of elements from the cycles of legends which later grew up about these characters. These legends originated in particular families or at particular religious centres, with the aim of authenticating their various interests or claims, or of glorifying personalities connected with them. Cycles of this type include that concerning *sBa gSal snang* (which stands at the centre of a famous work, the first part of the *sBa bzhad*[6]), and the cycles of *Sang shi*, Padmasambhava and Vairocana. Fragments and reworkings of this literary genre are preserved in later writings; they comprise a mixture of historical and religious elements, of folk history and family chronicles. All the same this literature gives us an idea of the extremely complex situation in Tibet at that period, and of the opposing forces which were at work.

Given these political and cultural relations with China, some social strata were disposed to a close collaboration with Chinese culture. Thus there came about the adoption of some characteristic motives from Chinese Buddhist hagiography. For example, the golden statue of Sakyamuni brought to Tibet in the dowry of *Srong btsan sgam po*'s Chinese wife recalls the golden statue which according to some Chinese traditions was the first sign of Buddhism in China. Again, the episode concerning the monk *Hwa shang*, who left behind one of his shoes when forced to leave Lhasa by anti-Buddhist ministers, reminds one of the shoe which was found in the empty tomb of Bodhidharma. Another factor which needs to be taken into consideration is the rivalry which existed between the families who had the duty of supplying from among their numbers the ministers (*zhang*, *zhang blon*, *blon chen*, *blon*; *zhang* are the ministers belonging to families from which the kings customarily chose their wives, such as *Tshes spong*, *sNa nam*, *mChims*, *'Bro*). These families were to have a decisive role throughout the whole of the dynastic period of Tibetan history, as the effective directors of policy. The kings themselves possessed relatively limited authority. Their office was surrounded by religious prestige, but in practice the priestly class of *Bon*, and the aristocracy, hindered their exercise of sovereignty. The great families from which the *blon chen* were descended, and the families of the queen mother's clan (often the family of the queen and that of the *blon chen* were one and the same), made their influence felt in all directions. All this harmed the king's authority critically. *Srong btsan sgam po*'s father and grandfather had broken with this tradition, but the leading families had not however given up their privileges. The long-lasting and deep opposition between the king and his followers on the one side, and his opponents on the other, divided Tibet into two parts, one faithful to the king and the court, and the other preoccupied with keeping their personal privileges. One or another of these great alliances alternated in controlling the country.

The inner struggles can be deduced from the large number of kings and princes assassinated by their own mothers or step-mothers. *Khri srong lde brtsan* himself expressed his inclination to Buddhism from an early age, which doubtless indicates that he was supported by a powerful group working in this direction, that of the *Mang* and the *'Bal*. The first assault by this pro-Buddhist party was unsuccessful. The opposing group, headed by *Ma zhang Khrom pa skyes*, temporarily seized the upper hand. The families favouring the adoption of Buddhism then resorted to violence to secure the success of their policy, and the leaders of the opposing party were exiled or removed (*Ma zhang Khrom pa skyes* was murdered). Even this, however, did not bring victory. Tibet was struck by grave natural disasters, which one of the aristocratic factions, incited by the *Bon po*, used for its own purposes. The *Bon po* saw their privileges threatened, and hoped to win all with the aid of the group of nobles who supported them. Thus they sought to make the introduction of the new religion responsible for all the misfortunes. The renowned Indian religious teacher Santaraksita, who had just arrived in Tibet, had to leave the country, and it was several years before he could return again, and before the king was able to publish his edict and the foundation of the monastery of *bSam yas* could take place (775).[7] We possess only scanty documentary reports and brief descriptions of all these events, although there are numerous legendary accounts from later periods, adhering more or less closely to the real events. It is clear anyway that the conflict between the opposing groups of forces must have been very violent. Other powers were certainly at work in addition to the two parties in direct contest. China had watched the rise of Tibetan power with anxiety, seeing in it a threat to her own expansion into Central Asia. She could scarcely remain indifferent to the events in Tibet. China sent a series of missionaries to Tibet, who were probably not exclusively concerned with matters of religion. So it came about that Tibet in the second half of the seventh century, after having conquered extensive territories in Central Asia, began to succumb more and more to the enchantment of Chinese culture. Members of the Tibetan aristocracy went to China to study, and there became acquainted with new, more sophisticated ways of living, with more appropriate administrative techniques and political institutions, and with a maturity of thought which had previously been inaccessible to them.[8] Thus there took place in Tibet at this time a phenomenon analogous to what was happening simultaneously in Japan.

2 Co-existence and conflict among the various tendencies at the time of the first introduction of Buddhism into Tibet

To the complexity of the political background described above must be added far-reaching conflicts among the supporters of Buddhism themselves. They agreed in demanding official recognition for the Buddhist teachings, but not on the form of Buddhism which was to be adopted. From the very beginning two tendencies were clear, one favouring Indian Buddhism, the other Chinese. We will first give an overview of the historical events, and then present the ideas which lay beneath them.

gSal snang of *sBa* (it may be presumed that this is the same person who in the following period adopted the religious name *Ye shes dbang po*) went to India and Nepal, and arranged for an invitation to be issued to Santaraksita. *Sang shi* on the other hand, who was the author of translations from the Chinese, was sent to China (on one occasion in company with *gSal snang*, though this was after the first arrival of Santaraksita). Santaraksita had no success at first and therefore advised that Padmasambhava should be sent for as the only person who would be able to overcome the demons hostile to Buddhism.

The details given seem to indicate the existence of two opposed groups, each wishing to gain pre-eminence for its own teachings. In this contest even suicide and murders carried out for religious motives were not unusual.[9] China supported her official missionary, the *Hwa shang*, who attempted to introduce the school of Ch'an,[10] not without a degree of success according to some reports. Santaraksita's second visit, and the coming of Padmasambhava, seem to show that success was not denied to the pro-Indian group either (the group of *Ye shes dbang po*). Admittedly the sources disagree concerning both the mission attributed to Padmasambhava and his stay in Tibet. If we follow some accounts, he would seem to have stayed in Tibet until the consecration of the monastery of *bSam yas*, while according to others he would have left the country before this, after overcoming the demons. According to this latter version the building of the monastery of *bSam yas* was supervised by Santaraksita, and after his death he was replaced as abbot by *gSal snang* (*Ye shes dbang po*). *Ye shes dbang po* occupied this post, however, for only a short time, and was succeeded by *dPal dbyangs*.[11]

Ye shes dbang po had evidently gone too far in his demands. He had claimed for the abbot of *bSam yas*, and so, indirectly, for the religious community, a position superior not only to that of the aristocracy but also to that of the ministers. As the advocate of the Indian school, he aroused the opposition of the pro-Chinese group, who favoured Ch'an. The opposition against *Ye shes dbang po* was again led by a representative of the aristocracy, *Myang Ting nge 'dzin*.[12] It can be presumed that he was moved to act not only by the resentment which he shared with other high dignitaries at the pretensions of the religious leader, but also by his inclination to the Ch'an sect.[13] There were probably connections between the revolt of *Myang Ting nge 'dzin*, the more or less forcible banishment of *Ye shes dbang po*,[14] the naming of *dPal dbyangs* in *Ye shes dbang po*'s place, and the sudden rise to prominence of the *Hwa shang* Mahayana, who defended the Ch'an tradition and challenged the school of Santaraksita to battle. Nor can one neglect the fact that *Myang Ting nge 'dzin*, whom King *Khri srong lde brtsan* had chosen as the guardian of *Khri lde srong brtsan*, continued for a long time after to exercise a considerable influence on the political and religious affairs of Tibet, and that the *rDzogs chen* school regard him as one of their patriarchs.

Ye shes dbang po fought back, giving a response which suggests too the general arousal of tempers. He followed the counsel which Santaraksita had given him before his death, and called Kamalasila from India.[15] However, even the subsequent council at *bSam yas* (792-4), in which according to the Tibetan sources the *Hwa shang* was defeated, could not bring the strife to an end. It seems that Kamalasila was murdered.[16] Vairocana, a follower of Padmasambhava, whose teachings were related to those of the Indian Siddha schools, was banished. These events once more show the turbulent history of the beginnings of Buddhism in Tibet. It was not a question of a conversion to a new doctrine brought about by purely spiritual factors. Everywhere there were also political motives involved, which had also economic implications, in view of the donations to the monasteries. Such conflicts between particular material interests went hand in hand with conflicts of a doctrinal nature. In short, the beginnings of Tibetan Buddhism did not follow the straight-line path which the orthodox tradition describes. Only a systematic examination of the history and origins of the *rDzogs chen* will enable a judgment to be made upon how far the tradition regarding these events must be subject to revision.

It can also be inferred from the sources that Padmasambhava played a smaller role than that ascribed to him by later tradition. As already mentioned, he had little or no part in the construction of *bSam yas* according to some sources. Other reports admittedly maintain that he was involved in the building of this monastery, but they speak of him variously as staying in Tibet for some months or for many years. They agree only in connecting his departure with threats or attacks against him. In short, everything in the tradition concerning Padmasambhava seems contradictory or obscure. A legendary halo soon grew up about his personality as well, a cycle of stories which came to include also King *Khri srong lde brtsan* and the introduction of Buddhism into Tibet in general. Some parts of this cycle were added only much later, perhaps in the fourteenth century, together with embellishments, chants of praise and so on. All this provided the basis for well-known works such as the *Pad ma thang yig*, *bKa' thang sde lnga* and other *gter ma* (cf.p.38).

It was only after the second diffusion of the Buddhist law that the figure of Padmasambhava the miracle-worker grew to gigantic proportions, and that he was spoken about as if he was a second Buddha, along with extravagant exaggerations of all kinds. This provoked the attacks of the *dGe lugs pa* sect. In the earlier literature the references to him, as mentioned above, are extremely modest. The *sBa bzhad*[17] says of Padmasambhava that he was recommended by Santaraksita as a great exorcist who would be able to overcome the local demonic opponents of Buddhism. These details attest that even then, in the Tibetan environment, suppositions and elements could crystallize about his person which were suitable for the foundations of an epic literary cycle on themes of religion and exorcism.

However that may be, Tibet opened its doors to new forms of thought and life. Behind this there stood significant missionary activity from both India and China, and also the Tibetan conquests in Central Asia, which led to Tibetans living together with peoples of a considerable level of culture. As a result a steady expansion of Buddhism began to take place. Of course this process must be understood correctly. There can be no question here of an all-embracing penetration which encompassed the entire population. Rural and nomadic groups are, as is well-known, the most resistant and conservative in matters of religion. The missionaries who came from India, China and Central Asia (including the Tantric masters) were for the most part highly educated men, thinkers, dialecticians, grammarians.

It could be objected that we only know these elements, since the literary sources say nothing about what was happening in the lower levels of the population. There is no doubt that the original interest in Buddhism lay with the upper, the more educated classes, both for the reasons mentioned, and in view of the difficulty of an adequate and generally accessible understanding of the doctrines of Buddhism. The rest of the population remained faithful to their rites of conjuration, their ceremonies and their exorcists. The impetus for the whole movement came from above, and the re-education due to the new religion brought about a significant raising of the cultural level of the new converts.

The scriptures introduced in the early days can be classified into two groups. In the first there are the texts translated by specially chosen and appointed persons (*lotsava*), working in collaboration with

Chinese, Indians and Central Asians, and which were intended for the education of the monks after the foundation of the various religious communities. Second, there were general compendia intended for the conversion of the public at large, such as the *dGe bcu'i mdo*, *rDo rje gcod pa*, *Sa lu'i ljang pa*, books which were it seems introduced by *Sang shi*,[18] and other short summaries of the teachings similar to those cited in the edicts of *Khri srong lde brtsan*.[19] According to these edicts, in the version cited in No.85[20] (*ja*, pp.108b, 110a), it appears that Buddhism at the time of its first diffusion was restricted to the essential doctrines: veneration of the Buddha, of Bodhisattvas, Pratyekabuddhas and Sravakas;[21] rebirth in the hells or into unfavourable destinies for those who do not honour the Three Jewels (the Buddha, his Law, the monastic community); the doctrine of karma; the doctrine of the twofold accumulation of merit (virtue and knowledge); the practice of the ten moral commandments; the Four Truths; the law of moral causation (*pratityasamutpada*); special emphasis on the teachings of Nagarjuna. A true picture of the Buddhist literature accessible to the Tibetan community can be drawn from the catalogues of the royal libraries–which admittedly date from various times and, it must be accepted, are not free from later alterations. They include even works on logic. These catalogues also reveal a gradual decrease of works translated from the Chinese.

3 Ordination of monks, foundation of monasteries, donations to monasteries

Within Indian Mahayana Buddhism speculative thought and ritual had already become indissolubly linked, and thus it came about that the ritual side of Mahayana Buddhism began to prevail in Tibet, thanks also to the tendencies to magic already present within Indian ritual. In a society already very receptive to such things, this led to the wide diffusion of writings of an exorcistic nature, although according to one source (included in No.85, *ja*, p.105) there was at the beginning a tendency to translate Chinese works of a different kind, and to show some mistrust towards the Tantras, especially those whose liturgy prescribed sexual acts and the use of alcoholic drinks.

The religious orders now began to be introduced, and, perhaps in 779, the first monastic ordinations were celebrated. This made it necessary to form religious communities on a large scale, and to found monasteries as cult centres, schools of religious education, and centres for the translation of the Buddhist works which were to be made available to the new adepts. These monasteries represented a new factor in the political structure of Tibet. Until then the political organization of the country had been primarily military in character. The state was responsible for defence and offensive action, and all subjects were liable without exception for taxation, for military service and for labour obligations, in accordance with their various qualifications and abilities. There now arose, however, an entirely new institution, in the form of the monastery, which developed outside the state structure. It was provided with special donations by the king.

King *Khri srong lde brtsan* made 150 families, along with their estates and property, responsible for supporting the temple of *bSam yas* and the performance of the prescribed rituals. A further hundred families were responsible for the maintenance of the monastery as such. The produce of the estates and pastoral land had to provide everything necessary: 75 measures (*khal*) of barley annually (according to other sources monthly) for the abbot, who had also to receive 1,500 ounces of butter, a horse, paper, ink and salt. The monks devoted to meditation, the *sgom chen*, were entitled to 55 measures of barley and 800 ounces of butter, the Indian masters (*acarya*) living in the monastery to 55 measures of rice and 100 measures of butter, those not obliged to live permanently in the monastery (*bandhya*) to 800 measures of barley, and to paper and ink, the pupils to 25 measures of barley and pieces of cloth.[22]

Thus it can be seen that the monastery formed a self-governing economic unit. Its spiritual organization also became steadily clearer. At its head stood the *chos ring lugs*,[23] representative and guardian of the Buddha's Law, who was chosen by the king and exercised the function of abbot (*mkhan po*). He was given quite substantial powers. The creation of these spiritual dignitaries provoked ever more bitter conflicts between the court, which immoderately favoured the religious community now coming into being, and the traditional political organization.

The same sources report on a branch establishment of the monastery of *bSam yas*. This was *mChims phug*,[24] 'the cave of mChims', which was reserved for the *sgom chen*, the followers of the ascetic schools. A college and seminary (*chos grwa*) was also formed to educate the newly converted further and to introduce them to the study of the sacred texts. Also associated with the monastic community were monks and ascetics without special duties (*rang ga ma*).

The *Pad ma thang yig* (No.3) demonstrates the co-existence of monasticism and Tantric tendencies. Different rules applied to the followers of the two streams. The non-Tantric monks had to be vegetarians, to live in the monastery, to abstain from alcoholic drinks and to follow the rites prescribed in the Sutras.[25] The others did not have to observe these precepts; their ceremonial was centred about the *mandala*; they lived in the meditation-cells or *sgrub khang*. The precept of chastity applied to both groups of monks.[26]

Numerous documents confirm in detail the growth of a new juridical person, the monastery, which possessed estates and moveable goods. In addition it possessed a number of servants of the religious community, *lha 'bangs* (called later, and up to our own day, *lha bran*); these are mentioned not as individual persons but as heads of families (*khyim pa*). As a result we can no longer establish the exact number of persons dependent upon the monastery.

These particulars emerge clearly from the documents found in Turkestan.[27] In Central Asia at the time of Tibetan domination the monasteries possessed property and servants, they carried out businesss transactions, and so on. Particularly noticeable for their activity are the *bandhe* (called *bandhya* in the charters), monks not directly linked to a monastery, forerunners of the later wandering lamas of the *rNying ma pa* sect.

The example set by the king must have been extensively imitated. The principle of virtuous action, continually inculcated in the sacred writings, places the virtue of generosity, of munificence, in the foreground as the first of the perfections (*phar phyin*, Skt. *paramita*). Practised with understanding and piety, it is said to lead gradually to the level of Bodhisattva, or to entry into one of the paradises. It promotes and reinforces the positive factors in the process of maturation of karma. The figure of the donor (*sbyin bdag*, Skt. *danapati*) acquires a more and more definite outline in Tibet too. Donations to the Samgha, the Community; the erection of consecrated buildings; contributions to each of the three receptacles (*rten*) or supports of the sacred (*sku*, *gsung*, *thugs* = body, speech, mind) in the form of donations of images, copies of books, and temples–all these bring about an accumulation of merit indispensable for the attainment of deliverance. Deliverance is the result of two inseparable factors; the method used, the practice (*thabs*, Skt. *upaya*) and 'higher cognition' (*shes rab*, Skt. *prajna*). The attainment of Buddhahood is the most difficult of all; less hard to attain is the state of Bodhisattva, or of exaltation into a paradise.

The means to attain these latter aims (to be discussed later in more detail) represent the easier way, a way of gradual purification and preparation for that radiant clarity which shines out during the transition from the temporal plane to the timeless plane of *nirvana*. The means (*thabs*) is the practice of the six perfections, of which generosity is the first. It is not the sublime sacrifices of the Buddha which are in question here, such as when in his past lives he was Prince Visvantara (the subject of a sacred drama of Indian origin which regularly moves spectators to tears in Tibet) or Ksantivadin. It is rather a matter of generosity towards the Buddhist community, a practice more easily accessible to ordinary men. When the Tibetan makes a donation, his generosity represents an easy way of acquiring merits.

When the followers of the Chinese Ch'an school also began to spread in Tibet and to raise their influential voice in the person of the several *Hwa shang*, the reaction of the Indian religious teachers working in Tibet, and of their followers, was inspired not only by doctrinal reasons but also by practical considerations. If Enlightenment could be brought about through a sudden, momentaneous *ictus*, if it could be born from a sudden act of deliverance in which the Buddha-nature of each individual was revealed, then practice (*thabs*) lost its value. The world, and everything achieved in the world, including those acts intended to bring about a gradual accumulation of merit, became of no significance. Such an attitude had serious consequences; one could arrive from these premises at an individualistic position which threatened the existence of the Samgha at the root (though in time the followers of Ch'an organized themselves in monasteries too, so as to derive a prosperous revenue from the generosity of those sympathizing with them and their path). In any case the monastic rules (*'dul ba*, Skt. *vinaya*) first reached Tibet only at a time when many of these precepts were becoming meaningless in India itself. For example, the rule of monastic poverty (renunciation of material possessions) had already lost its incontestable validity. The growth of the monastic institution led to contact with the world becoming ever closer; the monastery became, as a result of the donations it received, an economic entity which could supervise its property adequately and guard its own interests.

> It is forbidden for the monk of the Small Vehicle to possess gold or silver, but for the monk who is a Bodhisattva (*byang chub sems dpa'*), that is who has renounced *nirvana*, it is no sin, for he is striving for the good of his fellow men. (No. 77, 4a.)

Tibet had at the beginning an economy closed in on itself, hunting, pastoralism and agriculture, which could develop only slowly through a system of irrigation which was perfected with difficulty. The conquests in Central Asia, and the wars against China, extended not only the political and cultural horizons, but also the economic horizon. The penetration of Tibet into Central Asia, which owed its prosperity principally to trade, awoke new economic interests and brought about new social orientations.

The monastery did not only own property; it was also involved in trade. The *bandhe* occupied themselves with business and commercial relations.[28] Beginning with the foundation of the monastery of *bSam yas*, and continuing during the reign of King *Ral pa can*, a steady growth of donations can be seen; the number and wealth of the monasteries constantly increased. Thus there grew up within Tibetan society a new power, which opposed the old feudal families ever more strongly. The persecution of the Buddhist community which was unleashed by King *Glang dar ma* (838-42) arose not merely from religious motives. Just as in China, there were many important interests at play here. The attitude of *Glang dar ma* was doubtless in part formed by the concern he must have felt at the growing economic power of the monasteries, at their privileges and their arrogance. The steady extension of the religious community brought the existence of the state into serious danger. In addition there was the monasteries' freedom from taxation, the continual increase of their property through the assignment to them of estates and pastures, and the growing proportion of the population working for them in agriculture or as herdsmen, and therefore exempted from military obligation and compulsory labour. Also, donations did not only go towards the building of a temple; in addition they had to support the monastic community belonging to the temple, so as to secure for all time the performance of the ceremonies directed by the donor or testator in accordance with his will. This development deprived the state of considerable resources in both men and revenue, and this too at precisely the time when the threat from China was steadily growing as the Tibetans lost their Central Asian territories. The story of *Glang dar ma*'s opposition to Buddhism, which the orthodox tradition explains as the result of a demon having taken possession of the king, thus had a very real political and economic foundation.

4 The Indian and Chinese currents

The Indians who came to the Land of Snow did not all belong to the same school, and they did not all teach the same things. There were already profound differences between Santaraksita and Padmasambhava. The former was a great dialectician, though certainly as was appropriate for every Mahayana follower he was experienced in Tantric practice, if not to such a degree as to be a match for an exorcist. Padmasambhava was in the first place an exorcist, and after him other followers of the Siddha tradition also came to Tibet. The school of the Siddha, the 'Perfected Ones', was then at its apogee in India; the miraculous powers its followers boasted brought them disciples in Tibet too. The difference between the Siddha tradition and the Ch'an school lay not so much in their respective doctrinal positions as in the characteristic emphasis placed by the Siddha on the practices of yoga and magic. There were no insurmountable contradictions between their theoretical assumptions. Santaraksita and Kamalasila, on the other hand, began from doctrines as fundamentally opposed to those of the Siddha as they were to the teachings of Ch'an.

The decisive difference here lay in the fact that Santaraksita considered the achievement of Buddhahood to be the end-result of a long drawn-out process, which necessarily went through different stages before the conclusion was reached, while the Chinese school of *Hwa shang* preached the uselessness of 'means', and therefore of actions such as donations and so on, which are obligatory for the school founded upon the Prajnaparamita teachings[29] (of which more will be said later).

Some Mahayana schools had affirmed that the Buddha and all living beings were identical in essence.[30] Our essence, they held, is luminous spirit, defiled by transitory impurities. These impurities, which have arisen from a primeval impurity existing *ab initio* (comparable to the *avidya* of the Saivite schools), represent an original, congenital ignorance which increases further through our successive lives. If, then, in the depths of our being, this light of consciousness, which is identical to absolute being, shines, what need is there (the school of the *Hwa shang* asks) for such an enormous expenditure of effort? If our nature is pure in essence, then it will be defiled by any concept, good or bad. A white cloud will obscure the sun as much as a black one. Thus progressive purification is unnecessary; the infinitely long career of the Bodhisattva can be dispensed with. A spontaneous, direct awareness of our essential purity, of the light which we are, is enough. A re-cognition, an *anagnosis*, of our innermost being will suffice to eradicate all that is not luminous, all deception, ignorance and error. This overturning of the planes of existence does not result from the performance of any routine. It is rather the gift of an instantaneous flash of insight.

These are the principal characteristics of the two points of view, those of Kamalasila and of the *Hwa shang*, which clashed during the Council of *bSam yas*, called by King *Khri srong lde brtsan* in order to decide which of these points of view, the Chinese or the Indian, was correct.

It is of course scarcely to be supposed that the king and his ministers were able to understand the subtleties of these speculations in detail. At that time few Tibetans indeed would have been able to grasp the nuances of these doctrinal positions. According to the Chinese tradition, the king would seem to have decided in favour of the Chinese.[31] However, there are contradictions between the reports given in Tibetan and Chinese sources. We are led to distrust the Tibetan tradition more than the Chinese since the Tibetan reports originate from a relatively recent period, and were evidently first compiled when Buddhism in Tibet had already taken on the form it was to preserve in its essentials to the present day. In addition, *Khri srong lde brtsan*'s declaration that the teachings of Nagarjuna were to be followed is not enough to characterize his attitude unambiguously. Nagarjuna's ideas form a cornerstone of the Mahayana edifice, and no explicit inference can therefore be drawn from this declaration of the king.

From the time of *Ral pa can* (*Khri gtsug lde brtsan*, 815-38) onwards a significant decrease in the followers of Ch'an can be detected. In the catalogues of books in the royal libraries, books on Ch'an become ever rarer. The Indian school has visibly gained the upper hand; in this the influx of new teachers must also have helped. This does not mean however that the defenders of the Ch'an school have vanished completely.[32] In addition to the religious teachers living both in the houses of the translators and in the monasteries, there had also come to Tibet representatives of the Siddha school, which had, as already mentioned, points of contact with Ch'an, at least at the level of theory.[33] The rapid way of salvation ascribed to the Siddha, accompanied with miracles, and not far distant from magic, must have exerted a significant attraction upon less educated people and the broad masses of the populace. In short, it seems that Tibetan Buddhism, which was certainly far from homogeneous from its outset, already by the time of King *Glang dar ma* carried within it the seeds which in the further course of history would produce the profusion of doctrines later to be found.

Within the *Jo nang pa* and *rDzogs chen* sects a significant part of the heritage of the *Hwa shang*'s ideas, combined with those of the Siddha, was able to come to maturity, be consolidated, and then be transmitted on in further adaptations.

Myang Ting nge 'dzin, who has already been mentioned, was counted as one of the patriarchs of this movement[34] and is recognized by *rNying ma pa* monks to this day as one of their religious teachers. The *rNying ma pa* consider King *Khri srong lde brtsan* to be one of their protectors and patrons. Some books (*gter ma*) of this school are composed in the form of responses which Padmasambhava gave to the questions of King *Khri srong lde brtsan* on the occasion of a great ceremony at *bSam yas*.

The close relationship which existed between the *rDzogs chen* sect and the teachings of the Ch'an school is confirmed by a significant fragment preserved in the *bKa' thang sde lnga* (No.110). Among the several Ch'an teachers here mentioned, some are also known from the Tun-Huang documents.[35] *Hwa shang* is given as the seventh patriarch of the school, the first being Bodhidharma. This document, like the Chinese sources, has the disputation of *bSam yas* result in the victory of the *Hwa shang*. The *rNying ma pa* also seem to have continued certain aspects of the Ch'an teachings in their doctrines, thanks to one of the first Tibetan monks to be ordained (*sad mi*), *Nam mkha' snying po* from *gNubs*,[36] who is known to have been a Ch'an teacher.

One must guard against oversimplifying forms of religious experience and doctrinal statements. They do not develop in straight lines, least of all in times of considerable social upheaval, and of contacts with other cultures on many levels. The Buddhism entering Tibet came not only from India (by which is to be understood not only India proper, but also its border regions Nepal and Kashmir) but also from present-day Afghanistan and Gilgit, from the cities along the caravan routes of Central Asia (then known as the Silk Routes), and from China. Buddhism has never refused to accept, rework and transform the ideas of other peoples. In the territories bordering on Tibet there existed numerous religious forms in a picturesque juxtaposition which favoured exchange and reciprocal borrowings. The Chinese translators of Nestorian and Manichaean texts borrowed technical expressions from Taoist and Buddhist terminology, and indeed they borrowed more than just terminology. Vajrayana (gnostic) Buddhism developed hand in hand with Saivism. It is probable that in these ways, through the mediation of Buddhists influenced by other streams of thought, or for that matter directly, ideas foreign to Buddhism could be introduced within it, and gradually be merged into a developing doctrinal structure.

In any case Buddhism must have already, from its first entry into Tibet, undergone much modification and weakening. It cannot be denied that the local cults and beliefs persisted to a large degree, and that there were powerful centres of *Bon* resistance throughout the country.

Equally, it is certain that the Buddhist communities were forced to adopt some of the ancient rituals, which were indigenous and deep-rooted, and therefore ineradicable; even if these were furnished with new forms, in a similar way to the old gods of the country who were incorporated into the Buddhist Olympus after their conversion by Padmasambhava (cf.p.164). Similarly *Khri srong lde brtsan*'s inscription mentions *g.yung drung*, the svastika of *Bon*, and *gnam chos*, the law of heaven, characteristic concepts of the *Bon* religion. Local demons came to be accepted as Buddhist divinities who acted as avengers of broken vows. In the peace treaties too, for example in that between *Ral pa can* and China, the rituals which accompanied the concluding of the treaty and guaranteed its endurance were performed with animal sacrifices, and in an unmistakable context of *Bon*.[37]

TWO

THE SECOND DIFFUSION OF BUDDHISM

1 The revival of Buddhism

The persecution carried out by *Glang dar ma*, who died in 842, dealt a devastating blow to the Buddhist community, which not only lost the protection of the court, but was also deprived of all its property. Its estates were confiscated and its possessions seized. The Buddhist religion was outlawed, and its entire organization shattered. With *Glang dar ma*'s death the political unity of Tibet began to crumble; an era of decay and dissolution commenced. The state of anarchy lasted for two centuries, and led to Tibet being split up into a number of little states. The intellectual contacts with India were broken off. Even the royal tombs were desecrated.

Nevertheless, the destruction of the organization of the Buddhist community did not mean the end of Buddhism as such. Certainly Buddhism was no longer directed from religious centres, it became subject to arbitrary interpretations, and the controlling authority of the monasteries and religious communities no longer stood over it. The Buddhism that remained deviated more and more from the line of orthodoxy. In such circumstances a tacit agreement with *Bon* and with the folk religion had to be arrived at, all the more so because the religious attitude of the Tibetans still remained basically the same. A revival of the earlier religious ideas, not fixed through scriptures and varying from place to place, was inevitable; the *klu*, the *sa bdag*, the spirits of the soil, of the mountain, of the air continued to be venerated and feared as real powers.

The description given in the sources of the state of Buddhism immediately after the collapse of the dynasty and the end of *Glang dar ma*'s persecution cannot be too far removed from the truth.

A letter attributed to *Byang chub 'od*, an eleventh-century ruler in West Tibet (No.81, p.393) shows how literally the followers of the Tantric schools at that time were accustomed to take some of the ambiguous teachings in these scriptures. The Tantras contained arguments of the following kind (No.82, *Kha*, p.3a): Since the

Buddha-nature exists in everyone, we are all capable of attaining permanently a state beyond good and evil, provided that we can recognize this reality present within us. Consequently none of our subsequent actions, of whatever kind, will be sinful. This led to the triumph of the doctrine of the five *makara* (Skt.), the 'five *ma*': meat (*mamsa*), Paredra (*mudra*),[1] alcoholic drink (*madya*), fish (*matsya*), sexual union (*maithuna*). These were taken in a grossly exoteric and literal sense, not according to the esoteric interpretation (cf. the *gSang ba'i 'dus pa*, Skt. *Guhyasamaja Tantra*). The gods were worshipped through offerings of sperm, blood and excrement. Understandably *Byang chub 'od* felt disgust at practices of this kind, which offended both religious sentiment and morality.[2]

The revival of Buddhism took place only gradually. In their desire to demonstrate always an unbroken connection between the old communities and those of a later period, the sources frequently disagree concerning the details of the revival. The connection can be maintained only through the ordination of monks carried out in accordance with the precepts of the Vinaya, and therefore recognized as fully valid.

According to the chronicles, *Rab gsal* of *gTsang*, *g.Yo dGe 'byung* of *Bo dong*, and *dMar Sakyamuni* of *sTod lung* came to know of the persecutions of *Glang dar ma* during their meditation at *dPal chu bo ri*. They took up the Vinaya texts which they always kept at hand, and set off on a dangerous pilgrimage. Having miraculously escaped the Qarluq,[3] they travelled through the territory of the Hor and eventually reached East Tibet. There, among the nomad pastoralists of *rMa chu*, they came across a young man who bore the unmistakable signs of an innate inclination to the true faith (*mos pa*, Skt. *adhimukti*). Their example and their words spurred him to yet higher fervour. First he asked for the ordination of a lay disciple (*dge bsnyen*, Skt. *upasaka*), and then demanded to be given the full monastic ordination. According to the prescriptions of the Vinaya, to carry out this ceremony the presence of at least five monks is necessary: the instructor (*mkhan po*), the teacher (*slob dpon*, Skt. *acarya*), the master of esoteric secrets (*gsang ston*) and two assistants. Since this minimum number was not available, the youth could not receive a proper ordination. He then travelled to *dPal gyi rdo rje*, the monk who had murdered *Glang dar ma*. There could be no question of him participating in the ritual of consecration, however, because he was defiled by the murder. Nevertheless he enabled the novice's wish to be fulfilled by obtaining the services of two *Hwa shang* monks as the required assistants. Together with the three masters already named this gave the prescribed total for the ordination. The youth, who had taken the name of *dGe rab gsal* as a lay disciple, from the names of his most important religious teachers, *dGe 'byung* and *Rab gsal*, later became famous under his monastic name of *dGongs pa rab gsal* (832-915?).[4] He could be considered as being the official representative of the faith in *mDo khams* (East Tibet). However, a revival of Buddhism was beginning to take place in the Central Tibetan provinces of *dBus* and *gTsang* also. Five young men from *dBus* and the same number from *gTsang*,[5] who had heard of the events already described, came to East Tibet and asked *Rab gsal* of *gTsang* for full ordination according to the precepts, so that they could act as apostles of the Buddhist revival in the Land of Snow. *Rab gsal* refused at first, saying that he was too old; then they went to *dGongs pa rab gsal*, who however could not fulfil their request, because the five prescribed years had not yet passed since his own ordination, and he was not therefore qualified to invest novices. However, in consideration of the special circumstances the old master authorized an exception to this rule. In this way the five youths from *dBus* and the five from *gTsang* were ordained in proper form. Then the group dispersed to create new religious centres in various places. Each centre took on the name of the religious teacher founding it, as for example *'Dar tsho*, 'the masters of *'Dar*', founded by *Sa kya yon tan* of *'Dar*, and so on.[6]

Thus runs the account transmitted by *Bu ston* (No.113). Its accuracy is certainly open to doubt. *Bu ston* and his predecessors had reason to draw a picture not entirely corresponding to the actual course of events. Their labours were directed towards validating the installation of the masters to whom the existence of the new centres of the Buddhism which *Glang dar ma*'s persecutions had not totally destroyed was traced back. Thus *Rig ral*, for example, whom *Bu ston* cites for polemical reasons, describes the events in a rather different light. He inserts an intermediate period between the time of the first diffusion of the faith, which ended with *Glang dar ma*, and the second diffusion, which began with the revival of the religion and reached its climax with *Rin chen bzang po*, *rNgog lotsava*, Atisa and *Mar pa* (No.113, p.211). During this intermediate period the doctrine was not studied or preached properly, but was spread only in a falsified form. Also, the narrative reproduced above shows certain discordances. It is scarcely plausible, for example, that three monks meditating in solitude would have taken with them only the bulky volume of the Vinaya text (the book of discipline).[7] In general, monks devoting themselves to meditation are not only interested in questions of discipline. The group of ten young men in all from *dBus* and *gTsang* seems equally questionable, with its symmetrical division into two fives; behind this there evidently stands the intention of dividing the priority equally between these two provinces, which have always had an open or hidden rivalry. The intervention of *dPal gyi rdo rje* too is to be judged with a certain caution. Taking into account the difficult times, and the exceptional situation which presented itself, one could counter his refusal to take part in the ordination with the Mahayana Buddhist argument that murder is in some cases necessary, not only for the sake of the doctrine, but even for the salvation of the man to be killed, for he will be prevented through his death from committing even worse sins. In any case, the ordination of the five youths from *gTsang* and *dBus* by *dGongs pa rab gsal* was itself in violation of the rules. All in all, the narration of *Bu ston* appears to us to be almost certainly an attempt, accepted by posterity as a historical account, to demonstrate an unbroken continuity between the first and second diffusion of Buddhism in Tibet (the *snga dar* and the *phyi dar*). The ordinations performed between the first and second period could thus be judged as fully valid from the point of view of the doctrine. In this way too the orthodoxy of the little monastic centres which arose in the intermediate period, and which were linked to the old tradition by dubious connections, was confirmed.

Leaving aside these details, which are of purely formal interest for us, though they would have been of fundamental importance for *Bu ston*, there can be no doubt that the persecution carried out by *Glang dar ma* did not lead to the total destruction of Buddhism in Tibet. At most it caused a decline. From what has been narrated here in brief, and from other records, it is clear that in the Eastern provinces conditions were favourable for a revival of Buddhism in accordance with its authentic tradition, and rejecting the deviations and distortions previously mentioned. *dGe rab gsal* could be consecrated because in *Khams* the essential number of monks for the ordination could be gathered together. In *Tsong kha*, too, Buddhism put up a successful resistance in the tenth and eleventh centuries. In the Eastern provinces the school of the teacher Vairocana, who had been exiled there, had gathered numerous disciples. In *Khams* itself (in Jyekundo) Smrti, who came from Nepal, had brought a school into life. He was the teacher of *'Brom ston*, the founder of the monastery of *Rwa sgrengs* (Reting, 1057, cf.p.35). On the western borders of the country *Rin chen bzang po* and Atisa were both at work; more will be said of them below. In the frontier regions, contact was never entirely broken with neighbouring countries, which had a long Buddhist tradition even if it was now being placed in question by the changed historical situation.

After the expulsion of the Tibetans from Turkestan it is certain that there was a massive return to Tibet of Buddhist lay people, merchants, officials and so on, and surely also monks. If therefore the tradition insists on the continuity of Buddhism in Tibet, despite the events during and after the reign of *Glang dar ma*, we can acknowledge it as on the whole correct, with the above reservations. Buddhism survived this period of crisis in two different forms, one lay and the other monastic. The lay or semi-lay form had a mainly magical orientation, and was characterized by a subjective reading of the texts, particularly of the Tantric scriptures which were now taken literally, and not according to the esoteric tradition of interpretation established in India and later transmitted to Tibet. Along with this, old ritual customs which had little or nothing to do with Buddhism were often put into circulation again in Buddhist dress. This brought about a growth of immoral practices such that one could speak of 'bandit monks'.

This movement was followed, at a slightly later date, by a revival of monasticism, thanks to the founding of little temples (*lha khang*), around which gathered the spiritual heirs of a religious teacher whose name the community bore: feeble sparks gradually shining up once more. These *lha khang* were probably chapels like those which one can still come across today in Western Tibet; they have for the most part been destroyed in Central Tibet, as a consequence of the more violent history of that region. They consisted of a rectangular *cella*, at the centre of which was an altar with the image of the god to whom the shrine was dedicated. In many cases there ran about this *cella* a corridor intended for ritual circumambulation (in a clockwise direction). In front of the building there was an atrium.

2 *Rin chen bzang po* and Atisa

A further impulse towards the so-called second diffusion (*phyi dar*) of Buddhism took place in West Tibet, in the province of *mNga' ris*, which covers the regions of Ladakh, *Zangs dkar*, *Pu hrang* and *Gu ge*.

According to the tradition, these Western regions, which had been under Tibetan rule from the earliest years of the dynasty, had at this period fallen under the control of certain families descended from the former kings of Tibet. As my researches in North-West Nepal have shown, a new dynasty, the Malla, belonging to the Khasia tribe, had already come to power there at an early period, at least in the region around *Pu hrang*. This dynasty established its capital at Semja[8] in Nepal, and from there extended its control over *Pu hrang*. Even if the point in time at which this dynasty originated is uncertain, it can be accepted that it was already ruling in North-West Nepal by around the tenth century. Although this princely house showed itself to be extremely tolerant in its Nepalese domain, favouring the local cults everywhere and even showing Saivite leanings, after its conquests in Tibet it became a supporter of Buddhism. The kings of the first dynasties were probably led to favour Buddhism by political considerations as well as by their inclination to the faith of their ancestors. They found themselves in the middle of a conquered and partly hostile country, a region from which several influential *Bon po* teachers had originated or where they had taught, a country in which the indigenous religious traditions maintained themselves stubbornly. The pro-Buddhist policy of the Malla kings arose then, apart from religious convictions, from motives not unlike those which had formerly led King *Khri srong lde brtsan* to propagate Buddhism. The most significant figures of this dynasty are *Ye shes 'od* and *Byang chub 'od*. *Ye shes 'od* chose several youths and sent them to Kashmir to study the Buddhist teachings. One of these youths was later to become prominent under the name of *Rin chen bzang po* (958-1055). Kashmir was an appropriate place not only because of its nearness, but also because the last splendour of the Buddhist schools then held sway there, and famous religious teachers preserved both the speculative and logical tradition, and the practice of Tantra and ritual. At the end of their education, the youths returned from Kashmir to their homeland, along with teachers and also some artists, and they began to propagandize their faith over a wide region under the protection of the court.

Rin chen bzang po operated on two parallel levels: the erection of numerous chapels (*lha khang*) in the lands under the rule of the King of *Gu ge* and in neighbouring regions (the tradition speaks of no less than 108 chapels (*lha khang*)[9]), and an intensive work of translation. In all *Rin chen bzang po*, alone or along with collaborators, translated and revised 158 texts, both long and short, which were included in the *bKa' 'gyur* and *bsTan 'gyur*.[10] A school formed itself around him. Buddhism expanded through West Tibet, and made a breach in the *Bon* community. The king wished to invite a luminary of the doctrine from India to his country. His choice fell on Atisa, one of the four directors of the great University of Nalanda.

The powerful stimulus which *Rin chen bzang po* and Atisa brought to the revival of Buddhism in Western Tibet is an indisputable fact. Precisely at a time when dark clouds were gathering over Buddhism in India, Indian teachers from Kashmir and Nepal began to flow into these regions of Tibet.

The largest of the temples built in Western Tibet at that time, that of *mTho gling*, was erected, according to the tradition, on the model of Otantapura in India (of course this refers only to the *dkyil 'khor lha khang*, used for initiation; the whole complex of religious buildings is the result of a long development). In these circumstances it goes without saying that it was not only sacred texts and Buddhist teachers that came to Tibet. The Buddhist temple is unthinkable without its decoration. In order to perform the ceremonies, a chapel also had to possess statues of wood, bronze and stucco, and the liturgical instruments required for a form of ritual which was carried out strictly in accordance with precise rules. The frescoes decorating the walls illustrated the liturgical acts carried out in the Tantras, or portrayed the offering goddesses (*mchod pa'i lha mo*)–a hypostatization and transposition into human form of the most important components of the ritual, flowers, lights, even smiles and so on. The paintings on linen or cotton base, which already had a long history in India, and were especially favoured by the Buddhists, would not have been lacking either. These were called *pata* in India, in Tibet *sku thang* (or *thang ka*, generally known as 'Tibetan banners', or Tibetan temple standards).

The religious fervour soon spread to Central Tibet too. In this connection the continuous stream of Tibetan pilgrims to India was of great importance, and in particular the *lotsava* or translators who were part of it. These men visited the sacred places of Buddhist tradition in India in order to collect books, to study in the schools of Indian teachers, to be initiated by them into Tantric liturgy and to be instructed in the oral tradition of the mystical, ascetic and yogic texts, and in Tantric practice. However, Indian teachers also were now crossing the Himalayas more frequently in the opposite direction, as a result of the revival of Hinduism in India, and the Muslim invasions. They brought with them, of course, their books, and their protective deities.

So it came about that Atisa too came to the heartland of Tibet, to Nethang (*sNye thang*), only a few kilometres from Lhasa. He died at Nethang in 1054. His work had included not only the diffusion of the doctrine which had already been codified, but in particular a new emphasis on the cult of the goddess Tara, to whom he was especially devoted. He wrote concise texts to serve as introductions leading on to a more profound study of the Buddhist doctrine of salvation.

During the period of transition, Buddhism had become a religion in which the laity were taking a more and more central role. It was in view of this that the masters of the 'second diffusion of the teaching' emphasized the necessity of a solid tradition of teaching, which could remove the possibility of arbitrary interpretations of the sacred texts. The authority and validity of the doctrine had to be guaranteed through direct transmission from master to student. When *'Brom ston* asked Atisa which was more important and more basic (*gtso*), the text of the scriptures (*bka'*, Revelation, and *bstan bcos*, Skt. *sastra*, the books written by Indian masters), or one's teacher's instructions (*bla ma'i gdams ngag*), Atisa replied that direct instruction from one's teacher is more important (No.78, p.160). So it came about that the first two schools of Buddhism to appear in Tibet, those which trace their origins back to Atisa and *Mar pa*, both bear the name *bka' brgyud* (*Jo bo rje'i bka' brgyud*, No.78, p.185b). These schools, at least with respect to the esoteric tradition, recognize the same Indian teachers. The school which *Mar pa* founded still retains the name of *bKa' brgyud*, while the followers of Atisa, the *bKa' gdams pa*, also called themselves *bKa' brgyud bka' gdams pa*. The direct instruction (*gdams ngag*, *zhal gdams*) of the disciple by the master was held to guarantee both the correct interpretation of the scriptures, and the right understanding of the spirit concealed behind their words, thus enabling the Buddha's word to fulfil its mission of salvation. It is clear from the *bKa' gdams pa* literature that the objective of the first teachers was to create a solidly based school, to gather round them tested disciples who would be capable of transmitting the tradition to later generations. The teaching was mostly in the form of discourses, which were based on such condensed presentations as those of Atisa (No.78), *'Brom ston* and *Po to pa*, or sometimes on the responses which these masters had given on various occasions to students or inquirers. The teaching made use of illustrative stories (*gtam*). Its essential features were classified into groups (*tshan*) of three, five, six or seven topics, which were in their turn again sub-divided, evidently for ease in memorizing and to provide a framework for discussion (cf. No.78, p.185b).

The teaching aimed in the first place at the purification of the mind (*blo sbyong*), at the realization of the ethical and esoteric principles of Buddhism. Much less time was devoted to Buddhism's highly-developed theoretical side. Essentially this instruction was limited to leading the disciple to a better understanding of his own mind and to the achievement of insight into 'voidness' as the limiting state of things (*mthar thug*), together with compassion. The thought of Enlightenment from the point of view of ultimate reality is equated with 'voidness', while compassion results from the same thought when considered from the standpoint of conventional truth (No.78, pp.161, 167). 'Voidness' is the 'body of essence', compassion the 'body of form'.

A number of these *bKa' gdams pa* masters were given the title *dge ba'i bshes gnyen* or *dge bshes* (also spelled *dge shes*), corresponding to the Indian *kalyanamitra*, that is one who is able, owing to the profundity of his doctrine and of his wisdom, to lead others on the way of salvation. The esoteric tradition (*sngags*) too was in no way neglected. The renovators of Buddhism in Tibet would have been led to take the Tantras into consideration both through their own educational background, intellectual and spiritual, and through the correspondence of these teachings to the Tibetans' characteristic propensity towards the magical and esoteric (No.79, p.12b). The Nepalese teacher *Tsan du hang ngu* used to say that the Tibetans did not pay sufficient attention to his explanations of the Prajnaparamita teachings (Tib. *Pha rol tu phyin pa*, *Phar phyin*), but whenever he expounded the secret mantras their astonishment knew no end. At any rate the function of the master, the Lama, became more and more indispensable, and his superior status was no longer open to question. His qualities, the relationship between him and the student, the spiritual advantages derived from this relationship, were described ever more insistently. However, it should be noted that the spiritual life of Tibet was not simply attached to the Indian tradition in a nominal way. A discipline was imposed upon the revived Buddhism of Tibet, and its validity had from now on to be continually tested through comparison with the Indian tradition. This was especially necessary for the Tantric practices which these masters reintroduced into Tibet, for here the danger of misunderstandings and false interpretations had already become obvious. In fact these practices were from this time on to be restricted to initiates; their transmission took place more orally than through commentaries or exegetical writings. All the same, the existence of exorcists, or adepts of esoteric schools, is attested by the *bKa' gdams pa* sources themselves, where several masters are designated by the term *yogin* (Tib. *rnal 'byor pa*).

Starting from these premises, and considering the particular spiritual nature of the Tibetans, it is understandable that the monastic community, and each individual monk, came to be considered as sacred. It was the ordination, or in the case of the Tantric schools the initiation (*dbang*), which conferred this quality upon them. The initiation was thought, as will be seen later, to confer supernatural power, and to place its bearer outside of the realm of the ordinary. The initiated did not only achieve special experiences, they also often acquired powers which would have recalled to the believers the power (*mthu*) which had been ascribed in a high degree to the exorcists. Here there came into play expectations and beliefs which form the common heritage of Tibetan religion, whether *Bon po* or Buddhist. In addition, the monks of the little reconstituted communities represented, in their place in the chapel (*lha khang*), the mental body (*thugs rten*) of the Buddha. Thus they became imbued with the aura of sacredness which radiates from the physical body of the Buddha (represented by his image) and his verbal body (in the form of the sacred scriptures).

Texts attributed to the Buddha himself, as well as the commentaries of the masters, had praised the blessings which resulted from the construction of religious buildings, temples or *stupa*,[11] and the beneficial influence which was assured for anyone who commissioned ritual paintings or images, or who caused the sacred scriptures to be copied, recited or read out in public. Such meritorious acts were able to influence the course of karmic acts for the better and even to guide them on to another path. A *stupa*, a statue, a book, the reading of a sacred text: all these set into motion automatically a quantity of merit, effective beyond and in addition to the actions accomplished in daily life. Ideas of this sort had already come to maturity in India. They arrived in Tibet in the form of already codified rules, and found there soil particularly suited for their growth. Observance of these precepts, and generosity towards monks and religious dignitaries in general, was regarded as especially beneficial for both the spiritual and material well-being of the donor. They created a kind of guarantee, a sort of talisman against the dangers threatening from all directions. It is clear that from the beginning there had been a close reciprocal alliance between the religious community and the lay world. The monastic community was supported by the lay world; it conferred on it its own spiritual support and protection, and received from it in exchange its necessary material security and the assurance of future prosperity. In this way the basis was created for the reconstruction of the monastic communities as institutions of economic power, and therefore as decisive factors in Tibetan history. It is not by chance that the new propagandists for Buddhism joined caravans of merchants (No.113, p.203). From the start of the revival, all appropriate attention was given to the commercial aptitudes of the adepts (loc.cit: 'Ding [*'Bring*], as he is skilful in transacting business, is to be the custodian of the place'). The reviving community in Central Tibet enjoyed the aid of a prince, or rather a landed nobleman of *bSam yas*, just as *Rin chen bzang po* and the movement emanating from him was encouraged by the favour of the kings of Western Tibet.

Alongside the specifically monastic movement, the little communities undertaking the discipline (Vinaya), created with the support of kings or local potentates, there grew up the movement of the 'Perfected Ones' (*grub thob*), linked with the Siddha school of India. These *grub thob* were Tibetan ascetics who rejected all the orthodox and conventional forms. These monks did not feel themselves bound to any discipline. They preferred a wandering life, and were not obliged to be celibate. They taught that only the practice of yoga, and *hatha yoga* in particular, brought about the consubstantiation, the sameness of essence, with the radiant Mind of the Buddha. This emphasis on the technique of yoga did not in general exclude a theoretical preparation, as will be shown in Chapter 4. The Tantras, which lie at the base of these currents, recognize the necessity of a doctrinal training following the basic outlines of the system of Nagarjuna, or of the *cittamatra* teachings (cf.p.31). In practice, however, the special and arbitrary methods for the achievement of ecstasy which are peculiar to this school, along with the oddness of the ways of behaving which it prescribes, led to a deep antagonism between the two tendencies, the logical and doctrinal, and the gnostic, and this opposition also found its expression in a fundamentally different outlook on life.

This asceticism of the Siddha or *grub thob* school spread after the second diffusion of Buddhism. It is enough to recall the masters of two schools of this kind who had significant success in Tibet; *Mar pa*, representative and interpreter of the initiatory tradition going back to the Indian teachers Tilopa and Naropa, and head of the Tibetan school of the *bKa' brgyud pa*, and *Pha dam pa Sangs rgyas*, to whom the *gCod* school traces its origins. As elsewhere, there existed in these schools also a spiritual transmission from master to disciple, which soon, however, became institutionalized into monastic organizations. In the course of this process, the master gradually became the supreme head of a religious community. Financial interests were not absent in this process; indeed one can truly speak of greed in the case of some of these ascetics (*grub thob*). Following the example of the Indian masters, they did not dispense their initiatory teachings without an appropriate payment. This, however, was not demanded as a payment—spiritual things, it is said, have no price. It was to be seen, rather in the manner of the *daksina*[12] in India, as an obligatory expression of thanks on the part of the student, or as a sign of his willingness to make sacrifices. The biographies of *Mar pa* and the other *lotsava* are very enlightening in this respect. Before they set out for India on the search for their master, their *guru*, for initiatory consecrations or books, they had had to accumulate gold and riches. After their return to Tibet, they naturally expected the same treatment from their disciples. Thus riches accumulated about the masters. Their property brought about the need for an organization. Certainly, as in India, there were exceptions to this rule; Tibet too could show examples of unselfish teachers, who shunned any contact with the goods of this world.

3 The foundation of the great monasteries

The foundation of the monastery of *Zha lu* took place in the year 1040, that of *Rwa sgrengs* (Reting) in 1057, that of *Sa skya* in 1073. *Thel*, which was later generally known under the name of *gDan sa Thel* (or *Thil*), was brought into existence in 1158 by *Phag mo gru pa*, a disciple of *sGam po pa*, himself a student of *Mi la ras pa*. Other monasteries founded at about this time include *'Bri gung* (or *khung*), 1167, whose monks were long rivals of the *Sa skya pa*, *Tshal*, 1175, also in rivalry with *Sa skya*, and *mTshur phu*, 1189. All of these monasteries had important religious figures for founders or patrons. Each master emphasized his own tendency, doctrinal, mystical or yogic. The continually increasing secular power of the religious communities created antagonisms much more violent than theological differences of opinion. It released to a growing extent a militant attitude which aspired to hegemony in the temporal world as well as in the spiritual.

After centuries full of unrest and social disorder, a whole new situation came into being. The great religious communities arose out of a symbiosis of sacred and secular power. From now on the history of Tibet would be created by the abbots, as in the case of the *Sa skya pa*, or by the great landowners who, as the 'helpers' and secular protectors of important religious teachers, founded monasteries in their names. Since these powerful families concentrated their attention upon their particular monastery, their interests came to merge with that of the monastic community into an indissoluble unity.

Thus we arrive at the time of the creation of the first Mongol empire, that of Cinggis Khan. When the danger of the Mongols approached the borders of Tibet, there was called, according to ancient custom, a kind of assembly, at which it was decided to parley with Cinggis Khan. *Jo ga* and *Kun dga' rdo rje* of *Tshal* were entrusted with negotiating the Tibetan submission. By this time the *Sa skya pa* monks had already achieved great authority, but the other most powerful monasteries were also competing for the favour of the Mongols. The *Sa skya pa* emerged from this competition as the winners. Links of a special kind were formed between the court of the Yüan dynasty (the Mongol rulers of China) and Tibet. *'Phags pa* of *Sa skya* conferred on Qubilai Khan the initiation of *Kye rdo rje* (Skt. *Hevajra*), and in exchange the emperor granted to him sovereignty over Tibet. Emperor and abbot entered into a firm arrangement, resembling that between some emperors and some popes in European history. The territory of Tibet was divided into thirteen districts (*chol kha*), and these were subdivided into myriarchies (divisions of 10,000, Tib. *khri skor*). A census of the population was carried out for the purpose of tax collection, corvée, tribute assessment and troop recruitment. This system of administration continued to exist also under the *Phag mo gru pa* rulers (cf. Chapter 3).

To check the power of the abbots, officials called *dpon chen* were appointed, military commanders responsible to the Yüan emperor for security and peace in the country. They were also answerable for the keeping of amicable relationships between the monastic communities and the secular nobility, who often engaged in violent feuds among themselves. The myriarchies put into operation once more, although with new content, the military organization which had existed at the time of the kings. The myriarchs were appointed by the Mongol emperor, but these nominations in general only confirmed the situation already in effect. The investiture was of a purely formal character; the intervention of the Yüan dynasty and of the following Chinese dynasties was restricted to conferring the titles of appointment from time to time, and receiving the gifts of particular chiefs on specified occasions. Nevertheless the fundamental confirmation of Tibetan rulers here in question was to have important consequences for the future.

THREE

GENERAL CHARACTERISTICS OF LAMAISM

1 Fundamentals

Lamaism had reached its definitive form, and its doctrinal structure and ritual had been irrevocably determined, by the end of the fifteenth century (*Tsong kha pa* died in 1419). All of the schools and doctrinal movements had taken part in this evolution, which had lasted for several centuries, and in its course they too had reached their full maturity.

First of all, it should be remembered that the Tibetan expression of Buddhism, commonly called Lamaism, absorbed many ritual elements and magical attitudes, as well as a whole series of local spirits, all of which had been established in the Land of Snow long before the entry of Buddhism. Thus the divergence between some of the liturgical forms and concepts of Lamaism and the Buddhism found in Indian literary texts is entirely understandable.

At the same time, we should not lose sight of the fact that we are acquainted with Lamaism primarily from its still living ritual forms. What we know of it is based not only on literary accounts (although these exist in great abundance) or on the biographies of its most important figures (although these give us a tangible idea of how Lamaism was lived by men of different times). It comes above all from the direct observation of religious practice within Tibetan society and within the monastic communities which the Buddhist tradition regards as sacred.

By contrast, we know Indian Mahayana Buddhism in its late and extreme forms (as transmitted to Tibet) only in some of its doctrinal aspects and in its basic liturgical forms, and even for these we are limited to the schematic treatments which have come down to us in Sanskrit, or in Tibetan or Chinese translations. If we were in a position to reconstruct the gnostic and magical Buddhism of the Indian Vajrayana in the form in which it was understood and practised by, for example, the general public of Uddiyana (Swat) or Bengal between the eighth and eleventh centuries, then we would surely be able to establish many more analogies with Lamaism than we can see at present. The rich magical heritage transmitted in the Tantric literature, derived from many sources, fell in Tibet upon extremely fertile soil, in which it could continue to prosper.

In discussing Lamaism then we have first to distinguish between Buddhism, and the pre-Buddhist beliefs, myths, rituals and invocatory formulae of Tibet, which Lamaism has skilfully reworked, and embodied into its own religious world. This magical–religious heritage which was received by Lamaism was certainly not introduced in its entirety from India, though it was often codified into Indian-influenced ritual schemes. It will be dealt with in a later chapter (Chapter 6), devoted to the folk religion; it is this side of Lamaism which provides the Tibetan people with their support and defence against the powers of evil.

On the other hand monastic Lamaism, both in its teachings and its ritual procedures, has always to be considered in relation to the Buddhist tradition. This does not mean that Lamaism should be seen merely as a kind of appendix to Indian Buddhism, or that one should regard it as consisting only of the expositions of Indian Buddhist teachings. Such an oversimplified approach is certainly inadmissible. There is no doubt that the Indian tradition of thought lies at the base of the Lamaist interpretation of the relationship between the world of appearances and the world considered to exist in reality. Lamaist thought, however, is individual in many respects, and particular aspects of speculative thought and of practice have received special emphasis in the course of the development of its various schools. It is precisely these individual cases of emphasis or convergence that are of special interest to us here. If in the present account of Lamaism we, too, are often forced to repeat things that are well known to those familiar with Buddhism in general and Indian Buddhism in particular, we wish, however, to try to illuminate certain problems to which Tibetan Buddhism has devoted particular attention. We will have to be concise, although the extremely complicated details of the way to salvation, of the homologies between the stages of contemplation and ecstasy on the one part, and the corresponding steps of ascetic purification on the other, deserve a more detailed treatment.

In considering this restriction, it must always be emphasized that the Indian Buddhism of which the Tibetan Buddhist teachings represents the continuation and development was that professed by the Buddhist communities of India, Central Asia and China, on the eve of the collapse which occurred in the first two regions as a result of historical events (the Muslim invasions) or inner decay. What this implies is that Buddhism, at the time of its entry into Tibet, brought with it not only mutually divergent doctrinal statements, but also heterogeneous, if often parallel, concepts, of a more or less clearly formulated nature. It also carried with it a many-layered liturgical structure, interpreted through the most subtle symbolism, mystical and yogic practices for the easier acquisition of special modes of experience, and a notable heritage of magic, extremely varied in its forms and fed from sources lying far in the past. Such a system was, as already indicated, well able to meet the expectations of the less educated masses of the people.

The monastic ordination, and the monastic regime as a whole, was defined in all its details by a whole armoury of regulations. An immense literature contained minute prescriptions for these matters. The rules of discipline (Vinaya, Tib. *'dul ba*), formed a part of the scriptures, and had to be accepted without question. This was true also of the *mdo* (Skt. *Sutra*) and *rgyud* (Skt. *Tantra*), in other words those scriptures in which the revelations of the Buddha or of his disciples are contained and transmitted.

On questions of doctrine, however, discussion was permitted. Doctrine was dominated by a relativistic view according to which nothing has real independent existence, all is 'void' (*stong pa*, Skt. *sunya*), everything conceivable in empirical experience is held to be without an individual essence, all that appears superficially real can be shown to be without substance at the level of absolute truth. This was the position of the Madhyamika school (Tib. *dbu ma*), the system developed by Nagarjuna, who was the central figure of the doctrine in Tibet also. An alternative way which was open was that of Cittamatra, of 'thought-only' (Tib. *sems tsam*[1]) ascribed to Asanga and Vasubandhu. According to this, apparent reality is nothing more than a representation made by our mind (*sems*, Skt. *citta*), which produces all representations from out of itself, yet is in its own nature also pure radiance.

The Tibetan schools waver between these two positions, and avoid fixing themselves definitely upon one system to the exclusion of the other. However, the following can be said; while Nagarjuna always remains the central figure of the doctrine in Tibet, the *bKa' brgyud pa* and *rNying ma pa* schools tend to emphasize Cittamatra more strongly, while the *dGe lugs pa* hold more strictly to Nagarjuna and the Madhyamika position.

Logic (*mtshan nyid*, Skt. *nyaya*) can be considered as an auxiliary to the understanding of the doctrine, and therefore as a tool assigned for the goal of salvation. It had been developed to the height of perfection by Dinnaga and Dharmakirti, and the *dGe lugs pa*, followed in part by the *Sa skya pa*, affirmed its indispensability as the foundation of the teachings. The other schools however regarded it as only a preparatory study.

When considering the practices through which the goal of salvation, as defined in the Buddhist teachings, is to be realized, the problem can be defined as the choice between the immediate way and the gradual path. Is liberation brought about in an instantaneous moment of awakening, or is it the result of a progressive conquest? As mentioned in Chapter 1, the dispute on this subject had already broken out at the time of King *Khri srong lde brtsan*, between the Chinese teacher, or *Hwa shang*, who followed the Ch'an school, and the disciples of Santaraksita and Kamalasila. It was concerned with a fundamental question: is luminous intuition, blazing unexpectedly from out of our nature, by itself sufficient to bring about salvation, or must this saving vision be prepared for by a specific practice, that recommended by the Prajnaparamita teachings? The discussion involved, then, the two fundamental concepts of Buddhist mysticism, 'higher cognition' (*shes rab*, Skt. *prajna*) and the 'means', the practice (*thabs*, Skt. *upaya*). These are traditionally seen as working closely together with each other, as indissolubly intertwined. Another problem was closely connected to this. This was the problem of our identity, in other words the question of whether there exists an identity between the Buddha and all living beings. Does this inexpressible essence, this luminous mind, in each of us, shine out directly like a lightning flash and free us from error? Or can the attainment of salvation be the fruit only of a long-lasting process of both spiritual and ethical purification? This question inevitably led to a discussion of mind (*sems*, Skt. *citta*), and the problem of its connection with the light to which it is identical in essence (*sems = 'od gsal*), and to the void (*stong pa*); it also brought up the problem of the relationship between the mind which is imprisoned through its actions in the world of experience, and that radiant mind or 'void' which has independent existence.

The Tantra offered countless different paths, emphasizing variously gnosticism, liturgy or yoga. These paths are expressed through symbologies and rituals differing from one Tantric cycle to another. The single basic form of the meditation is subject to infinite variation in detail. In it, the individual deities, represented through their symbols, are brought into existence, that is made visible to the mystic, either externally, in an objectification in front of him, or within his own body. These divine forms are evoked not only for the attainment of salvation, but also for liturgical or magical reasons. Four, or sometimes five, magical actions (Skt. *karma*) are distinguished, usually *zhi* (calming offended deities), *rgyas* (increasing wealth), *dbang* (driving out hostile powers) and *drag* (acquiring the power of inspiring terror). Each deity is described in a prescribed text (*sgrub thabs*, Skt. *sadhana*) which gives its form and attributes, and thus enables the meditator to evoke it and cause it to merge with him. Its 'essential voidness'[2] must be recognized following the evocation, since nothing exists apart from pure radiant mind. Mind is without any form, though all forms emerge from it in their apparent manifestations. Here we are in the realm of a freedom of mystical experience on which no limits can be imposed. Out of it new formulae of meditation and invocation constantly arose and proliferated; for each meditator left his state of ecstasy in the certainty that he had been granted the revelation of a unique divine manifestation. The methods of evocation (*sgrub thabs*, Skt. *sadhana*) used to create the state of ecstasy flourished in Tibet on the fertile soil of the ascetics' aptitudes to visions.

2 The most important schools*

Divergences were acceptable between various interpretations of the revealed word and the commentaries, as long as the limits of the faith were not transgressed. Tibetan authors of theological treatises often mention the classical Indian grouping of Buddhist schools of thought into eighteen, but this classification is of dubious value and of mostly historical interest, and it can scarcely be justified with respect to Tibetan Buddhism.[3] In reality the schools of thought within Lamaism can in no way be traced back to these eighteen schools.[4]

One has to bear in mind always the profound division between *mdo* (Skt. *Sutra*) and *rgyud* (Skt. *Tantra*), and between their corresponding doctrinal systematizations. Of course Sutra and Tantra are not mutually exclusive, and frequently meet. The Sutra teachings always form the speculative framework, as we have already emphasized: Madhyamika relativism (in its two particular forms, Svatantra and Prasangika), and Cittamatra (in which only *sems* exists). Speculative thought never extends outside the boundaries of these two principal positions.

With respect to the Tantric teachings, a distinction has to be made between the orthodox Tantra, and those Tantric texts considered by other schools to be dubious, or entirely inauthentic. These latter are the Tantras (*rgyud*) accepted by the *rNying ma pa* school, as contrasted with the 'new' *rgyud* (*rgyud gsar ma*) newly introduced, or revised, after the second diffusion of the teachings, and which could be validated through recognized Sanskrit originals, and interpreted in accordance with a tested Indian tradition.

An adequate sub-division of the Lamaist schools would require yet further criteria. The Tibetans classify them according to the mon-

* This section is primarily directed to Tibetanists; non-specialists can go on to the next section.

asteries in which particular traditions of interpretation were cultivated, or on the basis of the religious teachers to which particular schools can be traced back, or according to the religious or exegetical tradition preferred within a particular school. In the division proposed by No.82 (4,1) for example, *Sa skya pa*, *Jo nang pa*, *Shangs pa* and *'Bri gung pa* are terms derived from the names of places or monasteries, *Kar ma pa* and *Bu lugs pa* (= 'disciples of *Bu ston*') are named after teachers, and *bKa' gdams pa*, *rDzogs chen*, *Phyag chen* and *Zhi byed pa* refer to the school's secret initiatory doctrines or to its emphasis on particular traditions or types of experience.

The teachers representing each of these schools are extremely numerous. There is little point in enumerating them in detail, especially as their originality is mostly very limited. Some are distinguished through their organizational talent, or because the impulse for the founding of famous monasteries, or the creation of important schools of exegesis, is ascribed to them, or for their activity as writers and commentators. Very rarely is it a question of a creative mind who has attempted to break through the framework of a tradition regarded as sacrosanct in order to open up new avenues for speculative thought, or to impose new disciplinary forms upon the religious community. *Tsong kha pa* (1357-1419) was an exception of this kind. Others again possessed considerable political authority, as with the first *Sa skya pa* abbots, who during the period of their pre-eminence, which lasted somewhat less than a hundred years, were involved everywhere in the struggles then taking place in Tibet.

If we restrict ourselves then to the most notable figures, then in the *Sa skya pa* school the so-called 'Five Greats' can be mentioned. The first of these was *Kun dga' snying po* (1092-1158), whose studies concerned primarily the Tantric cycle relating to Hevajra, the patron deity of the *Sa skya pa*. *bSod nams rtse mo* (1142-82) worked on a systematic ordering and classification of the Tantric literature, and also provided summary expositions of the teachings. *rJe btsun Grags pa rgyal mtshan* (1147-1216) was the author of numerous works of Tantric and doctrinal exegesis, as well as of medical treatises. *Sa skya Pandita* (1182-1231) turned his attention primarily to problems of doctrine and logic (*Tshad ma rigs pa'i gter*), basing himself upon the *Pramanavarttika* of Dharmakirti; he was also interested in rhetoric. *'Phags pa* (1235-80?), finally, was an extremely prolific writer who discussed all conceivable doctrinal, Tantric and liturgical topics, and also addressed numerous letters to Mongol princes in which he summarized the basic elements of the Buddhist teachings.

Bu ston rin po che (1290-1364), of the monastery of *Zha lu* in *gTsang* (founded by *lCe* in 1040) undertook a thorough revision of the entire doctrinal and liturgical literature. His particular achievement was to establish and arrange, in a virtually definitive form, the writings of the Indian interpreters and commentators, in the pages of the *bsTan 'gyur*, for which he also supplied a catalogue. He undertook the immense task of exegesis and commentary on all the fundamental texts of Buddhism, both those on disciplinary precepts (*'dul*, Vinaya) and the revelation proper (*mdo* and *rgyud*, Sutra and Tantra). This huge enterprise, in which he revised the entire religious literature and arranged it in a systematic form left permanent traces, which can also be seen in the arts; the wall paintings of the *mchod rten* of Gyantse, and those of many other monuments, were undoubtedly influenced by his precise descriptions of the various *mandala*[5] and of the individual Tantric cycles. His descriptions formed an indispensable foundation for the iconographical schemes (*bkod*) which inspired the painters. The school of the *Bu pa* (named after *Bu ston*), also called *Zha lu pa* after the monastery where his activity took place, goes back to this master. The differences between this school and the *Sa skya pa* are insignificant.

The *bKa' gdams pa* (cf.p.23) trace themselves back to Atisa, who came to Tibet in 1042 and died at *sNye thang* in 1054, and to *Rin chen bzang po*, in other words to the 'second diffusion of the doctrine'. The school was given a significant impetus by *'Brom ston rGyal ba'i 'byung gnas* (1003-63 or 64), the most important disciple of Atisa. It can also boast other well-known religious teachers: *Po to pa Rin chen gsal* (died 1105), the founder of the monastery of *Po to*, *Blo gros grags pa*, founder of the monastery of *sNar thang*, *Phu chung pa gZhon nu rgyal mtshan* (1031-1100) and *sPyan snga Tshul khrims 'bar*, founder of the monastery of *Lo* (1095). While not rejecting the Tantric exercises of the Vajrayana, this school developed them intelligently, opposing the aberrations and heresies into which the followers of Tibetan Buddhism had fallen. One of the Tantras particularly cultivated by them was the *Tattvasamgraha*, and it is the cycles of gods of this Tantra, dedicated to a particular form of Vairocana (*Kun rig*, cf.p.197) among others, which predominate in the chapels founded by *Rin chen bzang po* in West Tibet. This school exerted a significant influence upon the development of the teachings in Tibet, for its masters enjoyed great prestige, and in consequence followers of the other sects studied with them attentively. At this time there took place the editing of the great collections of the *bKa' 'gyur* and the *bsTan 'gyur*, massive compilations of all the texts translated into Tibetan. The original redactions of these collections, which contained the translations of India's literary and spiritual heritage to Tibet, were made at *Zha lu* and *sNar thang*.[6]

The *bKa' brgyud pa* school gives particular emphasis to Tantric exercises, and to the practice of yoga (or *mahamudra*, cf.p.71). This school is connected with the Indian Siddha Naropa through his student *Chos kyi blo gros* of *Mar*, better known as *Mar pa*, or as the *lotsava* of *Mar* (1012-96).

In general, the Tibetans divide the students of *Mar pa* into three groups: those entrusted with the interpretation and explanation of texts (*bshad bka' 'dzin*), the ascetics (*grub bka' 'dzin*), and the students whose task it was to transmit the esoteric practices for transferring one's consciousness into other beings, particularly into dead bodies (*'grong 'jug bka' 'babs*). *Mar pa*'s son *Dar ma mdo sde* received this secret teaching from his father, but taught it to no one in his turn, and it was lost at his death. *Mar pa*'s most important student was *Mi la ras pa* (1040-1123), whom the master initiated into his mystical exercises. The poems of *Mi la ras pa* were composed on the model of the *Dohakosa*, in which the Indian Siddha wrote down the doctrines of their school and the technique of their mystical exercises in allusory language which is often difficult to understand.

The most important students of *Mi la ras pa* were *Ras chung rDo rje grags pa* (1084-1161) and *sGam po pa* (1079-1153). *Ras chung* was sent by his master to India to penetrate more deeply into the yoga which has the so-called 'Six Laws of Naropa' for object. *sGam po pa* was the composer of a kind of *Summa* of Buddhist thought (No.116), which anticipates the later work of this kind written by *Tsong kha pa*, and gives a careful and extremely clear introduction to Buddhism. The treatise 'The Six Laws of Naropa' by *Mar pa*'s teacher enjoys special fame; there is no school among which it is unknown, not even that of the *dGe lugs pa*, since it summarizes the fundamental principles of Vajrayana soteriology in concise form, and has therefore particularly attracted the interest of commentators. A very significant literature thus crystallized about these 'Six Laws', of great psychological interest.

The *bKa' brgyud pa* school split up later into numerous branches, among whom the *'Bri gung pa* deserve special mention; as already noted they entered the political arena in order to contest with the *Sa skya pa* for pre-eminence. They owe their name to the monastery of *'Bri gung*, which was founded by a student of *Phag mo gru pa*, himself a disciple of *sGam po pa*. This monastery however had its greatest success at the time of the *'Bri gung rin po che* (1143-1217). In addition one should mention here the *sTag lung pa*, so named after the monastery of *sTag lung*. *sTag lung bKra shis dpal* (1142-1210) counts as the most important leader of this school. The *'Brug pa* represent another branch, named after that country where they particularly took root, Bhutan (*'Brug yul* in Tibetan); they were founded by *Gling ras pa Pad ma rdo rje* (1128-88). One of the most notable polymaths of Tibet, *Pad ma dkar po* (1526-92) belonged to this school. Also to be mentioned are the *Kar ma pa*, a school which traces its origin to a disciple of *sGam po pa* named *Chos 'dzin dge 'phel Dus gsum mkhyen pa* (1110-93), the founder of the famous monastery of *mTshur phu*. This school, which came to be of great importance, was itself divided into two branches frequently in conflict with each other, which were called red hats (*zhwa dmar*) and black hats (*zhwa nag*) after the colour of the hats worn by the heads of the schools.[7] Another sect also attached to the *bKa' brgyud pa* is that of the *Shangs pa*, founded by *'Ba' ra pa rGyal mtshan dpal bzang* (born 1310). This school traces its origin to a *Bon* follower converted to Buddhism, *Shangs khyung po rnal 'byor pa*, who had studied with numerous Indian masters.

The *Sa skya pa* sub-divided too, giving rise to the *Ngor* school, so called after a monastery in the province of *gTsang*. This school goes back to *Kun dga' bzang po*, who founded the monastery in 1429.

The *bKa' gdams pa* school flowed into that of the *dGe lugs pa*, whose followers also bore the name *bKa' gdams pa gsar ma* ('new *bKa' gdams pa*'). This movement culminated in the synthesis brought about by *Tsong kha pa* (1357-1419), with whom the history of the reformed school (*dGe lugs pa*, *dGe legs pa*), also known as the 'Yellow Sect', begins. In his work *Lam rim chen mo* (which was formally conceived of as a commentary to a short work of Atisa, the *Byang chub lam rim sgron me*) *Tsong kha pa* provided the *Summa* of Lamaist doctrine as he saw it. He made this text the basis of the 'Yellow Sect', and it has become a kind of Bible for them, to which they constantly refer in the form of excerpts, explanations and commentaries. In his *sNgags rim*, *Tsong kha pa* presented a survey of the Tantras recommended to his students, along with an account of the liturgy and of the correct interpretation of the gnosis which brings salvation. *Tsong kha pa*'s work was continued by his two most important students, *Dar ma rin chen*, better known as *rGyal tshab* (1364-1432), and *mKhas grub rje* (1385-1483). Along with their master, these two form an indivisible triad, known as the *yab sras gsum* (the 'father', i.e. the master, and his two 'spiritual sons'; they are always presented as three). This triad brings the development to a final end. While there were a vast number of prolific writers after the time of these three masters (it is enough to recall the literary activity of the Fifth Dalai Lama, *Blo bzang rgya mtsho* (1617-82), which verges on the miraculous), the exegesis of this later period does not have the same definitive character; it is more concerned with the clarification of already assured positions than with enriching the intellectual heritage and opening new ways for thought.

The *Jo nang pa* school, founded by *Shes rab rgyal mtshan*[8] (1292-1361), placed its major emphasis on the *Kalacakra Tantra* and on the doctrine of the *Tathagatagarbha*. Its followers were often regarded with suspicion, because they advocated certain opinions which as we will see, were considered as heterodox by the other schools (cf.p.69). The most important figure of this school was *Taranatha* (born 1575).

The 'Old Ones' (*rNying ma pa*) still remain to be considered. They were so called to distinguish them from the 'New Ones' (*gSar ma*), that is the followers of the 'new Tantras', improved and selected after the second diffusion of the doctrine–the Tantras, that is, of the time after *Rin chen bzang po* and Atisa, and which had been declared valid by the great *Sa skya pa* commentators and by *Bu ston*.

The most eminent figure in the *rNying ma pa* tradition is Padmasambhava (Tib. *Pad ma 'byung gnas*, cf.p.5-7), a master regarded by them as a second Buddha. Many books were attributed to him, and were alleged to have been hidden by him or by his students in order to be rediscovered and diffused in later, more favourable times. This literary genre, which is extraordinarily rich in works, is called *gter ma*.

These extremely numerous *gter ma* were put into circulation at different periods. Each of them was supposedly found by one of a series of discoverers, on whom are bestowed the title of *gter ston*, 'revealer of *gter ma*'. Often these discoverers claim not only to have found the texts, but also to have translated them into Tibetan. In these cases the texts in question were writings on rolled-up yellow leaves (hence the name *thang yig*, *thang*, rolled-up writing, scroll) in non-Tibetan languages, such as Sanskrit or the language of Uddiyana (Swat, the homeland of Padmasambhava). One of the most famous *gter ston* was *O rgyan gling pa*, to whom is ascribed the discovery, in *Shel dkar*, of the *Pad ma thang yig*, a book which contains a testament of King *Khri srong lde brtsan* (cf.p.7), and the narrative of the successive incarnations of Padmasambhava, along with his adventures in Tibet, and numerous prophecies. *O rgyan gling pa* also discovered the *bKa' thang sde lnga*, a book consisting of five chapters. This latter work in particular is of great significance as it contains elements which are indubitably ancient, if much reworked. The *Pad ma thang yig*, on the other hand, was constantly revised, and therefore exists in various versions. It is not without interest that the most important *gter ma*, such as the two books mentioned, were 'discovered' and put into circulation at the time of the first *Phag mo gru pa* king (*O rgyan gling pa* is a contemporary of *Byang chub rgyal mtshan*, died 1373, the founder of the political power of this family, cf.p.40). These texts cannot be separated from the cultural renaissance of which the *Phag mo gru pa* were creators and promoters, nor from the political aspirations of the region of *Yar klungs* where their power was centred. The distribution of the *gter ma* (which were believed to contain the teachings of Padmasambhava and of his divine and human assistants) naturally lent new prestige to the *rNying ma pa* sect, and an authority which corroborated its teachings, to such a degree that at this time the *rNying ma pa* Tantric texts were codified in a vast collection (the *rNying ma rgyud 'bum*). This collection represents a Tantric tradition independent from that regarded as valid by the other sects.[9] This tradition too, and its introduction to Tibet, was ascribed to great Indian masters, contemporaries, collaborators or students of Padmasambhava.

This literature, including the *gter ma*, contains much inauthentic material, but also original texts and liturgical and magical elements to which parallels and analogues exist in the writings of the other schools, for they move in a circle of ideas which is similar although not the same as that of the other schools.

Apart from the *gter ma*, the most important basic text of the *rNying ma pa* is a famous Tantric scripture, the *gSang ba snying po*, in a translation made during the first period of the introduction of the doctrine. The *rNying ma pa* sect reached its apogee in the *rDzogs chen* school, whose most significant representatives were *Nyang ral Nyi ma 'od zer* (born 1136), *Gu ru Chos dbang* (1212-73), and *Klong chen pa* (1308-63). The last of these is the translator of one of the most famous texts of the *rDzogs chen*, the commentary on the *sNying thig*, a text which was allegedly revealed at the time of *Khri srong lde brtsan* by Vimalamitra to *Myang Ting nge 'dzin*.

The *Zhi byed* school, 'the pacifiers' or, better, 'those who pacify suffering' (*sdug sngal zhi byed*), originated with an ascetic from South India, *Pha dam pa Sangs rgyas* (died 1117),[10] who visited Tibet no less than five times (in the course of his fifth journey he also visited China). One of the objectives of this school was the liberation of living beings from suffering in all its forms. The *Zhi byed* school produced a remarkable literature in the course of its development, but it eventually merged with the other schools. However, another school, known as *gCod*,[11] which originated with the same master, survived successfully. Its teachings, which are based on the *Phar phyin*, were taught by *Pha dam pa Sangs rgyas* to *sKyo ston bSod nams bla ma*. It divided into two branches, 'male *gcod*' (*pho gcod*) and 'female *gcod*' (*mo gcod*). The latter was founded by a woman, *Ma gcig Lab sgron ma* (1055-1145), who owed her training to the same *sKyo ston* school; she was met by *Pha dam pa* on the occasion of his third journey to Tibet. Word of some scriptures of this school reached *rDo rje gdan* (Vajrasana), Bodhgaya in India; the books were said to have been brought there by Indian masters and translated into Sanskrit.

3 The conflicts between the schools and their significance for the political history of Tibet. The office of Dalai Lama

We have outlined above the most important tendencies within Tibetan Buddhism. The schools representing these tendencies were concerned to continue in Tibet the tradition which had come from India, even if they were prepared to make compromises between the indigenous liturgical and mythological heritage and the ritual systems of India. These schools, as a totality, constitute the world of Lamaism, in all its various aspects. They were, however, also capable of intervening in the political life of the country in a decisive manner, and thus determining its history.

The entire story of Tibet is characterized by a contest between centrifugal forces on the one side and strivings for unity on the other. The divisive tendencies rest upon the antagonisms between the great families who possessed the estates and pastoral lands. A first attempt to unify the country was made by the dynasty which collapsed with *Glang dar ma*; after it Tibet fell back into new division. The *Sa skya pa* school's attempts at a second re-unification had some success, thanks to the favour which the *Sa skya pa* abbots enjoyed with the Yüan dynasty, but this was more an apparent hegemony than a case of real domination, since there were equally powerful forces at play opposed to the *Sa skya pa*, for instance the *'Bri gung pa*. The myriarchies which the Mongols created were opposed to any centralized control or ambitions at overall power, and thus contained the seeds of a further dissolution. Monastic organizations took the place of the land-holding aristocracy, or allied themselves with them. In this way there came into being communities of interest, and also conflicts whose causes are not always to be sought only in *odium theologicum*; indeed religious differences were often only a pretext. The power of the abbots perceptibly came to replace that of the hereditary feudal nobility as a driving factor in the history of Tibet. The monasteries of the various sects became organizations both economic and political in nature, sometimes opposed to each other, sometimes united in temporary unions for specific ends, although always in reality guarding their independence. This development necessarily led to the aristocracy becoming, in an increasing degree, the secular arm of these powers, to whom they were bound by common interests. A new impulse towards hegemony is bound up with the name of *Byang chub rgyal mtshan* (died 1373), of the family of *Phag mo gru pa*. He began with a revolt against the *Sa skya pa*, who had lost their patrons and protectors with the fall of the Yüan dynasty. The *Phag mo gru pa* were originally *bKa' brgyud pa*, but they were extremely eclectic with respect to religion, and were closely connected to the *bKa' gdams pa* and the *Sa skya pa* also. They rapidly developed into a major power. However, they created the basis for a new fragmentation by assigning the hereditary office of governor (*rdzong dpon*) of the territories they had conquered to certain families who had assisted their rise to power. The *Phag mo gru pa* were dominant on both the secular and the religious plane, and with them a double succession was customary, with the religious power being inherited on one side and the secular on the other. The two powers were, however, quite often united in the same person. Their hegemony was in fact restricted to only part of the country, to *dBus* (Central Tibet), the area where the dynasty which brought about the original unification of Tibet had emerged, and where the *Phag mo gru pa* too now centred their dynastic power. *gTsang* (West-Central Tibet), however, remained outside the realm of their power. Indeed it opposed the *Phag mo gru pa*'s strivings for dominance, placing itself behind the rulers of *bSam grub rtse* and siding with the *Kar ma pa*. The feud between *dBus* and *gTsang*, Central and West-Central Tibet (East Tibet stayed as yet outside this conflict) characterized the events of Tibetan history for two full centuries. During this period a steadily growing circle of leading families was led by deceptive hopes, or under pressure, to favour one or another faction. In the meantime the Yellow Sect was able to consolidate its position; at the time when *bSod nams rgya mtsho* (1543-88) converted the Mongol followers of Altan Khan, the office of Dalai Lama came into being.

The title of Dalai Lama was originally conferred by Altan Khan on *bSod nams rgya mtsho*, who then raised his predecessors *dGe 'dun grub* (1391-1475) and *dGe 'dun rgya mtsho* (1475-1542) retrospectively to the same dignity. These Lamas were regarded as successive rebirths of the same person, according to a theory further discussed in Chapter 5 (pp.134-5). The successive Dalai Lamas were also regarded as incarnations (*sprul sku*) of the Tantric god Avalokitesvara, thus building upon the *Ma ni bka' 'bum*, a *gter ma* text dating probably from the fifteenth century in which Avalokitesvara is described as a kind of patron deity of Tibet, who had already appeared in incarnate form in Tibetan history, for example as King *Khri srong lde brtsan*. The fifth Dalai Lama, *Blo bzang rgya mtsho* (1617-82), was not only concerned with acquiring the widest possible recognition for his sect; he was also attempting to bring about a settlement of the internal strife that was devastating the land, and to re-establish its political unity, not indeed any longer under secular rule, but under the supremacy of the Dalai Lama himself.

In view of the weakness and internal disruption of the *Phag mo gru pa* regime, the Dalai Lama called in the help of the Qosot Mongols. This led to the murder of the king of *gTsang*, and the re-establishment of Tibetan unity through foreign assistance. The way had thus been opened for the interference of foreign powers in the fate of Tibet.

The prestige of the *dGe lugs pa* school (also called *dGa' ldan pa*) received a new impulse in the time of the fifth Dalai Lama through the appearance of a second supreme spiritual dignitary alongside the Dalai Lama. This was the *Pan chen* (from the Sanskrit term *Maha-*

pandita, 'great scholar'); his monastery was *bKra shis lhun po*. The *Pan chen* are re-incarnations too, in that the divine presence of *'Od dpag med* (Skt. *Amitabha*, the god of Infinite Light) takes up his earthly dwelling in them. The theory of the *Pan chen* incarnations was introduced by the fifth Dalai Lama in order to raise the rank of *Blo bzang Chos kyi rgyal mtshan* (1570-1662). In this case too, retrospective validity was conferred upon the theory, and the series was held to begin with *mKhas grub rje*, so that *Blo bzang Chos kyi rgyal mtshan* became the fourth incarnation. As already indicated, this evolution indicated a noticeable growth of the prestige of the *dGe lugs pa* school, who now claimed as their own three supreme religious dignitaries: the Dalai Lama, the *Pan chen* and the *Khri rin po che* (*dGa' ldan khri pa*) or grand abbot of *dGa' ldan*. In the course of political events, however, dissensions frequently occurred between the *Pan chen* and the Dalai Lama, since the *Pan chen* were often not inclined to fall in with the political directives of the Dalai Lama, and preferred to guard their autonomy in the territory of *gTsang*, where they resided and enjoyed greater authority.

Sporadic and futile attempts at resistance took place now and again in subsequent years in this formerly so disrupted land, but in the period following the fifth Dalai Lama a sovereignty which could be described as theocratic became more and more consolidated. The highest governmental power (although restricted as a result of the long-lasting Chinese interference) was vested in the Dalai Lama. Numerous monasteries of other sects were confiscated. The aristocracy retained the privilege (and the obligation) of service in the government; the country was divided into prefectures, which were generally headed by two officials in each case, one civil and one religious. The centrifugal tendencies were stifled for ever, and all power concentrated in the Dalai Lama, at whose side there might, but did not necessarily, stand a kind of regent (*sDe srid*) and an advisory organization. All the same it can be stated that this development by no means led to a general climate of intolerance. While the *dGe lugs pa* school naturally enjoyed the greatest privileges, the other sects were allowed to live in peace, and their monasteries too continued to grow or to decline according to the degree of support from their adherents. If certain sects, like the *rNying ma pa*, were to enjoy less popularity in the future in many parts of Tibet, everyone was nevertheless free to follow the school corresponding to his own convictions.

In this connection, one should not forget that the differences between particular schools were not always very deep. They resulted for the most part from particular features of the method for attaining salvation, from differing theoretical premises, from a preference towards a particular Tantra or from differences in interpreting the experiences revealed by the Tantra in question. In some cases too there were emphases characteristic of particular schools and these only, as with logic (*mtshan nyid*), which was a principal discipline in religious education among the *dGe lugs pa* but did not, however, play the same role in other sects.

With respect to the numerous texts contained in the *bKa' 'gyur* and the *bsTan 'gyur*, however, one cannot say that the same development took place in Tibet as in China, where various texts gave birth to quite different schools, each of which gradually took on a more and more clearly characterized independent existence, taking into themselves significant parts of Chinese thought. The texts preferred by the Tibetans were almost always the same. Tibetan exegesis was influenced in particular by the following: Prajna, Madhyamika, the works of Nagarjuna and of various followers and of Asanga and Haribhadra (who was not translated into Chinese), logic (in China only an elementary text by Dinnaga was translated), and other texts related to Prajna. Those schools concerned particularly with yoga, ascetic practices and *mahamudra*, like the *rNying ma pa* and *bKa' brgyud pa*, devoted their attention especially to all the classes of Tantra.

In spite of such differences in detail, the most respected masters of most schools willingly agreed that disagreements of such kinds could never affect the unity of the faith. The multiplicity of opinions was to be understood as the co-existence of equally valid paths, one easier to negotiate while another is harder, one straight while another is indirect. All, however, lead to the one goal worthy of pursuing: 'liberation from suffering'. Each individual in his particular life chooses the path which is the best and the most suitable (at least as it appears to him) but everyone is guided in such a choice by karmic conditions, which determine one's greater or lesser spiritual maturity, one's higher or lower ability to understand and to actualize the supreme truths taught by the Buddha.[12]

Viewed in this light, the co-existence side by side of monasteries of different schools (*chos lugs*), which is fairly often found, makes sense, although those schools, such as the *rNying ma pa* and the *Jo nang pa*, which were considered as deviant by the dominant orthodoxy, were all the same excluded. In Gyantse the *Sa skya pa*, *Zha lu pa* and *dGe lugs pa* shared in the same sacred precinct, and similarly in Tsethang. Individual masters had no misgivings about visiting the most prominent scholars of other schools, who had made a name for themselves as highly valued representatives of a particular tradition of interpretation or of religious exercises. *Tsong kha pa*'s case can be taken as typical; he owed his doctrinal and spiritual training to visits to the most famous masters of his time, without any sort of prejudice with respect to their school.

4 The figure of the religious teacher (*bla ma*)

The preaching of the doctrine in Tibet was the work of numerous individuals originating from the most diverse parts of Buddhist Asia. Individual preachers were bound at that time by no control from a church or religious authority accepted as generally binding. Each considered himself the interpreter of a particular school of thought or liturgical method.

The considerable prestige of some teachers led to the development of various modes of tradition and oral transmission (*brgyud*), each expressed in a series of texts or specified exercise. The great number of interpreters who arose in this way was increased yet further by the individualistic tendency dominant throughout Mahayana Buddhism. The highest authority, as has already been said (cf.p.22), is that of the master; he alone is in a position to make the teachings of the sacred texts accessible and to allow them to become operative. One glance at the Tibetan historical work *Deb ther sngon po* (No.115) is enough to convince one of what has been said.

Lamaism, in its continuation and emphasis on the Indian tradition, places the figure of the master, *bla ma*, at the centre point. It should be noted here that not all monks, indeed relatively few in view of their great number, count as real *bla ma*. In the Indian tradition, in those schools which can be designated as magico-gnostic, whether Buddhist or Saivite, the master (Skt. *guru*) forms the pillar supporting the whole mystical experience. If Siva becomes angry (so the Saivite texts teach) 'then the guru can pacify him, but if the guru becomes angry, then no one can pacify him'. Similarly in Mahayana and Vajrayana Buddhism the *guru* (Tib. *bla ma*) is enabled, through living, direct contact, to transmit the letter and the spirit of the teaching, and to awaken the sparks out of which blaze forth the fire of mystical experience. The bond between master and disciple is a father–son relationship of a spiritual kind (*thugs sras*), and as such incomparably more important than the bonds of blood relationship. Master and disciple are called *yab sras*, father and son. This spiritual continuity linking master and disciple is called *sampradaya* in India, *brgyud* in Tibet; through it both become links in a chain which guarantees the continuing existence of the doctrine and of the mystical experience. Word (*lung*) and power (*dbang*) are transmitted from the one to the other in their indissoluble unity. Words and experiences are passed on like living things, in accordance with the norms of *govatsanyaya* holding among Indian ascetics, that is, like the 'vital link between the cow and the calf nourished and raised on its mother's milk'.[13] An instruction based simply on the written word, without the participation of a *bla ma*, is not only ineffective; it can even lead one away from the right path and be destructive.

If this chain is broken, then the teaching, now contained only within the texts, loses its efficacy; it has become like a corpse, and no power in the world can assist it to new life and to new validity. In the figure of the master, of the *bla ma*, two functions then are joined, although both aspects are rendered by the same word and can be united in the same person. On the one hand the *bla ma* transmits the word (*lung*), he passes on the teaching; on the other hand the *bla ma* is the master who confers power (*dbang*) through initiation or consecration (also *dbang*). In India too we meet alongside the *siksa-guru*, the master of the teaching, the *diksa-guru*, the master of the initiation.

In certain special cases the revelation can take place in a dream, or by direct communication on the part of a deity. We should not be surprised at this; the dream has a special significance in the mystical experience of every religion, and most particularly in Hinduism and Buddhism.

In Lamaism then there are always two sides to be distinguished. One is the world of religion, of monasteries and hermits, interested according to school or inclination in doctrine or liturgy, in ascetic practices or yoga, subject to fixed rules, practised in the teachings and the rituals, introduced through the initiations into mystical experiences. On the other side, outside such a communal life, stands the lay world. Outside it, but linked with it in the closest possible manner; it breathes the same religious and spiritual air. Of the three sets of vows (*sdom*) which can be taken, those of monastic discipline (*so thar*), of the Thought of Enlightenment (*byang chub sems*), and of the initiatory formulae (*sngags*), the first is reserved to the monk. In so far as the layman (*'jig rten pa*) lives in the midst of the world, he is not able to obtain and develop that particular religious experience accessible only to those who have chosen the monastic life and received ordination. The life of the layman is therefore a preparation for the life to come, or for the attainment of paradise. He should be preoccupied above all with the accumulation of merits, merits obtained through the worship of the 'Three Jewels' (*dkon mchog gsum*; Buddha, Doctrine, Community) and the taking of refuge in them, and also through the vow to strive for supreme Enlightenment—the necessary prerequisite to be able to count as a follower of the Great Vehicle.

Certainly the dividing line which results from the taking of initiatory vows, and compliance with traditional disciplinary procedures (*so thar*, Skt. *pratimoksa*), always remained between the layman and the monk. If however these consecrations separated the layman from the monk (for all the diversity of the monastic community (*rab 'byung*) itself) the observance of the ethical norms sanctified by Buddhism of old brought about a certain softening in the everyday life of the

Tibetan. These precepts, consisting of the five 'abstentions' (not to kiii, not to steal, not to speak falsely, not to commit adultery, not to become intoxicated) are valid without exception for both the lay follower (*dge bsnyen*, Skt. *upasaka*) and the monk in the older tradition.

In the following period, the more tolerant Mahayana rules gradually prevailed. The Mahayana places the main emphasis on the vow to strive for Enlightenment, and it is therefore also defined as the Vehicle of the Thought of Enlightenment (*byang chub theg*). The Mahayana precepts establish three basic moral norms: the vow of abstention from evil, the accumulation of good works (*dge ba chos sdud*), and activity for the welfare of all living beings (*sems can don byed*). These norms are valid for the layman as well as for the monk. For the monk, these three norms are merged with those of the monastic discipline. According to the Esoteric Vehicle (*sNgags theg*), the Vajrayana, these norms are actualized simultaneously in individuals of a superior disposition, through a spontaneous, free acceptance (Indrabhuti is cited as the classical example); in those of a lower nature they are achieved more gradually. Thus it comes about that the vows of chastity and of abstention from meat and alcoholic drinks are not imposed even on the monks themselves in all schools.

FOUR

THE DOCTRINES OF THE MOST IMPORTANT SCHOOLS

1 Assumptions common to all schools

In spite of the difference which we have referred to, the schools are entirely in agreement on many points. Which are these?

The existence of suffering,[1] and man's consequent desire to overcome this suffering and to reach the state referred to as 'liberation' (*thar pa, rnam par thar pa*), is the point of departure, and a fundamental premise. Liberation coincides with omniscience, which represents a limiting state (*mthar thug*), because only he who has attained omniscience has overthrown the plane of illusory existence and thereby found himself on that other plane where omniscience, truth and reality merge into one. This goal, however, cannot be reached as long as the 'means' leading to liberation are not known, or are not applied correctly.

The world of our perceptions and experience (in this connection it is all the same whether it is conceived of as real or, after deeper investigation, seen as 'void' (*stong pa*) and without any essence of its own) can be reduced to elementary factors, point-moments called *chos* (skt. *dharma*), separate from one another, but connected to the momentary content of the process of perception. Their true nature, which is that they are an ephemeral illusion, is revealed only to 'higher cognition' (*shes rab*, cf. pp. 62-3). Higher cognition is the penetrating to, and cognizing of, the true nature of these appearances, of these forms created by our discursive knowledge, these products of a false dichotomy (*rnam par rtog*) between subject and object. Only this higher form of cognition can eliminate the defilements or imperfections (*nyon mongs*) which obstruct the way to liberation, whether they be inborn or acquired, of a moral or of a spiritual nature. The most important basis for this process of liberation is the Doctrine, the Law (*chos*) revealed by the Buddha. This Law, however, is not just to be accepted simply as it is, but to be thought through and argued out in one's mind, so that each person who takes this Law upon himself must be clearly aware of its true meaning. The dialectical process which leads to the liberating state of cognition is based upon the sacred texts (*lung*) on the one hand and critical examination (*rig*) on the other. The cognitive state must be combined with a particular mode of life and of action. This practical aspect of the path is defined by two complementary factors: that which is to be accepted and followed (*blang*) and that which is to be renounced or abandoned (*'dor*). Thus the way to liberation starts off from several basic factors: a particular way (*lta*) of seeing and understanding things, and a way of behaving (*spyod*) appropriate to the goal to be achieved, in other words the meditation (*sgom*) through which that goal is to be transformed into lived experience. All this requires a method, a 'path' (*lam*) to be followed, which is able to bring together in a harmonious form the individual ethical, cognitive and meditative elements which lead to the desired goal. Each system (*grub mtha'*) and each school has the task of bringing together in an organic whole, of testing and examining these individual elements, of investigating their mutual relationships, of evaluating their validity and accuracy by reference to tradition and the words of the Buddha; in short, of creating a conclusive interpretation. The final objective remains the awakening of that higher cognition, that *shes rab*, Skt. *prajna*, in the adept's consciousness, which enables him to survey the ultimate nature of all things with the clarity of direct insight; in other words, the transcending of the subject–object dichotomy.

What then is the special nature of the Tibetan Buddhist view of the world? It has four main elements. (1) Everything is connected to everything else, nothing has individual permanence. (2) All things and all concepts (except those arising from the Doctrine) are causes and consequences of suffering, and are indissolubly bound up with suffering. They continually give new nourishment to suffering, in that they cause and promote the continuation of existence. (3) All the things and concepts that we think of as real, before we attain spiritual and intellectual maturity, are without true existence, are mutually bound to each other, and therefore 'void' (*stong pa*). (4) There exists a state beyond suffering and beyond the world of appearance which has fallen to our lot and to which we remain attached for as long as we do not perceive our true nature. This state beyond the world of appearance is *nirvana*. This term refers to a situation which is beyond description, beyond both ordinary existence (*srid*) and that state of peaceful detachment (*zhi*) attainable in certain moments of meditation (*srid zhi gnyis mtha' dang bral*). It is the supreme, irreversible identification with that state which is called Buddhahood.

When we have acquired this fourfold certainty, our whole life must be transformed in accordance with it. As will be recalled, the taking of refuge in the Buddha, the Teaching and the Community stands at the beginning of this path. This taking of refuge divides the Buddhist from the non-Buddhist. This must be followed by the awakening within oneself of constant energy (*brtson 'grus*), and its application for the fulfilment of the obligations which have arisen from the recognition of the fourfold truth; obligations both concerning what must be done (*blang*) and what must be renounced (*'dor*). As a third step there follows the decision (*nges par 'byung*) to overcome the world of relativity, suffering and impermanence, and along with this decision the taking of the vow to strive for Enlightenment (*byang chub sems bskyed*). This solemn promise has the power to bring about, in the distant future, the transformation of the believer into a Bodhisattva, into a potential Buddha, provided that the believer continues to think and act in accordance with the obligations arising from the vow. Above all, the vow does not allow him to be concerned only for his personal salvation (*rang don*) as is characteristic of the Lesser Vehicle (*theg dman*, Skt. Hinayana); he must work also for the salvation of others (*gzhan don*). This is the path unique to the Great Vehicle (*theg chen*, Skt. Mahayana), and which distinguishes it fundamentally from the Lesser Vehicle. The latter did not find a favourable environment in Tibet and never spread there. The Great Vehicle represents the second revelation of the Doctrine, especially in its condensation in the *Phar phyin* scriptures (Skt. Prajnaparamita). This stage is followed, but only for the most mature individuals, by the revelation of the gnostic–magical vehicle, the Tantra (*rGyud*), the vehicle of *sNgags* (Skt. *mantra*), also called *rDo rje theg pa* (Skt. Vajrayana), the Diamond Vehicle. This division into vehicles is based on the construction of the path of the Teachings in successive stages in accordance with the moral, intellectual and karmic qualifications of the initiates.

The assumption of a clear or correct view (*yang dag lta*) is characteristic of the Great Vehicle. This view is that of the Madhyamika system (*dbu ma*). The principle of a correct view, implicitly contained in the *Phar phyin* (Prajnaparamita) scriptures, was placed by Nagarjuna at the centre of his doctrinal system. It states that all that can be thought and known is relative and 'void', is not Being-in-itself; this inability to qualify the apparent world is itself its transcendence. This certainty becomes an experience unfolded in five phases or 'paths': (1) The path of the 'accumulation of virtue' (*tshogs lam*), forming an indispensable preparation, the overcoming of the moral and intellectual defilements which are inborn in us and grow steadily in the course of our lives. A purifying ethical practice and intellectual understanding are required to counterbalance these defilements. (2) The phase of practice (*sbyor lam*), of the putting into practice of the truth postulated by the Mahayana, of reflection over the previous path and on the path to be entered upon in order to achieve Buddhahood, that final stage to which the thought of Enlightenment should lead us. A precondition for this is the inner realization of the Bodhisattva state by means of successive and always more complete purifications, the so-called 'Earths' or 'ascensions'. This practice takes place in two parallel phases which are however indissolubly united: (3) The phase of vision (*mthong lam*) and (4) The phase of meditative refinement (*sgom lam*), by means of two modalities which finally coincide, peaceful detachment (*zhi gnas*) and higher vision (*lhag mthong*).

Aside from these four phases, and beyond them, there exists a further phase, (5) The state of he who no longer needs to learn (*mi slob*), of the Buddha. This is the path which gradually leads to the tenth 'Earth', at which all defilements are dissolved, including the most subtle (defilements are divided into two groups, heavy, gross (*rag*) and subtle (*phra*)), and the attainment of the state of Buddhahood is thus prepared for. Thus far we are taken by the *Phar phyin* scriptures and by their doctrinal commentary (Madhyamika, *dbu ma*) and the practical handbooks of meditation based upon them. As already mentioned, the growing spread of the Tantric schools of the various streams of Buddhist thought introduced a further problem. How was the Tantric–gnostic experience to be incorporated into the doctrine? The Buddha, it was said, had preached the doctrine not only at Bodhgaya (Lesser Vehicle) and at the Vulture Peak, Ghrdrakuta (Great Vehicle); there exist also many other preachings, some on this earth, others in the paradises, in which the Buddhas, whether Sakyamuni, *rNam par snang mdzad* (Vairocana), *Kun tu bzang po* (Samantabhadra) or many others, have revealed the doctrine of salvation.

2 The vehicle of the Mantra

Thus to the revelation granted in the *Phar phyin* (Prajnaparamita) followed that of the esoteric formulae (*sngags*, Skt. *mantra*), in other words of the Tantras. The concept of Tantra includes a literature and a totality of experiences described in detail in the books bearing this title. In my writings I have referred to these currents, whether they be Buddhist or Hindu, as 'gnostic', for they present numerous traits in common with the gnostic schools, for example the bringing into being of an esoteric wisdom which is not intellectual cognition, but rather an ecstatic, blissful consciousness, the actualization of which is aided by liturgical ceremonies having the power to release the emotional impulses which are to renovate and transform the individual. Thus the individual attains step by step to a higher plane of existence. This process, thanks to the actualization which has been referred to, takes place within the individual himself and exclusively on the basis of his own powers and his own will, without any assistance from divine acts of grace. The literature concerning this process, and the actions prescribed within it, are surrounded by secrecy and closed to the non-initiate. There arises therefore the imperative need for an initiation, and of an overcoming through this initiation of inborn or acquired ignorance, of an ever more perfect conquest of every dichotomy. The Tantras, all the Tantras, offer their assistance in this process, thanks to a revelation of the Buddhas, transmitted through direct teaching from master to master. In schools of this kind extremely ancient mythical elements are called into service to indicate in symbolic form the various phases of the ascent; throughout the preparatory or liturgical procedure there occurs the momentary apotheosis of mystical states, or even of individual factors in the ritual. If we hold the opinion, on these and other grounds, that Tantrism can be considered as forming part of the gnostic movement, we are not in this way maintaining that it is a kind of offshoot of the gnostic currents of the West, although it is difficult to deny the possibility, even the fact, of mutual influence between Western and Eastern gnosticism. Essentially it is a question rather of homologous attitudes, of the effort, in both East and West, to substitute a lived experience of salvation for purely rational processes, to transcend the spatio–temporal experience through a flight into absolute space, and absolute time, an *ex-cessus mentis* into the indefinable 'Void' which contains all. It should however be born in mind too that the content of the Tantra has by no means been exhausted by what has been said. There are also purely magical elements to be found in the Tantra, as in much Western gnosticism also (e.g. *Pistis sophia*), elements that indicate the close links between Tantrism on the one side, and popular traditions uninfluenced by orthodox theological schools on the other side. Such aspirations have been particularly active at times of political and social crises, at times of breakdown of traditional values, when the longing in men for contact with the divine and for faster paths to salvation becomes manifest. The Tantras of the 'superior class' are above all addressed to men in whom non-religious impulses, especially those of a sexual nature, are at their most powerful. These practices have the goal of bringing about a 'transfer' of emotions, of becoming free of passion through passion, through a psychological technique anticipating the latest achievements of psychoanalysis. The ordinary man is born from desire (*'dod chags*) and bound to desire, yet desire can become a means to liberation. With the help of the Tantra the passions can be changed into forces assisting in the work of salvation (No.101, p.13b).

It should be held in mind that the path of the *Phar phyin* (Prajnaparamita) and of the Tantra differ in two ways. In the first place, there is an external difference, concerning the lesser or greater difficulty of the training, and consequently the shorter or longer duration of the corresponding path (*lam*). While the followers of the *Phar phyin* require two or three incalculably long aeons (Skt. *asamkhyeya*) to attain the state of Buddhahood, he who chooses the way of *sNgags* can achieve it even within a single life. There is also an internal distinction; many commentators define the *Phar phyin* as the Vehicle of the Cause, in other words as a propaedeutic vehicle, in that it explains the necessary premises to achieve the 'fruit', revealing that they consist of the four supreme purities corresponding to the Earth of the Buddha. However this vehicle does not offer the possibility of enjoying the 'fruit' while one is traversing the 'path', in other words in this individual existence (*gzhi*). The vehicle of Tantra or Mantra (also called the Vehicle of the Means, *thabs*, or the Diamond (*rdo rje*) Vehicle) is by contrast the Vehicle of the Fruit (*'bras*). But this vehicle in its turn is also the cause, in that it leads to the immediate enjoyment of the 'fruit', which is represented in the form of the four supreme purities attainable at the end of the ascent, during the journey, in other words during the meditation practice in this very existence.

It still remains to explain what these supreme purities of the Earth of the Buddha consist of, what is meant by the 'fruit' to be attained, and also by what means these purities can be experienced during the process of purification through the help of the Tantric vehicle. First it should be said that there are three essential phases in the process of purification: the phase or state in which the meditator is reflected in his ordinary nature (*gzhi dus*); the phase of the 'path', or of the meditation process, in which the meditation proceeds according to the prescribed methods (*lam dus*); the phase of the 'fruit' (*'bras dus*), of the state to be achieved as a result of the experience. Here we speak of a 'meditation process', because we are concerned with situations which are realized within the meditating subject himself. It must however, be kept in mind that from the standpoint of the experience realized as a whole, these situations can no longer be localized either in space or time, because space and time belong to the apparent world, which does not exist. These situations are destined to dissolve into a non-temporal transcendence. Both the experience granted in the phase of the 'path' and in the phase of the 'fruit' consist of a coinciding with pure consciousness, in respect of which none of our categories of thinking can be applied. In this essential reality there is no duality between a Here and a There, between a Now and a Later; such a dichotomy is only a fleeting, unreal rippling of waves over the immobile radiance of that consciousness without content. The dichotomies are always unreal appearances (*snang*), but they manifest themselves in infinite gradations and qualities, from the dichotomies of the world in which we exist to those which manifest themselves progressively on the path of ecstasies.

With respect to the two groups of problems still to be discussed the following can now be said:

A *The four purities*

The four supreme purities are the following: (1) purity of the Earth of the Buddha, realized through transcendent consciousness (*ye shes*), consciousness which illuminates itself; (2) supreme purity of the *maya*-body (*sgyu ma'i sku, sgyu lus*, cf.pp.56, 58): coincidence (*zung 'jug*) of the plane of things having form (*gzugs*) with the spiritual plane (*sku thugs gnyis su med*). This is not a physical body belonging to the sphere of the material (*gzugs*, Skt. *rupa*), but an image; (3) supreme purity of co-fruition (*longs spyod*),[2] the peak of bliss (*bde*), transcendent consciousness free from impurity (*zag med ye shes*); (4) supreme purity, supreme excellence of action, thanks to which one is continually pre-occupied with the good of others whose salvation is thus made possible.

B *The experience of the four purities*

(1) First purification must be attained by traversing the common path (*thun mong*) which the *Phar phyin* also recognizes. Then the *yogin* (Tib. *rnal 'byor pa*), who is now traversing the Tantric path (*sNgags*), must progress through a multiplicity of experiences, always following the methods and the successive stages of the Tantra chosen by him as guide. This choice of a particular Tantra is not made at random, but in conformity with the master's decision and the master's testing of the intellectual and spiritual maturity of the disciple. The mystic perceptibly frees himself from the illusory appearances, creations of discursive and dichotomizing cognition, which are at work in the empirical world (the world (*snang*) which erroneously appears as real), reflected in infinite combinations which bring about ever deeper entanglement with it. The neophyte purifies himself by virtue of the certainty which he has attained through experience: that every possible aspect of thought, whether it be of the external world, or of the world of creatures that live within that world (*snod bcud*) is nothing but 'voidness' (*stong pa*). This 'voidness' is the essence of wisdom, it is the non-duality 'of the profound and the radiant'. Its forms are the purified worlds that can be seen and enjoyed in the meditation process, the supreme purification of the 'bliss-bringing Buddha-Earths': in them the Buddhas preach to choirs of the blessed. Such purification, which is otherwise achieved as the 'fruit' or result, is here

anticipated and lived during the phase of the 'path'; these 'Earths' are contemplated in the glory of paradise, as for example the paradise of *bDe ba can* (Skt. Sukhavati) and many others, according to their traditional descriptions.

(2) In the next stage the yogin sees the dissolution of his present body (*gzhi dus*), the result of karmic maturation, into the 'Void-Light' (*'od gsal, stong pa nyid*).

Thus the yogin already experiences Buddhahood in a transitory way while going along the 'path'; the same Buddhahood, recognizable through its characteristic marks, its ten associated powers and so on, which is then attained in the 'fruit' phase. Pursuing his meditation further, the mystic takes part in another exalted state of insight, in which he recognizes three certainties within himself: with respect to his body, the certainty that it is capable of transformation into the deity; with respect to his speech, the certainty that it is the sacred formula, the Mantra (Tib. *sNgags*) of miraculous power, conclusive in its sonority and infinite in its power; with respect to his mind, that it is infinite spiritual potentiality. By virtue of these certainties he lives during the 'path' phase that which he will attain in the 'fruit' phase, the limiting state of bodily existence: for example the body of *'Od dpag med* (Skt. Amitabha), which is the synthesis of two limiting states (*mthar thug*), the purity of the *maya*-body with its appropriate signs and marks in the clarity of the *sems*, which in its essential nature is the same as the light (*don gyi 'od gsal*).

(3) The mystic dissolves into the 'void' the real or imagined ritual objects and instruments. After he has changed himself into a god, he emanates these objects from his mind until they fill the whole of space. In this way these ritual accessories reveal themselves as what they are, in other words a form of transcendent consciousness, through which an unlimited capacity for 'bliss' is released. Although this power represents the condition and end-result of the process, it is here already experienced during the 'path' phase.

(4) Finally the yogin radiates from his deified self an infinite quantity of light which spreads out through space and alleviates the sufferings of living beings. Indeed the beings themselves are transformed into gods and goddesses which emanate from his transcendent consciousness (*ye shes lha* and *lha mo*). Then the mystic reabsorbs the rays of light into himself again, dissolving them into his heart. This stage is very important, because it is thanks to its repeated exercise that the mystic achieves the supreme purity of 'action', the fullness of which opens to living beings the path of liberation. The purity of 'action', which otherwise comes to maturity as a 'fruit' of the state of Buddhahood, is here experienced as a stage of the 'path'.

If we take into account what was stated above (p.52), we can state that the experience of the four supreme purities during the 'path' phase does not only represent an anticipation of their actualizing in the 'fruit' phase. Through prolonged and continuous practice, rather, this experience becomes a preparation and preliminary training for the 'fruit' phase, in that it brings to life a new level within the neophyte. Here we are dealing with a fundamental feature of the Mantra (Tib. *sNgags*) vehicle. It uses meditative, contemplative, psycho-physical and yogic techniques to evoke in its disciples a state of ecstasy and of transcendence thanks to which the state of consciousness proper to Buddhahood is experienced, if only in a temporary way. At the same time it is also a kind of confirmation (or better preliminary testing) of the goodness of the 'fruit', a participation in the supreme glory and power that is proper to the Buddha realized within this life–realized while still on this side of that outermost limit, beyond which exists the inexpressible luminous essence, the Alpha and Omega of all things.

The advantage of the Mantra (Tib. *sNgags*) path over the way of rationality emerges clearly from what has been said; while the latter requires an extremely long period of time for the attainment of the goal, the former offers the shortest path for the achievement of Buddhahood.

Schematic summary of the two paths

*A Path of the Prajnaparamita (*phar phyin*)*

The Prajnaparamita, the fundamental text on which is based the Madhyamika (Tib. *dbu ma*) elaborated by Nagarjuna, is centred upon the lack of essential nature in itself of all things related to others and of the dichotomizing process of our thought. Other central concepts: the person as made up of five components (*phung po*); sense-organ, sense-perception, sense-object, organ or activity of apperception or of apprehending (*manas*, Tib. *yid*), vow to achieve enlightenment, Buddhahood. It is meritorious, however, to remain a Bodhisattva because in that way one can contribute through example or preaching to the conversion of others, and to propagate the Buddhist Doctrine.

Observance of 6 or 10 'perfections' (Skt. *paramita*): generosity, patience etc.; method of meditation, contemplation and concentration which gradually ascends becoming more complex and complete, allowing he who follows it with vigilant and attentive mind to pass gradually from one to another of the ten states called Earths (*bhumi*, Tib. *sa*); each of which represents a state of purity and spiritual achievement superior to the preceding one; with the achievement of the tenth Earth the omniscience of the Buddha, the essence of the Buddha, the Dharmata is actualized; the meditation which brings about such an ascent is very complex, but is carried out through a *bhavana* (Tib. *sgom*), a continued meditative exercise which produces a gradual, progressive and gradually more refined spiritual and mental cultivation through a dialectical process centred about two principal phases: *samatha* (Tib. *zhi gnas*) 'spiritual serenity' and *vipasyana* (Tib. *lhag mthong*) 'superior vision'.

B Path of Mantra

A

Individual in his psycho-physical reality located in a particular time and place (*gzhi dus*).	1 material body (*rag pa'i lus*): *sems* + 5 components of the personality, sense-organs, related perceptions, mental functioning, faculty of cognition (*yid*, Skt. *manas*). 2 subtle body (*phra mo*): channels (*rtsa*, Skt. *nadi*) through which move the power of vibration (*rlung*, Skt. *prana*) and the subtle (*phra mo*) *sems*. 3 most subtle body and *sems* (*shin tu phra pa'i lus* and *sems*) called the innate body (*gnyug ma'i lus*) and the innate *sems* (*gnyug ma'i sems*). 4 body of mental cognition, *yid lus* (in state of dreaming or of intermediate existence (*bar do*), a modification of body and *sems* in a more subtle (*phra pa*) state).

B

Path (*lam*) towards the process of exaltation achieved in part by the method of evocation (*bskyed rim*) and in part by the method of achievement (*rdzogs rim*).	Isolation of the body (*lus dben*) followed by the five stages of the method of achievement (*rdzogs rim*) 1 isolation of the word (*ngag dben*). 2 isolation of the *sems*; at this stage one attempts to discover what the *sems* actually is (*ngo bo*); together with meditation on the Light (= *sems*); its real nature is not revealed, but rather its reflex (or better its germinal state, *dpe 'od gsal*). 3 *maya*-body (*sgyu lus*), transformation of the innate power of vibration (*gnyug ma'i rlung*) and the innate *sems*. 4 (a) body of transcendent consciousness (*ye shes pa'i lus*); *ye shes* = *sems shin tu phra mo*, extremely subtle *sems*; such a body is awareness of its own true nature, transcendent consciousness. (b) light in its absolute reality (four degrees); *don gyi 'od gsal*.

5 convergence (*zung 'jug*) of the *maya*-body (*sgyu lus*) and of light in its absolute reality (*don gyi 'od gsal*). pure *maya*-body (*dag pa'i sgyu lus*). diamond body (*rdo rje sku*), light in its absolute reality (*don gyi 'od gsal*).

C

Effect or fruit — *Chos sku*, body of infinite spiritual potentiality. *longs sku*, body of co-fruition in the paradises etc., as with the five Buddhas of the pentad preaching in their various paradises. *sprul sku*, apparent body, in the phenomenal world as with Sakyamuni.

3 Investiture and consecrations

Before the process summarized above is discussed in detail, we still have to describe how the practice of Tantra or *sNgags* is actually performed. It is absolutely necessary to have previously undergone the preparatory school of the vehicle of the *Phar phyin*, which is addressed, as seen above, primarily to the intellectual faculties. To this must still be added two things of decisive significance: an appropriate spiritual investiture, which can be described as a consecration (*dbang*), and a body of rules (*dam sdom*) resulting from that investiture.

The neophyte obtains the investiture through a ritual performance centred around the symbol of a particular god. From this moment on it is his duty to meditate on the visible aspect (*sku*) of this god as specified by the tradition, and to follow strictly the path corresponding to this special meditation, striving throughout in all ways to actualize the appropriate mystical experiences (*dngos grub*). The various 'consecrations'[3] can be reduced to four principal types. They concern the defilements and contaminations accumulated in us through the three 'doors' of body, speech and mind (*lus*, *ngag*, and *yid*), which make up the psycho-physical totality on the unpurified level (on the purified level they are described by the corresponding 'honorific terms', *sku*, *gsung*, *thugs*). These three kinds of defilement in their turn can be seen as particular aspects of defilement itself. In this way we can speak of four defilements, which correspond to the four principal consecrations. Each of these gives to the consecrated person the ability to purify himself from the corresponding defilement, an ability which he did not previously possess. These consecrations are called *bum dbang*, *gsang dbang*, *shes rab ye shes kyi dbang* and *tshig gi dbang*: investiture through the 'vessel', investiture through the secret, investiture of transcendent consciousness through higher cognition (this is a conjunction of the first two investitures in the sense that the second is actualized at a higher level, while the first has not yet attained its limiting scale) and investiture through the word.

The investiture through the 'vessel' purifies the defilements adhering to the body. This consecration confers the power for carrying out the process of evocation (*bskyed rim*, cf. pp. 94-5) during the 'path' phase, it sows a seed, creates a receptivity for the obtaining of the body of manifestation (*sprul sku*, Skt. *nirmanakaya*), which is actualized in the result phase, and thanks to which the Buddhas can carry out their mission of teaching in the world–as in the epiphany of Sakyamuni.

The second investiture conveys the ability to eradicate the defilements adhering to the power of speech. During the 'path' phase it makes one able to meditate on the *maya*-body (Tib. *sgyu lus*, cf. below), an attainment acquired through the 'method of achievement' (*rdzogs rim*, cf. p. 75); the seed is thus sown for the body of co-fruition (*longs spyod sku*, Skt. *sambhogakaya*), which appears in the result phase and becomes a reality in the paradises, where the Buddhas silently, eternally reveal the doctrine of salvation to the elect.

The third investiture brings about the ability to overcome the defilements attaching to the mind (*yid*). During the 'path' phase it gives the power of meditation on the radiant light (*'od gsal* = *ye shes*). This meditation takes place in the 'method of achievement' and sows the seeds of the body of infinite spiritual potentiality (*chos sku*, Skt. *dharmakaya*), which again is actualized in the 'fruit' phase.

The fourth investiture confers the ability to eliminate defilement as such, in other words to remove the contamination *per se* which is at the base of the three named types of defilement. During the 'path' phase it becomes the meditation on the 'method of achievement' (*rdzogs rim*) which culminates in the convergence (*zung 'jug*) of light (*'od gsal*) and of the *maya*-body, and thus brings about the seeds of that Body into which the other bodies dissolve (*ngo bo nyid kyi sku*). This is the absolute realization of convergence, the ineffable identity of which was spoken, the consciousness of Being-in-itself which becomes reality in the 'fruit' phase. This signifies that the four consecrations create a disposition for the attainment of the three existential states and for their dissolution into the indissoluble unity of Consciousness and Light.

4 The Tantric process of transcendence: mental body, *maya*-body, body of transcendent consciousness

Our repeated reference to the *maya*-body (*sgyu lus*) leads us here to consider a very important point: the existence of a body of very fine substance, distinct from the material body composed of the five psycho-physical components (*phung po* etc.), but inherent within it, which represents the continuity between the different possible forms of existence[4] of the individual.[5]

Within the material body[6] in which the vibration of life and the *sems*[7] are present in their coarse state, is present an innate body, the *gnyug ma'i lus*, which the material body supports and sustains. This innate body is not of coarse material nature, but is a psycho-physical complex *sui generis*, consisting of a breathing or fine vibratory power (*rlung*) which tends to expand outwards into the realm of objective things; it is the vehicle of a mental energy (*gnyug ma'i sems*) which perceives objects, unleashing the dichotomizing faculty I–Not I. Although *rlung* and *sems* are of the same nature (*ngo bo*), in that they inhere in one another, they have different effects; their relation is like that between fire and flame, or fire and warmth.

These two principles (*sems* and *rlung*) are the true shapers of human destiny; of the two, *sems* is the more important. *Sems* is described as the creator (*byed po*) of *samsara*, of the unending cycle of successive births and deaths, but it is also the creator of that which is beyond (*'das*) *samsara*. This is because it is on the one hand the instrument of objectification, but on the other has the capacity to transcend itself, in other words to change into transcendent consciousness (*ye shes*) and in this way through the attainment of pure consciousness to transcend duality (No.84, p.11a).

This transcendent consciousness emanates from a mental body (*yid lus*), which in its described structure travels from life to life, driven by its karmic inheritance (*las*) and by the defilements (*nyon mongs*) which burden it. In terms of its nature it cannot be distinguished from the innate mind (*gnyug ma'i sems*). The yogin can transform this *yid lus* into a body of transcendent cognition (*ye shes lus*) through his meditation, experience and practice. The distinction between the two can be compared to that between earth and a vessel; the vessel, made from earth, having earth as its material basis, is however not identical with earth, it has a different function and destination. Besides, the *yid lus* is 'contaminated' (*zag bcas*), it experiences pleasant and painful sensations, and also it owns as a body numerous demonic beings, or rather conditions of being endowed only with this corporeality (such as the demons *'dre* and the gods *lha*). By contrast the body of transcendent consciousness (*ye shes lus*) is free from any kind of defilement (*zag med*), and it is not perceptible to an ordinary man. Although the wish to work for the benefit of one's neighbour, as prescribed by the Mahayana, can be present within the *yid lus*, it is not free to give itself up to this impulse, for it is bound and hindered by the force of karma. The body of transcendent consciousness (*ye shes lus*) by contrast is free to accomplish good, as in the case of the great ascetics. As we will see, it abandons the body to its fate at the moment of death, for it is able to ascend to the Pure Lands (*zhing khams*, Paradises) or alternatively to descend to the Impure Places, into the hells, in order to accomplish its task of the salvation of beings.

For a better understanding of this complex of ideas it should be noted that in light sleep and at the moment of death the vibratory power born together with the *sems* produces the *yid lus*. The *yid lus* becomes autonomous during sleep, since the six forms of sensory experience (*rnam par shes pa*) are inactive, and also at death, when these forms of sensory experience dissolve into the faculty of perception (*yid rnam par shes pa*), in individuals who have not undergone the practice of liberation. The mechanism of this process is conditioned by the different relationships in which the vibratory potentiality of the breath of life (*rlung*) and the *sems* stand in juxtaposition to each other, according to which one or the other factor acts as primary cause (*dngos nyer len*) or as contributory cause (*lhan cig byed rkyen*). This mechanism, summarized in the Appendix to this chapter (pp.106ff), takes on an even more complex form during the moment of Enlightenment because of the shining out of the radiance (*'od gsal*) proper to the *sems*.

Both *sems* and the breath of life or vibratory power in the subtle state have their seat in the so-called 'point' (*thig le*, cf.p.262) which is visualized as being in the heart, of the size of a sesame seed, and which signifies absolute potentiality. *Sems* and vibratory power are the precondition of the *maya*-body (*sgyu lus*), which can purify itself to become the body of transcendent consciousness (*ye shes lus*) when through contemplative practice the continuum of consciousness is cleansed. This practice is divided into the two phases already mentioned: peaceful detachment (*zhi gnas*, Skt. *samatha*) and higher vision (*lhag mthong*, Skt. *vipasyana*). For the disciples of the special (*thung mong ma yin pa*) path of Tantra this purification is accomplished through the four consecrations mentioned above (cf.p.57) and the exercise of two methods: that of evocation and that of achievement (*bskyed rim*, *rdzogs rim*).

In this connection it is necessary to respect the wide range of expressions used by Tibetan theory and mysticism to indicate the various instruments, aspects and stages of the cognitive process and of the transformation and transcendence which are gradually brought about. The point of departure is naturally formed by the five modes of perception (the five *rnam par shes pa*) which come together and are integrated in the faculty of mental perception or apprehension (*yid rnam par shes pa*). This latter faculty transforms the perceptions as it apprehends them and thus forms a sixth sense. (Other schools also introduce the 'store-consciousness', *kun gzhi*, Skt. *alayavijnana*, a kind of unconscious both collective and individual, an inexhaustible substratum in which all experiences are deposited and from which they emerge again; they also speak of 'contaminated' perception, *nyon mongs rnam par shes pa*.) *Yid* is synonymous with *sems* when *sems* is in its crude state and not yet capable of transcendence. From this *sems* originate mental and psychic states and reactions (*sems byung*). As already explained, *sems* cannot be separated from the very subtle breath which penetrates through our entire body, the vibratory power of the purest kind (the same in essence and kind as the universal respiration or breathing), which can be considered as the 'mount' of the *sems* itself.

This *sems* or mental energy is transmuted into transcendent consciousness (*ye shes*) as a result of a transformation caused by particular states or moments of thought. These are moments essentially permeated by a conviction which accomplishes within them an overcoming (*nges par 'byung*) of this illusory world, a liberation. In other words: the breath of finest nature which vibrates in us and the *sems* which is inborn (*gnyug ma*) in us are identical in nature (*ngo bo*), and co-exist in all of us in every moment of *samsara*. As a result of meditation and practice the *maya*-body (*sgyu lus*) is achieved, the vibration and the mind-light coincide. In the course of further practice the *maya*-body is transformed into a pure body, the limiting state of bodily existence. The light becomes pure consciousness (*thugs dag*),[8] in other words it is transformed into the limiting state of essential light (*don 'od gsal*), which is experienced in its immediate character and is therefore different from that light (*dpe 'od gsal*) which was conceived abstractly at the preceding stage, the stage of 'learning'. The integration of the two stages in the state of non-duality is called the convergence of those who have no more to learn (*mi slob pa'i zung 'jug*); it is the state of Buddhahood.

In other words again: the *maya*-body (*sgyu lus*) is gradually freed from every contamination, and finally even from the 'engrams' of latent defilements. In this process the vibratory force and the mind-light work together, serving alternately as primary and contributory causes. In successively higher stages the *maya*-body is transformed into the subtle *maya*-body (*sgyu lus phra mo*), into the transcendent consciousness of the *maya*-body (*sgyu lus pa'i ye shes*), into the pure *maya*-body (*dag pa'i sgyu lus*). During the ascent towards the Tenth Earth, the culminating stage of the path of learning (cf.p.50,53) the transcendence is accomplished into absolute cognition, into the pure body (*sku dag pa zung 'jug*), into the 'diamond body', and finally into the body of unlimited spiritual potentiality (*chos sku*), into light: the long process of elimination from oneself of all objectification and of every impulse towards objectification has reached its goal. This extremely complex process is presented in schematic form in the Appendix at the end of this chapter (pp. 106ff).

In this process of the dissolution of objectification, brought about through mystical experience, the state of death is experienced: the eight signs (*rtags brgyad*) of the gradual reabsorption of the components of ostensible materiality are visualized one after another; their apparent manifestation is dissolved into pure existence: the element of air into the element of water (= illusion); the element of water into the element of fire (the field of vision is entirely filled with a subtle smoke); the element of fire into the element of wind, like sheet-lightning into space; the element of wind into sensory perception (*snang ba*), in two phases, the first like the blazing up of a lamp, the second like the autumn sky permeated with moonlight; all appearance dissolves into a diffuse light like the orange-yellow colour of the setting sun; the diffuse light dissolves into an inner gleam of light (*nyer thob*) as at twilight; the inner gleam dissolves into light (*'od gsal*) like the colour of the sky at dawn. Throughout this sequence we are considering a process of dissolution which is not happening in reality but which is visualized in the meditation process as successive appearances and culminates in visions ever more sublime, until at last every appearance vanishes in the colourless, pure radiance of the essential purity of light. In other words, the total elimination of all that arises and appears takes place in radiant cognition of essential being. The experiences or meditations of the moment of death lead then to the attainment of that state which can be defined as the pure and complete voidness of non-being, the essential precondition for reunification with the transcendent undifferentiated light.

Mental states and psychic processes (*sems byung*) are by contrast, cognitive functions of the individual: by cognition here is to be understood a faculty of discrimination which is also capable of purification through gradual cleansing from the cognition of ordinary rationality to higher cognition (*shes rab*, where *rab* = higher). This cognition is a discriminative faculty different from the simple response to a stimulus (*shes*), such as the sensations mentioned above and the perceptions connected with them. It is present in all living beings and causes animals, for example, to search for water when they have thirst and for shelter when they are cold. Higher cognition (*shes rab*) has for its object everything that can be an object of thought, it is the ability to discriminate, but also the ability to resolve in itself successive mental situations or manifestations. This cognition is of two kinds: 'contaminated' (*nyon mongs can*) and uncontaminated. The former leads to misfortune, the latter can lead to truth, that is it is capable of entering into unison with the real nature of things, and thus eventually leading to liberation. Both these cognitive abilities are present in all. The second divides into two branches: ordinary *shes rab* and special *shes rab* (*khyad par can*). Only in this last case can one translate the Tibetan expression literally as higher (*rab*) cognition (*shes*). It too divides into two sub-species: cognition which is inspired and purified through the Buddhist revelation but is not yet illuminated through the doctrine of 'voidness' (the 'Middle Way', *dbu ma*), and cognition which by examining objects or ideas (*chos*) through the doctrine of the 'void' has arrived at the certainty that it is impossible to make assertions about the true nature of objects, that in other words the content of our ordinary experience is empty. Some achieve this higher cognition without attaining to that even higher summit, cognition which becomes identical to the *Shes rab phar phyin* (Skt. Prajnaparamita, 'perfection of cognition'). Others, however, do achieve this; they have recognized the impossibility of attributing to an object of any kind a specific, permanent and really true character (*mtshan med*). Even these are not yet detached enough to be able to reach[9] the supreme goal. They are the Bodhisattvas of the First to Seventh 'Earths'. Those, finally, who have not only realized that no assertions can be made about phenomena but have attained complete detachment become Bodhisattvas of the Eighth to Tenth 'Earths'.

While we can define *sems* as an energy of thought closely bound up with the breath of life or the vibratory capacity (*rlung*, Skt. *prana*), *shes rab* (Skt. *prajna*) represents a cognitive function, which (in its purified form too) always represents an instrument of liberation. *Shes rab* is not given any ontological significance, but it is a necessary coefficient of the process of transcendence. Its indispensable correlate is formed by 'means', which is identified with compassion (*snying rje*) and thus with action for the good of beings. The combined effect of these elements brings about the overturning of the planes, transcendence to the body of infinite spiritual potentiality. This higher cognition is hypostatized in Tantric symbolism as the 'paredra' of the deity. The work or means is conceived of as the father (*yab*), higher cognition as the mother (*yum*); illumination, identical in its nature to absolute cognition, is born from their union. In conformity with the personification of a *nomen* as a *numen*, a much-used process in the Mahayana and Vajrayana, the mother, visualized alone, becomes the mother of Buddha, the supreme Matrix.

5 *Sems* and light

In the entire course of the religious experience of Tibetan man, in all of its manifestations from *Bon* religion to Buddhism, a common fundamental trait is evident; photism, the great importance attached to light, whether as a generative principle, as a symbol of supreme reality, or as a visible, perceptible manifestation of that reality; light from which all comes forth and which is present within ourselves. Already in the cosmogony this originally pure, undifferentiated light is transformed into coloured light, white and black, from which springs forth the twofold creation (cf.p.214). The greatest *Bon* divinity is *gShen lha 'Od dkar*, 'the White Light'. The blessings of saints are also conveyed through the luminous energy of the rays of light which emanate from them (*'od zer shugs*–No.2, p.28a). In the *Bar do thos grol*, in the literature that is which is dedicated to the technique of transformation of the life-principle at the moment of death, photism is a fundamental element. The consciousness of the spiritually mature person becomes identified with the light which shines out at the time of death, it perceives the identity between that light and its own radiant essence.

Sems then is not only mental energy, but also light, and light too is the breath (*rlung*) on which it 'rides', for the breath also is made of five shining rays of light (*'od zer*). Once *sems* has been transformed into transcendent consciousness, its presence makes possible transfiguration into the 'diamond body' (*rdo rje sku*) of which we have already spoken. The essence of this 'diamond body' is formed by the five forms of consciousness (*ye shes lnga*); it represents the limiting state of existential reality. This metamorphosis is accomplished thanks to the luminous potentiality which is present in germinal form in the breath (*rlung*) and *sems*. The *sems* is light (*'od gsal*), because if it were not, then it would not be possible to cognize, or to see, and it would not be possible for it to be transformed into transcendent cognition. The light which is identical in essence to the *sems* can be considered from two different points of view, as object (*yul*) or as subject (*yul can*). Light as object is voidness itself (*stong pa nyid*), it is that which cannot be an object of thought. As subject it corresponds to the voidness of the subject which shines forth once objectification has been transcended. This light (*'od gsal*) has to be distinguished from luminosity (*gsal*), the capacity to emit light from the mind (*sems*) and from the mental states (*sems byung*) present within the psycho-physical continuum. The connection between light and mind (*'od gsal* and *sems*), which is defined as 'non-duality of the profound and the luminous' (*zab gsal gnyis med*), characterizes the state of transcendent consciousness (*ye shes*). The various schools diverge noticeably on this subject and on the related conception of the connection between bliss (*bde*) and 'voidness'. This can be understood if one considers that the connection between *sems* and light, and the identity of these two terms, forms the basis of Buddhist soteriology in Tibet. This is not the place to enter into the subtle debates set off by this problem. Instead some of the opposing theses in the argument will be briefly outlined.[10]

According to the view of the *Sa skya pa* school luminosity is the characteristic sign (*mtshan nyid*) of the mind, while the essence of the mind is voidness. Voidness does not detract (*'dor*) from luminosity, nor does luminosity detract from voidness. The coinciding of luminosity and voidness, which represents an inexpressible state of pure objectivity (*'dzin med*), defines the limiting state (*mthar thug*) of the *sems*, its essential state. In other words, *sems* in itself is voidness, and its limiting state is precisely this voidness. According to *rJe btsun bSod nams rtse mo*, the *sems* is without beginning, duration or end, it exists *ab initio*, beyond any dichotomizing mental process and any discursive cognition (*rnam rtog*, subject–object), analogous to infinite space. The *sems* can be characterized above all by three immanences (*lhan skyes* = born in us): Cause, 'Path' or *iter*, 'Fruit' or result. (a) In each of us the inborn *sems* (*gnyug ma'i sems*) is luminosity and its essence is voidness. Luminosity and voidness are not derivable from one another, but they flow together (*zung 'jug*). (b) The 'path' aspect concerns the yogin in his aspirations to follow the prescribed way, concerns the disciple of the Tantra of the superior class (*bla na med*, Skt. *anuttara*). Here luminosity corresponds to the method of evocation (*bskyed rim*), voidness to the method of achievement (*rdzogs rim*, cf.p.74). Transcendent consciousness (*ye shes*) which is born from the coincidence of these two aspects is attained through repeated practice of meditation. (c) In the 'fruit' or result, the culmination of the meditative process, luminosity corresponds to the apparent body (*sprul sku*), voidness to the body of infinite spiritual potentiality (*chos sku*), while the body of co-fruition (*longs sku*) represents the coincidence of the two aspects. Through meditation of this kind is created the consciousness of Being of the innate *sems* and thus the necessary condition for the attainment of the three 'bodies' in the moment of effect. Thus the process of salvation pivots around the *sems*.

The experience (*nyams len*) follows; all that appears to exist (appears, that is, only within the *sems*, for no object exists outside of it) is nothing but the luminosity of the *sems*. However, since the real nature of the *sems* transcends all duality, all that appears is deception, magical play (*sgyu ma*, Skt. *maya*). In this consists its voidness (*stong pa*). The realization that derives from this corresponds to the coincidence of luminosity and emptiness. This is the precondition for the experience (*nyams len*).[11]

In the meditation mentioned above we are in fact dealing with various modes of being, various forms of the same essence, just as a nugget of gold can be made into various shapes, into vessels or other objects of use, which however do not cease to be gold in their basic essence. Apart from this doctrine of salvation, which is practically identical with that of the other schools, the *Sa skya pa* teachings emphasize a special point of their own. This is that luminosity is a characteristic sign of *sems*. The *dGe lugs pa* reject this position. According to their view, luminosity is not the characteristic sign of *sems* but the actual essence of *sems*. Luminosity is a characteristic sign of the cognitive faculty (*shes pa*). Thanks to this luminosity, which is inherent in all the cognitive states of our continuum, we are able to see (*mthong*), hear (*thos*) and comprehend (*rtogs*) the object of cognition. Were this not so, there would be no difference between us and the material world (*bem po*, Skt. *jada*).

To understand these ideas better we need to recall the difference between the luminosity we are considering here and that of, for example, the sun's rays. The sun's rays enable us to see, in that they illuminate objects, but they do not see themselves. The luminous cognitive states on the other hand do not only illuminate what is cognizable inside and outside us, they also illuminate themselves as objects of luminous cognition. Thus it comes about that in the cognitive process (*shes pa*) luminosity and cognition belong essentially to each other. If the luminous states as a result of adventitious defilements do not illuminate the objects proper to them, they still possess as cognitive states this power within themselves. Therefore when the light (*'od gsal*) is not *per accidens* affected by defilements, and emerges in its natural purity, it is not a characteristic sign but an essential quality of the *sems*.

Two different basic situations thus result: *sems*, and the derived mental states or psychic processes (*sems byung*). *Sems*, on the one hand, comprehends and perceives things in themselves by virtue of the function proper to it; on the other hand the mental states derived from *sems* comprehend the particular characteristic signs of these things (cf.p.64). If we see an object which possesses form (*gzugs*), in a luminous manner, then we perceive at that moment only the essence (*ngo bo*) of the object in its general aspect; this is the function of *sems*. When, however, we see the individual qualities of the object, for example its blue colour or square shape, then we are in the realm of the derived mental states. The cognitive process includes both aspects, *sems* and the derived states, each of which is operative according to the circumstances. Thus every object of perception for the *sems* is also an object of perception for the derived mental states. In the continuum (*rgyud*) of each being, luminous thinking energy (*sems gsal*) is innate, both in fine (*phra*) and coarse (*rag*) forms. This luminous mind bears within itself, as we have shown, the power of gradual perfection until it is finally able to rest within its own essential nature (*rang bzhin gnas*), in Buddhahood.

According to this doctrine, a potentiality innate within us enables us to attain Buddhahood, in that our *sems* is basically voidness, pure consciousness empty of all content, even if we do not perceive it. However the attainment of this state presupposes continuing practice and meditation, that is a gradual uninterrupted purification.

The conclusion at any rate is that Lamaism, developing perhaps more amply principles already inherent in the Indian Mahayana,[12] asserts the existence within us of a mind or spirit (*sems*) which represents an interior entity. This *sems* can rise from its impure, conditioned (*samskrta*) state to a progressive purity which is 'voidness', because beyond all thought that results from thinking, but is also omniscience, Buddhahood. Thus this Buddhahood is *in nuce* within us until it rises to a transcendence which is unconditioned (*asamskrta*) as such, but also conditioned (*samskrta*) in that it is the result of a successive ascent of gradually higher stages of which the last is conditioned by the experience of the preceding ones. However, absolute purity, absolute potentiality of Being, once it has been attained, is *asamskrta*, no longer conditioned, because it can no longer fall back from its situation at the limit. This revelation, this limiting situation, absolute potentiality of Being, is also Being itself, consciousness and light: 'void' in its condition of non-perfection in that it is related to an other; 'voidness' when no longer subject to relation.

6 Substantialism of the *Jo nang pa* school

Here the doctrinal contrasts between the *Jo nang pa*[13] and *dGe lugs pa* schools emerge particularly clearly. The representatives of the *dGe lugs pa* school admit, certainly, that the *sems* can be transformed into Buddha as a result of meditative practice, but they deny that this transformation is inevitable. Here their path parts from that of the *Jo nang pa*. According to the teachings of the *Jo nang pa* what can be cognized does not exist; the only thing that truly exists is that which is named the 'essence' of the Tathagata (*bde bar gshegs pa'i snying po* = Skt. *tathagatagarbha*, *chos nyid*), Being or 'true truth' (*don dam bden*).

Voidness is the being in self of *sems*; luminosity is the word, the identity of both is consciousness (*thugs*). This division is equivalent to that of the three bodies: the true essence of *sems* is the body of infinite spiritual potentiality, luminosity is the body of co-fruition, its manifestation and appearance is the apparent body. When transcendent consciousness arises, illusory appearances cease. Conversely, when illusory appearances manifest themselves, transcendent consciousness ceases. The world of things is without any essence; things are no more than appearances, and appearances are the result of *sems* alone. The meditating person is not in reality present, nor is there anything to be meditated on, because both meditator and object of meditation are nothing but the luminous power of thought. Consequently a practice of meditation to be followed does not exist, for there is no goal towards which it could be aimed.

Being, called by various names, is innate in all things and in all living beings. It is present as consciousness both in the enlightened Buddha and also in the psychic continuum (*rgyud*) of all beings, whether or not they are conscious of it. Absolute identity exists between the various Buddhas; all the Buddhas of the past, the present and the future proceed from the *tathagatagarbha*, the matrix of Buddhahood. This primary cause of Buddhahood is present at all times and outside of all temporality, in all places and beyond any spatial determination; there is only the body of infinite spiritual potentiality (*chos sku*). The distinction made between cause and effect concerns only the relationship, not the essence. The path to be travelled to the attainment of Enlightenment can be described as 'cause' only as a manner of speaking, and equally one can speak of 'effect' only as a verbal convention, for the 'effect' is present within the 'cause' before any beginning. There are possibilities of comparison here between this doctrine of the *Jo nang pa* and that of the Hindu Samkhya philosophy.

In this context one cannot speak of an overcoming of defilements, since these do not in reality exist. If from the point of view of the individual one can speak of the possibility of the attainment of Enlightenment (*sangs rgyas*), one cannot say that anything new has in reality been won or acquired. It can be a question only of a complete release and separation (*'bral*) of Being from all its defilements, and even that is not really so, because there is not in fact anything here to eliminate; the state of Being exists *ab initio* as absolute purity. As such Being is designated *rtag brtan g.yung drung*, the eternal, which stands beyond time, the unalterable; *g.yung drung* (Skt. *svastika*) is a technical term to indicate Being in the *Bon* religion. Being rests in itself and is therefore without any emanation and beyond all illusory appearance (*'khrul snang*).

Empirical reality (*kun rdzob*) is by contrast nothing more than the totality of defilement. If it is true that its content has no reality, then it can no longer be the original cause of defilements. The matrix of the Buddhas, the *tathagatagarbha*, is *ab initio* empty in itself (*rang stong*). Therefore the *tathagatagarbha* is all that is real, conceived of as void of everything of any other kind (*gzhan stong*). This gives the fundamental distinction between the two truths; while relative truth, the apparent world, is empty in itself, absolute truth, Being, is void of anything different from itself.

The two truths are illustrated through two examples. In the first the empty being of the cognizable is like a coiled rope which is taken for a snake in bad lighting. The snake is not present in the rope, and it is only through error that it is taken to exist; consequently it is without any individual existence. Emptiness in the second example is like a garment on which one discovers accidental stains. The garment is washed, the stains vanish, and the garment again achieves its original state, free from those stains which do not belong to it by nature.

If the defilements were real, then where did they come from? If they were innate in the *sems*, then this too would have to be eradicated, since the defilements are overcome in the course of the 'path' and the meditation.

One cannot exclude the possibility that this substantialism of the *Jo nang pa* school, which was regarded as equally heretical by almost all Tibetan schools, contains an echo of the Saivite schools of Kashmir.[14] Knowledge of these schools may have penetrated into the border regions of Tibet, the more so as in India at that time there were also conspicuous points of contact between Tantric, Saivite and Buddhist teachings. The principal objection of the *dGe lugs pa* to the *Jo nang pa* is the following. It may well be true that for the essence of the *sems* and the luminosity proper to it, despite chance defilements, a development is possible through meditation and the 'path' which will eliminate such defilements. However, the eradication of the defilements does not involve the suppression of the *sems* which they have been obscuring. The *sems* is so to say homologous and of the same nature as the family of the Buddha, for it can change to Buddhahood through the prescribed 'path'; this however does not imply that the *sems* capable of such transcendence is necessarily the Buddha himself, as can be seen from the following illustration: if a prostitute bears a son to a world-ruler, it is by no means certain that the son like the father will become a world-ruler. In addition the *dGe lugs pa* maintain that the *Jo nang pa* teaching is in contradiction with the fundamental assumptions of the Buddhist doctrine.

Continuing this argument, the *dGe lugs pa* school refuses to recognize an identity of the three states (the moment of beginning, the 'path' and the 'fruit'), because the non-duality of the two truths, conventional and absolute, is defiled at the beginning within the meditating individual. In the 'path' phase this non-duality, although it is made free of the defilements (*kun brtags*) deriving from our momentary illusions and concepts, is still subject to the defilements innate to it as mental inclinations. As a result, however, of the convergence of the two truths brought about in the instant of the 'fruit', these truths cease to conflict. Consequently we are dealing here with a substantial difference and not one of form only.

If we speak of the two truths in this context, the conventional or relative truth and the absolute truth, it is understood that we mean not just two modes of cognition, but rather two global situations. What we see, grasp and conceive is fundamentally only names and designations, not realities endowed with their own proper being, with a being that would be able to exert an influence on the *sems*. The *sems* for its own part, although empty, is still light that illuminates particular objects, and so is to be regarded as the basis for all that appears within and outside *samsara*. It would be a mistake here to postulate two different aspects, for both are of the same nature. It is only in so far as they appear as two that they cause the two truths, the conventional and the absolute. Since they are in reality one and the same, they form the essential precondition for their identity: their individual being is founded purely in conceptual thought and not in true Being.

The voidness of the *sems* is not negative voidness, because absolute voidness does not have a something opposed to it which has to be negated; it is voidness, nothing-ness—and that is all. Although what is cognized in empirical experience is nothing but words and names, it comes to be falsely considered as real thanks to the conventional truth which engenders and directs the empirical world. Conventional truth consequently appears to attach this or that function to things. That the world of objects is void of any substantial self-nature, and that it appears clothed with functions of all kinds, points to the convergence of the two truths, the relative-conventional and the genuine or absolute. The limiting point is not negation, but voidness which transcends negation itself: that which cannot be qualified, that which cannot become the content of thought.

7 The *bKa' brgyud pa* school

The *bKa' brgyud pa* school also lay stress on luminosity as the characteristic sign of *sems*. On this point their teaching does not diverge from that of the *Sa skya pa*. With respect to the interpretation of the limiting state of *sems*, however, various views exist within this school, all of which agree in holding that *sems* has not arisen from nothingness, does not consist of nothingness and does not vanish into nothingness; it stands outside of birth, cessation and duration, and thus outside any spatio-temporal limitation. To identify with *sems* in the meditation process therefore comes to signify the bringing about of the limiting situation. The many discursive trains of thought dominating our consciousness must be forcibly checked until they vanish. In the completion of this process consists liberation, the dissolution of dichotomizing cognition into the body of infinite spiritual potentiality (*chos sku*). Neither the existence of the cognizable from the standpoint of relative truth, nor its non-existence from the standpoint of absolute truth, is to be affirmed. As soon as every process of conceptualization and dichotomization is brought to a standstill, the *sems* will rest in its own self-being. This is the highest meditation. In this way the intuitive, non-rational insight is gained that all cognizable is nothing but deceptive appearances (*snang*) of *sems*. This intuition coincides with the limiting state of *sems*.

According to *Mi la ras pa* the clouds of the *maya*-body form themselves in the infinite potentiality of the *sems*-voidness. Its origin is the voidness of *sems*, its reabsorption (*thim*) is reabsorption precisely in *sems* as voidness. He who is not conscious of this allows empty, illusory structures to appear and grow. The goal of the yogin is liberation from the world of illusions; to achieve this he must make use of the double path of higher cognition and meditation, of ethical and cognitive accumulation and of practical exercise. These provide the help which not only enables insight into voidness but also gives a basis from which to realize this process within his own self.

The cessation of every passion, of every thought attached either to the state of *samsara* or that of peaceful detachment (*srid zhi*) is designated *nirvana*. Here too, however, we are dealing only with a concept which emerges from the mind-voidness, because all that can be cognized, all that can be affirmed or denied, sought for or rejected, is nothing but appearance arising from *sems*; reality is voidness. The state of rest (cf.p.65) overcomes the streams of dichotomizing concepts, of discursive cognition; supreme vision is the actualization of this limiting state. The two processes reach a balance, like a pair of scales coming to equilibrium; the dichotomizing impulses which had previously existed reach a standstill and the birth of new divisive tendencies is brought to an end. Such a supreme catharsis is called the Great Seal (*phyag rgya chen mo*, Skt. *mahamudra*); everything converges into the supreme consciousness of being. The authors of treatises divide it into 'impure', when it is cognized but not yet fully actualized, and 'pure', an inexpressible radiance like the sun in a cloudless sky. The word 'seal' can, it is true, have a double sense, for a seal presupposes an object on which it leaves its mark. In fact what is in question here is an inexpressible experience without object or subject, for both coincide: one does not exist without the other, and both dissolve as supreme consciousness is achieved.

8 Tantric practice according to the tradition of the *Bla na med rgyud*

In Tantric practice there are different kinds of exercise depending on the individual carrying them out. The Tantras containing these and describing how to carry them out are divided according to their contents into four classes or groups. These are (1) *bya* (Skt. *Kriya*), liturgical performance; (2) *spyod* (Skt. *Carya*), praxis; (3) *rnal 'byor* (Skt. *Yoga*), yoga; (4) *bla na med* (Skt. *Anuttara*), the highest group, beyond which there is no further.[15]

The first two classes are based on the assimilation and practice of the 'path', which is founded upon the non-duality of voidness and light. In the Tantras of the first class (*bya rgyud*), however, external ritual acts (making offerings, recitation, purificatory baths etc.) predominate over internally accomplished yoga. Liturgy, offerings, recitation of formulae are more important here than meditation (*sgom*). In the Tantras of the second class (*spyod rgyud*) by contrast, external act and interior yoga are in balance. The third class, that of the Yoga Tantras (*rnal 'byor rgyud*), aim at the assimilation and exercise of the 'path' on the basis of the non-duality of bliss and voidness. They place more importance on yoga accomplished internally than on external action.

The principal aim of the Tantras of the last class (*bla na med rgyud*) is to provide a method by which *sems* can be held under control, since all that is done and said, action and word, is always determined by the *sems*.

Once the mystic has actualized through his practice the *maya*-body mentioned earlier, in the form of the 'pure' *maya*-body, he experiences the limiting point of the *maya*-body, and light (*'od gsal*) in its pure radiant plenitude. In other words, the limiting point of light, the state of non-duality, is then experienced as a concurrence which transcends all appropriation, all taking possession and so on. When this state appears the dissolution of the two planes of existence (the plane of *samsara* and the plane of peaceful detachment, *srid zhi*) takes place and Buddhahood is experienced.

The Tantras of the fourth class (*bla na med rgyud*) place special emphasis in this connection on the teaching that breathing or vibratory ability (*rlung*[16]) and *sems* can be controlled once the circuit is interrupted which the two describe continuously in the two principal 'channels' and which causes the defilements producing *samsara*. These 'channels' are two imagined passages, without any physical reality, which run on the right and left side of the body; the right channel (*ro mo*) corresponds to hatred, the left (*rkyang ma*) to attachment. These two principal channels (*rtsa*, Skt. *nadi*) are connected to a third *nadi* (called *dbu ma*, Skt. *avadhuti*), which runs along the length of the spine, through a three-stage process which consists of breathing in (*gzhugs*), holding of breath (*gnas*) and breathing out (*thim*, in other words flowing back of the individual breath into the cosmic universal breath). Only as a result of this process does *sems* cease its movement and become the necessary precondition for the realization of that unique state (*thun mong ma yin pa*) that prepares for the coming of Buddhahood. Of course this process requires the previous practice of the *Phar phyin* vehicle, which forms an indispensable foundation. Otherwise it would be as if a completely inexperienced person wished to ride upon an untamed elephant. This at any rate is the view of the *dGe lugs pa*, the *Sa skya pa* and the *bKa' gdams pa*. Other schools such as the *rDzogs chen pa* prefer immediate entry to the Tantric path and regard the detour through the *Phar phyin* as dispensable.

The variety of contents of these Tantras of the fourth class (*bla na med rgyud*) has led the scholiasts to divide them into two sub-classes, 'Father'-Tantra (*pha*) and 'Mother'-Tantra (*ma*), a division which the *dGe lugs pa* have also taken over. The *Sa skya pa* add a third sub-class to these two, the Tantra of non-duality (*gnyis su med*), that is of the equilibrium of the two aspects (No.84, p.34b).[17] The *rDzogs chen* school, however, has a completely different division of the *rgyud* (cf.pp.77ff.). The basic distinction between 'Father'-Tantra and 'Mother'-Tantra relates to differences in doctrinal and ritual content. These can be summarized as follows (without going here into the hairsplitting discussions set off by this question): the two approaches place the stress differently with respect to the central principles of the entire fourth Tantra group (*bla na med rgyud*), the *maya*-body and light. In the 'Father'-Tantras the *maya*-body, which corresponds to the 'means' (*thabs*), to action, has the upper hand, while the role assigned to light (*'od gsal* = *shes rab*, higher cognition) is secondary. Examples of Tantras of this sub-class are *gSang ba 'dus pa, rDo rje 'jigs byed*, and so on. With the 'Mother'-Tantras the balance is reversed. Examples of this sub-class would be *'Khor lo bde mchog* and *Dus kyi 'khor lo*.

The mystic experienced in the teaching and practice of the fourth Tantra class (*bla na med rgyud*) thus has as the goal of his meditative and ascetic practice the rapid transformation of the *yid lus* (cf. above, pp.59-60) into a *maya*-body (*sgyu lus*), so as to anticipate already during the 'path' phase the various stages of the catharsis of salvation. If candidates for salvation through the 'Mother'-Tantras do not complete the prescribed contemplation of the supreme light-consciousness (*'od gsal* = *shes rab*) during the 'path' phase, then the attainment of absolute *sems*-purity (*thugs* = omniscience, Buddhahood) is denied to them at the 'fruit' phase. Equally if those seeking salvation through the 'Father'-Tantras do not place the *maya*-body (= *thabs*) at the central point of their contemplation and meditation during the 'path' phase, they will be unable to achieve the purification of body which is revealed at the stage of the result as the 'diamond body' with its characteristic marks.

The practice used by the schools can be characterized briefly as follows: for seekers after salvation who appear spiritually still immature the method of 'evocation' or 'production' (*bskyed rim*) is recommended for the maturing of their thought, while for those who are already spiritually mature the method of achievement (*rdzogs rim*) is prescribed. On this theme there was a continuing dialogue between the various schools, each of which sought to render prominent the superiority of its own particular goals and methods. The first method (*bskyed rim*) is intended, briefly, to bring about the transformation as understood by the doctrinal system of the school concerned into one of the three Buddha-bodies mentioned repeatedly above: body of infinite spiritual potentiality, body of co-fruition, apparent body (*chos sku*, *longs spyod sku*, *sprul sku*).

The basic precondition is the state of the mystic in each of his karmic experiences. Here three principal phases are to be distinguished: birth, death and the intermediate period (*bar do*) between death and rebirth. These three states represent the foundation of purification (*sbyong*), in so far as the goal of the meditator consists precisely in overcoming these states, the existence of which is ascribed to the continuity of karma, the persistence of error and all the appearances which so fatally accompany them.

In the 'path' phase the purifying presence of the three bodies is lived through as a result of the practice of meditation. At the end of this process the state of purification is attained as 'fruit', as soon as according to the circumstances and the particular aptitude and perseverance of the mystic one of the three bodies is achieved. When death approaches, the human being is on the point of succumbing to the pressure of karmic forces. The hierophant then comes to his aid. The hierophant has through observance of and prolonged meditation according to the precepts of this Tantra class (*bla na med rgyud*) transposed them into reality. At the moment of death therefore the karmic 'engrams' formed in the dying person are purified and a coincidence brought about between the light (*'od gsal*) realized in past meditations and the new light revealed in the instant of dying. The two lights, identical in essence, are now transferred into the body of infinite spiritual potentiality (*chos sku*).[18] This coincidence of the two lights is usually called the coincidence of the 'Mother' light with the 'Son' light.

For those who have not yet achieved this goal there follows upon death the state of intermediate existence (*bar do*) between dying and new incarnation. It is the fate of the ordinary human being to fall prey to a new existence with all of its inevitable sufferings. The mystic, however, evokes at the instant of death the experiences realized during the 'path' phase, so as to actualize the state called 'body of co-fruition' (*longs sku*). These experiences purify the karmic 'engrams' which provide the impulse for the intermediate existence (*bar do*), and so bring about the passage to the state of the 'body of co-fruition'. Persons of lesser maturity again, who are not able to overcome the state of intermediate existence, finally succumb to the compulsion of new rebirth, to a new immersion in the cycle of *samsara*. The yogin, however, brings about as a result of the experiences described earlier the state of the apparent body (*sprul sku*).

In reality the method of 'evocation' is much more complicated than this. In particular it makes use of the technique of breath control (Skt. *pranayama*) mentioned above, and so opposes to each karmic force (*las stobs*) a state engendered by the exertion of all the forces of ascetic practice (*sgom*).

The problem of the 'method of achievement', of its interpretation and of its practical aspect, has led to considerable differences of opinion between the schools. These have naturally been particularly deep between the *dGe lugs pa* and the *rNying ma pa*. Here it is a question of divisions already formed previously in the Tantric schools of India, which were further deepened and stressed by the Tibetan Tantrics. The premise and foundation of the whole process remain throughout the three moments of breathing (*rlung*, cf.p.64). The adherents of the *Dus kyi 'khor lo* (The Wheel of Time) prefer a sixfold yoga. In the *bDe mchog* schools, however, the 'method of achievement' based on the four voidnesses (voidness, great voidness, total voidness, extreme voidness) was adopted. Other procedures are the 'method of achievement' of four yogas of the *rDo rje 'jigs byed* and the 'deep way' of the *gSang ba 'dus pa*, which is followed by the *dGe lugs pa*.[19] All methods, however, equally tend to a practice which sets for its goal the passage from the *samsaric* and temporal plane to the extra-*samsaric* and atemporal plane; the passage that is from the phase of learning (*slob*) to that beyond learning and beyond all experience capable of being analysed and defined.

The process takes place through epiphanies, anticipations of the 'fruit' phase. In it, five aspects of perfection and purification are actualized: the state of perfection and purification (1) of the body; (2) of the word, of sound-potentiality in its own right, which expresses everything in all sounds and in each sound; (3) of the mind (*thugs*), equivalent to omniscience, to absolute, eternal omnipresence; (4) of action, enabling one to lead living beings on the way of salvation; (5) of efficacy (*phrin las*), enabling the adoption at will of any desired form suitable for the conversion of living beings, until the end of *samsara*. In such a manner the mystic who has been reintegrated into the wholeness of the consciousness of Being experiences in himself the extratemporal glory of divine powers in the moment in which he turns into an archetypical emanation.

We have had to restrict ourselves to the most basic points regarding the actual contents of the 'Father'- and 'Mother'-Tantras, the sub-classes of the Superior Tantra (*bla na med rgyud*). This subject is fundamental to Lamaist soteriology and is deserving of a more comprehensive treatment. We look now at the *rNying ma pa* school, whose formulations of doctrine and meditation are in many cases noticeably different, although there are frequent points of connection with the other schools none the less, since many doctrinal premises are the same, and also many fundamental experiences correspond in a certain sense.

9 The *rNying ma pa* school

The doctrinal synthesis produced by the *rNying ma pa* is much the most individual, both from the point of view of the doctrine itself, and with regard to the Tantric tradition on which the school is based. As we will show, their views on *sems* (the kernel of soteriology) are altogether individual. Besides this the Tantric texts of the *rNying ma pa* (cf.p.38) and the experiences described within them vary considerably from those of the so-called 'new' schools (*gsar ma*), which were developed after the second diffusion of the teaching. In the first place the number of 'vehicles' now rises to nine (*theg pa rim pa dgu*), each of which corresponds to the karmic and spiritual situation of a particular group of men.[20] Buddhist experience is divided into three groups, each of which is further sub-divided into three. Thus the first three 'vehicles' (those of the Sravaka, of the Pratyekabuddha, and of the Bodhisattva) are intended for beings of lower abilities, the next three (Kriya, Upa-yoga, and Yoga-Tantra) for those of medium ability, and the last three (Maha-yoga-Tantra, Anu-yoga-Tantra and Ati-yoga-Tantra) for those of highest ability.

The followers of the *rNying ma pa* schools have devoted an extensive literature to this subject, frequently concerned with defending this system against the other schools. The distinctions which they argue against the other schools are concerned with (a) the texts relating to the particular 'vehicles'; (b) the preparatory actions; (c) the mode of conceptualization; (d) the meditation; (e) the practice; (f) the result and the 'fruit'.

The lower valuation given to the first three vehicles, the Lesser Vehicle, the Vehicle of the Pratyekabuddhas, and the Greater Vehicle (Mahayana), represents nothing new. The religious experience of Buddhism in no way comes to a close with the Mahayana, and indeed its most efficient soteriological inspiration appears precisely within the realms of the 'Diamond Vehicle' (Tantra). The *rNying ma pa* recognize six Tantra classes (corresponding to the fourth to ninth 'vehicles') rather than four, and the terminology relating to these classes also differs somewhat from that of the other schools.

Of course even the *rNying ma pa* do not reject the general doctrinal structure of the Mahayana. The background still remains the concept of 'voidness', but in developing these theoretical foundations further, *rNying ma* mysticism places the centre of gravity differently. The 'Earths' to be traversed in the course of the catharsis (cf.p.50) now become thirteen. By following the Kriya-Tantra the Thirteenth 'Earth' can be reached within only seven lifetimes from the first step; by following the Upa-yoga-Tantra it can be reached within five lifetimes. Through the third Tantric class, the Yoga-Tantra, the initiate is able to attain Enlightenment in the *'Og min* paradise within three lifetimes. With the assistance of the Maha-yoga-Tantra one can attain the apparent body (*sprul sku*) in the existence immediately following the present one. The Anu-yoga projects the body into Great Bliss at the instant of death. The Ati-yoga leads directly to the outermost limit, to the goal, to definitively actualized consciousness of Being.

The content of the Tantras can be sketched briefly as follows. They are divided into two groups each with three sub-divisions (Kriya, Upa-yoga, Yoga; Maha-yoga, Anu-yoga, Ati-yoga).

Group A

I Kriya (a) Preparatory acts: rituals, purificatory baths, offerings etc.; (b) mode of conceptualization: the existence of gods is acknowledged (if in a purely relative manner) and the relationship between god and men is viewed as like that between king and subjects; (c) meditation (*sgom*): on the gods, as if they actually existed; (d) practice: purification of body, speech and mind. Of the defilements, anger is particularly to be overcome; (e) fruit: the goal is the attainment of the glories of the three gods called *mGon po*, a 'fruit' which is already anticipated in the experience of the 'path' phase, although its attainment requires from a minimum of seven to a maximum of thirteen lives.

II Upa-yoga (a) Preparatory acts: concentration[21] (*samadhi*) on the convergence of the two truths (cf.p.69-70); (b) mode of conceptualization. Although it is recognized that from the absolute point of view one cannot speak of birth, it is still accepted at the level of empirical truth. Similarly one can speak of the evocation and bringing to manifestation of gods (cf.p.94); the relationship between god and man is viewed here as like that between master and servant; (c) meditation: on the five 'families' of gods, the pentads[22] (cf.p.97), with the aim of bringing about the convergence of contemplation and practice; (d) practice: with the aim of the performance of good works for one's neighbour through the four modes of magical action, along with the overcoming of envy; (e) fruit: the goal is a state analogous to that of the pentad, and its experience is again anticipated in the course of the 'path'. The result may be achieved in from five to thirteen lifetimes.

III Yoga (a) Preparatory actions: meditative coincidence of work and concentration or 'synentasy' (*samadhi*); (b) means of conceptualization: leading the mind to absolute truth; on the plane of conventional truth, action for the transformation of the self into a god, or evocation of the god in front of the meditator (*ye shes lha*, *dam tshig lha*, cf.p.95); (c) meditation: on the prescribed *mandala*, with reference to the five Enlightenments, beginning from concentration on body, speech and mind–the state of the hypostatization of the transcendent consciousness of these deities; (d) practice: actualization of the *ye shes lha* state (cf.p.95) for the good of living beings, bringing about the fusion of the 'Means' (*thabs* = Father) with transcendent consciousness (= Mother), overcoming of pride; (e) the goal is the attainment of the glories of *rDo rje 'chang*, and the experience of this deity is anticipated in the 'path' phase; from the third life on, rebirth in the *'Og min* paradise is possible.

The three Tantric classes discussed so far are particularly concerned with body, speech and mind respectively. Their result in the phase of fruition is the body of co-fruition (*longs sku*).

Group B

I Maha-yoga Here it must first of all be mentioned that the four consecrations (the same as those described above, p.57) stand at the centrepoint of the experience of the following three Tantra classes. They are repeated in each class with a different and progressively higher effect. The consecration of the 'vessel' transfigures itself and everything else onto the divine plane. In the second consecration ambrosia (= transcendent consciousness) descends on the head of the person being initiated. In the third consecration fusion (= Non-Duality) takes place between teacher and disciple. In the fourth, the non-reality of the meditator is accomplished, in that reality is situated beyond any individuality. Such an initiation has four advantages over the consecrations of the Tantras previously described: (i) in the earlier Tantras, the *mandala* was sketched on the earth with coloured powders, while here a book takes its place; (ii) in the lower Tantras colours were used to depict the figures, while here the creative phonemes (*mantra*)[23] of the deities are used; (iii) in place of reproductions of the deities visualizations are used; (iv) in place of the various objects with which the *mandala* was adorned there is the *mchod rten* (cf.p.80). (a) Preparatory actions: consecration of the 'vessel'; (b) mode of conceptualization: in the Maha-yoga, the individual components of the human personality (*phung po* = Skt. *skandha*; *khams* = Skt. *dhatu*, sensory sphere; *skye mched* = Skt. *ayatana*) distinguished and classified by the traditional doctrinal system are deprived of their fictive materiality and considered as of divine nature. Thus they become identical to the divine plane, in that, through an esoteric homology, they demonstrate the presence of divine forms co-ordinated with particular moments of the actualization of being; (c) meditation: on the *mandala*, to fuse together the two moments of the evocation, *ye shes lha* and *dam tshig lha* (cf.p.95) in perfect non-duality; (d) practice: what are defilements in the uninitiated are now transformed, and thus liberated, through the passage to the state of transcendent consciousness (*ye shes*); (e) fruit: the aim is the attainment of the apparent body, and appropriate meditations are employed in the 'path' phase. In this way the purification of the body takes place, which assures the attainment of the apparent body (*sprul sku*) in the following existence.

II Anu-yoga Here we have to deal with an extremely complex set of concepts, since it encompasses both Tantra sub-classes, Father- and Mother-Tantra. The consecration here is on a higher level than that described earlier. (a) Preparatory actions: 'emanationless' secret initiation (*gsang dbang*), and the initiation of transcendent consciousness resulting from higher cognition (*shes rab ye shes dbang*) which is termed 'emanationless in the highest degree', meaning that the dichotomizing power of thought is interrupted (cf.p.47). Each of these consecrations includes all the four kinds mentioned above (consecration of the 'vessel' etc.), with different meanings and a different liturgy. Thus there are eight kinds of consecration presupposed by the two sub-classes of Tantra brought together in this class. The most important aspect here is the union of the Father (*yab*) and the Mother (*yum*), that is of the master and his paredra[24] in intimate embrace. The symbolic power of this process, in which Enlightenment is equated with the semen resulting from the union, permeates the whole scheme. The same is true for the second set of consecrations, those called 'emanationless in the highest degree' (*shin tu spros med*), in the course of which the initiand himself becomes the actor, for he unites himself with the paredra (*phyag rgya*, Skt. *mudra*). In the secret initiation, when the Thought of Enlightenment[25] (*byang sems*), here equated with the semen of the *bla ma* embracing the paredra, is placed on the tongue, then this is the consecration of the 'vessel'. When one tastes it, the secret consecration is granted. When the instruments of yoga ('channels', breath, 'drop' or *thig le*, cf.p.72) are filled with bliss, the third consecration is accomplished. The fourth is experienced when the identity of bliss and voidness is perceived. In this way the defilements of the plane of the Word are purified and effectiveness is achieved in the meditation, an effectiveness which rests upon the control of the breathing and of the 'drop' (cf.p.262). In the next existence the body of co-fruition can be attained. In the second set of consecrations, the initiation of transcendent consciousness called 'in the highest degree emanationless', when the initiand contemplates in his meditation the *bla ma* and the paredra and worships them as gods, the first consecration takes place. The second corresponds to the fall of semen = Thought of Enlightenment. The third takes place when the experience of great bliss begins, and the fourth when the union of bliss and voidness is accomplished. The superiority of the secret initiation lies in the complete reversal of the liturgical structure which takes place in this Tantra class; the *bla ma*'s body here replaces the book in the 'vessel' consecration. In the second consecration the paredra takes the place of the *bla ma*, while in the third the deification of the *bla ma* and his paredra united in sexual embrace replaces the invocation of deities. In the fourth the three planes of the *bla ma* himself (body, speech and mind) replace the *mchod rten*.[26] The superiority of the second initiation of transcendent consciousness over the secret initiation is also fourfold: the *bla ma* is no longer situated on the exterior, since the body of the initiate becomes identical with that of the *bla ma* transformed into the *mandala*. The paredra does not stand outside the initiate in the second consecration, but is united into one with him. The Thought of Enlightenment = semen does not fall outside in the third consecration, but is absorbed back into itself. In the fourth the state of pleasure is derived not from external causes but out of itself; (b) mode of conceptualization: transcendent consciousness and the plane of potential existentiality (*dbyings*) as non-duality; (c) meditation: voidness = luminous transcendent consciousness; (d) practice: all is illusory play of transcendent consciousness; (e) fruit: the experience of the enjoyment of 'great bliss' can be realized whenever one wishes during the 'path' phase. Mental defilements are purified. At the moment of death the 'body of great bliss' is attained.

III Ati-yoga (a) Preparatory actions: 'emanationless consecration in transcendent form'. This includes the four named consecrations, each of which now reveals through intuitive vision that all that appears as pure, contentless consciousness is *sems*, that *sems* is voidness, that voidness is bliss, and that bliss transcends any possibility of definition, stands beyond all thought. This initiation is distinguished from the previous consecrations of the Anu-yoga in that the *mandala* on which one meditates is here transformed from the body into the *sems*, and the union with the paredra is replaced by attaining coincidence with transcendent consciousness. Instead of a flow of delight, there is produced here a delight without flow; instead of a state of grace being received from the exterior, the mystic is situated in a state beyond all thought; (b) and (c) mode of conceptualization and meditation: everything is beyond definition, there is nothing to hope for or fear; (d) practice: no concepts may arise, just as little liberation from concepts; nothing is to be received, nothing is to be abandoned. All defilements are purified in transcendent supreme consciousness; (e) fruit: the aim is the achievement of the 'perfected body', and its qualities are experienced in the 'path' phase; the defilements of the physical, verbal and mental plane are all completely removed; integration with voidness-light-Being. As a result the body of Being is already attained in this life.

All this can naturally only be given here in a schematic form. We must content ourselves with indicating that at this point the complex heritage of yoga and Tantrism (whether of Buddhist or Saivite character) breaks in again on the world of experience of the *rNying ma pa*. It can be recognized in the ever increasing stress laid upon 'great bliss' (*bde chen*, Skt. *mahasukha*), which plays a decisive role in the Saivite schools and in their special interpretation of *ananda*, 'bliss',[27] which along with Being and Consciousness is one of the three inherent properties of the real in Saivite philosophy.

Erotic symbolism takes over control of Tantric experience. Thus the presence of the paredra becomes an essential element of the ritual. The equation of semen with Thought of Enlightenment, light held captive within the body, dominates the liturgical process. Of course this is in no way a Tibetan innovation; it is rather an Indian tradition traceable in its origins to the most ancient times, although one cannot exclude the possibility that its later perfecting may have occurred under the influence of gnostic and magical currents in the border regions of Tibet and India. This does not mean however that the symbolism is to be taken literally. The paredra, the 'Mother', is evidently transcendent consciousness, and her union with the 'Father' in its various stages represents the dynamics of the relationship which develops between these two elements of liberation. Liberation, initially an object of contemplation, progresses from a convergence simply learnt or suggested by the teaching of the master, to visual conceptualization according to the schemata of the *mandala*, then to participation in transcendent consciousness, in order finally to arrive at a definitive synthesis in the mystic himself. He has no further need of reflection, nor of meditation, nor of objectification (either conceptualized or suggested); rather he lives in himself this *mysterium magnum*. Nevertheless the ritual procedures in certain ceremonies suggest memories of literal interpretations, for example semen = Thought of Enlightenment, Transcendent Consciousness, is represented by curdled milk which is to be drunk from a skull bowl (genuine or made from metal). It was in this form that it was offered to me, too, when I obtained the consecration of *Kye rdo rje* in *Sa skya*.

We should remember throughout that in this Tantric literature we move among symbols, that the words do not have their ordinary meanings and are scarcely ever able to be translated adequately into our logical language. All this is secret, and each word or action evokes states that have to be experienced directly.

The doctrinal standpoint of the *rDzogs chen* (the *rNying ma pa* tantric school) is as already indicated (p. 14) different from that of the schools discussed previously. It posits the existence of a state of absolute voidness, uncreated, without origin, without beginning, in which exist neither Buddhas nor beings that might strive towards Buddhahood. This state is called the 'body *in se*' or quintessential body (*ngo bo nyid kyi sku*). In it the various modes of being flow together, and thus it transcends both the samsaric and nirvanic states. In its actualization it unfolds spontaneously as pure intelligence, Gk. *nous* (Tib. *rig pa*); its symbolic name is *Kun tu bzang po*. We ourselves, at the basis of our being, are this *rig pa*, and if we recognize it as such in the 'path' phase, then it will be transformed in the 'fruit' phase into great transcendent consciousness (*ye shes chen po*). If, however, it is not known to be *rig pa*, to be voidness illuminated *ab aeterno*, then it becomes clouded through adventitious defilements, and is changed into non-intelligence (*ma rig*). This non-intelligence is the cause of the deceptive dichotomies through which the chains of samsaric experience hold us captive. These dichotomies are produced by the *sems*, which thus has to be distinguished carefully from the *rig pa*. The *rig pa* is undefiled *ab initio*; it is only as a consequence of lack of insight into its nature, and the error which this causes, that the deceptive process of *sems* and its activity takes place.

A famous series of *rDzogs chen* verses runs as follows:

> *rig pa* is reality. Since it is voidness, it cannot be asserted of it that it is eternal. Since its nature is luminosity, such a definition sets no limit to it. It is boundless compassion, from which endless manifestations flow. Although its three aspects can appear as distinct, in reality one is dealing with the same thing. In its essential state it is emanationless *ab initio*. It is not being, for even the Buddhas cannot see it. It is not non-being, for it forms the foundation for the samsaric and extra-

samsaric world. It is neither something positive nor something negative, therefore it goes beyond any defining in words.

Such is the basis for the appearance of the objective part, that in deceptive manner appears as a part of the *sems* (*snang cha*). Whatever appears as the objective world outside the mind (*phyi rol*), including the *sems* when it becomes its own object (*yul*), is unreal, is insubstantial. The *sems* as subject (*yul can*) either recognizes its real nature, in other words absolute voidness, or else it does not recognize it. If it does not recognize it then it is non-intelligence (*ma rig*), then it succumbs to the dichotomies, the disintegrations into series of oppositions, which are however basically derivable from a single pair of opposites, *samsara* and *nirvana*. The consequence is that the *sems* remains attached to the plane of illusory existence.[28] We remain throughout here in the realm of a function of the mind (*sems*), one of the functions creating the immeasurable network of illusions (*'khrul*), a network which thanks to the confused play of concept-bound cognition unfolds ever more extensively. Once an end is put to this play of illusion, the comprehension of pure intelligence (*rig pa*) follows. The spontaneous and direct actualizations of pure *rig pa* can also be designated Enlightenment (*byang chub*, Skt. *bodhi*); it is without quality, form or colour, an indefinable, absolute identity. This vision is gradually opened up through the meditation and successive purifications undertaken in the course of the initiatory practice. Apart from this gradual (*rim gyis*) actualization an immediate (*gcig char*) revelation of the truth can occur, such as that which was granted to *dGa' rab rdo rje* and other ascetics already spiritually mature.

The same thing then happens to *rig pa* as to a human being when he falls from the waking state into the state of dreaming, and the most varied dream images then pass before him. However, as soon as *rig pa*, substrate of all that appears in or beyond this world, acquires intuitive consciousness of itself as such, it is released and freed. When it does not recognize itself, when its view is obscured, it creates out of its own free activity an apparent duality—the foundation of the characteristic illusion of *samsara*. In reality there is nothing outside *rig pa*, therefore there is nothing to be received or overcome, nothing to assert, nothing to deny.

The mechanism of illusion (*'khrul*) comes into action as a result of the three primary causes (*rgyu*), thanks to the three aspects of non-intelligence (*ma rig*) and the four contributory causes or accompanying circumstances (*rkyen*). The first primary cause is cognition itself, in that it does not recognize that the cognizable, the apparent world, is derived from itself. The second is the innate non-intelligence (*ma rig*) that conceals within itself the ability to recognize itself or not to recognize itself. The third comes down to the fact that this non-intelligence (*ma rig*) does not recognize that all that can be asserted is nothing but its own illusory emanation. The four contributory causes consist in the non-recognition that subject and object result from non-intelligence (*ma rig*), in the acceptance of the appearance of non-intelligence (*ma rig*) themselves as objects, in the appropriation of the apparitions by the subject, and finally in the simultaneity of these three forms of non-intelligence (*ma rig*).

Light, on the other hand, forms an essential factor in the process of manifestations and actualization of the *rig pa*, or conversely in the process of illusory appearance (*'khrul snang*), and precisely because of its immanent and free activity (*rtsal*). Light-intelligence is manifested through its immanent action by means of five rays[29] (*'od zer*) which in their pure part or aspect appear as the 'five families' of the body of co-fruition.[30] In their impure part or aspect they appear as the five constituent parts of the human personality, the supports of *samsara*.

These five luminous bodies reveal themselves in the individual, in his state of illusory appearance, as the five constituents of his illusory personality. The five aspects or modalities of transcendent consciousness (*ye shes lnga*) appear through the process of spatio–temporal individuation as the five moral 'infections'; the five lights appear as the five elements and consequently as the five sense-objects, five senses and five modes of sensory perception. In this way the mechanism and technique of progressive deliverance is thrown open to the yogin, for not only are there precise correspondences and homologies with respect to the individual aspects of the illusory emanation, but these correspondences suggest to the mystic the content of his progressive stages of meditation and thus actualize the reversal of the planes.

Conversely the five 'poisons', the five sins out of which the illusory texture of *samsara* is woven, transform in the limiting phase of the 'fruit' into the five forms of transcendent consciousness, while the five components of the human personality are transfigured into luminous, divine forms. *Rig pa*, the Light-Voidness, is recognized as such in the meditation at the 'fruit' phase, and the body of infinite spiritual potentiality (*chos sku*) is actualized. When its luminosity shines out in its full radiance, the body of co-fruition (*longs sku*) is actualized, and when 'compassion without restriction' appears, the apparent body is actualized. In this way the actualization of the three bodies comes about at the 'fruit' phase, each according to the circumstances. These three bodies are imagined as present and actually operative in the body of the mystic at the moment of the supreme initiation of the

Ati-yoga, and their existential mode of Being is integrated into the pure body *in se*.

Two of the long and complicated procedures designed for liberation from the error causing the perpetuation of *samsara* deserve mention here. Through one of these, *khregs chod*, the meditating individual (*gzhi dus*) is able to recognize the intelligence present within himself. The second phase leading to such a reconquest of the Light, *thod rgal*, is a procedure taking place through an articulated structure of meditation and of yoga which draws within its power all the modes of psycho-physical activity of the meditating individual.

In both cases (*khregs chod* and *thod rgal*) we are concerned with a process of meditation based upon the Light (*'od gsal chen po thod rgal*, No.103, p.21b), but there is a fundamental difference between the two. Seven 'superiorities' of *thod rgal* over *khreg chod* are mentioned: only *thod rgal* opens up a vision of transcendent consciousness (*ye shes*) and of the pure light[31] and brings about a convergence of transcendent consciousness and the limitless sphere of existentiality (*dbyings*). The first method represents a state of preparatory tension, in which the process of meditation and yoga (*rtsa rlung*) is not yet refined, while nothing coarse (*rag pa*) remains in the all-dissolving light of the second method. In *khregs chod* the body can be represented as transformed into a particle of dust or an atom, but it does not vanish into the light. Using the first method alone the *sgyu lus* cannot reach its limiting state, the diamond body therefore cannot be achieved either, and one cannot succeed in bringing about the salvation of others in a complete manner.

In the *rDzogs chen* school, as in all the yoga schools, the body is seen as an essential instrument of salvation.[32] It is provided with 'channels' or 'centres' (*rtsa*, Skt. *nadi*) within which the vibratory potential or respiration (*rlung*) moves, as does the action of the inner intelligence (*nang rig pa*), which must be found again (*ngo sprod*) before the light of the essence can shine out (No.103, p.26). Five significant things (*gnad*) have thus to be kept in mind: (1)-(3) the body with its three particular postures, (4) speech and (5) mind (*sems*). The three postures of the body are those of the lion, the elephant and the ascetic (*drang srong*). The first of these corresponds to the body of infinite spiritual potentiality (*chos sku*), the second to the body of co-fruition, the third to the apparent body. In the first manner liberation is brought about from the troubles caused by illusory appearances, in the second the enjoyment of Being as such is attained, as distinct from the being of such and such an object, while in the third this Being manifesting itself in its freely chosen appearances is viewed with the eye of the doctrine (ibid., p.29b).

With respect to the word (*ngag*) the most important thing is not to speak, for from words arise the dichotomies with their antagonistic consequences. With respect to the *sems* it is a question of giving up, through control over the vibratory faculty or respiration (*rlung*) the conception of oneself as a thing, and thus bringing about the convergence of potential existentiality (*dbyings*) with intelligence (ibid., p.28).

The decisive factor with respect to the *rig pa* is liberation from all that appears as existing; the intelligence must be visualized as infinite or as reabsorbed into celestial space, upon which a dark blue line appears in its midpoint; this is the exterior sphere of the existential (*phyi dbyings*): the emanation of the five lights with their five colours from that light is the interior sphere of the existential (*nang dbyings*). Although an exterior and an interior sphere (*dbyings*) are spoken of separately, the two are, however, indissolubly bound to unity, like the lightning which is visible in the sky in its full illuminating power, but when seen from inside a tent appears to illuminate it from the inside (ibid., p.31). This duality is only appearance (*snang*).

The *thod rgal* meditation aims at the dissolution of the physical and mental world into creative light. It is practised in the morning or the evening, and consists in fixing one's gaze on the sun or on a light. After repeated attempts and experiences, whose duration differs according to the subject undertaking the practice, a point appears. If one continues to fix one's eyes upon the sun, then this point divides into five concentric circles which are considered to be manifestations of the five lights mentioned. The midpoint (*thig le*) is regarded as a symbol of the void (*stong pa*). If one meditates on it intensively, then the divine forms appear, each one characterized by its own symbols and signs. If this point is kept as the centre of contemplation, it spreads out until it penetrates through infinite space. Thus all distinction between subject and object disappears.[33]

The result of the light-meditation carried out in *thod rgal* is that the physical body dissolves and is transformed into a radiant body, the 'rainbow body' (*'ja' lus*). Deceptive appearances, all things which appear to our mind as an object (*snang yul*), become one with absolute potentiality (*thig le = chos sku*). The light appearing in the 'path' phase becomes one with the *rig pa ab aeterno* visualized in the 'fruit' phase; this is the vision of *Kun tu bzang po*. This identity is called 'meeting of the mother and son lights'. The convergence between voidness, liberation from all that can be expressed, and luminosity, the identity of voidness and light, transcends all possibility of definition and can therefore never be content of the intellect. It is the state-in-itself of the undefiled mind, all-penetrating consciousness of Being, beyond time and space, the essence-body, the body of light without limit.

The *rNying ma pa* also divide their doctrinal structure into three groups: (a) the group concerning *sems* (*sems sde*) which culminates in the Maha-yoga Tantra; (b) the *klong* group (*klong sde*) whose principles are explained in the Anu-yoga Tantra and form an initiation into the *khregs chod* described above; (c) the group of 'formulae' (*man ngag sde*), the quintessence of the teaching (*rDzogs chen*), presented in the Ati-yoga Tantra: the introduction into the practice of *thod rgal*. While it is possible with respect to certain masters to establish agreements and correspondences between the Maha-yoga and Anu-yoga Tantra on the one hand, and the 'Father'- and 'Mother'-Tantras of the other schools on the other hand, the *rDzogs chen* adherents affirm the absolute superiority of the Ati-yoga Tantra, to which they assign a special state of pre-eminence.

10 The *gcod* tradition

The *gcod* school, which constitutes a monastic tradition in its own right, merits a special mention. Its teachings are, however, accepted by other schools too, although these schools diverge from *gcod* with respect to practice and method. The chief *gcod* monastery is situated in *Ding·ri*. Its theoretical premises are connected with the *Phar phyin* (Skt. *Prajnaparamita*) scriptures, and in particular with the chapter on Mara. The Prajna, called '*mantra* which heals all ills', is the text which *Ma gcig Lab sgron ma* used to recite (*klog*) continuously. The theoretical basis of *gcod* certainly stands in opposition to that of the teachings of the other schools. While they take the view, as we have seen, that suffering is removed after the destruction of the moral defilements (*nyon mongs*) which cause it, the disciples of *gcod* insist to the contrary that the destruction of suffering brings about the destruction of the moral defilements.

The practical side of *gcod* has the aim of cutting through (*gcod*) the process of thought (*rnam rtog*). This process causes the duality of the apparent world in that it presupposes a thinking subject and an object which is being thought of, and thus also an act of thinking. It is at the basis therefore of all egotism and of the emergence of all emotional and thinking activity (*bdag tu 'dzin*, No.2, p.11b). The pure state of Being cannot be attained without the suppression of this process. *gcod* is intended therefore to cut off the discursive process at the root and so directly (*gcig char*, ibid., p.8b) help bring about the insight that in reality nothing exists. Out of this flows liberation from all dichotomies of good or bad (*bzang ngan med pa*, ibid., p.11b) and thus from all the fears of life, including the fear of birth and of death (*skye 'chi*, ibid., p.12a), and therefore from all deceptive appearance. The meditation takes the form of a sacrifice, an offering of body and of life, a destruction of the five constituents of the human person (*phung po lnga*). The goddess who watches over *gcod* is called 'She who rejects every process of life' (*lus srog gzang du bor ba'i ma*, loc.cit.). The offering or sacrifice is here symbolically conceived as the task of the five senses–the doors which allow deception its entry into the world of concepts and through which this deception unfolds. In this sense the goddess is the hypostatization of infinite potential existentiality (*chos dbyings*, Skt. *dharmadhaṭu*), but she only plays a provisional role as a support (*dmigs*) of the meditation process, during which she is conceived of visually in her own form. In invoking her as Mother and thus ascribing an instrumental value to her the meditator temporarily forgets that he is concerned here only with a symbolic representation through which human finiteness attempts to represent the inconceivable and inexpressible. The spontaneous hymns born out of this experience are not inferior in their poetic force to the poems of Indian mystics such as Rama Prasad. He too evokes Kali as the divine dispenser of life and death, Kali who symbolizes at base the secret principle of life subject to the laws of universal development. Similarly the Tibetan mystic describes himself as a son calling upon his mother to liberate him from all vanities and errors:

> Mother, when you are there (near to me),
> I am at peace.
> When you go away, my heart
> Is full of sadness (ibid., p.12b).

And he implores her for her blessing (*byin gyis brlab*), the mother's blessing, as if the reintegration he desires is to be owed to her grace and not to his perseverance and energy in meditation. In this sense one cannot speak of grace, for the divine symbol itself has its origin in the thought of the meditator, and consequently no grace can descend on the mystic from the outside. Certainly we should never lose sight of the fact that we are dealing here with a drama which can shake profoundly the mental and emotional structure of he who gives himself to the meditation, and in the course of which the givens of the ordinary world of experience are reduced to nothing.

In its totality the process described possesses great psychological significance. There are two distinct elements in its actualization and course up to the limit of the transition to the other plane. These are a preparatory element, in which the deceptive assumption of the existence of gods and demons is made, and a second element which brings about the certitude that gods and demons are nothing but emanations of our own thought. Through the joint action of these two contradictory elements, the meditation process takes form until its dissolution. This takes place when illusion yields place definitively to the certainty, now lived through and experienced and not just given by the intellect, that in these representations one is dealing only with symbols and not with essences or realities. A process of evocation lies at the basis of this drama, the voluntary calling forth of a hallucinatory state during which gods and demons appear visibly before the meditator. This state results from intensive meditation on the 'seed' or mystic syllable, the germ or embryo of every divine form which finds its expression in a particular phoneme from which a light shines that can solidify into a divine or demonic form.

A significant fact here is that *gcod* customarily prefers to concentrate on fear-evoking deities, on the *gnod sbyin*, *gdon*, *dregs*, *'dre* and so on, in their terrifying, bloody and death-dealing forms of manifestation.

To pave the way for this emotional crisis and for the required visualization, the *gcod* teachings recommend that the appropriate exercises should be carried out in cemeteries (*dur khrod*) and amongst corpses. The meditator must be equipped with a trumpet made from a human tibia (*rkang gling*) and the *damaru*, the shaman's drum. The preferred time is the 'dark fortnight'. In this fear-inspiring atmosphere the mystic is placed alone, with the conviction acquired from his daily meditation on the Prajnaparamita and from the teaching of his master, but with all the archetypal fears in his subconscious of humanity in general and the Tibetans in particular. At the moment of invocation the certainty that the images standing before him are creations of his own mind comes to his aid against the outbreak of primeval fears. Certainly a merely intellectual assurance is not sufficient to convince him that these forms do not exist in themselves, but are mere illusory products of thought-processes not yet brought under control. The meditator has to absorb them in their primal 'seed' and let this 'seed' disappear into his heart. Only thus does he attain, thanks to continually renewed practice, the lived certainty that these manifestations are not real, but illusory images emanating from himself. In this way also he acquires the conviction that each thought, each experience, each form, each thing is no more than the play of uncontrolled thought, which disappears at the breaking forth of that luminous undifferentiated consciousness, out of which the unreal flows.

Two ways are open to man. One leads to a state which may be human or even divine, the state of being subject to joy and grief. Its content or duration may vary, it is still always the path of *samsara*. The other way is the path of Enlightenment (*byang chub*, Skt. *bodhi*), the path of liberation (*thar lam*). In order to traverse it, *gcod* must cut off the basic causes of the cycle of *samsara* at their roots. This process begins with two erroneous views (*ldog*), one general, abstention from evil and so on, and one particular, the performance of good actions: even this latter does not liberate one from the cycle of *samsara*. Both good and bad must be overcome and in this way the lived certainty must be reached that there is neither subject nor object. Thus every bondage to one or the other can be blocked immediately at its root. These premises are already familiar to us, but here their practical expression is different and above all much more intense.

The theoretical basis of the meditation practices is formed by the idea that there are many domains of the world of demons (*bdud*): demons here are embodiments of the illusions to be overcome. Some 'demons' presuppose a contact (*thogs bcas*), in other words one is concerned here with the senses and the objects of the senses. Other 'demons' do not depend on such contact: they reign over the objects of thought-activity, the causes of hopes, fears, satisfactions, attachment to virtues practised in the 'path', attachment to all means of relief against illness, punishment or injury by supernatural powers, and also hesitations and doubts concerning one's own abilities and so on. Such illusory powers, conceived of as demons, can be suppressed on the plane of quiescence, and there dissolved through that supreme intuition according to which there is nothing that can be overcome or striven for, neither demonic beings nor things, nor indeed elimination or aspiration as such. If a fear-inspiring phantom arises, there is no point in avoiding it; one must look it boldly straight in the eye, and indeed look through the meditation on non-existence at both the object causing the fear and also the subject experiencing the fear, and the fear itself as such. The meditation is particularly strengthened by the offering of one's own body as food or plunder to fear appearing or manifesting itself in demonic form. In so far as the mystic continually holds the instructions given to him in his mind, and imbues them with the recognition that nothing exists that has self-existent being or is other than deception, he extricates himself from the situations possible to the dichotomizing operation of thought, and leads everything to its dissolution in the void. All that appears to us as an external world then vanishes; our psychic continuum no longer knows what it desires to actualize or overcome; the psycho-physical components of the personality disappear, and with them also age, illness and death, similarly every thought of sin, blame, evil, suffering and so on is swept away.

Manifestations of *maya* (*cho 'phrul*) of the kind described above are regarded by unenlightened men as the work of demons (*bdud*, *bgegs*). As soon as such phenomena take place, one is instructed to direct one's contemplation upon one's own body, and beginning from this to undertake the transition to Being standing beyond all individuation. For this purpose the mystic is ready to place himself in the worst conditions: he resorts to spots and places where corpses are exposed, where the demons (*gnyan*) live, in order to commence the path of meditation there. Nor does he offer gifts or prayers to the protective gods (*srung ma*), for it is enjoined upon him to act alone, to stand the test on his own, to prove to himself that the teachings imparted to him are not merely a theoretical concoction. Thus he allows his imagination full play: terror-evoking delusions rise before him, the heavens break apart over him and the waters break forth beneath him, while demonic monsters press in on him from all sides. But it is given to him to confront these illusory forms born from his own mind without fear: steady and imperturbable, he remains in his place as if he was at home, he remains serene in the consciousness that these gruesome visions are nothing but illusions of the deceiving imaginative power of his mind.

Once the mystic has reached this stage, the tumult of illusions comes to a halt. It can even happen that they no longer arise at all, though in his subconscious certain latent fears, potential dispositions for such visions, still remain. In this case the yogin (*rnal 'byor pa*) has recourse to stronger practices of concentration (Skt. *samadhi*), practices that are able to dissolve even the subtlest illusions of *maya* into nothing. Through this means any idea of fear, or even of a person seized by fear, vanishes (No.24).

Error too appears ever more rarely, finally to evaporate in a limiting state in which error is purified so to speak with a kind of artifice of error, concepts purified with the aid of concepts. The dichotomizing thought process in its infinite ability of projection and reflection thus creates itself within itself and finally finds voidness again, beyond all duality, in the limiting state. Actually it is a question here of a rediscovery, not of an attainment, for there is nothing to attain.

The ritual performed here unfolds in four successive phases, each with a name of its own: (1) 'white sharing' (*dkar 'gyed*): one's own body is conceived of as transformed into ambrosia and offered to the 'Three Jewels'; (2) 'multicoloured sharing' (*khra 'gyed*); one's own body is conceived of as transformed into a garden, into foods, into clothes, into desirable objects, which are offered to the gods called 'Protectors', who are able to overcome all of the hindrances standing in the way of the attainment of Enlightenment; (3) 'red sharing' (*dmar 'gyed*); one imagines the flesh and blood of one's own body being dispersed throughout all of space and offered to the demons, *'dre* and *srin*; (4) 'black sharing' (*nag 'gyed*); one imagines that one's own sins and those of all beings are absorbed into one's own body, as an enormous accumulated sin, and that the body is offered to the demons as a ransom for this sin and for all the sufferings and misfortunes arising out of it.

The following implements are required for the performance of these rituals: a trumpet made of a human tibia (*rkang gling*), which renders *lha* and *'dre* submissive; a *damaru* (the shaman's drum); a small bell; hair woven into a tuft and a piece of Persian cloth (*stag gzig gi ras ma*); human skin or skin of a wild animal with the claws intact: this serves to subdue the demons (*dregs*).

The familiarity of the followers of *gcod* with demonic powers (which are thoroughly real in the eyes of simple people) and the emphasis placed by them on everything macabre and gruesome has brought about an ever stronger movement of the sect towards an attitude which links them, perhaps genetically too, apart from the specific content of their teachings, with certain Indian sects who were concerned with proving their total indifference to common opinion through ever stranger practices. The rules which they observed bear witness to a marked disdain towards everyday customs, indeed a total lack of concern and insensitivity (*phyogs ris med*) with regard to them. These people would eat the food of lepers and beggars and wear their clothes, and live in their company rather than in the monasteries (No.83, p.23b). This attitude went along with the penchant widespread among many circles of adepts for exorcistic activity, so that it is hardly surprising that many followers of these schools concern themselves, apart from the conjuration of demons, with, for example, scapulimancy (divination by means of shoulder-blades) and other magical divinatory rituals. In East Tibet *gcod* was practised above all in two *bKa' brgyud pa* monasteries, *rGyu ne* and *sKyabs che*, where the monks, once they had finished the appropriate Tantric training and taken the relevant tests, received the title of master of *gcod* (*gcod pa*).

When epidemic disease breaks out, it is the *gcod* adepts who attend to the transport of the corpses to the cemetery (they are believed to be immune to any infection) and to the cutting through and breaking up of the bones. Their services are called upon to protect against epidemics: if an infectious disease has broken out in a village, they carry out their conjurations using a ball of *tsamba*[34] into which is mixed various substances like black grain, black sesame seed and so on. Then the village population gathers on a meadow and a great fire is kindled. The exorcists perform a dance accompanied by *damaru* and *rkang gling* while reciting appropriate magical formulae. Finally they throw the *tsamba* ball into the fire with great force; flaming up and scattering sparks it whistles away over the heads of the assembled people. Thus the epidemic is overcome. This ceremony is called *me zhags*. Another goes under the name *gshed 'dur*; *gshed* is a demon who accompanies a dead person, obstructs his entry into paradise and can also be harmful to his relatives and friends. These monk-exorcists can be recognized from the fact that they wear a special hat of rectangular form.

11 Conclusion. The special nature of the Lamaist teaching of salvation

If we look back over the brief characterization given in the preceding pages of the doctrinal opinions held by the various schools, then one fact which we have already mentioned deserves attention above all else. Despite all their differences in detail, the schools have a definite common group of premises, even if some particular traits receive greater or lesser emphasis here or there, or are modified in various ways. Common to all naturally is that indispensable propaedeutic, without which one cannot speak of an acceptance of Buddhism: the vow to traverse the path of salvation, the taking upon oneself of the practice of salvation leading to this goal, the recognition of the contingent nature, and consequently of the voidness of every possible object of thought, and so on. It is evident that, beyond these general premises, the magical and gnostic foundations of Tantrism lend their unmistakable imprint to the whole Lamaist way of thinking and practice. This applies not only to the liturgical structure but also in the formation of the entire mode of living directed towards the goal of salvation. It would be a grave error, and reveal an insufficient understanding of the special nature of Tibetan Buddhism, if one were to disregard the soteriological goals permeating and dominating it. It is not a question here of a purely intellectual process, not of the acquisition of theoretical knowledge, but rather of the alignment of the entire cognitive activity towards the goal of salvation. All along the line intellectual understanding remains subordinate to lived experience. The discovery and testing of truth and rational insight into it has to withdraw in the face of the lived possession of certainty. The intellect can at most pave the way for salvation; it cannot bring it about. To help the experience become reality, Lamaism calls in theoretical teaching, spiritual ecstasy and yogic technique in all their forms. Only in this way can the complete reversal of the planes of existence which is at the centre of the Buddhist revelation be actualized. All that can be thought is indeed relative and 'void', but this 'voidness' is void only in so far as Being cannot be encompassed by our thought. This voidness is equated with Bliss (*bde*) and with Light (*'od gsal*) and goes beyond the unending alternatives of the thinkable. True and untrue, empirical and absolute truth, *samsara* and *nirvana*, all dichotomies in short, are only arbitrarily made signs and designations, and as such contaminate the inexpressible, non-objectified Light-Voidness. Although the origins of Non-Being, of the qualifiable out of the non-qualifiable, remain a mystery which cannot be penetrated even through the doctrine of defilement, man (who is himself too no more than an illusory manifestation) can overcome thanks to his *sems* his own illusory appearance as object, as well as the world of things which is given an objective character only by conceptualization. This extremely subtle *sems*, carried by the respiration, is made of a special substance not comparable with ordinary matter: it is Light, its state of existence is pure luminosity, objectless consciousness of Being. In order to remain firm in its plane of existence situated beyond all defilement, the *sems* must raise and purify itself and become *sgyu lus*, *ye shes lus* and 'diamond body'. At this point the soteriological structure is completed by the doctrine of the four 'bodies'; the body *in se* and the three repeatedly mentioned above: the body of infinite spiritual potentiality (*chos sku*), the body of co-fruition (the heavenly body which reveals itself to he who can bring himself into harmony with this body preaching throughout all eternity in the paradises) and the apparent body of the *katabasis* into the world of *samsara*, for the preaching of the Word and to serve as an example to mankind. The goal of esoteric experience is the transformation of the I which has descended within the confines of space and time. It is, however, precisely this spatio–temporal foundation (*gzhi*) on the basis of which the reversal of the planes leading to one of the three Buddha bodies takes place (No. 102, p.94). By means of its transformations the *sems* acts as intermediary between everyday reality, the meditating being (such as he is, with all his karmic heritage, in his localized spatio–temporal aspect) on the one side, and those possibilities on the other side which continually indicate higher forms of being. The path leading to these special modes of being stands open to the truly initiated mystic. In this way the apparent discontinuity between voidness, consciousness of Being, the endless sprouting forth of divine figures in the so thickly populated Buddhist pantheon, and the apparentness of all that presents itself as existent and conceivable is closed. Here we witness a unique process of emanation and reintegration: the emanation of the illusory existentiality of the world of appearance, and its disappearance back into the voidness of Being. The theory and mysticism of Buddhism provide 'technical' apparatus for this latter process. Through the liturgical and meditative phases, the mystical individuality of the innate *sems* of the adept reaches a breakthrough, it effects an entry into those higher planes, into the marvellous fusion through which the distance between those planes and that of humanity is abolished. The mystic himself becomes able to transform himself temporarily into a god (*lhar bskyed*), a process familiar from Indian liturgy: *na adevo devam arcayet*, 'he who does not change himself into a god cannot worship a god'. This principle has developed in an altogether extraordinary manner in the Vajrayana and within Lamaism. Beginning from the meditation formulae which describe the aspect and symbols of particular gods, the meditator concentrates on an individual form chosen by him, he transforms within his mind the place where he is into a paradise until this actually appears before his sight. In its centre is the palace of a god. At its centre there is a white lotus in the case of a radiant, benevolent god, or a red lotus for a bellicose and fear-inspiring god. He contemplates the magically generative primal syllable (*sa bon*) as upon this lotus or upon a corpse (in the case of an evil deity). This primal syllable is a symbol in sound in which the essence of the god concerned is represented. If *Phyag na rdo rje*, for example, is to be evoked, then the meditator will concentrate upon the 'black' syllable *hum* in his heart, until he becomes one with that god in the particular aspect evoked by him. When he has transformed himself in this way into *Phyag na rdo rje*, he meditates on the white syllable *om* (generative phoneme of the Body of all Buddhas), visualizing it within his head, on the red syllable *ah* between his shoulders (creative sound on the plane of Speech), and on the blue syllable *hum* in his heart (creative phoneme on the plane of Mind). Such a transformation of oneself into a god is called *dam tshig sems dpa'* (Skt. *samaya-sattva*), 'being resulting from the vow'. It is prescribed in particular for rituals of exorcism directed against demonic powers: *Phyag na rdo rje* has the power of making demons obedient. The transformation of oneself into a divine being (*bdag bskyed*) is common to all schools, although the liturgical procedures which bring it about through a series of stages vary in form. A sudden onset of the transformation is also accepted, especially by the *rNying ma pa*, and is called *lha krong bskyed*. When the transformation takes place the evoked god can also appear opposite one's actual self (*mdun bskyed*), in other words it is projected spatially in front of the beholder. Alternatively one speaks of creation 'out of transcendent consciousness' (*ye shes sems dpa'*, Skt. *jnana-sattva*). Out of the generative sound associated with *Phyag na rdo rje*, appearing at the centre of the heart of the meditator who has become *Phyag na rdo rje*, luminous rays spring forth which reveal *Phyag na rdo rje* residing in his divine palace in his paradise (*lCang lo can*). They strike his heart, lead upwards his *ye shes* (his transcendent consciousness) and bring him in front of the meditator. This is the point at which the mystic offers to the deity the prescribed ritual offerings (*mchod pa*). A further kind of evocation bears the name 'being of synentasy' (*ting nge 'dzin sems dpa'*, Skt. *samadhi-sattva*). This takes place when the hierophant, who is already transformed (as *ye shes sems dpa'*) to *'Jam dbyangs* (Skt. Manjusri) visualizes in his heart, for example the creative syllable *dhih*, in which the essence of *rDo rje 'jigs byed*, the active and ferocious aspect of Manjusri, is represented, in order then to bring about the transformation from the first aspect of Manjusri into the second. However, it can also happen that some of these transformations result successively from each other. For example, the meditator may visualize himself as 'vow-being' (*dam tshig sems dpa'*), with the 'being of transcendent consciousness' (*ye shes sems dpa'*) situated in his throat, and then in the heart of that being the 'being of synentasy' (*ting nge 'dzin sems dpa'*).

Other variants of these rituals are, for example, evocations by means of a vessel (*bum bskyed*[35]). Meditations of this type can lead to regular proliferations of *mandalas*, when the meditator conceives of and visualizes himself under various forms, for example as *rNam par snang mdzad*, and emanates out of his being transformed in this way complete infinite chains of deities, and absorbs them again into himself. Again the mystic may evoke infinite Buddhas out of infinite space, in order to receive the initiatory consecration from them, and then dismiss them again into the space identified with his own heart.

On the subject of invocations of gods there exists in India as in Tibet an extensive literature, concerning which the views of individual teachers and schools differ from each other in major respects. Many, for example, deny the transformation of the self into the deity in the *bya rgyud*. In general it can be said that the individual elements of the invocations result in extremely complex forms: one begins from the seed-syllable in one's own heart, created out of voidness; the seed-syllable is transformed onto a moon or sun throne conceived of as situated in space; this is followed by concentration on the sounds forming the *mantra* of particular deities, and then on the letters forming these *mantra*. During the recitation of these formulae various parts of one's own body must be touched. This process is called *phyag rgya* (Skt. *mudra*), and corresponds to the *anganyasa*, 'placing the hands upon the parts of the body', of Indian liturgical practice. During this the conviction that one has become god (*nga rgyal*) must be constantly strengthened.

The facts given can serve as especially noteworthy examples of the aptitude of Indo-Tibetan religious masters for setting loose psychic states of intense experience in which the meditator goes outside his self. These examples attest their capacity for seizing upon the mechanisms working at the deeper levels of the psyche, and so releasing paranormal states which the masters can then direct appropriately. In any case the most essential and decisive of these processes consists of the dissolution of all appearances into voidness; all forms must be purified through their disappearance into the 'void'. In that the mystic renews in himself the universal metamorphosis, he creates according to the plan of the meditation used by him all possible forms on a purified plane, in order to allow the pure forms thus achieved to dissolve once more into that same inconceivable matrix. All this is directed to a single goal: to reproduce in oneself the process of emanation and reabsorption, and in this way to divest all appearances of their pretence of reality.

Each individual is assigned a guardian deity (*yi dam lha*), a particular divine form with which he is in harmony and which through this connection directs the actualization of his catharsis on the proper path. The sudden apparition of the *yi dam* is of decisive significance to him who receives it, to whom the theophany is revealed by his personal *bla ma*, in a dream, or through a mysterious sign right at the beginning of the initiatory process (for example through the casting of a flower onto a section of the *mandala* drawn or painted on the floor of the temple; the falling of the flower on the section where a particular god is represented reveals the mystical relationship between the initiand and that god). The choice of a *yi dam* is determined by the number of families (*rigs*) into which the pantheon is divided (and therefore human beings too are classifiable). Each god and each man is assigned to one of the five 'families'[36] (*rigs lnga*), which are conceived of differently according to the different Tantra classes. Although the five families, the pentad, belong to the body of co-fruition, they are also in a certain sense bodies of apparition, in so far as they appear in other forms, although higher than human, and must stand in connection with others. As already stated, in us too there exists at the 'fruit' phase, because of the possibility of a transformation of each individual component (*phung po*) of our psycho-physical personality into one of the five Buddhas of the pentad, the potentiality of the transformation of these our components, indeed our very defilements, into divine forms, on the basis of secure correspondences. We equally are formed of five components, although these appear contaminated through the condition of *samsara.* These components are form (*gzugs*), sensory perception (*tshor*), conceptualization (*'du shes*), karmic impulses (*'du byed*) and the principle of consciousness (*rnam par shes pa*), and to each of these components there corresponds an emotion which is capable of transfer to the divine plane: hate, mental delusion, envy, sensual indulgence, passion (the state of passion as such). At the moment of transition these five constituent elements of our personality are transformed through their purification, each into a god of the pentad: *rNam par snang mdzad* (Skt. Vairocana), *Rin chen 'byung ldan* (Ratnasambhava), *'Od dpag med* (Amitabha), *Don yod grub pa* (Amoghasiddhi) and *Mi bskyod pa* (Aksobhya). This transformation is the passage to their real essence (*ngo bo*). The *yi dam* is a kind of symbol under which this progressive deliverance is accomplished. Not only does each person have his own *yi dam*; each school also possesses *yi dam* of its own. The most important *yi dam* of the *Sa skya pa*, for example, are *Kye rdo rje*, *bDe mchog* and *rDo rje rnal 'byor ma*. Those of the *rNying ma pa* school are *dGongs 'dus* and *Phur pa bka' brgyad* (cf. No. 27, pp.33ff.). Those of the *bKa' brgyud pa* are *dGyes pa'i rdo rje*, *bDe mchog* and *rDo rje rnal 'byor ma*, while those of the *dGe lugs pa* are *gSang 'dus*, *bDe mchog*, *'Jigs byed* and so on.

This long list gives only a few examples, and many others could be cited. In addition, it is possible to meditate on each of these *yi dam* in various ways and according to particular methods (for example, *bDe mchog* according to the system of the yogin *Lu i pa*, or that of *Nag po pa*, or that of *Dril bu pa*), each according to the techniques of evocation and performance in use in different Tantra classes.

The meditation processes indicated above abolish the distance between the world of men and the divine sphere. They evoke the divine being and draw him down on to the human plane through the creative phonemes appropriate to him and the attracting effect of the light, and at the same time they raise the human being to a plane beyond human existence. This transformation or ecstasy is brought about through the *sems* being purified to the level of transcendent consciousness (*ye shes*), creating at the same time a plenitude of light which envelops and overwhelms the meditator and irradiates his visions. The experience he lives through is directed towards a single goal: to enable the meditator, to actualize in a moment of ordinary time that state of divine corporeality situated beyond the human. *Sems* serves the meditator as his *logos* in this process. Without *sems* there could be no contact between the human and superhuman planes, no transformation or movement from one plane to another. It is the innate *sems* which through meditation attains to dimensions beyond our normal senses, and it does this not only in anticipation of that which is awaited in the 'fruit' phase, but above all in order to prepare for that state, to be equipped for it.

After the death of a man who has followed the teachings of salvation three ways are open to him: to enter the *chos sku*, the body of co-fruition or the apparent body. In addition there exists the possibility of a re-entry into *samsara*, which contains divine existences as well as human, demonic and animal.

Certainly it can happen that after the state of contemplation of the experience of one of the higher planes in the 'path' phase, the *sems* can fall back into the sphere of influence of illusory appearance. Only constantly repeated meditation practice creates the preconditions for the definitive bringing about of the blissful moment in which the overcoming of existence and suffering is actualized.

Thus we can understand the great significance which all schools, especially the *bKa' brgyud pa*,[37] attribute to the 'six principles' (*chos drug*) of Naropa, teacher of *Mar pa*: (a) *gtum mo*, a yogic process which manifests itself physically through the voluntary raising of the body temperature; (b) *sgyu lus*;[38] (c) dream (*rmi lam*); (d) light (*'od gsal*); (e) transference into other forms of existence (*'pho ba*); (f) *bar do*.[39] The first principle serves primarily as a technique of Hatha-yoga which accomplishes the process of the 'four consecrations' through a difficult control of breathing and a visual contemplation of fire and of the sun in various parts of the mystic's body, and which leads into the hallucinatory vision of one's own body being completely in flames. The second and third of Naropa's six principles are closely linked together, in that they try to bring dream images into the service of the way of salvation. If our daily conduct of life does not conform to the precepts of the teacher then the karma accumulated in us in the past ensnares us in the illusions it awakens, while we add new illusions to those already stored up. Such illusions also affect the images in dreams, which are contaminated by them. Being perpetuated in this way, this state affects also the state of intermediate existence after death. The effect of impure apparent reality thus spreads over three realms: illusion as action of karma, the extending of such illusion into dream life, and the influence of the impure illusory states on the mental body (*yid lus*)[40] when it seeks a new incarnation at the moment of death. Against this triple realm of 'impure' illusion (cf.p.107) can be opposed a triple realm of 'pure' illusion, which is created through meditation on one's own body as the divine body–into which one's own body can be transformed through the prescribed methods because of its lack of real substance. This 'pure' illusion guards the dream state against the images caused by impure concepts. In the intermediate existence which takes place between death and new reincarnation the *yid lus* is transformed into a body of co-fruition. The meditation here relies on a yogic technique which culminates in the identification of the meditator with *rDo rje 'chang*, or according to the teachings of others, identification with *bDe mchog* in union with his paredra (*yab yum*). Then the meditator visualizes a triangle (*chos 'byung*) under his navel. This triangle, white on the outside, red on the inside,[41] is a symbol of the archetypal Matrix; within it one visualizes those beings who do not perceive the true nature of things on their endless wanderings. Then these beings dissolve again into the light, flow back, disappear, and only the triangle remains. A meditation of this kind has its effect on dreaming too, which can thus be made usable for the goal of Enlightenment. The illusory perceptions of the day are of the same stuff as dream-images; if one can control one, one has power over the other too. Dream and not-knowing, *ma rig*, are related; both are causes of illusory apparent images of the mind. Out of this certainty results the quiescence of all concepts; all that appears springs forth from the defilements already present *ab initio*. Because these operate from the waking state on dream-concepts, one is instructed to grasp the dreamlike nature of the two apparent worlds through the insight that all is like a dream. Yogic technique adds the idea that the respiration flowing in the upper part of the body condenses itself into a white 'point' (*thig le*), the 'father-semen', and that in the lower part of the body condenses into a red point, the 'paredra-blood'. Both of these points are situated in the heart. Progressive meditation on these two points creates the same state in the adept as the four consecrations: the first consecration takes place when the two points are in movement; the second when they touch; the third when the bliss resulting from their touching is experienced; the fourth when the two points fuse into one. The importance of the fourth of these phases can scarcely be surprising in view of what has been explained previously. In this phase the light (*'od gsal*) in its identity of essence with the *sems* radiating out of it is concentrated, like a lamp illuminating both itself and other objects without aid from outside. The light-mind, *'od gsal-sems*, is that force which flows forth at the 'fruit' phase into one of the three bodies. It rests beyond duality in unending radiance, and in an inherent sonority which contains in potential all possible sounds. Its luminous plenitude is limited in no way by any spatial surface. It is radiant voidness, out of which streams forth the infinity of luminous concepts, but these illusory images are nothing but the intrinsic power of the void in itself. In distinction from the light of day, the light of dream is not projected onto the exterior in illusory apparent forms, but is lived in its own proper Being-in-itself.

The fifth of Naropa's topics, transference (*'pho ba*), takes place at the moment of death, but this process too must be integrated into the practice of the way of salvation. For if this art of transference has not already been practised in one's previous life one cannot have recourse to it at the moment of dying. Of course the actualizing of this experience during the 'path' phase does not mean that transference is already actually brought about, but rather that an experience is practised as preparation for the events of the moment of death. At death three possibilities then become open. The first and highest is transference into light, the second transference into a body of co-fruition or an apparent body (cf.p.99); the last (for individuals of lesser ability) is the method of evocation (*bskyed rim*). In this meditation the meditator must conceive of himself as being a god, for example as *rDo rje phag mo* or some other analogous female goddess, above which he visualizes *rDo rje 'chang* in the form of his own *bla ma*, in order to represent the continuity of the revelation of salvation. The transference of the *sems* takes place through pronouncing the syllable *hik*. Repeating this syllable in the prescribed manner causes the *sems* to pass through the fontanelle, the suture at the top of the skull. When one pronounces the syllable *ka* it returns to its place. In such a way contact is brought about between the human plane and that plane which transcends the human. The practice must be repeated three times, until the moment when blood or moisture flows out of the fontanelle.

The further development of this ritual (*'grong 'jug*) and the intermediate state (*bar do*) have already been mentioned.

These theoretical and yogic elements bear witness to the directing of all experiences or modes of being that are possible towards a single purpose, salvation. The same can also be said of the rituals performed at the time of death, though here it could also be a question of a further development of primitive magical beliefs in a philosophical and mystical form. In these various rituals the mechanism of transference between various human states for soteriological purposes is perfected. This results in a grandiose attempt at transfiguration, in which the variable and contradictory conditions of the apparent world are integrated into the actualization of supreme consciousness. In this process there is no break in the continuity; what happens in us is an event for the totality; apparent temporality dissolves itself for the initiate into an eternal moment.

The examples given above (cf.p.64) confirm again that Lamaism, dominated by gnostic-magical Tantra (*sngags*), postulates a radiant mind-light (*'od gsal–sems*) present within us, which is capable of successive gradual purification until it is raised to the state of omniscience, 'knowledge of all forms', proper to the Buddha. It is this condition of absolute purity from every defilement, this quiescence in the limiting state of Being, that we may designate, in an analogical mode of expression, as the Supreme Reality.

Nevertheless this in no way requires the presence of the *tathagatagarbha*, the undefiled essence, in our cosmic continuum, as the *Jo nang pa* would assert. Such an assumption would lead Buddhism back towards Saivite characteristics. The luminous, undefiled absolute consciousness of Being is not immanent, but nevertheless only the purification of the *sems* can bring about the reversal of the planes, whether this purification takes place in a gradual or immediate fashion (according to the individual case and the school). Despite the diversity of ways in which the problem is described, it can, however, be affirmed that the Tibetan who has grown up among such gnostic and magical practices is imbued with the conviction that he is able to change into modes of being progressively higher in nature until he is dissolved into the nameless. The levels of existence already traversed on the path of meditation will enable him in the moment of death, thanks to the abilities he has acquired and the mental equipment he has gathered, to attain a Buddha-like or at least paradisial existence.

This process takes place in a progressive flashing forth of ever more radiant visions which appear to the mystic as the object of his contemplation but are no more than the experience of his own gradual purification and self-transcendence.[42]

An important meditation process is double in nature: the visualized evolution of the divine plane (*rjes gzhig*) and its dissolution (*ril 'dzin*) into pure light. This leads to the supreme convergence. Once the equivalence of light and voidness is actualized, quiescence into the supreme silence takes place. The two processes (*ril 'dzin* and *rjes gzhig*) contribute equally to the total overcoming of dichotomizing appearance in the light of Being. According to some doctrinal systems the essential difference between the two is that the former method proceeds from a concentration on one's own person, the latter from concentration on the external world (*snod bcud*, 'container' and 'contained'). The elimination of one's own illusory ego seen as a fixed individual is brought about by the former process. In the course of it the process runs on the one hand downwards from the head and on the other hand upwards from the feet, each meeting at the boundary between the two parts of the body, as represented by the heart. The two parts of the body are absorbed into the heart, and then the heart in its turn is absorbed into the phoneme *hum*, this phoneme into the point of absolute potentiality (*thig le*), and the point finally into voidness.

The following image is given of this process: if one breathes against a mirror, one's breath clouds the whole surface, but the mist eventually disappears going inwards from the outside, covering an even smaller area until only a point remains, which also finally dissolves.

The second of these processes of reabsorption consists of the drawing back within of all of the forms outside of us, which consist of undetermined luminosity. An image for this process is a handful of snow thrown into a fountain of water and gradually dissolving within it (No. 95, pp.248ff.). All this, as always, is only to serve as a symbolic representation. The details of this exercise vary according to the particular sources used.

A process such as this, in which the identification of the object of vision with the seeing subject is brought about until it leads to the transcending of this dualism on a plane beyond all perception, is in no way an uncontrolled shining forth of images. It is rather a spiritual dynamic controlled by the meditator striving for his catharsis. This dynamic moves within the rigid architecture of the doctrine, which in its vigilance constantly imposes postulated equivalences in a progressive order: each moment represents the summation of all the preceding elements and the necessary precondition of all the elements that will follow. The vision does not come from the outside, it does not descend from above; it springs from the inside and is accomplished within the meditating subject, for only the subject moves in the sphere of influence of his own ecstasies. If vision, and the willed, controlled discipline of meditation, meet here in an indissoluble unity, we can then see in this one of the most profound and most original contributions of Vajrayana Buddhism and its Lamaist exegesis to the consciousness of the world of mystical experience. This contribution consists above all in posing the question of the possibility of the purification of given reality. Tantric experience with remarkable boldness does not so much propose the eradication of the unavoidable and inexorably given weaknesses of man (the innate inclinations traceable to certain fundamental affects, cf. above, p.51) as attempt their transference on to a higher plane. The passions are not to be suppressed, they are a fact related in nature to our own being. Through progressive purification (cf.p.61) they become the instrument of their own transcendence, they become the basis of a reintegration, assuming that the correct mode of dealing with them is assured. This is precisely what the *sNgags* or Tantra has to offer, as we can read in the *rDo rje gur*: 'Man, such as he lives in the world, is born as a result of passion, but through passion itself he becomes free again' (No. 84, p.14a).

The bipolarity between man and woman serves as a precondition of the transfer as well as one of the essential principles of Tantric experience; it is an undeniable fact characterizing the whole of existence. The same is true for the homology between sexuality and liberation, provided that both fundamental facts are held under the control of purifying consciousness. Sexual experience (in its usual fourfold division) is the object of a symbology both complex and therefore incomprehensible to the layman. Sexual experience is placed in relation to the esoteric process of Tantra in such a way that the individual phases of this process correspond to situations of rising sensual intensity. The glance which plays over female beauty, the smile of contentment, the holding of hands, the sexual act ending in fulfilment: these four situations correspond to the four Tantra classes (*bya rgyud*, *spyod rgyud*, *rnal 'byor rgyud*, *bla na med rgyud*).

The Tibetan teachers, especially those of the *rNying ma pa*, do not exclude the requirement of the presence of a female being in the initiatory rite, as the symbol of *shes rab*. Besides, even *mKhas grub rje* states that an experienced scholar of the sixty-four methods of love is needed for the performance of this ritual. Here it can be seen that we move in a sphere which is not essentially different from the world of Indian Tantra. However, it is to be noted how in Tibet (especially in the *dGe lugs pa* schools) this evidently delicate sub-structure, although subject to the strongest initiatory propadeutic has built over it a super-structure understood in a primarily symbolic sense, saturated with all the symbolic power of yogic technique. Despite this, one can scarcely deny that the *bla na med rgyud* would not rule out an interpretation of this kind, which would not be out of line with its origin, and the prescribed initiation could also be taken in an entirely literal sense. Nevertheless the *bla na med rgyud* can be considered the high point of the religious experience and esoteric expression of Tibetan soteriology. This school incorporates in its totally organic structure that ardent longing of the true Vajrayana disciple (and thus of Tibetan Buddhism in general) for an ascent to higher planes of existence, for the actualization of 'Buddhahood', towards which Buddhism appears to be directed in all of its expressions, if by various ways and through various means.

Inevitable consequences result from such premises, in particular the predominating significance of vision as one of the building blocks of the contemplative process. This favours the tendency for the outward projection of the concepts standing before the mental eye, in order, through their expressive immediacy, to make easier the visual evocations of the mystic, and to direct them along specified paths. In this way the immense richness of visual imagery in Lamaist cult life becomes understandable, and similarly the objectification of Tantric experience in buildings and pictures, as is present in the so-called '*stupa* of a hundred thousand images' (*sku 'bum mchod rten*). These images attempt to capture in visual symbols the Tantric cycles which indicate ways of salvation. They form a significant attempt to make the mysteries of the gnostic way visually present, including for example the heavenly choirs which have appeared to the meditator in the course of his radiant journey through the infinite worlds of his inner experience. The artist is restricted to putting fixed colours on to the schematic forms which appear to the mind of the mystic. The abundance of sights, almost explosive in its appearance and verging on the miraculous, is forced through painting into patterns fixed by ancient tradition. The gnostic background from which they have issued assures for these forms a rich symbolic content. At the same time these figurative representations become a kind of key for the understanding of the mysteries of the literature to which this imagery remains bound, and which is itself only accessible with difficulty.

As in the books the literal meaning is to be distinguished from a deeper, symbolic content, so the images represent not only a deity corresponding to a certain name and form; they represent a content which is accessible only to the initiate. Only if the images in question are 'read' in this special manner do they acquire saving value, do they open the way to the meditation concerned. The images of the Lamaist pantheon are unusual, unhuman, often consisting of monstrous, fantastic gods with many heads and arms, holding in each arm weapons and liturgical utensils, adorned with necklaces or diadems of human skulls and resting on corpses which are crushed underfoot. The masters of the Vajrayana 'read' this iconography, absurd at a first glance, as a symbolic writing in images, alluding to a hidden content of experience. The double images so common in Lamaism, the so-called 'Father-Mother' (*yab yum*) representations of pairs in sexual embrace, are explained, as mentioned above (cf.p.80), in the following way by the *bla na med rgyud* or the Ati-yoga. The father as 'means' (*thabs*), as the *maya*-body, is able through gradual adaptations to the four voidnesses and the four kinds of bliss to be transformed into consciousness of Being. The mother, his paredra, embracing the father in the sexual act, represents higher cognition (*shes rab*). *sGyu lus* and transcendent consciousness are the indivisible aspects of enlightenment and reintegration flowing together on the plane of ultimate reality. The great pleasure in coitus corresponds to 'great voidness', to entry into consciousness of Being, itself situated beyond any qualification. The tendency to concretization favours the creation of an abundance of visual supports to the processes of meditation and evocation. To this need can also be traced back the visual imagery associated with particular elements of the ritual and with set formulae. In the invocation *Kye rdo rje*, 'Oh! *rdo rje*' (*rdo rje*= 'diamond', 'diamond state') a deity identical in essence with Aksobhya is called upon. The cult objects too, lamps, bells, vessels acquire divine forms: during the process of evocation they serve in an appropriate costume as bringers of offerings to the deities summoned, forming a kind of chorus (*mchod pa'i lha* or *lha mo*). Whatever can serve the process described, as a base or support, is incorporated into it.

This height of mystical contemplation, this wondrous attempt to transcend into gnostic visions a lofty philosophical experience and a heritage of folk concepts and magical fears rooted in the depths of the past was however not accessible to all. Its hidden meaning was reserved to a minority, while the great majority took the visual representations at their face value. In the case of the holy scriptures things were different; people had less direct contact with them. The images, however, stood visibly before all eyes in the monastery temples, and also in private chapels. Their secret meaning therefore had to give way to the significance which could be perceived directly, as happens with all symbolic concretizations of the divine. In place of esoteric understanding there arose practices of conjuration, lay piety, offerings to implore protection and favours from the gods. In the religion of the broad masses primitive folk beliefs and formal ritualism continuously carried off the victory. Certain divine figures enjoyed particular favour as helpers of mankind. In moments of danger they were invoked, in the extreme situations of life they were called on for defence, as also for protection against evil after death in the intermediate state. *sPyan ras gzigs* (Skt. Avalokitesvara) accompanied and comforted the Tibetan on his entire path through life, with the holy formula *om ma ni pad me hum* whose magical power flows inevitably out of the sound of each of the syllables. *sGrol ma* (Tara) like *sPyan ras gzigs* sheltered men from the eight kinds of danger.[43] The 'great compassionate one', Sakyamuni, had preached the law of salvation to men. *Gu ru Rin po che* (Padmasambhava) is the subduer of the demons, the enemies of the Buddhist preaching in Tibet; through his magical power, which neither men nor demons can withstand, the great exorcist not only converted them but transformed them into guardians and protectors of the Law. Thus the division became ever deeper between an esoteric form of Lamaism accessible only to a few, and which assumed a hard path of purification and uncommon qualities of character, and a folk religion whose ideas and customs succeeded in penetrating also the daily liturgy of the monasteries, with its conjurations, its magical formulae and its sacrificial offerings. Lamaism could not remain indifferent in the face of the fundamentally magical attitude of the Tibetan people, and all the less so as the Vajrayana literature itself, at least in its literal interpretation, encouraged such inclinations and hopes to a significant degree. In this folk-religious practice only certain fundamental traits of learned Lamaism remained, and within their structure mythological ideas, ceremonies, magical and cosmological concepts and so on were inserted. These Buddhism had already found on its entry into Tibet, in rich abundance and varying from place to place; not only did it not suppress them, but it wished to admit them into its own system as a venerable, anonymous heritage of the past.

APPENDIX

The process of transformation of *Sems* and *rLung*

What follows is very complicated and particularly difficult to condense into a few words. In general, it can be said that in this introduction to the process of psychic metamorphosis the basic elements (body, speech, mind) are presented as in their ideal situation, as residual preconceptions from our empirical world; they have to be eliminated one by one, in such a way that even thinking itself is eliminated from our mind. Since mind is light (*'od gsal*) the meditation on its luminosity is considered under a double aspect: as *dpe*, that is as a reflection or image of the nature of an example rather than real; or as *don*, in other words in reality.

Normal state of the individual (*gzhi dus*), Samsaric state (*Dasein*) (*gnyug ma'i lus* = breath or energy which moves the *gnyug ma'i sems*, cf.p.65).

Breathing and *gnyug ma'i sems* are of identical nature (*ngo bo gcig*); between them exists a relation identical to that between fire and flame; although inseparable, they can be distinguished with reference to their function: *gnyug sems* has the function of perceiving objects; *gnyug rlung* is the vibratory impulse in the direction of the object; in the normal state of life (*gzhi*) they are found in the 'point' (*thig le*) situated in the heart (cf. note 16, p.262).

State of sleep and dreaming

In the state of deep sleep *gnyug rlung* and *sems* are scarcely active; in the state of light sleep *rlung* and *sems* produce the *yid lus* (mental body), capable of movement (see above, p.60), in which arise fantastic images corresponding to dreams. In the moment immediately preceding the dream, the individual sensory perceptions (*rnam par shes*) cease; when the very subtle *gnyug rlung* comes into action and becomes the primary cause (*dngos kyi nyer len*) while the *gnyug sems* acts as contributory cause (*lhan cig byed rkyen*) the *yid lus* of the dream is produced. When the *gnyug sems* of the moment immediately preceding the dream acts as primary cause and the *gnyug rlung* as contributory cause, the state of dream-*sems* is produced.

Moment of death and during *bar do* (intermediate state between death and new life)

gnyug sems and *rlung* project themselves out of the 'point' (*thig le*) in the form of a mental body (*yid lus*) searching for a new birth, experiencing the illusory phenomena of the intermediate state (*bar do*); the mental body (*yid lus*) is a subtle body provided with all the senses and identical to *gnyug sems* + *rlung*.

In the moment immediately preceding death, when sensory perceptions (*rnam par shes*) cease and the *gnyug rlung* is projected outside the 'point' (*thig le*) in the heart and acts as primary cause while the *gnyug sems* is contributory cause, the *yid lus* of the *bar do* is actualized.

In the moment following immediately on that of the *sems* of the moment of death, when the *gnyug sems* acts as primary cause and the *gnyug rlung* as contributory cause, the *sems* of the *bar do* is actualized.

The connection between the two moments

As far as the *rlung* and the *sems* are concerned, the connection (*mtshams 'byor*) between the moments preceding and following sleep and dreaming is determined by the 'engrams' (*bag chags*) of events and of the dichotomized state of everyday life; the connection between the moments preceding and following the last *sems* of death and the *lus* and *sems* of the intermediate existence is determined by the engrams of the individual's actions and emotions.

Sgyu lus and its progressive purification

This body can also become the 'body of transcendent cognition' (*ye shes lus*). This is achieved by the yogin through his practice of the Tantra of the highest class (*bla na med rgyud*). First of all the purification must be accomplished through meditation on the teachings of the *phar phyin*, and then on those of the *rgyud*, especially the *bla na med rgyud*, including the teachings on the four consecrations and on the vows which arise from them. Finally the method of evocation and the method of achievement (*bskyed rim* and *rdzogs rim*) (cf.p.74) are put into practice, and so finally the yogin enters into full possession of the teachings.

Then the three isolations are practised (cf. note 8, p.261; *lus dben, ngag dben, sems dben*). At the limit of the isolation of the *sems* (*sems dben*) the experience of the *dpe 'od gsal* takes place (cf.p.61), then the yogin devotes himself to meditation on the eight signs (*rtags*, cf.p.62) as a result of which the wind of karma is reabsorbed into the heart-'point', as happens at the moment of death. Then the subtle *gnyug rlung* (the 'mount' of the *sems*) coincides with the moment immediately following the *dpe 'od gsal* functioning as primary cause, while the last moment of the *dpe 'od gsal* acts as contributory cause; in this way the subtle *sgyu lus* is attained, still in part not purified, and shining like a rainbow.

Then the last *dpe 'od gsal* moment of the isolation of mind (*sems dben*) acts as the primary cause, and the *gnyug rlung* (its 'mount') as contributory cause, leading to the attainment of the transcendent cognition of the *maya*-body (*sgyu lus ye shes*).

At the climax of the *rdzogs rim*, when the actualization of the *don gyi 'od gsal* takes place (cf.p.56), through the successive appearance of the eight signs which accompany death, *rlung* and *sems* in the coarse state[44] are absorbed by the subtle *rlung* and *sems* of transcendent consciousness (*ye shes*), which is situated within the heart. The subtle *rlung* of transcendent consciousness, identical in nature to that of the *don 'od gsal*, then acts as primary cause, while the *don 'od gsal* acts as contributory cause, leading to the attainment of the pure *sgyu lus*. Then when the light (*'od gsal*) functions as the primary cause, and the breath (the subtle *rlung*, which is however identical with it in nature) as contributory cause, the transcendent cognition (*ye shes*) of the *maya*-body is produced.

The pure *maya*-body (*sgyu lus*) is the body of transcendent consciousness (*ye shes*); it is without any defect; this does not, however, mean that it is free also of every defilement. The *sems* of this body of transcendent consciousness, emanating from the coarse mind of the body of karmic maturation, acquires the capacity to perform many kinds of miracles for the good of others; and also even while it remains in the normal body it possesses infinite faculties for the good of others. Thus the yogin achieves the Tenth 'Earth'. When the subtle *rlung* of transcendent consciousness (*ye shes*) (the 'mount' of the *'od gsal* immediately after the last moment of the *don 'od gsal*, limiting point on the path of cognitive development) acts as primary cause, and the *'od gsal* of the extreme limit of cognitive development acts as contributory cause, the two forms of contamination (moral and mental) are finally overcome.

In this way convergence into the pure body or diamond body (*rdo rje sku*), which represents the ultimate limit of experience, is accomplished. When, at the extreme limit of the path, the moment immediately after the *don 'od gsal* acts as primary cause and the subtle breath ('mount' of the transcendent consciousness) acts as contributory cause, the extreme limit of transcendent consciousness, which cognizes all that is knowable, infinite potentiality, the *chos sku*, is achieved.

FIVE

MONKHOOD, MONASTERY LIFE, RELIGIOUS CALENDAR AND FESTIVALS

1 Organization of monastic community: hierarchy and offices

The organization of monastic communities deserves particular attention within a study of Tibetan religious life. Not only were the monasteries highly respected and extraordinarily fruitful centres in which Tibetan Buddhism received its impetus and from which it spread itself; the entire political and cultural history of Tibet was dominated by the monasteries. From the standpoint of the teaching the various regulations collected in the Vinaya disciplinary code (*'dul ba*), particularly the rules of the *so sor thar pa* (Skt. *pratimoksa*) held for the monastic communities of Tibet as for those elsewhere. With few exceptions, all doctrinal schools followed the *pratimoksa* prescriptions concerning monastic ordination. Only after completing this ordination could the monks take on the vows and obligations required for either of the two paths now open to them: the vows of the Thought of Enlightenment (*byang chub sdom*) for the Mahayana, or the Tantric vows (*sngags sdom*) for the Vajrayana. Some schools, for example the *rNying ma pa*, did not regard the *pratimoksa* ordination as obligatory for all. According to the *rNying ma pa* the vows of the Thought of Enlightenment and those for Tantric practice can be taken without the preceding detour through the *pratimoksa* precepts, assuming participation in the everyday liturgical life of the monastic community. This possibility does not exist for the *dGe lugs pa* monks. Once a monk of this sect decides on marriage, or renounces the rules of the order which he took on through his consecration, he must annul his vows (*rab 'byung sdom slar phul*). The two vows mentioned for which observance of the *pratimoksa* is not required (*byang chub sdom* and *sngags sdom*) are, according to both the *Sa skya pa* and *rNying ma pa* school, also open to laymen (*khyim pa*). It is thus possible for a layman too to attain to the supreme experiences and to become a 'Possessor of the Diamond' (*rdo rje 'dzin*). This leads to three groups of descending spiritual level: monks (*dge slong rdo rje 'dzin pa*), novices (*dge tshul rdo rje 'dzin pa*) and finally laymen (*khyim pa rdo rje 'dzin pa*). The conditions and demands of everyday life, as well as the continual growth in power of the monasteries as they became more and more involved in secular activity had necessarily to lead to a considerable softening of the originally strict monastic observance. Of the Vinaya literature, which is present in numerous translations in the Chinese canon, representing among them the various schools and their different versions of the disciplinary code, the school represented in Tibet is that of the Mulasarvastivadins.

All of humanity falls naturally into two groups: the *nang pa*, that is 'those situated inside', in other words inside the Law of the Buddha, and the *phyid pa*, 'those standing outside', that is those who do not follow the Buddha's word. Among the *nang pa*, however, two further groups can be distinguished: on the one hand the *dge bsnyen* (Skt. *upasaka*), lay adherents for whom only the first five precepts are obligatory (not to kill; not to steal; not to live unchastely; not to lie; to drink no intoxicating beverages), and on the other hand the *dge tshul* (Skt. *sramanera*), the novices, bearers of the lower consecrations, and the *dge slong* (Skt. *bhiksu*), ordained mendicant monks, who have to fulfil all of the ten precepts. (The additional five are not to eat at a time when it is not permitted; not to take part in dance, song, music, theatrical spectacles; not to use any garlands, perfumes or adornments; not to sleep on a high or large bed; not to receive gold or silver.)

While the precepts for monastic consecration and for entry into the orders are in principle the same everywhere, these basic norms are overlaid by the predominance of Tantric practices, as indicated above. The consecration (*dbang*) awakens a spiritual maturity of another kind in the recipient, the maturity of one who has actualized the mystical practices prescribed in the various Tantric schools (*sgrub bla*, *grub thob*, Skt. *siddha*).

The rules and precepts valid for the monks and for the internal organization of the monasteries thus differ significantly from those of the original Vinaya. The title of *dge bshes* or Doctor of Theology, as it is now understood in the *dGe lugs pa* schools, is also a special creation reflecting the particular teaching methods of that sect, which give special weight to logic as a basic formative discipline (although the title itself is connected with a simpler one, that of *dge bshes gnyen*, Skt. *kalyanamitra*, spiritual friend, counsellor and model on the path of salvation, cf.p.23).

With respect to monastic organization, to avoid a mass of examples we will explain primarily the arrangements existing in the *rNying ma pa* and *dGe lugs pa* schools. The organizational differences between the monasteries of these two schools do not go very deep. In general the divergences between the two forms of monastic organization rest on the greater or lesser significance given to *sngags*, to Mantra, ritualism and the practices of Tantra, on the one hand, and to *mdo*, the revelation of the Buddha as given in the Sutras, on the other. However, it must be remembered here that these two branches, into which religious literature is divided, are not to be sharply distinguished in the Lamaist view; they are rather to be seen as parts of a whole. It is true that in the practice sometimes *sngags* is specially emphasized and *mdo* recedes into the background, and sometimes the reverse is true. It is, however, always a case of a different placing of the emphasis, of a stronger or lesser commitment or preference, and never of a complete exclusion of the other area. Bearing this in mind, we can say that some schools have an emphasis on doctrine which affects all areas, and stress in particular the *Phar phyin* (Prajnaparamita) and *mNgon rtogs rgyan* (Abhisamayalankara) texts and the study of logic (*mtshan nyid*), while other schools are primarily attracted to liturgy and mysticism. Besides this, however, there exists within particular schools some freedom regarding the traditions prevailing in some monasteries, in view of the prestige of their founders, or their especially glorious past. Quite often many variations appear in liturgy and doctrine within a particular school or sect, as for example with the *Ngor pa*, a sub-sect of the *Sa skya pa*, or (to a greater degree) among the various sub-divisions of the *bKa' brgyud pa*. Among the *dGe lugs pa* two slightly different tendencies exist in the form of the monks following two different Tantra schools (*rgyud grwa gnyis*), one called 'upper' (*stod*) and the other 'lower' (*smad*).[1] This division appears to go back right to the time of *Tsong kha pa* himself. According to the tradition *Tsong kha pa* directed *Shes rab seng ge* to go to Upper *gTsang* (*gTsang stod*) in order to spread the reformed teaching (*stod rgyud rnying pa*) there. In the course of his work *Shes rab seng ge* founded a teaching establishment in *Lhun po rtse* in *gTsang stod*. Later he reached Lower *dBus* (*dBus smad*) where he formed a new school in the neighbourhood of Lhasa (*rgyud smad grwa tshang*, 'Lower' Tantric College).

Afterwards his disciple *Kun dga' don grub* founded a further college at *Byams pa gling* in *dBus stod*. Of this teacher it is reported that he was able through his magical powers to banish a dangerous flood threatening Lhasa. In recognition of his merits the district of *rGya btab Ra mo che* was granted to him (cf.p.1), and it was here that the college of *rgyud stod grwa tshang* ('Upper' Tantric College) came into being as a successor organization to that of *gTsang* (No. 81, p.300).[2]

Although both traditions derive from the teachings of *Tsong kha pa*, there are various differences between them. Both have the same guardian deities (*yi dam*), *gSang 'dus*, *'Jigs byed* and *bDe mchog*, but there are some differences visible concerning the methods for actualizing the experiences embodied in the Tantric cycles, as well as the formulae and liturgical rituals shaped by them (for example, in the way the *mandala* is drawn).

Another difference is that *Dam can chos rgyal* is the most important protective deity (*srung ma*) for *rgyud smad*, while *mGod po phyag drug* is for *rgyud stod*. In addition many external peculiarities can be mentioned, for example in the clothing: members of *rgyud smad* wear a yellow monk's vest (*grwa lan*) and brightly coloured (*skya po*) shoes, while members of *rgyud stod* wear a dark red vest (*dmar smug*) and shoes of the same colour. These are certainly not profound differences, but it can nevertheless be seen that even within the bounds of orthodoxy there is here a certain freedom which contrasts with the uniformity usually found. A similar spirit of freedom is unmistakable with some other schools, such as the *bKa' brgyud pa* and the wandering lamas (*sngags pa*). The connection between the followers of these schools and the monasteries appears to be less strict, and their mystical practices do not rule out the possibility of personal variation and individual aspects. The life of continuous wandering and the preference for solitary places of these monks would also be conducive to a more independent religious life. Stable residence in monasteries, the obligation to participate in the divine services with their fixed timetable, the strict regulation of all external aspects of life, the memorization of the basic rules and their mastery in conformity with the study precepts—all these tend to force the life of the community into a fixed structure, and to preserve the supremacy of the community as a collectivity over its individual members. This supremacy is liable to be weakened, however, when it is a question of acquiring inner experiences (*sgrub*) rather than participating in a ritual act or applying oneself to study or teaching. The same process took place in India as more and more methods developed for the attainment of a particular mystical state. It was never true that the path revealed by individual masters or the special ascetic methods linked to particular deities made it impossible for other, newer methods to be introduced (cf.p.33). The basic principle of Buddhism, that truth emerged or revealed itself in accordance with the spiritual maturity of the devotee or mystic, always retained its validity. Only experience itself, and the revelations and inner enrichments flowing from it, procured for the contents of the experience directly lived and undergone the value of authentic truth for those situated in an analogous spiritual condition.

We will now proceed to describe the monastic organization characteristic of the *rNying ma pa* school and of those related to it such as the *bKa' brgyud pa*. In these schools monastic organization has a double orientation, or more exactly a double mode of training. On the one hand, there is a ritualistic and intellectual training while, on the other, practice and yoga are placed at the central point. The former corresponds to the seminary or college (*bshad grwa*) where the liturgical and doctrinal texts are explained and commented on, while the latter is concerned with instructions for the methods for achieving mystical experience (*sgrub grwa*). This is however a formal distinction only; no genuine insight can have merely intellectual value, it must always tend to become a living spiritual experience.

Those studying in the *bshad grwa* divide into two groups. There are the students living in the monastery itself and for whose upkeep the monastic community is fully responsible during their obligatory period of study of at least five years. Then there are those students who defray their expenses from their own resources, and do not come under the monastery rules. The two classes are called *phogs zan*, those who receive their subsistence, and *rgyab sdod pa*, those who live apart.

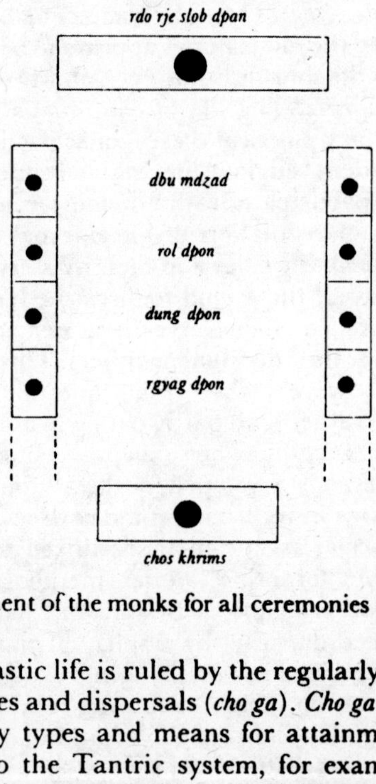

Figure 1 Arrangement of the monks for all ceremonies (*rNying ma pa* school)

The entire monastic life is ruled by the regularly repeating cycle of liturgical assemblies and dispersals (*cho ga*). *Cho ga* means 'liturgy'. It encompasses many types and means for attainment of the desired goal. According to the Tantric system, for example, *cho ga* is the meditation in which one's guardian deity (*yi dam*) is visualized before one. The apotropaic and exorcistic ceremonies are also *cho ga*, as are the rituals accompanying monastic consecration, the rituals for opening the summer period of retreat and so on. The liturgy of *cho ga* is usually divided into a series of common observances, in the course of which the prescribed ritual compendia are recited. Fixed hand gestures (*phyag rgya*, Skt. *mudra*) form part of this performance, as does the accompaniment of special liturgical instruments, of which two are absolutely indispensable, the small bell (*dril bu*) and the *rdo rje*.[3] The hand gestures (*phyag rgya*) act as commentary on the recited text and thereby lend it a corresponding efficacy.

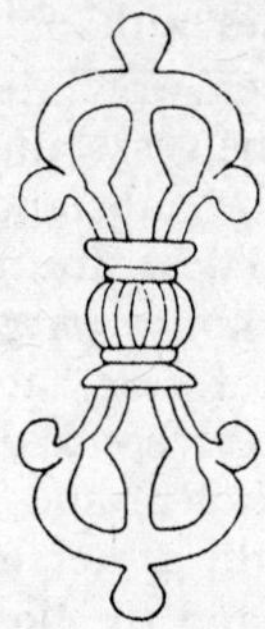

Figure 2 *rdo rje*

The cult act (*mchod pa*) is composed of scriptural recitation (*zhal ton* or *zhal 'don*) and liturgical performances. Its goal is to pacify or to give pleasure to (*dgyes*) a deity, or sometimes to promote the deity's actualization (*sgrub mchod*). This point requires an explanation. From the doctrinal point of view it is of no concern to the gods, in the bliss of their states of meditative absorption in the various paradises, whether a cult act is addressed to them or not. However, as far as the faithful are concerned such a cult act serves as a means of purification and promotes the accumulation of the two kinds of merit, karmic and spiritual. Similarly the doctrine provides an explanation of the exorcistic rites (*gtor zlog*). Thus it is said that in these rituals the sacrificer evokes his own evil actions or thoughts, or those of other people, in front of him in the form of demons (*bgegs*). Thus the offering given to the guardian deities (*yi dam*) is considered to be a means to overcome or chase away these demons. Again, the *mandala* ritual (*dkyil 'khor cho ga*) aids one to enter the divine fields which it depicts visually through the process of meditation and evocation. Besides these there are liturgical acts which are concerned with immediate ends, in a more direct way: for example, the attainment of certain benefits or practical advantages such as long life or health, to be attained in this life for oneself or others. These rituals are called *sku rim* (or *rim gro*). In all cases the possibility of obtaining liberation from the performance of rituals alone is excluded. The accumulation of good brought about through them gives them a purely purificatory and accessory value.

An essential element in many rituals is the *gtor ma*, a heap of barley-flour kneaded with butter. Sometimes it is coloured, and it can also be made in various forms, according to the ritual for which it is intended. The liturgy distinguishes five aspects of the *gtor ma* offering: (a) the person offering the *gtor ma* or for whose benefit the *gtor ma* is offered. This person can be anyone who has taken the three vows (*sdom*) already mentioned, though all people can benefit from the ritual; (b) the vessel (*snod*) in which the offering is placed. Vessels of iron or leather are excluded. The *dGe lugs pa* also exclude vessels made of human skulls or skull-bones, although the *rNying ma pa* allow them. Vessels of gold, silver, copper, wood, terracotta (*rdza*) and brass are recommended. The rim of the vessel must have no fault and the base must have no holes; (c) the substances (*bcud*) which are offered together with the *gtor ma*. These are milk, barley and butter (*dkar gsum*) or sugar, treacle and honey (*mngar gsum*), and *tsamba*. Among the *dGe lugs pa* meat and beer (*chang*)[4] are prohibited; (d) the entity to which the offering is made. Here a distinction is generally made between offerings proper (*mchod*) and gifts (*sbyin*). The former are made to the 'Three Jewels', the protective deities of the sect (*mgon po*), the god of wealth (*nor lha*) and the 'lords of the earth', the gods of dwelling-places. The latter are for powers of a demonic kind and beings created for lower destinies (hells and so on); (e) the manner of the offering.

In the course of the *gtor ma* ritual the following elements are significant: the person of the offerer is conceived of as transformed into a deity. Infinite gifts are summoned out of space and transformed into ambrosia. Goddesses emanated out of the offerer's own body pay homage to the offerer transformed into a god, and his purification is carried out by the Buddhas who have hastened from all points of space bearing vessels in their hands.

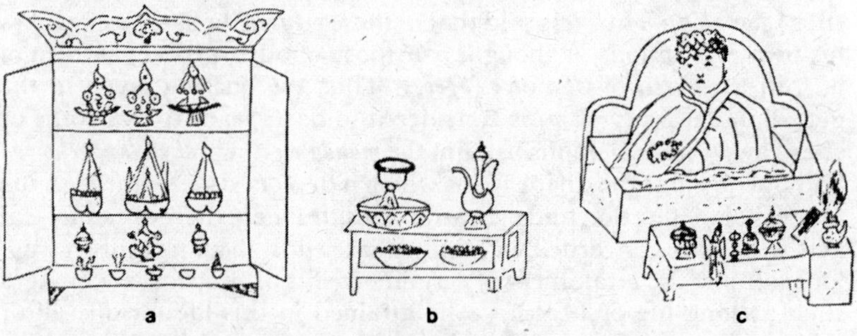

a b c

Figure 3 A *sngags pa* performing a ritual of the Tantric liturgy
For this the following are required:
(a) a small cupboard with two or three shelves. On the top shelf are the three essential *gtor ma*: the *gtor ma* of the monk's Tantric master, of his guardian deity (*yi dam*) and of the *mkha' 'gro ma*. These are needed in the *rNying ma pa* and *bKa' brgyud pa* schools; the others require only the *gtor ma* of the guardian deity (cf.p.97). On the middle shelf there are three additional *gtor ma*; on the lowest

The process described proceeds in thirteen successive phases, each corresponding to various groups of gods and demons to whom the offering is directed. The offering itself is always visualized as transfigured into ambrosia or into a jewel. Through it the powers are to be made satisfied, and thus rendered disposed to ward off evil and overcome misfortunes threatening the individual person or living beings in general. Both those to whom the gifts are directed and the gifts themselves vary very much in accordance with the individual case. If it is a question of demons, the offerings can even be imagined as nauseating substances (meat and so on). However, the presuppositions of the offering are always retained in its schematic construction: the Thought of Enlightenment, the Refuge in the 'Three Jewels', the possibility of transferring the merit of the offering to other beings, the hoped-for action of atonement. Here reality is transformed onto a plane of the imagination which is attributed by virtue of meditation a new, more real and more intense reality than normal everyday existence. An imaginary plane is reached, on which both the sacrificer and the whole feast (*mgron*) to which the imagined divine guests are invited come together in an apotheosis transcending space and time. This series of interconnected visions however always remains within the structure of the ritual architecture of a supranormal world which opens before the participants in these meditations.

Necessary ingredients of the *mchod pa*[5] are offerings of water, flowers, foods (*zhal zas*), lamps (*mar me*) and perfumes. Each of these gifts is placed on the altars in front of the images in an appropriate vessel. In the course of the prescribed divine office this takes place during the recitation of hymns (*bstod pa*), with the accompaniment of prescribed musical instruments, of which the following are the most important: cymbals (*sil snyan*, or in a smaller version *ting shag*); conch (*dung dkar*); shawm (*rgya gling*); drum (*rnga*), both the large drum used in the temple and the small drum in the chapels where the cult of the protective deity (*mgon po*) of the sect or monastery concerned is carried out.

is the fivefold offering (cf. Fig. 5(c)) and behind it the medicinal herbs (*sman*) and blood (*rakta*) to the right and left of the central *gtor ma*.
(b) *gsol phud*: the offering. On a silver plate (*pad sder*) in the form of a lotus-blossom (*pad ma*) is placed a cup containing offerings (*phud phor*); in this are tea, *chang*, milk and also various kinds of seeds. At its side is a special ampulla called *mchod thib* with offerings of various kinds mixed with *chang*, tea or milk. (Cf.p.269, n.6.)
(c) Monk on his seat. Before him a small table, on which are medicinal herbs, the red *gtor ma* which represents blood (*rakta*), the double-headed pellet-drum (*damaru*), the bell, etc. At the beginning of the ceremony he places a round hat on his head, the *thugs dam zhwa mo*, the 'hat for the guardian deities'.

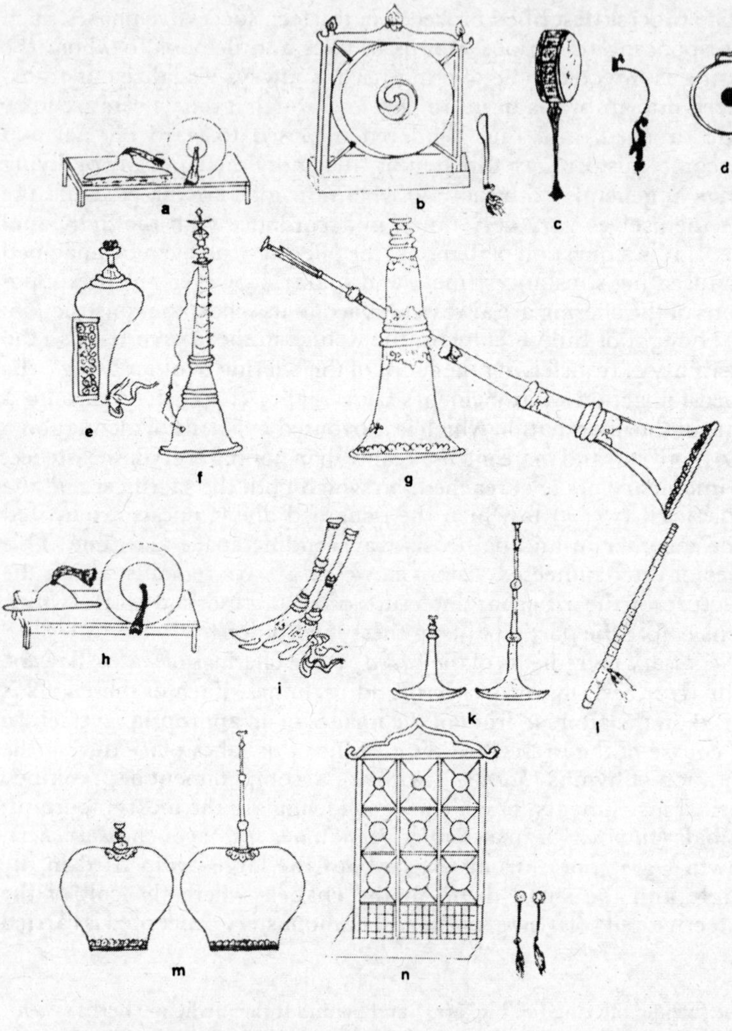

Figure 4 Musical instruments used in the liturgy
(a) *sil snyan*: cymbals, essential for all offering rituals, and in ceremonies carried out both in accordance with the *mdo* (Skt. Sutra) and in those of the Tantras of the lower classes.
(b) *rnga chen*: large drum. This is beaten in the temple at those ceremonies (*tshogs pa*) in which the entire monastic community takes part, and also during the most important Tantric practices. It is sometimes beaten from high up on the roof or balcony of the temple in order to summon the monks together. The drumstick is to the right.

The kind of musical instruments used (*mchod rol*) depends both on the particular nature of the liturgy employed and on the deity to whom the ritual is addressed. If the liturgy is carried out according to the rituals of the three lower classes of Tantra, for example, the various objects required to celebrate a guest (*mgron chas*) must be placed in front of the master (*slob dpon*) on the altar. These include the vessel with grains of various kinds (*'du phor*), the water vessel (*ril pa spyi blugs*) for washing the face (*zhal bshal*) of the image, the vessel surmounted by peacock feathers (*bum pa*), the short cord (*gzung thag*) for establishing the connection between the officiant and the water vessel which is required for the ritual, incense (*spos*), the conch-shell with perfume (*dung phor*), the little bell and the *rdo rje* (cf. Figure 5 (a)).

In the ceremonies of the first Tantric class (*bya rgyud*) the *mandala* is also used. This *mandala* is called *tshom bu'i dkyil 'khor*, because a heap of grain (*'bru'i tshom*) is placed on its decorated surface for each deity present in the *mandala*. In front of it seven cups made of copper or silver are placed. The first two of these (*mchod yon* and *zhal bsil*) are filled with water, the third with flowers and grain, the fourth with incense for burning (*spos*), the fifth serves as a lamp (*mar me snang gsal*),

(c) *lag rnga* or *rnga chung*: pole drum. This is used in the *mgon khang* and during the ceremonies of the lower Tantra classes, especially during the *gto* or exorcistic rituals (cf.p.176). Usually the pole drum is beaten by two rows of monks (*rnga gral*) placed opposite one another. Drumstick to the right. Among the *Sa skya* monks this drum is used by the *dbu mdzad* to introduce the ceremony.
(d) *rgyal rnga*, *'khar rnga*: gong, used especially to announce the time and hour of the monastic assembly.
(e) *dung dkar*: white conch-shell trumpet, an important accompanying instrument in religious ceremonies.
(f) *rgya gling*: shawm, used in all ceremonies except the rites of exorcism (*bzlog*).
(g) *dung chen*: long trumpet, used primarily in the Tantric ceremonies of the higher class; among the *Sa skya pa*, the *rNying ma pa* and the *bKa' brgyud pa* this instrument generally does not take part in the performance of hymns (*bstod*).
(h) *rol mo*, *sbub chal*: large cymbals, used primarily in the ceremonies connected with the 'terrifying' deities.
(i) *rkang gling*: short trumpet, a much-used wind instrument, indispensable for ceremonies of invocation (*spyan 'dren*).
(k) *kar gling*: wind instrument of Chinese origin, used at festivals, is also blown from the upper storey of the temple; one of the nine good signs (*bkra shis dgu rtsegs*).
(l) *khred gling*: transverse flute, also belongs among the good signs.
(m) *sbu phag*: a kind of trumpet, another of the good signs; of Chinese origin.
(n) *drwa ting*: an instrument consisting of nine *'khar rnga* or gongs (cf.d), another sign of good omen. Beaters to the right.

the sixth again contains water (*dri chab*) and the seventh various kinds of food (*zhal zas*).

The most frequently used cult utensils are the mirror (*me long*) as symbol of the visible, small cymbals (*ting shag*) representing the world of sound, a shell filled with perfumes, standing for smells and perfumes, all kinds of foods (*zas sna*), symbolically representing the world of taste, and a piece of silk (*dar*) standing for the sense of touch (cf. Figure 5 (e)). These five objects form a symbolical offering of the person concerned, who is represented through his five senses. The mirror has a second symbolic value: it is often held that placing it before the images of the gods signifies that all things, including the figures of the gods, are only a reflection created by our imagination.

The form of the liturgical act varies according to which Tantric cycle is to be employed and whether a peaceful and serene (*zhi*) or a terrifying (*drag po*) deity is concerned. For example, an entire skull (genuine or reproduced in metal) or cranial bone may be placed in front of the master, provided with the 'five ambrosias' (*bdud rtsi lnga*) or medicinal herbs, and also the small bell and *rdo rje*, a vessel with peacock feathers, a *damaru*, another skull, blood (*rakta*) and the 'five kinds of flesh' (*sha chen lnga*)[6] (cf. Figure 5 (b)).

Figure 5 Examples of the arrangement of liturgical utensils at Tantric ceremonies.
(a) For ritual performances in accordance with the lower Tantras, the following instruments are always required: cymbals, great drum, conch, *rgya gling*, bell. The *ting shag* (cf.p.266) and *damaru* are not absolutely essential. The utensils are arranged as shown in (a) before the *slob dpon*: (from left to right) a covered bowl (*'bru phor*) to contain grains of various kinds, a bell, *rdo rje*, vessel for consecrated water (*ril pa spyi blugs*), a vessel with peacock feathers, a small cord which can be held by pupils or assistants, incense, a conch containing pleasant-smelling substances.
(b) For ritual performances such as those relating to the higher Tantras the following musical instruments are provided for ceremonies directed to the peaceful deities: cymbals, drum, conch, *rgya gling*, *damaru* and small bell. From left to right in the diagram: perfumed medicinal herbs, i.e. the so-called five kinds of ambrosia (*bdud rtsi lnga*) in a skull-shaped vessel, bell, *rdo rje*, *damaru*, vessel with peacock feathers, *raktá* (blood with the five kinds of flesh) in a bowl-shaped vessel.
(c) Six vessels which are placed before a *mandala* drawn with coloured earth. From left to right: water (not always required), flowers, incense, lamp, water, various foods.
(d) *gtor ma* used in the rituals directed to terrifying deities. These represent (from left to right) a skull (the five senses), incense (= human fat), a lamp fed with butter (= *zhun chen*, liquid of a decomposing corpse), water (bile), food (= flesh and bones). Note the equating of the *gtor ma* with parts of the human body.

a

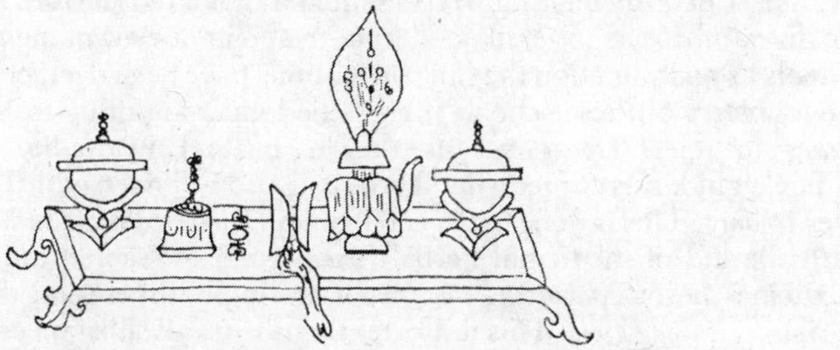

b

c

d

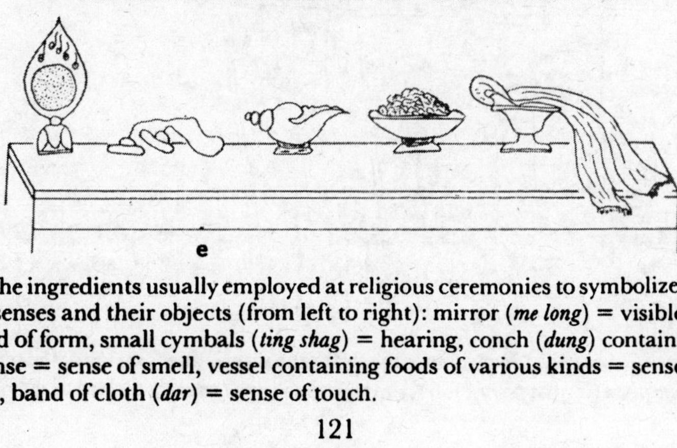

e

(e) The ingredients usually employed at religious ceremonies to symbolize the five senses and their objects (from left to right): mirror (*me long*) = visible world of form, small cymbals (*ting shag*) = hearing, conch (*dung*) containing incense = sense of smell, vessel containing foods of various kinds = sense of taste, band of cloth (*dar*) = sense of touch.

In the ceremonies devoted to the terrifying gods the vessel for the foods (*zhal zas*) contains an offering (*gtor ma*) which represents blood and bones. In this case a water-vessel containing bile (*mkhris pa'i dri chab*) is used, along with a lamp containing fat (*zhun chen kyi mar me*) and an incense vessel from which comes the smell of melted fat (*tshil chen gyi spos*). Another implement used here is a black, triangular piece of cloth (*g.yab dmar*) which has a *rdo rje* fixed to its apex and two pieces of red cloth (*phan lce*) attached to its two lower corners. The trumpet used in the *good* ceremony (cf.p.91) is made from a human tibia (*rkang*); the upper part is ornamented with silver and gold.

The use of filthy offerings (represented by coloured *gtor ma*), as with the 'five ambrosias', is explained from the point of view of the Siddha schools as an indication that all conventions have been overcome. For the followers of these schools there is no longer anything to 'accept' (*blang*) or 'reject' (*spong*) because they are beyond any duality.

The eight kinds of medicinal herbs can also be mixed with Tibetan beer (*chang*). This is done in the ceremonies called 'mystical realization with the aid of medicinal herbs' (*sman sgrub*) or 'sacred ambrosial medicinal herbs' (*bdud rtsi chos sman*) or simply 'liberation through pleasure' (*myong grol*). This indicates that the use of substances which cause intoxication and ecstasy is not excluded; these states can be regarded as preliminary signs of the desired *excessus mentis*. Pills (*ril bu*) or ambrosial pills (*bdud rtsi ril bu*) are formed out of the ingredients mentioned; a whole literature exists on the methods for making them. These pills are received during the act of consecration (*dbang*), and also, because of the efficacy they possess, in illness or in the death-agony. Frequently the medicinal herbs are replaced by *chang* and the 'blood' by tea.

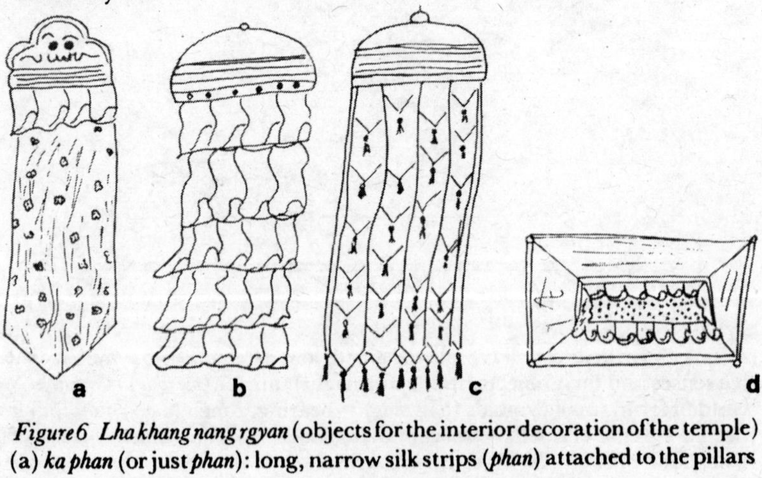

Figure 6 Lha khang nang rgyan (objects for the interior decoration of the temple) (a) *ka phan* (or just *phan*): long, narrow silk strips (*phan*) attached to the pillars

As we have seen, the structure of the liturgical action is fairly complex. Its domain extends from the offering each day of substances in the individual vessels before the images (substances which correspond symbolically to the five senses and their objects) to the extremely complicated Tantric rituals. These latter rituals are subject to numerous modifications, according to the *mandala*, the particular kind of meditation, the master, the gods, the aims associated with the Tantra, and so on. These practices have a very significant emotional component. They bring about special emotional states, hopes and ecstasies, through which it is hoped to induce the rapid, if only momentary, abolition or stoppage of the dichotomizing process, which has been so often spoken of above.

The offerings during the ceremony (*mchod*) are generally designated cult substances (*rdzas*, *mchod rdzas*) although this term frequently refers to the liturgical objects as well. The 'container' or 'support' (*rten*) of sacredness, which may be a reliquary, a book, an image or a temple, is always conceived of as one of these *rdzas*. These 'supports' can in general be divided according to the 'three planes' of body, speech or mind. Thus there are 'supports' of the body (*sku*), such as images (though 'body' here must be understood in the sense explained in the previous chapter, cf.p.57), 'supports' of the plane of the word, for example the Buddha's word as contained in the scriptures, and 'supports' of the mental plane, such as a *mandala* or a temple. The various kinds of 'supports' can also be classified as outer, inner and secret. The outer are visible and readable, like an image or a book. The inner generally cannot be seen, as with reliquaries, or special sacred objects in the temples, closed to the public, which can only be viewed if one receives special authorization, in exceptional circumstances. The secret 'supports' are inaccessible to all who have not received the 'consecration of the secret'. The *bla ma* can only allow insight into these secrets to the initiated.

(*ka*) of the temple; under the dragon's head (*'brug mgo*) there are five five-coloured strips called *'ja' ris* (rainbow design); underneath there are rolled-up strips of cloth (*phur mang*), and under this again a piece of silk of the same length as the pillar or column.
(b) *phur mang*: cylinders of cloth rolled together in five successive rows. Above there is a parasol-shaped cover with five strips of various colours beneath it. Hung on the ceiling, between the pilasters or columns.
(c) *phye ma*: decoration hung from the rafters, in the form of a long parasol, with the usual five five-coloured strips, to which are fastened little bands of white cloth (*dung phreng*). The upper part consists of cloth of various colours and fringing garlands; on the lower end there are fringes and pendants.
(d) *bla bre*: piece of multicoloured cloth, quadrangular with hanging borders (*phur ma*), hung to cover the opening for light in the ceiling of the temple.

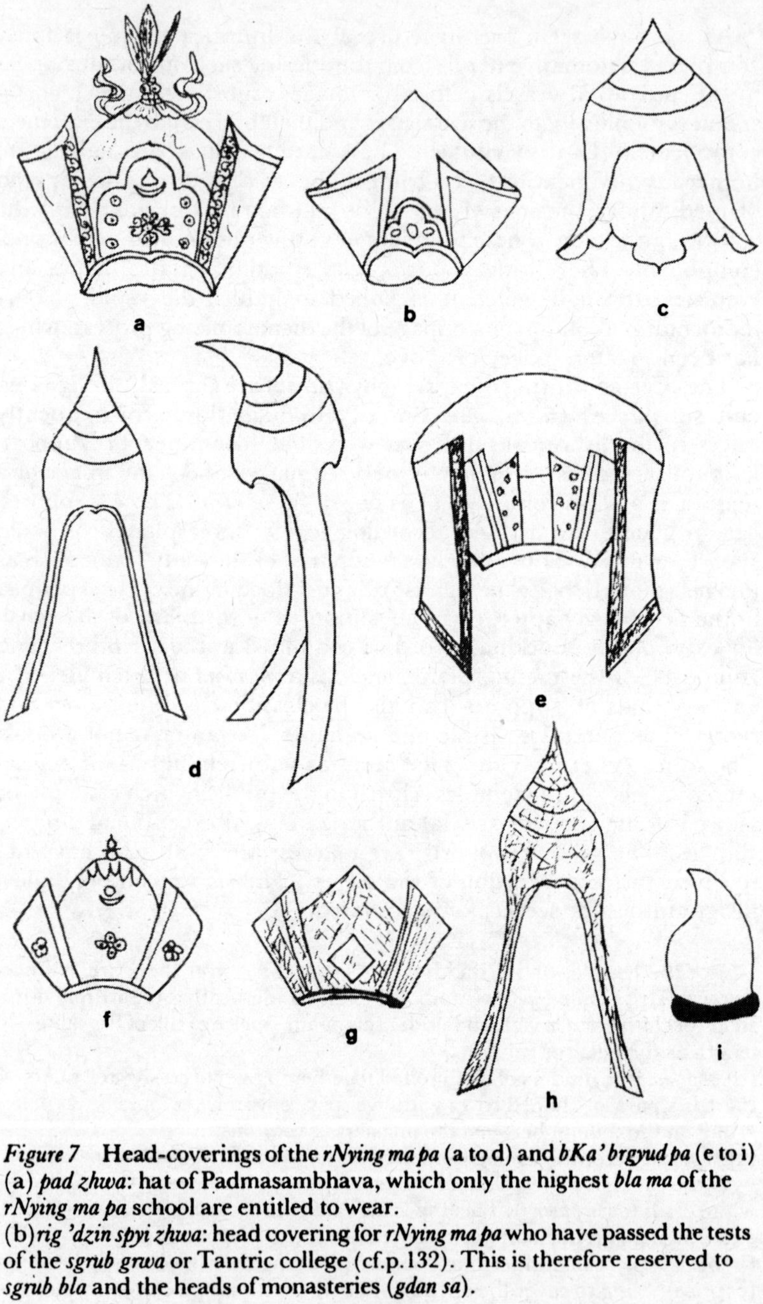

Figure 7 Head-coverings of the *rNying ma pa* (a to d) and *bKa' brgyud pa* (e to i)
(a) *pad zhwa*: hat of Padmasambhava, which only the highest *bla ma* of the *rNying ma pa* school are entitled to wear.
(b) *rig 'dzin spyi zhwa*: head covering for *rNying ma pa* who have passed the tests of the *sgrub grwa* or Tantric college (cf.p.132). This is therefore reserved to *sgrub bla* and the heads of monasteries (*gdan sa*).

In describing the ritual practices of Tibetan monasteries, I will attempt to give a generalized picture of the customs usual in the most important monastic communities. At about seven in the morning there takes place, for example, the meditation on the *mandala* of *sGrol ma* (Skt. Tara), (*sgrol ma dkyil 'khor*). This includes the recitation of the *sgrub* texts most appropriate for this ceremony. At about nine o'clock the monks again gather in the temple or in its forecourt, and sermons and learned discussions take place there. As soon as all the monks are present, the abbot (*mkhan po*) begins to interpret the doctrine on the basis of a scriptural text he has selected. This interpretation proceeds in two parts. The first is directed to the less schooled or less educated monks; after they are dismissed the esoteric part begins for the more advanced and spiritually more mature. When this teaching period has finished the monks (*grwa pa*) are free until the time of the common meal. From two to four in the afternoon they stay in their cells to study and learn by heart the textual passages which the abbot explained on that day. During this period a great silence has to reign within the monastery walls. It is supervised by an overseer (*chos khrims pa*) entrusted with the keeping of discipline. The beginning of these two hours of study is announced with a small drum. When the same drum announces the end of the study period everyone is free to visit the overseer and examiner (*skyor dpon*) of the students. He checks whether

(c) *pad ma sam zhwa*: reproduction of the hat of Padmasambhava, worn only by *mkhan po* and *sprul sku* or other *bla ma* of the *rNying ma pa* while expounding the doctrine.
(d) *pan zhwa*: the head covering proper to the *pan* (=*pandita*). The decoration consists of fine gold strips, whose number (1,2,3,5) depends on the number of collections of the sacred scriptures which the wearer has studied (or indicates. his deep study of the Five *rig pa* or branches of knowledge). The *bKa' brgyud pa* forms h and i are worn primarily during commentaries on the doctrine, or again serve to indicate the experience acquired through deep study of the doctrine.
(e) *dwags zhwa*: the name comes from the hat worn by *Dwags po lha rje* (*sGam po pa*). According to the legend, *Mi la ras pa* made him a gift of one of his shoes, which out of pious respect he used as a head covering; this explains the form of the hat.
(f) *zhwa nag*: 'black hat'.
(g) *zhwa dmar*: 'red hat'.
(h) *pan zhwa*: the hat proper to the *pandita* or scholar, used principally by the *mkhan po*, ornamented with gold threads as with the *rNying ma pa* (cf. d, above).
(i) *sgrub zhwa*: the hat used, according to legend, by *Ras chung*: only the *sgrub bla* (cf.p.132) are entitled to wear it. It is put on during interpretation of the doctrine or while preaching. This form of hat is used also among the *'Brug pa*, *Phag mo gru pa* and other *bKa' brgyud pa* sub-schools; they have several variants of it.

they have memorized properly the textual passages given to them. Under his control they master their tasks (*skyor sbyong*) ever more perfectly. At around six o'clock the great drum summons the monks yet again from above to a general assembly, at which the prescribed common ritual takes place in the temple. This consists of prayer (*gsol kha*) to the *chos skyong*, ceremonies for the deceased (*gshin po*) or prayers (*bsngo smon*) whose merit is to benefit those who have accumulated bad karma. From six to ten o'clock is a second period of seclusion in the cells for study. At about half-past ten the monks have fulfilled their ritual obligations and can go to bed.

During the three summer months the monks are, at least in theory, obliged to stay in the monastery. In the course of the year, however, the big local festivals take place, and the monks can apply for permission to go to their villages to take part in them, or to travel from village to village to perform particular ceremonies (*sku rim*) at the request of the inhabitants. Apart from the days of festivity prescribed in the calendar of feasts (which are discussed below) the anniversary of the death (referred to naturally as 'entry into *nirvana*') of the sect's most famous teacher is celebrated. On this occasion the various ritual acts are divided as follows: morning ceremony (*tshe lha rnam gsum*) in honour of *Tshe dpag med*, *rNam rgyal ma* and *sGrol ma dkar po*, and the solemn promise (*smon lam*) of ever more widespread diffusion of the doctrine. The afternoon is intended for questions to the teacher (*slob gnyer*), or the monks are given the time off. Among the *Sa skya pa* this yearly memorial celebration is for *Sa skya pandita*, among the *rNying ma pa* it is for *kLong chen pa*, and among the *bKa' brgyud pa* for *sGam po pa*.

In the course of these festivals an 'incarnation' (*sprul sku*) living in the monastery expounds the five situations (*phun sum tshogs lnga*) favourable for the attainment of salvation: perfection of place (*gnas*), of time (*dus*), of the teacher (*ston pa*), of the sermon of the law (*chos 'khor*) and of the gathering of the hearers of this sermon. These amount to the advantage of having been born in a particular place and at a particular time, when the appearance of a Buddha has revealed the Law and created the necessary preconditions for liberation. The exegesis begins at sunset and lasts the whole night, with discourse and reply between the commentator and particular monks especially advanced in their studies, whose names are noted on a special list (*ming tho*) of those coming under consideration for this honour.

At sunrise the solemn promise of continued diffusion of the Law (*bstan rgyas smon lam*) is repeated. A lamp is lit and each monk, beginning with the first of each row (the monks are arranged in two rows in the assembly hall, to the right and to the left; the abbot is situated in the centre in front of the altar) recites the formulae of blessing and good fortune (*bkra shis*). Laymen too can be present at this ritual act.

Among the *Sa skya pa*, the *rNying ma pa* and the *bKa' brgyud pa*, the basis for the *bshad grwa* is formed by the *gzhung chen bcu gsum* or 'Thirteen Great Texts'. These consist of the works of Nagarjuna and Maitreya, along with the Vinaya and Abhidharmakosa; the *Sa skya pa* also include writings on logic and some of the most important works of the great leaders of the school, headed by *Sa skya pandita*.

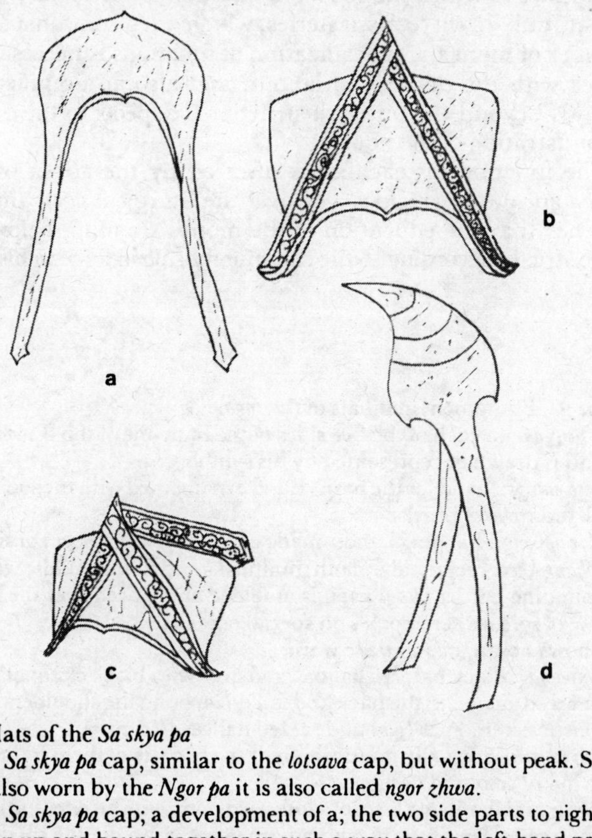

Figure 8 Hats of the *Sa skya pa*
(a) *sa zhwa*: *Sa skya pa* cap, similar to the *lotsava* cap, but without peak. Since this cap is also worn by the *Ngor pa* it is also called *ngor zhwa*.
(b) *sa zhwa*: *Sa skya pa* cap; a development of a; the two side parts to right and left are taken up and bound together in such a way that the left-hand part is turned to the inside and the right-hand part to the outside. The right-hand part (called 'ear' in Tibetan) symbolizes the sacred scriptures, the left mystical practices.
(c) *sa zhwa*: a variant of the preceding type, reserved only for the highest dignitaries.
(d) *pan zhwa*: *pandita* cap (cf. Figures 7, d and h). The ornamentation with fine gold strips indicated the various branches of knowledge mastered.

These books serve as the basis of the doctrinal positions of the various schools, but this of course does not prohibit, in fact it makes necessary, a study of the commentaries and treatises dedicated to these texts by the most important masters of the school concerned.[7] The interpretations given by these masters serve the students as a guide and a decisive touchstone. When their five years of study are over, the monks of the first group mentioned above (*phogs zan pa*) can remain further in the monastery in order to perfect themselves in the disciplines to which the school in question is particularly devoted.

Naturally in these monasteries, which often contain a considerable number of monks, a specialization of functions is necessary in accordance with the division of labour, and also an organization which extends beyond the purely instructional aspects to the ordering and administration of the house.

The function of teaching is directed by the abbot of the school (*bshad grwa*). He presides also over the liturgical acts, and in general watches that the education of the monks standing below him takes place strictly according to the community rule in force in his monastery.

Figure 9 Equipment and hats of the *sngags pa*
(a) *rigs lnga*: on each of the five sides of the tiara one of the Buddhas of the pentad is drawn or represented by his symbol.
(b) *rtsa chings*: 'band for the base'. Band ornamented with turquoises, pieces of coral and rows of pearls.
(c) *dar dpyangs*: hanging bands, made of five-coloured pieces of silk.
(d) *phang kheb*: rectangular cloth, multicoloured in the middle with a surrounding border (*lcags ri*); it is unfolded and placed over the lap in the course of solemn ceremonies on special occasions.
(e) shows how a, b, and c are worn.
(f) *zhwa nag*: black hat, i.e. hat covered over with black cloth; black strips of cloth are attached to the back and fall down on to the shoulders. It is used at exorcistic ceremonies (*gto*) and sacred dances (*lha 'cham*).
(g) *ber*: tunic, normally multicoloured; the borders of the skirt and the sleeves have many coloured designs.
(h) *sba le*: a collar in the form of a lotus-blossom, with an opening in the middle for the head. Usually dark, and ornamented with a double *rdo rje* (cf.p.115).
(i) *rus rgyan*: ornament made of bones held together by a cord, with representations in relief of gods or their symbols. This is used as a kind of armour on the occasion of the ceremonies mentioned above under f, and also at ceremonies accompanied by fire-offerings (*sbyin sreg*).
(k) *phang kheb*: black cloth apron, on which the features of a terrifying deity (*khro rgyal*) are represented. On the borders drawings of skulls and flames.
(l) shows how the various items of clothing are worn.

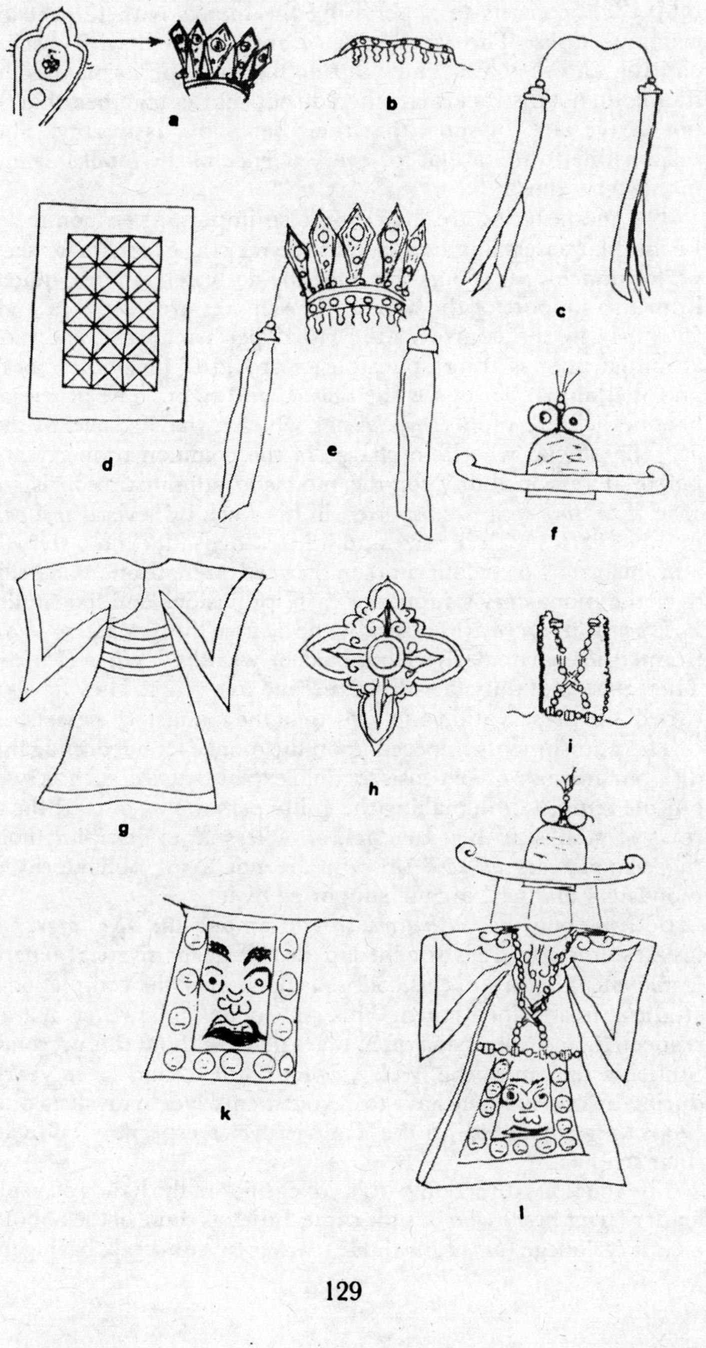
a
b
c
d
e
f
g
h
i
k
l

The task of the *skyor dpon*, who has already been mentioned (cf.p.125), consists in supervising the monks with respect to their religious tasks. The *chos khrims pa* are entrusted with disciplinary control, and they also watch during the ritual performances that the monks do not distract each other, do not chatter together, that they do not arrive late, in short that their behaviour is worthy. They are responsible to the abbot for every offence of the monks against the monastery rules.

The monasteries are, however, also important economic centres. From their assets and estates must be met the expenses for the ritual performances, as well as those for the daily ceremonies, quite apart from the support of the monks. The monks are given tea and soup (*thug pa*) in the course of the ritual performances. The monastic administration is also responsible for providing fuel, butter for the tea and the lamps, barley for the *tsamba*, and so on. The provisions are kept in the store-room (*gnyer khang*), which is watched over by the *gnyer pa*. The official who is in charge of the common property and has personal responsibility for the monastic administration is the *spyi dpon*. The *spyi dpon* is supported in his work by several *spyi pa*; their number varies with the size and importance of the monastery. These administrators meet four times in the year (or more often) to deliberate over the monastery's supply of cash, provisions and foodstuffs. The *spyi dpon* and *spyi pa* are chosen by the head of the monastery (*bla brang*) from either particularly rich monks or wealthy laymen (*khyim bdag*). Their period of duty lasts from three to five years. They have to take care of the preservation and growth of the monastery's assets.

The punishments imposed upon the monks for offences against the disciplinary code often consist of mild expiatory tasks such as sweeping out the temple, or in making the guilty person stay outside the seated rows of monks in the ritual action. A less strict discipline holds for those monks (*rgyab sdod pa*) who are not living obligatorily in the monastery and who are not supported by it.

Both among the *rNying ma pa* and among the *bKa' brgyud pa* the greatest importance is attached to the college for mystical experiences (*sgrub grwa*). Entry to this college is open after the completion of the studies already mentioned. This restriction is, however, not always respected, and admission often takes place without this precondition. Students remain in the *sgrub grwa* for not less than seven years, and during this period they have to devote themselves to mystical practices (*bsnyen bsgrub*) based on the Tantric cycles especially cultivated in their school.

The religious direction of this college lies in the hands of a spiritual leader (*sgrub dpon*) who has the same duties as those of the abbot in the ordinary college (*bshad grwa*). He teaches twice a week, basing himself upon a particular doctrinal text, which the students must study in two different ways. In the first morning study period they memorize the text and learn by heart the simple verbal meaning, while in the second study period they practise meditation (*sgom*) on the deeper content of the text's meaning. The whole day is divided into four *thun* or study periods; the first (*snga thun*) from five to eight in the morning, the second (*gung thun*) from nine o'clock to noon, the third (*phyi thun*) from three to six in the afternoon, and the fourth (*mtshan thun*) from nine to twelve at night. In summer and winter the first period is reduced by an hour and the second by half an hour. The recitation of mantras usually takes place in the evening (*phyi thun*). In the three summer months the vision of light practices (*khregs chod*, cf.p.85) are discussed in the *rNying ma pa* colleges, while the *bKa'* brgyud pa study the 'Great Seal' (*phyag rgya chen mo*, cf.p.71). In winter yogic exercises and breath control (*rtsa rlung 'phrul 'khor*), especially *glum mo* (cf.p.98), are the main objects of practice.

a b

Figure 10 *Rab 'byung chas* (equipment of all ordained monks)
(a) *lhun bzed*: bowl, used by the monks (*dge tshul* and *dge slong*) for their food.
(b) *chab blugs*: flask, used by the monks to purify their mouths on entering the temple. Usually enclosed in a piece of cloth, which is sometimes embroidered.

The spiritual director (*sgrub dpon*) is not only a master of ascetic practice; his supervision extends also over all the usual divisions of the school. Its inner administration is divided similarly to that of the non-Tantric college (*bshad grwa*). The overseer of provisions (*gnyer pa*) is here chosen by the monks, and the *spyi pa* selected from influential and prosperous people. With respect to the spiritual hierarchy in the college for mystical practices, in other words concerning the individual ranks accessible to its members, if the candidate finishes his studies successfully he is promoted to the rank of master of mystical practices (*sgrub bla*, or simply *bla ma*). Part of the promotion consists of the ceremonial conferral of a hat (*zhwa mo*) which other masters have already possessed, along with the presentation of a small bell and a *rdo rje*, which have again been used by past directors of the school (*sgrub dpon*). Only this investiture confers on the candidate the title of *bla ma*. The other monks continue to carry their title of priests (*grwa pa*), *bandhe* or novices (*dge tshul*), and are thus kept distinct even in title from the real Tantric master. The *sgrub bla*, after the completion of his intellectual, contemplative, liturgical and mystical education, now possesses all the necessary qualities to be able to carry out the extremely complicated ceremonies involving the use of the *mandala*, to handle successfully the tasks of a *bla ma* in the villages or of a family chaplain (*mchod gnas*); he can in short carry out every kind of ritual (*sku rim*).

The next higher rank is that of director of the music and song accompanying the liturgical acts (*rol dpon*). The playing of the cymbals is one of his tasks. He occupies this office for two years. Then he becomes *dbu chung*, that is provost (*dbu mdzad*) of the second grade, for a period of office of three years. The *dbu chung* opens and presides over the communal ritual performances (*tshogs*), except for those of the highest importance.

The next rank is that of provost of the first grade (*dbu mdzad*). He directs the most important cult acts (*sgrub mchod*). After three or five years he withdraws from this office and then receives the title of retired provost (*dbu zur dbu mdzad*); although no longer having to take part in the ceremonies, he possesses the same privileges as before. A further rank is that of *rdo rje slob dpon* (Skt. *Vajracarya*), master of the ceremonies which employ the *mandala*; he confers the consecration (*dbang*) on the adepts, and gives the instructions for traversing the path of salvation. It is his task to uncover the *mandala*, and to consecrate the prescribed offerings at ceremonies directed to terrifying gods. After five or seven years he ends his period of office and becomes a lama in retirement (*bla zur*). At this point he can also retire to a hermitage (*ri khrod*) or take over the office of *sgrub dpon* in another monastery.

Figure 11 *dbyar gyi rta zhwa* (hats worn in summer while riding a horse)
(a) *gser zhwa* (*nam mkha' rab 'byams*): reserved for 'incarnates' (*sprul sku*).
(b) *gser theb*: reserved for *rtse drung* (government officials) and the *dgon dpon* (cf.p.134).
(c) *zhwa khra*: multicoloured hat reserved for certain monks of the *bKa' brgyud pa* school. Dark blue basic colour, with white or red designs.
(d) similar to *gser zhwa*, but covered over with a white piece of woollen cloth; worn in general by the *mkhan po*. Those monks not entitled to wear a gilded hat

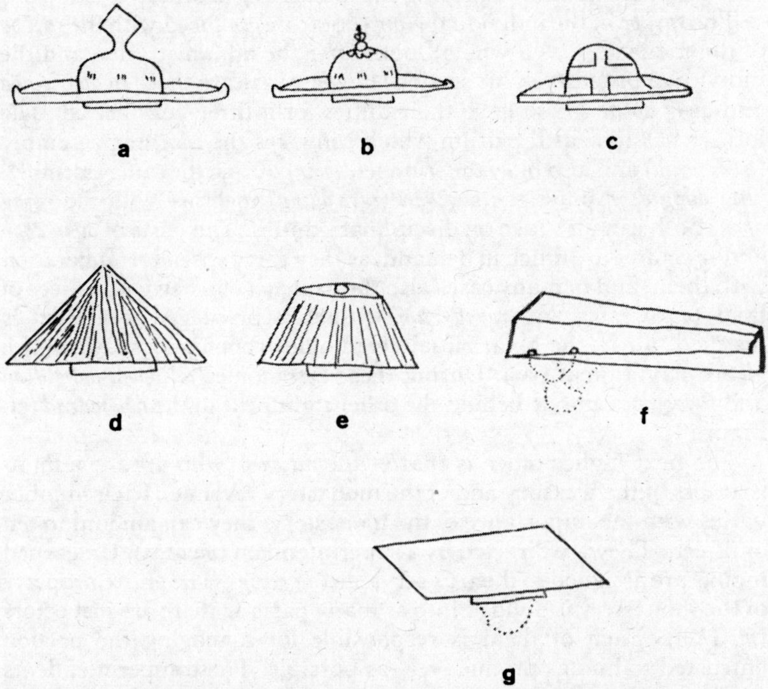

wear hats made of a wooden frame covered with white cloth. All monks can wear a hat of this kind.
(e) peculiar to monks of certain *Sa skya pa* monasteries. This hat is called *zhwa gya la*; it was originally worn by the ministers of Derge. It too is covered over in white.
(f) *nyi zhwa*: sunhat, the head-covering worn according to tradition by the *lotsava*, the 'translators', when they travelled to India to learn Sanskrit, to translate the secret texts and bring them back to Tibet with them. Another name of this kind of head-covering is *sho khal*. Nowadays hats of this kind are also worn by women.
(g) head-covering worn by those carrying out the *gcod* practice (cf.p.87).

The monastic organization also requires another series of offices which have little to do with the training of the monks but are important for the monastic life from the point of view of discipline and administration. The larger monasteries are mostly divided into various sections (*gling*), each of which is placed under the control of the leader of a ten-membered corporation (*bcu dpon*). In the larger monasteries further assistants, the *yang dpon*, are placed below the *bcu dpon*. These officials have the task of keeping the monastery in order.

The *spyi pa* of the individual *gling* (not to be confused with the *spyi pa* of the monastery as a whole) looks after the administration and the individual property of his section. Lower ranks are those of *dung g.yog* and *dung dpon*. These have their duties for a three-year period. The former has to beat the drum which convokes the morning assembly (*tshogs chen*) and also blow the trumpet (*dung*) during the same assembly. The *dung dpon* plays the shawm (*rgya gling*) together with the *rgyag dpon*. Both can also take on disciplinary duties. The posts of *dung dpon* and *rgyag dpon* are much in demand, as they carry special remuneration with them, and in many cases also the usufruct of a particular piece of land (*dung zhing* and *rgyag zhing*). Such a privileged treatment is justified, for in the great ritual ceremonies conch and shawm (*rgya gling*) play a great part. During these ceremonies *rol dpon*, *dung dpon* and *rgyag dpon* sit one behind the other right next to the *dbu mdzad* (cf. Figure 1).

The next higher office is that of the *mi chen*, who are the administrators of the treasury and of the monastery revenue. Their number varies with the importance of the monastery; they can amount to ten or fifteen. They are directed by a superintendent (*mi dpon*). Unlearned monks are assigned to them as servants (*mi g.yog*). The entire property of the monastery is divided into as many parts as there are inspectors (*mi chen*). Each of them is responsible for managing the portion entrusted to him as productively as possible. These superintendents can be monks or laymen. The *chos khrims pa* and *dgon dpon* are charged with disciplinary duties, but these offices are also very lucrative, since they are linked to special appanages in the form of the produce of the land (*chos zhing* or *dgon zhing*) allocated to them. They are conferred for three years. They are subordinate to the superintendent (*mi dpon*) surnamed *spyi zur*, deputy administrator, possibly an aristocrat (*mi drag*) resident in the monastery. These administrative posts are never occupied by a *rdo rje slob dpon* (*Vajracarya*).

The *phyag mdzod* is the director of the household for the residence of the monastery head (*bla brang*), who is usually an 'incarnate' (*sprul sku*). The *phyag mdzod* is assisted by a kind of treasurer (*gnyer pa*) who looks after his expenses and so on.

The prestige of a monastery derives in all cases from the 'incarnate' which it shelters within its walls. Although he does not interfere in any way either in questions of monastic discipline or in questions concerning the doctrine, the whole existence of the monastic community revolves about his person.

These *sprul sku* (the term has the primary meaning of 'apparent body', the third of the three 'bodies'. cf.p.263, note 18) are generally known in the books on Tibet as 'incarnate lamas'. According to the teachings of the *rNying ma pa* school it is a question in the first place of the reappearance of particular teachers, disciples or assistants of Padmasambhava. The Master prophesied that they would return on this earth, in order to restore the books which he had hidden (that is, to act as *gter ston*) or to re-establish the correct interpretation of his teachings according to the sense which he gave to them (*dgongs gter*). In this way and for the same purpose Vimala was to be reincarnated (cf. No. 3, p.379), and also Padmasambhava himself (ibid., p.380).[8] This older conception differs, however, from that of the present day. On the older model the incarnation had a somewhat discontinuous character; it could happen when the master concerned judged in his mental continuum that the appropriate moment for his new mission had arrived. Today it is a question of an unbroken chain of incarnations (*sku 'phreng bar ma chad*) occupying the same abbatial or monastic office and bound up very closely with this office. The same is also true for the position of Dalai Lama, as a consequence of a usage going back to the third Dalai Lama, *bSod nams rgya mtsho* (cf.p.41) and which was later transferred to the *Pan chen* lama too. This system came into use in Tibet at the time of the *Kar ma pa* lama *Dus gsum mkhyen pa* (1110-93, cf.p.36), who at the time of his death prophesied his future rebirth (*Kar ma pa kshi*).

The custom was adopted by all the sects which maintain monasteries in which reincarnations of the same master succeed each other, such as the *sprul sku* of *rDo rje brag*, of *sMin grol gling*, and so on, among the *rNying ma pa*.

The *sprul sku* of today (leaving aside the Dalai Lama, for whom an extremely complicated special etiquette exists) have the right to special signs of dignity denied to all others, for example to a red band (or two) for their horse, with a long tassel of hair (*rta gdam*) hanging down at the front. They may also wear the coloured hat with a large brim, the dome-shaped upper part of which is ornamented and which is held in place by a chin-strap (*gser zhwa*, cf. Figure 11). Another special hat reserved to *sprul sku* is the 'hat with long ears' (*zhwa mo rna ring*), which is so called because two pieces of cloth to the right and left hang down so low that they touch the shoulders. This head covering otherwise resembles a phrygian cap, except that it is encircled by three to five golden or gilded bands (*gser dkris gsum*, *lnga*). Such a hat is also known by its Indian name of '*pan chen*'s hat' (*pan zhwa*, cf. Figures 7, d and h, 8, d).

In the course of our brief description of the monastic organization of the *rNying ma pa* we have frequently made use of the word 'monk'. In this connection we need to recall what was said earlier, that for the *sNgags pa* the priestly consecration according to the Vinaya precepts is not an unconditional requirement. While the ordained monks wear

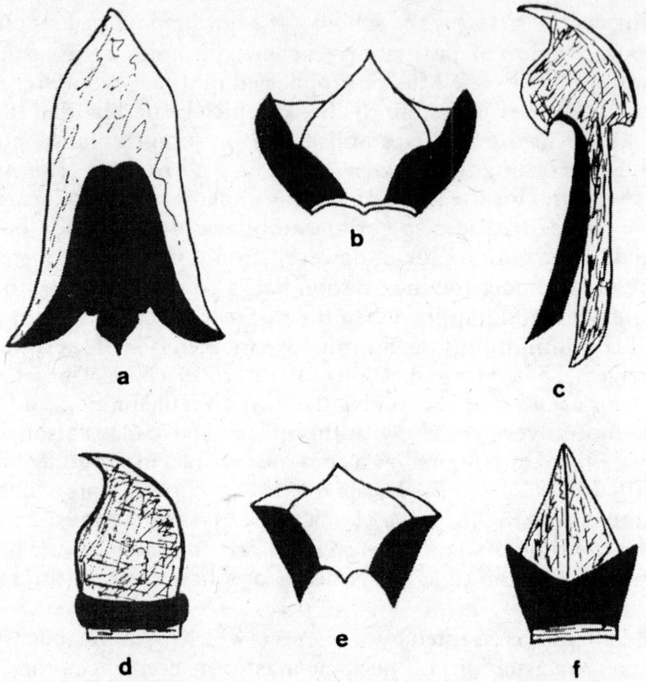

Figure 12 *dgun gyi rta zhwa* (hats worn in winter while riding a horse)
(a) is worn by *rNying ma pa* and *bKa' brgyud pa*. It is lined on the inside with fox-fur and reserved for great lamas and 'incarnates' (*sprul sku*).
(b) with raised side-pieces, otherwise exactly the same as a.
(c) yellow in colour; reserved for *dGe lugs pa* great lamas while riding.
(d) characteristic hat of *Sa skya pa*, *rNying ma pa* and *bKa' brgyud pa* monks.
(e) generally reserved for nuns (*a ne*). Coloured red among *Sa skya pa*, *rNying ma pa* and *bKa' brgyud pa*, yellow among *dGe lugs pa* nuns. Made of wool, lined on the inside with fur.
(f) used in the *gcod* practices. Made of red wool, surrounded with a high border of black cloth or black fur.

the usual red monk's clothing, the *Ras pa* are clothed in white, although this rule does not always hold. For the monks who have received the consecration the three-month summer retreat (*dbyar gnas*) is obligatory.

The ordained monks can of course always renounce their ordination (*sdom phul*) at a later date according to the appropriate precepts.

In the *dGe lugs pa* school the situation is not very much different, but we find here certain traits which can be explained either in terms of the new orientation going back to the founder, *Tsong kha pa*, or through the separate and more extended development of this school, which surpasses all the other schools in its great prestige, and even installs the head of the church, the Dalai Lama, to say nothing of the political power which it had before the Chinese takeover. The three great monasteries (*gdan sa gsum*) of Central Tibet (*dBus*), namely *Se ra*, *dGa' ldan* and *'Bras spungs*, along with *bKra shis lhun po* in *gTsang*, each used to contain several thousand monks. In these great monasteries the monastic establishments surround the chapel building (*tshogs chen*), the large hall intended for monastic gatherings and for the collective rituals performed together at least once each day.[9] This 'chapel' thus forms the central point of the entire monastery, and not so much in the material sense as in the spiritual, as a result of the rituals performed within its walls. These concentrate in this place the effective presence of the third of the 'Three Jewels', the Community. The rest of the very extensive complex of buildings is taken up by the colleges or teaching establishments (*grwa tshang*), which served for the training of the monks and in which their daily life takes place. The chapels (*'du khang*) of the individual teaching establishments, where the less important rituals and lesser liturgical performances take place also require mention. Then there are the hostels and hospices (*khang tshan*) for those monks who come from all parts of Tibet to these monasteries for occasional visits or for purposes of study. These hostels generally take their name from the place of origin of their temporary inhabitants. Thus there is a *dBus khang tshan* for visitors from Central Tibet (*dBus*), a hostel for those from *Khams* (called *sPom ra khang tshan* in the monastery of *Se ra*), a *mNga' ris khang tshan* for guests from West Tibet, and so on.

Each of these three groups of buildings (chapels, colleges, hostels) possesses its own assets and thus forms an economic unit. This common property is called *spyi*. The collective property of the whole monastery is called *tshogs chen*. This is used to meet obligations incumbent on the community as a whole, as distinct from the particular tasks of the individual teaching establishments and hostels, which have extensive reciprocal independence and economic autonomy, and therefore (as will be discussed later) have separate administrative responsibility.

In accordance with the organization of monastic teaching, three kinds of establishment can be distinguished within these large *dGe lugs pa* monasteries. These are (a) the establishment for teaching and interpretation of the sacred scriptures (*bshad grwa*); (b) that in which the monks are instructed in logic and the art of disputation (*rtsod grwa*, *chos grwa*); and (c) the division devoted to mysticism and to the theoretical and practical study of Tantra (*sgrub grwa*, *sngags grwa*).

Who now are the religious authorities (*dbu 'dzin*) who preside over the various divisions of this great monastic whole? Here there are two principal aspects to the monastic organization to be considered: the spiritual, educational, liturgical on the one hand, and the worldly (*srid*) and especially the administrative on the other. Taking the monastery of *Se ra* as an example, the spiritual authority, first of all, is concentrated in the hands of the abbot (*mkhan po*). With respect to the monastic discipline, the inspectors (*zhal ngo*, *dge bskos* or *chos khrims pa*) are responsible for its maintenance both during the ritual acts and in general at all times of day. Armed with heavy cudgels and accompanied by their assistants they watch over the observance of the monastic precepts and the monks' conduct in general, as was already mentioned with respect to the *rNying ma pa*.

It is the duty of the provost (*dbu mdzad*) to give the signal of commencement at the collective recitation (*zhal 'don*) of the sacred scriptures during the collective ceremonies. The texts which are recited on this occasion are called *chos spyod rab gsal*, a name which includes all the treatises regarded as indispensable to the liturgy, although their contents vary from sect to sect.

The overseer of the distribution of the monastery tea is also responsible for its good quality. This tea is in general called *gsol ja* (it bears this name in the chapel, but it is called *grwa ja* in the college buildings and *tshan ja* in the hostels), and it is given to the monks summoned to a ritual performance. The overseer carries out this office in the chapel under the title *ja dpon nang*, but not in the teaching establishments.

In the individual colleges and hostels the tasks of administration belong to the overseer of stores (*gnyer pa*) who has substantial powers.

The *phyag mdzod* takes care of the property of the individual teaching establishments as well as that of the abbot's residence (*bla brang*).

The *chab gtong ba* or *chab brim pa* offer water to the monks gathered in the monastery at the beginning and end of the ceremony (*snga chab*, *phyi chab*), although this is now no longer the custom in all Tibetan monasteries.

Among the ranks of the monastic hierarchy, that of *gzim khang pa* should also be mentioned. He is a kind of representative of the government chosen by turns from among the monks. He is called *sku tshab* in *Se ra* monastery, *pho brang sde* in *'Bras spungs* and *dpal chos* in *bKra shis lhun po*. In the last-named monastery, however, this functionary is not chosen by the monks but appointed by the government. In this case he is usually an official of the church authorities (*rtse drung*), an indication of the traditional mistrust of Lhasa towards *bKra shis lhun po*.

The *spyi gso* (many monasteries have two of these officials), the general administrator of the monastery, has the same powers as in the monasteries of the *rNying ma pa* school. He takes care of the goods and of the property (*chos gzhi, dgon gzhi*), in short the economic interests of the monastery in general. The distribution of the provisions needed by the community for their upkeep and for the ritual duties does not however take place directly through this official, but through his assistants and overseers of stores, although the overall control remains in his hands. In the hostels many teaching masters (*dge rgan*) carry out administrative duties.

In the great *dGe lugs pa* monasteries the office of abbot is as a rule entrusted to famous *dge bshes* (in *bKra shis lhun po* they are called *bka' chen*) on account of their spiritual merits and their learning. In these monasteries neither an incarnation (*sprul sku*) nor an ordinary monk (*grwa rkyang*) is called to this high office as a general rule. The qualification of *dge bshes* is however not necessary for other offices such as that of the overseer (*zhal ngo*) in chapel, the *gzim khang pa* or the administrator (*spyi gso ba*). In the less important monasteries, also, the rank of *dge bshes* is not an absolute precondition for elevation to the position of abbot. Appointments to the most important monastic offices are made after nominations by the monastic community, which puts forward after mature deliberation a list of the five or six most worthy candidates. This list of recommended candidates (*chos tho*) is then presented to the central office (*yig tshang*) responsible for the religious hierarchy in the Lhasa government (this office is directed by four high religious dignitaries, *drung yig chen mo*) and finally submitted by the Cabinet (*bKa' gshags*) to the Dalai Lama in person, with whom lies the final decision. The appointment is made by a decree bearing the official seal of the Dalai Lama. Of course this procedure operates only for the most important offices (*las sne*); lesser appointments take place directly through the abbot.

The monastic way of life in Tibet thus rests on spiritual communities containing very large numbers of monks (*grwa pa*). However, not every member of these communities is able to see through the prescribed course of studies to the end. Simpler tasks are required of bearers of lesser monastic grades. Such tasks include maintenance of the monastery buildings, lighting lamps on the altars, in short all the jobs that require no particular learning. These monks, called *ldob ldob*, make up the great majority of the monastic population; they correspond approximately to the lay brothers of the Catholic monasteries. In the monastery of *Se ra* they are recognizable by the long growth of hair on either side of the head. In *bKra shis lhun po* they are called *shar ba*. They are not bound to scrupulously precise observance of monastic duties and perform primarily manual work. In the monastery of *Se ra* they used to form a quite martial kind of monastic militia, which fairly often led to serious disturbances.

Study and training are thus the roots of a deep-penetrating differentiation between learned and unlearned monks. Proportionately it is only a few who are willing to take on such a difficult period of study. They bear the honorific title of 'literati' (*phyag dpe ba*) and, provided that they have the necessary aptitude, they have to study according to those methods which Tibet inherited from India, which involve the mastering of the five main divisions into which the enormous corpus of Buddhist scriptures is divided. These are (1) logic (*tshad ma*); (2) Prajnaparamita (*phar phyin*); (3) Madhyamika (*dbu ma*), the philosophical system of Nagarjuna; (4) Abhidharma (*mngon par mdzod*); (5) Vinaya, discipline (*'dul ba, so sor thar pa*). They form a very demanding curriculum. Understandably, not all of those willing to learn are able to immerse themselves in these studies equally deeply. Many come to a standstill in the middle and renounce a more extensive education. Remember that the entire period of study lasts for from twenty to twenty-five years![10]

If the student has passed the prescribed examination successfully, then two kinds of possibility of advancement are open to him. He can attain the rank of a *dge bshes* of second class (*dge bshes chung*), which is awarded by the college where he studies. Or he can obtain the rank of a *dge bshes* of first class (*dge bshes chen*), a promotion which is made by the government on the recommendation of the appropriate study establishment. The *dge bshes* is now qualified to carry out the most important and most difficult ritual performances (for example as *bsnyen bskur zab rgyas* in the general chapel, the colleges or the hospices). The *dge bshes* of second class can be transferred to the branch establishments of the monastery, where they in their turn can now teach the five branches of study.

The *dge bshes* of first class are divided into two groups *tshog ram(s) pa* and *lha ram(s) pa*.[11] The former are qualified to teach in the various monasteries, to expound the sacred scriptures on the occasion of major festivals (e.g. at the *tshogs mchod*, on the twelfth day of the second month), and to comment upon and to carry out public disputation on the five areas of study.

Some *dge bshes lha ram(s) pa* have the privilege of taking part in the

Figure 13 *sgrub pa'i chas* (items of clothing and equipment used by the lamas on the occasion of great ceremonies and festivities)
(a) and (b) *rgyag zhwa* (head-covering) and *rgyag gos* (clothing) which is worn on festal occasions in processions and on the temple balcony to the sound of the trumpets and the *rgya gling* (cf. Figure 4; among the 'nine signs of good omen'), especially by the monks playing the *rgya gling*.
(c) *dung gos*: 'clothing of the trumpet-player', is worn by the trumpet-players on the occasions mentioned.

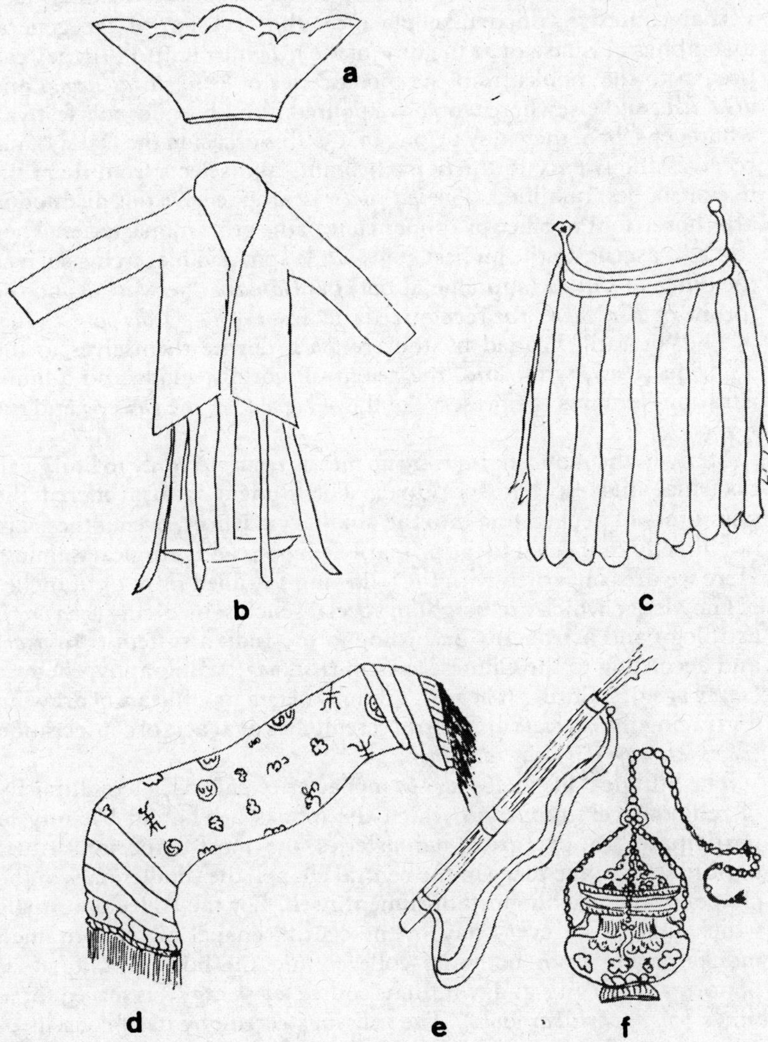

(d) and (f) *spos khebs*, incense-cover, and *spos phor*, incense-carrier. During the processions two monks precede all the others, they wear the *spos khebs*, slung from their right shoulder to their left armpit, and hold the incense-holders for the *bsangs* ceremony (cf.p.199).
(d) and (e). If a great lama is invited, one or two monks walk before him, wearing the 'incense-cover' and holding the *spos dbyug* (e), the 'incense-staff', in their hands. These monks walk behind the *rgya gling* players.

great debates on questions of logic or of themselves leading such verbal contests, which take place on the occasion of the general assemblies in Lhasa or at the time of the *sMon lam* (cf.p.149); they can preach to the monks from the monasteries of *Se ra*, *'Bras spungs* and *dGa' ldan* and elsewhere who have poured into Lhasa for this festival, whatever school they may belong to. On this occasion the Dalai Lama receives the twenty to thirty participants and selects from them the five or six best qualified. The *lha ram(s) pa* who receive this distinction are chosen for the office of abbot in one of the great monasteries. They can also ascend to the highest steps of the spiritual hierarchy, such as the office of *khri pa* (supreme abbot) of *dGa' ldan*, 'he who sits on the throne of *dGa' ldan*', the recognized successor of *Tsong kha pa*.

The 'literati', headed by the *dge bshes*, devote themselves to the doctrine (*chos*), while *srid*, the realm of worldly goods and administration, remains the preserve of the *phyag mdzod*, the *gnyer pa* and the *spyi gso*.

Study in the monasteries is by no means restricted only to liturgical, doctrinal and esoteric scriptures. The student is also offered the possibility of penetrating into the auxiliary sciences, even if these are not directly connected to the primarily religious and liturgical training. Here we are concerned with the following so-called *rig pa* or branches of knowledge which are taught in special schools: medicine (*sman rig*), astrology and astronomy according to the Indian system (*rtsis dkar*) and according to the Chinese system (*rtsis nag*); calligraphy; rhetoric (*snyan ngag*); painting (*lha bris*); grammar (*sgra rig*); the art of drawing for tracing the *mandala* at Tantric ceremonies or at acts of consecration (*dkyil 'khor gyi thig dang rdul tshon*).

The liturgical life in *dGe lugs pa* monasteries unfolds in a multiplicity of religious ceremonies in which the monks are bound by duty to participate. In the great monasteries the most important ritual performances take place in the central chapel, the smaller ones in the chapel of the teaching establishment itself. For the collective rituals which take place every day in the central chapel all the ordained monks gather from both the colleges and the hostels. The ritual performance begins at dawn. In its course tea (*mang ja*) is served three times (*sňga*, *phyi*, *bar gsum*). The religious ceremony itself consists of recitation of the sacred scriptures and of rituals fixed by precise rules. Such morning observances normally take place once daily, twice on festival days.

Apart from this daily liturgical activity, the life in the great *dGe lugs pa* monasteries is ruled by an intensive striving in another direction. The attainment of the longed-for grade of *dge bshes* demands an extremely deep study of the doctrinal writings, especially of the *mNgon rtogs rgyan* (Skt. *Abhisamayalankara*) and the *Lam rim chen mo* of *Tsong kha pa* which is based upon it, and above all of logic (*mtshan nyid*). An essential role in the monk's life is accordingly played by the *chos grwa* reserved for public disputation, a wide open place, often planted with trees, and of an inviting peacefulness, which is guarded by a wall (*lcags ri*) built around it. In the middle of the open space is a place for the throne (*khri*) on which the leader of the disputation takes his place and from where he announces his judgment on the ability and maturity of the participants in the contests. The study period is divided into eight sections, measured differently according to the seasons. Hours of study, of discussion of texts and of disputation alternate with periods of rest (*chos mtshams*).[12] Those who are assiduous in their studies dare not allow themselves any rest even at these times however, for during the rest periods they have to learn by heart those texts they have chosen for special study, they ask question of their teachers (*dge rgan*), and in fact they continue with their usual activity, admittedly with somewhat more freedom than during the ordinary school routine.

The studies in the *chos grwa*[13] begin immediately after the end of the *sMon lam* festival (on the twenty-fifth day of the first month). Debates can normally take place only in the appropriate place described above; only in exceptional circumstances can they be put on in the chapels of the individual teaching establishments, for these are reserved for liturgical performances and religious practice (*nyams len*, *nyam bshes*) while the *chos grwa* is intended specifically for dialectical disputation (*brtag dpyad*). Many of these verbal battles, in which the monks put to the test not only their erudition but also their presence of mind and their subtlety in argument, are of considerable interest. As an example here I will mention only the debating competition which usually takes place in the time between the second and the sixteenth day of the fifth month (*chos mtshams*). The event begins after one monk challenges his companions to disputation on themes which he proposes. To do this he goes to a college other than his own and writes his name there on a wall meant for this purpose. Upon this the contest of oratory begins. In the course of it he is obliged to answer all the questions asked by those of his colleagues and teachers who are present. This duel of oratory, which recalls similar customs in India, is called *rig che* (Great Test of Wisdom). It begins every second day at sunset and lasts without a break until dawn of the following day.

During the great summer period dedicated to the doctrine (*dbyar chos chen mo*), which lasts from the seventeenth day of the fifth month to the fifteenth day of the sixth, the abbots of the various *chos grwa* customarily comment on and interpret the *Lam rim chen mo* of *Tsong kha pa*.

The sixteenth day of the sixth month is a holiday in the *chos grwa*, although some *dge bshes* organize public discussions on questions of religious doctrine before the gate of the central chapel. In this case the debate is transformed into a real popular festival (*dus ston*), at which laymen are encouraged to give gifts to the monastery, and indeed to provide the cost of food for the entire monastic community for four days. On the occasion of this festival the other monks carry out a thorough cleaning of all the sacred utensils and gaily decorate the surroundings of the temple.[14]

The great winter festival of the doctrine (*dgun chos chen mo*, also called *byams smon lam dgun chos* or *bzang spyod chos thog*) takes place from the seventeenth day of the eleventh month to the sixteenth of the twelfth. During this festival four assemblies are summoned each day in the chapels of the individual colleges, where the debates last without a break for two days and two nights. On this festival too laymen compete in generosity to the monastic community.

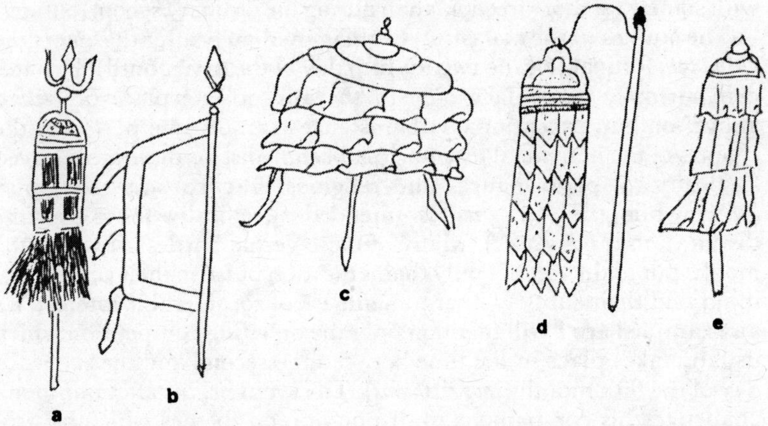

Figure 14 Temple ornamentation and objects carried in processions
(a) *rkya dar*: an object similar in form to the *thug* found on the temple roof. A cylinder made of black wool threads or yak hair, stretched over a central frame or structure, with a trident on top. The whole device is enclosed by vertical and horizontal strips of white cotton.
(b) *dar*: flag of whatever colour, quadrangular or rectangular, with fluttering pennants (*lce*) of indeterminate number.
(c) *gdugs*: parasol, somewhat smaller than the usual parasol.
(d) *phang tshar*: banner (cf. Figure 6).
(e) *rgyal mtshan*: another kind of banner, the top of which resembles a small parasol.
All these objects are used in processions; they belong to lamas invested with high dignity, or are used in special ceremonies (the setting up of a *mandala*, etc.) in which the presence of a great lama is regarded as essential.

As is apparent from the examples given, the activity of monks in the *dGe lugs pa* monasteries extends over two regions. On the one hand there is a liturgical life consecrated by custom, enveloped in ritualism, fixed by tradition, which has many traits in common with that of the other schools, even if it keeps clear of many of the outgrowths of esotericism which prevail there. On the other hand there is the deep doctrinal study, which is however, on account of its difficulty, only for a few chosen ones. Logic and disputation predominate here, and lead to the formally correct posing of a thesis being taken as a guarantee for its truth, and to preference being given to the cold logical architecture of scriptural interpretation over the emotions of inner spirituality.

If in the above account we have stressed primarily the role of doctrine and disputation among the *dGe lugs pa*, this should not give the impression that this tradition neglects Tantric study. The Tantras are, rather, cultivated by special schools, the *sngags khang*, which can only be entered after completion of a preliminary course of teaching (cf.p.137). However, what distinguishes this tradition from others is the smaller number of Tantric texts which they recommend and the stricter selection which they make.

It should be remembered in this connection that *Tsong kha pa* himself wrote not only the treatise called *Lam rim chen mo*, which deals with the non-Tantric teachings, but also the no less famous *sNgags rim* on the Tantras. One of *Tsong kha pa*'s students, *mKhas grub rje*, is known as the writer of one of the most important texts on the Tantric literature and its sub-divisions.

With respect to Tibetan monastic liturgy in general the following still remains to be said. Liturgical life in Tibet has many aspects and equally many formulations. In the works of the Tibetan polymaths ritualistic treatises (*cho ga*) are present in abundance, and particular texts among these have been accepted by the various monasteries. The daily liturgical action, in which the monks are bound to participate, is often an act of spiritual uplift only in theory. In reality it becomes a magical practice, though as such it is to be clearly distinguished from Tantric ritual, to which one cannot deny a higher emotional content. An active and automatically released power is ascribed to the continually repeated words and formulae (often in a more or less deformed Sanskrit incomprehensible to the monks themselves) and to each separate moment of the ritual drama. This power is innate in the liturgical act as such; it is released by it with the same inevitability as, for example, merit is released through the recitation of a sacred text.

In conclusion it should also be noted that the Tibetan monasteries can be divided into the following three groups, *gdan sa*, *gzhis dgon* and *gzhung dgon*. *gdan sa* are the central establishments of a particular school. In Tibet before 1959 these included, for example, *sMin grol gling* and *rDo rje brag* for the *rNying ma pa*; *Se ra*, *dGa' ldan* and *'Bras spungs* for the *dGe lugs pa* (cf.above, p.137); *mTshur phu* and *'Bri gung* for the *bKa' brgyud pa*; *Sa skya* for the *Sa skya pa*; *Rwa sgreng* for the *bKa' gdams pa*. Each of these monasteries has branch monasteries of the same sect attached to it; these are called 'dependencies' (*gzhis dgon* or *dgon lag*). Colleges (*grwa sa*) are found only in the central establishments, where monks are generally divided into 'local' (that is monks born in the neighbourhood of the establishment, who entered it in boyhood) and stranger monks (*byes grwa*). The latter come from the branch monasteries (*gzhis dgon*) to the central establishment in order to spend there the prescribed number of years of study for the completion of their education. During this period the college has to defray the food and lodging of these students. It also happens, however, especially when the monasteries concerned are not to be considered in a strict sense as 'dependencies' of great monasteries, that their monks visit the colleges of other larger monasteries according to old custom.

The branch monasteries (*gzhis dgon*) only contain a limited number of monks in general, and meet their expenses from the produce of their property and from donations from charitable persons. Often the monks support themselves from their private property. In West Tibet and Spiti it is usual for the family to assign a piece of land for this purpose to their son if he is about to enter a monastery. In such cases this property goes on his death to the member of the family with the right to inherit; otherwise it is incorporated in the monastery, except for the personal effects of the deceased.

The *dGe lugs pa* monasteries of *Se ra*, *'Bras spungs* and *dGa' ldan* are generally referred to as 'State Monasteries' (*gzhung dgon*) because, while they possessed their own property, they often received assistance from the State in case of need. This custom, however, was restricted to Central Tibet, as is the corresponding term.

2 Religious calendar and festivals

The daily existence of the monk, unfolding through ritual, study and disputation, is periodically enlivened by religious festivals and ceremonies, whose solemn rituals draw the entire monastery within their power.

Here one should distinguish between the celebration of the calendrical festivals, by the monks responsible for the cultic acts, and the participation of the laity in the festivals. The monks are actors, the laity are spectators, though spectators free to move. It should not be forgotten that, at least in theory, the laymen are always beneficiaries of these religious performances, since the ceremonies generate merit which spreads out over everyone. Through the transference of the result of a good action (Skt. *parinamana*) it brings profit to all. The believers are thereby encouraged to contribute to the fruitful performance of the sacred ceremony through donations and other services, since it is to their own moral advantage.

The Tibetan calendar of festivals goes back in its essentials to the precepts laid down in the Vinaya (full moon, new moon and so on) along with the various celebrations commemorating important events and actions in the life of the Buddha. Buddhist doctrine divides the Buddha's life into twelve 'acts' (*mdzad pa bcu gnyis*), a scheme whose influence is also felt in sacred art. These twelve acts represent a development of a more limited scheme which recognized only eight essential acts in the life of the Sublime One, each of which was celebrated through the erection of a *mchod rten* (Skt. *stupa*) of a particular shape.[15] As is well known, the religious calendar reaches its climax in four of the Buddha's acts: birth, Enlightenment, setting into motion of the Wheel of the Teaching, entry into *nirvana*. All of these four festivals are celebrated on the same day, namely on that on which the attainment of Enlightenment falls. To these principal moments in the life of the Master (*ston pa*) are added the memorial festival of his descent from heaven (to which he had ascended to preach the Law to his mother), and also that of the most famous of the miracles ascribed to the Buddha, that of Sravasti, where he multiplied himself into an infinite row of manifestations while flames streamed from his head and feet alternately. In this way he vanquished the heretics who had challenged him to a magical competition.

The following are the most important days in the Tibetan religious calendar:

First month: tenth to fifteenth days, anniversary of the great miracle of Sravasti, which follows on from the festival of the *sMon lam*, the Great Vow; it is the most important ritual event of the year. One can easily understand how the miracle of Sravasti, the Great Miracle (*cho 'phrul chen mo*), became inserted into the New Year's Festival (*lo gsar*); it recalls the defeat of the heretics, who were opponents not only of the Buddha but also, and above all, of the Law, and thus of the moral and religious order which Buddhism introduced into Tibet. It was a natural step therefore to equate these heretics with the forces of evil, with the world of Mara (Tib. *bdud*), a world which on Tibetan soil had been enriched by numerous new traits that India had not known. This world also included the intransigent forces of the indigenous religion which Buddhism had overcome. The Great Miracle thus became the symbol of the triumph of the *novus ordo* and the overcoming of its enemies.

Fourth month: seventh day, festival of the birth of the Buddha.

Fifteenth day, festival of the Enlightenment and of the entry into *nirvana*.

Sixth month; fourth day, feast of the first sermon.

Ninth month: descent of the Buddha from heaven.

Each of these days or series of days is, like the New Year's Festival, a festival, a 'great time' (*dus chen*).

The preceding enumeration in no way exhausts the religious calendar of Tibet. The fifteenth day of the third month, for example, is sacred to the memory of the preaching of the Kalacakra Tantra, a famous Tantric cycle first revealed at *dPal ldan 'Bras spungs* (Sri Dhanyakataka in East India). In addition, each monastery celebrates the day on which, according to tradition, the particular *rgyud* or Tantra to which the school concerned attributes special importance was revealed.

In the *rNying ma pa* school numerous festivals have important events in the life of *Gu ru rin po che* (Padmasambhava) for their subject. On the tenth day of the first month, his flight from the world, taking of vows, meditation in cemeteries, receiving of the name Santaraksita; tenth day of the second month, taking of vows and receiving the name *Sa kya seng ge*; tenth day of the third month, the occasion when, on being consigned to the flames by the King of Zahor, he changed the holy fire into water, and established himself in meditation on a lotus blossom which blossomed forth in the midst of the lake he had summoned by magic. On this occasion he chose Mandarava as his female companion, and took on the name Padmasambhava. A series of other famous episodes from his life are also commemorated on the tenth day of this month.

Among the *Sa skya pa* monks, the summer ceremony (*dbyar mchod*) takes place from the seventh to fifteenth days of the fourth month. At its centre stand the liturgical formulae sacred to *dPal Kye rdo rje*. On the fourth day of the sixth month the festival of the (sixteen or eighteen) Arhat (Tib. *gnas brtan*) is celebrated, also called *stong mchod chen mo*; at this festival a thousand lamps (*lha bshes*) are kindled. From the twenty-second to the twenty-ninth days of the ninth month the exorcism called *gtor zlog*, sacred to the *mgon po* Mahakala, is performed. This consists of the erection of a great *gto*, of which more will be said below (cf.p.155). On the occasion of this festival the ceremony called the great *ma ni dung sgrub* is also performed. This involves preparing a *mandala* of *sPyan ras gzigs*, at the centre of which is placed a vessel (*bum pa*). A thread comes out of this vessel, and is held in the hands of the monks celebrating the ceremony, who form a circle. The ceremony must last for seven days without the chain of monks ever being broken. If one of them goes off to eat or sleep he is immediately replaced.

The Tibetan liturgy is rich in variations which depend not only on the different ritual forms in the various sects but also on the particular character of the gods or festivals concerned. In addition there is a natural distinction between the general everyday liturgy and the very much more complex liturgy which precedes or accompanies mystical practices. There are however certain common elements, mostly forming a prelude to the sacred action proper, which are present almost without exception: the purification of the place provided, first of all, and then the elimination of all the forces and influences injurious to the performance of the ritual or the sacred condition of the locality.

The ritual performance is prefaced by the solemn pronouncement of the triple formula of refuge (*skyabs 'gro*) 'to the Buddha, to the Doctrine, to the Community'; on this follows the repetition of the vow to strive for Enlightenment, and the contemplation of the four 'immeasurables' (*tshad med bzhi*). The seven parts (*yan lag*) of the ritual follow: (a) act of homage or veneration (*phyag tshal*); (b) offering proper (*mchod pa*, cf.p.116); (c) confession of sins; (d) expression of rejoicing over the good deeds done by living beings and by the Buddhas, which benefit us all (*dge la rjes su yi rang ba*); (e) request to the Buddhas to preach the doctrine; (f) request to the Bodhisattvas to renounce their entry into *nirvana* and to continue their work of salvation in the world further; (g) allowing all living beings to share in the fruits of the ritual. All this is followed by the singing of hymns and the offering of *gtor ma*.

Many festivals result from the adaptation of old local celebrations to the world of Lamaism. Buddhism in Tibet, far from forbidding the festivals in honour of the various *dei loci* (*yul lha*, *sa bdag*, *klu*), has rather impressed its own imprint on the traditional rituals and festivals, which have been allowed to continue and to preserve essential features of their ancient forms. There is scarcely any place in Tibet where these old indigenous forms were not preserved from destruction by admitting them into the festal cycle of the Lamaist calendar. Even in such important festivals as the *sMon lam*, which took place in Lhasa from the fourth to twenty-fifth days of the first month, the ancient festival of the New Year, attested from almost everywhere in Tibet, is still clearly perceptible.

The 'Great Vow', *sMon lam chen mo*, cannot be separated from the exorcistic custom of driving out the evils stored up in the course of the preceding year (*gtor bzlog*). We are concerned here with an extremely complex series of public and private observances which accompany the onset of the New Year. The rituals and festivals concerned occur, with local variations, in all parts of Tibet. This period of time, always regarded as menacing, was celebrated through special cult acts in all areas and schools. In Derge, for example, the introductory ceremonies climaxed in a great liturgical performance (*sgrub chen*) centred upon the deity *dPal Kye rdo rje* and the seven *mandala* of the *Ngor* school.

At the end of the year the festival of good omen (*bkra shis dgu rtsegs*) is celebrated. This festival is intended to close one cycle and introduce a new period of salvation under favourable signs. The festival consists primarily of a musical performance at which the great trumpets and the shawms sound forth. It begins in the night of the thirtieth day of the last month of the year and is constantly repeated until the evening of the fifteenth day of the first month of the new year. The apotropaic character of this custom is evident, and it is equally clear why it lasts unbroken from sunset to dawn for two full weeks; during these nights the powers of evil lurking in the dark are at their most dangerous. In the second half of the last month of the year (on the 16th, 21st, 22nd, 23rd, 25th, 28th and 29th) the rituals of the *Phur bu*[16] cycle also take place, though the liturgical details vary. The feast of the twenty-eighth and twenty-ninth days is called *phur chen*, that of the twenty-first and twenty-second *phur chung*. The former are also called 'Upper action' (*stod las*) and the latter 'Lower action' (*smad las*). While the former festival is essentially positive in nature and is intended to ease the way to Enlightenment (*byang chub sgrub*) for living beings, the latter has the task of chasing away hostile powers (*dgra bgegs bsgral ba*). The climax of the ritual action is the expulsion of the powers of demonic destruction (*gto zor*). On these two occasions impressive ritual dances (*lha 'cham*) are organized, which for many parts of Tibetan society constitute the quintessence of the New Year festival.

Large-scale festal occasions like these are not only an affair of the monks. The functions of these ceremonies (exorcism of evil influences, invoking a better era, calling up good fortune for the year which is beginning) grant them an all-embracing range. The performance of this festival, with its common hopes and common struggle, not only for the welfare of the individual but for the good of the community, integrates the monkhood and the lay world into a social totality. It is not surprising then that this occasion has become a national festival of the whole Tibetan people. Even if the laymen are not called upon to participate directly in the cult, but are merely present as spectators, their presence underlines the participation of all in the central impulse of the monastic community. The layman bears an active joint responsibility for the efficacy of the rituals; he makes his contribution to the process of accumulation of good and wholesome powers, among other things by taking part in the ritual circumambulation of the sacred buildings, which also include the monastery press. Through such religious acts he pays homage to the word of the Buddha, the verbal body of the Buddha, and collects merit not only for his personal salvation, but also for the collectivity whose future welfare the communal ritual ensures.

The transition from one year to another represents a critical moment for the entire country, and thus requires, to balance this moment of danger, the common exertion of all positive forces so that the passage will turn out fortunately. One can hardly be surprised if on this occasion ancient indigenous customs of exorcism of harmful spirits come to the surface again and are reflected in the liturgy which Lamaism has adopted, even becoming tied up closely with the ethics of Buddhism. Thus it now becomes a question not merely of repulsing the adversaries which are threatening but also of an active performance aimed at accumulating good karma. The good karma arises from the co-operation between the monks performing the ritual ceremonies and the laymen giving their material support through donations and charity. Thus the karmic content of the festival does not remain isolated; it benefits all, and provides the ethical counterpart of an efficacious defence against evil, the result of a symbiosis between old and new, between the original religiosity of Tibet and the moral doctrine of buddhism.

Given this context, one can understand how it came about that the *sMon lam* celebration[17] introduced by *Tsong kha pa* was inserted into the total picture of the ceremonies described above. The *sMon lam* results from the incorporation of archaic rites of passage on the occasion of the change of year, which are found everywhere in Tibet, into Lamaist ritual, in this case through the mediation of the *dGe lugs pa* school. The *dGe lugs pa* also perform exorcistic rituals (*gtor bzlog*), but they have given the festival a more monastic character, along with the appropriate symbolism, without being able by this means to prevent the people from continuing to preserve their old customs in this new dress. The symbolism which has been grafted on to the old custom is in any case not understood by all. Given the existence of a ritual form regarded as indispensable for the common good and for future security, the old tradition had to be carried on, if in new clothing.

The overlaying of the old New Year festival by the *sMon lam* celebration emerges very clearly from the fact that the festival is now equated with the anniversary of the victory over evil and heresy in the miracle of Sravasti (cf.p.147). This struggle and victory over the forces of evil forms the principal theme too of the *lha 'cham* dances organized at the end of the year among all schools. It is true, however, that the spontaneous, popular character of the New Year festival is encumbered to some degree by the symbolism which serves to admit it within the doctrinal structure of the *dGe lugs pa* reforms.

In this context the *sMon lam* vow has (at least in theory) not only the task of ensuring the coming of a prosperous year. The *dGe lugs pa* have given it an additional, more secret meaning. The community is situated in a period of general decline, in which evil grows and the doctrine preached by Sakyamuni is becoming obscured. It thus becomes necessary to overcome or at least to lessen the evident marks of this period of time, plagues, war and famine, and above all to help the saving activity of the next Buddha, *Byams pa* (Skt. Maitreya) by preparing for his coming. The symbolism behind these ideas carries over into the liturgical and practical aspects: the government distributes medicinal plants (*sman*) to the monks as an antidote against illnesses, pieces of silk cloth (*dar 'jam*) for defence against the danger of weapons, and foods, meat, soup, money and so on against the threat of famine.

The liturgy is determined in all its separate sections by the doctrine. For example, the ritual circumambulation of the temple of *Byams pa* has the symbolic meaning that the new age of the doctrine, the descent of the divine word, is already an accomplished fact. Even the exorcism (*gtor bzlog*), which the *dGe lugs pa* too practise, here undergoes a transformation taking it far from its original sense. Having entered Buddhism from the indigenous tradition, it takes on speculative subtleties in this context, for example in the idea that non-knowing (*ma rig*), the origin of moral defilement (*nyon mongs*), and therefore also of the corresponding karma, is inborn in myself and all others and must therefore be burned up in the fire of transcendent consciousness (*ye shes kyi me*). The image which is at the centre of this ceremony is therefore intended to take non-knowing onto itself and is to be burned up in the fire of wisdom, which is represented in this way. In order not to depart too far from the usual concepts through such interpretation, the opponents of the religion and the country, the demonic powers, are also conceived of as conjured into this image (called *ling ga*). Through the ritual action they are overcome or killed, after their conscious principle (*rnam par shes*) has been driven away onto the plane of infinite spiritual existentiality (*chos dbyings*).[18]

All along the line a new interpretation of the traditional rituals has been undertaken under *dGe lugs pa* auspices. Instead of awaiting the New Year, it is the *annus magnus* whose coming is awaited; the short space of twelve months thus becomes a section of a chain stretching on into infinity, and thus bringing good fortune and blessings, worthy of the renewal of the doctrine, of the coming of the realm of Maitreya, whose epiphany will take place after the conclusion of the progressive decline of the present cosmic period.

Along with the *sMon lam* ceremonies there used to take place another New Year custom, analogues for which can be found in many other cultures. This is the temporary overturning of the social order such that power is placed for a short (or sometimes for a longer period) in other hands. On this occasion a monk from the community was chosen to be city magistrate of Lhasa. During the *sMon lam* festival he supervised the monasteries and also the city government, he inflicted fines and other punishments. A similar custom existed in Derge (where the monk chosen was not called *zhal ngo* as in Lhasa but *'du ba'i gsol dpon chen mo*).

One should always remember that in the exorcism (*gtor bzlog*) a positive act of driving out the evil is taking place in which the society must take part with all its energy. At this critical moment of transition from past to future the fighting spirit of all of society and of each individual must be called forth to the utmost possible degree. The participants in the sacred dances brandish weapons in their hands; horse races, archery competitions and athletic games complete the picture of the festival. This is certainly a question of very ancient, doubtless pre-Buddhist, traditions, in which an agonistic and military character predominates. The festival is celebrated at a time when war and hunting begin again. The competitions described are thus rooted in tradition to such a degree that they still today play a role of the first rank in the New Year festivities. This is especially true of the horse races which have represented one of the best-loved attractions of this festival since the most ancient times. With the easy excitability of spirits and the lowered discipline, however, these competitions do not pass off without some danger. According to the narrative of the *Pad ma thang yig* (No.3 pp.406f.), it was during these very horse races at the New Year's Festival that King *Khri srong lde brtsan* was killed by an arrow, after his ministers had forced him to ignore Padmasabhava's advice to abolish the old custom.

Faced by the uncertainty of the coming year, man chooses not to abdicate but to oppose his utmost power. The agonistic element thus becomes a decisive factor of this festival; it is reflected in the military ceremonies, in the gestures of the dances and so on. The Lamaist adoption of ancient customs is apparent in many of the New Year customs which were practised in Derge. At these festivals the usual rivalries between the sects were also temporarily attenuated. *Sa skya pa* and *rNying ma pa* share together in the ceremonies (the *drug cu*[19] or *tshogs rab* festival) from the twenty-third to twenty-ninth of the twelfth month, which form a rite of preparation for the *gto* on the twenty-ninth day of this month, a ceremony of evocation and propitiation of *dPal rDo rje 'jigs byed* according to the *Sa skya pa* method.

The *gto*, along with its meaning and significance, has been discussed already, and it will be returned to again later (cf.p.177). Here we will draw attention to the competitive games of all kinds, essentially similar to those described above, which are arranged at these festivals.

Lamaism could not remove these customs, which were difficult to uproot. On the occasion of these festivals martial games take place even in the course of the religious ceremonies. On the morning of the twenty-third, the first stroke of the powerful drum resounded from the balcony of the second storey of the temple, directly above the entrance gates. With loud shouts, and clearing their way with hands and feet, the monks gathered at the two gates to the right and left of the great temple, which had previously been closed by the two ministers (*blon po*) of the King of Derge. At the second stroke of the drum the two doors were pushed open by the officials mentioned, and the whole crowd of monks rushed out together riotously, as if completely beyond control, to crowd together again before the main gate of the temple. On its two wings were situated high up two metal fittings, on each of which a metal ring hung with a multicoloured silk scarf knotted on to it in such a way that the rings turned upwards. On the second drumstroke the monks rushed forward with their usual violence into a thick heap before the door. The competition which now began consisted in trying to be the first to put the metal ring back into its normal position, so that the scarves now hung from the lower half rather than the upper. Only the occupants of the monastery were admitted to these competitions, and not the guests who had streamed into Derge from other monasteries for the festival.

On the third drumstroke the great gate opened, and the tumultuous crowd moved into the inside of the temple. Each monk tried to be the first to reach the sitting-places situated right and left of the two principal pillars. There was a legend connected with these pillars. No one had been able to succeed in transporting them from the forest to the place where the temple was being built. One day, however, they were found already in their place, a deed of the *deus loci* (*gzhi bdag*) of Derge, *'Bri gnyan gdong*. He who succeeded in taking his place on the seats in front of these pillars, to the right and left of the throne (*chos khrims khri*) reserved for the King of Derge, received from the government a *mdzo* (a cow-yak hybrid) and a leopard skin. These pillars were therefore called *mdzo ka*, '*mdzo* pillars'. The taking of these seats was thus bound up with a competitive struggle which quite often developed into a real tumult (according to Professor Namkhai Norbu, to whom I owe these particulars). As soon as the King of Derge, his ministers and all the heads of the monasteries sat down on their thrones, and the king gave a signal with his hand, silence was established and the great gathering for the cult act began. Thus a popular element from the realm of the New Year festivities, in the form of the competitions, has crystallized about a purely liturgical cult ceremony belonging to a particular Tantric cycle.

While this festival was taking place from the twenty-third to the twenty-ninth in the *Sa skya pa* temple, the *rNying ma pa* sect simultaneously celebrated its rituals consecrated to *'Jam dpal tshe bdag* in other monasteries. Both liturgies pursued the same goal, to eliminate hindrances (*bar chad*), causes and occasions of misfortune (*rkyen ngan*) so as to assure good fortune in the coming year. This meaning emerges even more clearly from the festival which was celebrated on the twenty-ninth day of the same month. On this day the exorcism (*gto*) already mentioned of the *drug cu chen mo* (cf.p.153) was performed together by *Sa skya pa* and *rNying ma pa* monks. The *Sa skya pa* who streamed here from the principal monasteries and their branches went by in procession. Then the *rDo rje 'jigs byed* dance took place, after which the great offering (*gtor ma*) was brought to the bank of the *gTang chu*. Subsequently *Sa skya pa* and *rNying ma pa* gathered in the *Tshe bdag lha khang* and led the *gto chen* (cf.p.180) of the *Tshe bdag* on to the dancing place. The dance lasted the entire day till sunset. More than a hundred monks dressed as deer[20] took part in it, along with a further hundred in the dress of black women (the so-called *nag ga ma*). As evening fell, the great *gto* was led to the bank of the *gTang chu*, where the *Sa skya pa* had prepared the offerings (*gtor ma*). On the way the *gto chen* was turned towards a little valley (*Ngul chu*), then towards a rock (*rdo pha wang*). This custom rested on the idea that the power active in the *gto* had the ability to avert harm caused by water and mountains. Then the *gto* was brought to the bank of the *gTang chu* and a representation of the *ling ga*, drawn on a piece of paper, was proffered towards it. During these processes about three hundred richly dressed and ornamented men fired ancient muskets with gigantic barrels and fearful detonation.

The New Year celebrations, which are tied into the religious calendar, and on which the participation of the monastic communities confers a particular solemnity, are to be distinguished fundamentally from the primarily secular and popular festivals such as that of the harvest time. More will be said about these in the chapter on Tibetan folk religion. The New Year's Festival and the Harvest Festival apparently attest through their juxtaposition the coexistence of two calendrical systems of different origin. In the older calendar, that of the *lo gsar* (New Year) an echo of a society based essentially on hunting is still perceptible. At the first thaw the mountain paths became usable, the animals come out of their hiding places, every human activity becomes less restricted, and hunting and war begin again. Thus military dances, competitions, martial games and so on announce the new phase in the rhythm of communal life.

The feasts for the end of the harvest stand in another kind of cultural context. With the harvest a period of grace in the community's activity comes to an end and a new cycle of work, that of ploughing and sowing, begins. The type of ritual bound up with this is of a different kind, because determined by different religious and cultural premises. In reality the dividing line has become blurred in the course of time; the two modes of being standing alongside each other have affected each other, and reciprocal influence has become the rule. A unifying sacred order has been constituted and the inevitable fusion of elements of different cultural and social provenance brought about. Nevertheless the presence of two calendrical systems of different origins can still be clearly seen. The New Year, having become official through its adoption by the monastic community, is bound up very closely with the sacred regulation of the monastic life. The Harvest Festival is beyond such control, it is a form of expression of the agrarian life of the community, in which the banishing of hostile spirits by the village magician plays a more important role than the direct involvement of the monastery.

3 The hermits' way of life

Tibetan monks do not only live in monasteries. Apart from the monks in the monasteries, there are first of all the wandering lamas to be considered, whom it is true often merge into the class of exorcists (*sngags pa*). They offer their services wherever the formulae and arts which they consider to be their unique property are in demand. Another group of monks is that of the hermits (*ri khrod pa*). Monks of all schools practise temporary seclusion in hermitages intended for this purpose or in rocky caves more or less apart from their monasteries. Such seclusion is not restricted to those who have devoted themselves to a life of contemplation and to yogic exercises; it is also resorted to by those who wish to meditate or to write in solitude. In Tibet there were whole towns of hermitages which were attached to particular monasteries. Here we will mention out of many only the *Yer pa*, the hermitages in the neighbourhood of Gyantse, where each monk spent his life in his own narrow cell. The confinement can take on very severe and harsh forms, notably in the *bKa' brgyud pa* and *rNying ma pa* sects. In these cases it is no longer a question of temporary seclusion, but of complete withdrawal from the world, of the breaking off of all relations with mankind. Occasionally this hermit life recalls certain details of the Egyptian monasticism so exhaustively studied by Festugière (1965), so that perhaps the question of the origin of certain aspects of these penitential practices, for which parallels scarcely exist in India, should be raised again. In any case the confinement, which is chosen freely, is fully entered upon only after exhaustive preparation and the use of special liturgical formulae. The flight from the world is dominated here by the desire to participate in special mystic revelations through the aid of appropriate yogic techniques. The ascetic (*rnal 'byor pa*) must therefore first undertake the prescribed initiation under his master's direction. After this the 'four hundred-thousands' are recited among the *bKa' brgyud pa* or the 'five hundred-thousands' (*'bum ther*) among the *rNying ma pa*. This refers to the obligation to perform a hundred-thousandfold recitation of the refuge formula (*skyabs 'gro*; refuge in the Buddha, the Law and the Community), a hundred-thousandfold drawing of the *mandala*, a hundred-thousand prostrations (*rkyang phyag*, complete prostrations in which the forehead touches the ground, corresponding to the Sanskrit *astanga-pranama*) and a hundred-thousand recitations of the mantra formula of *rDo rje sems dpa'*.

This fourfold propaedeutic is extended among the *rNying ma pa* by a meditation to be repeated a hundred-thousand times by the candidates. These preparatory acts take place either in the hermitage (*ri khrod*) itself or in the colleges for yogic practice (*sgrub grwa*) which were mentioned above (cf.p.114). There the beginning hermit awaits after his vows the sacred assent of the guardian deity (*yi dam*) appropriate to his goal, namely *dPal 'Khor lo bde mchog*. Then in an isolated place, not far from a hermitage or small monastery apart from the world (*chos sgar*), he builds himself an earthen hut (*'dam sbyar*), or else he may seek refuge in a cave in the rocks (*brag phug*) large enough for him to walk, lie down and sit, and with a latrine in one corner. The cell is then completely closed, except for a small opening through which the attendant (*sgrub g.yog*) assigned to him passes him food and water once a day, at midday, without being allowed to speak a word. The food is passed to him by means of a kind of revolving basket of food which fits exactly into the opening, so that the servant cannot see the meditator's hand. If no answer comes from inside the cell for three days, this indicates the hermit's illness or death. Then the lama in charge is summoned. This lama is also present at the closing of the cell, which is accomplished by a special ceremony to banish any possible interference (*bar chad sel ba*). Then two to four heaps of stones (*mtshams tho*) are rolled before the entrance, and ritual gifts (*gtor ma*) offered for the *chos skyong*, and *rgyal chen*[21] and especially for the *deus loci* (*gnas bdag*).[22] Also the magical formula *hum* is written in ink on a wooden tablet and this is fixed in front of the opening of the cell.

The period of confinement usually lasts seven years, but it is at least for five. In case of illness the lama in charge of the hermitage can be summoned in order to banish the causes of harm (*rkyen sel*).

Concerning the *rNying ma pa* we have yet to add that the hermits of this school have themselves enclosed in cells or caves into which not even the smallest ray of light can enter. Such caves for hermits are called 'dark retreats' (*mun mtshams*). Their occupants perform a special type of yoga which equates the mind (*sems*) with light (*'od gsal*), and which we have already alluded to in Chapter 4. They hope that through this practice the inner light will break forth from the mind which is of the same nature as it and illuminate everything with its shining radiance. Some ascetics go so far as to let themselves be walled up without food or drink; to their spiritual faith the 'essence' of water (*chu'i bcud*) or the 'essence' of a stone called *cong zhi* will provide sufficient nourishment.

4 The property of the monastery and its administration

As already mentioned (cf.p.137) the property (*spyi*) of the monastery is of four kinds: landed property, herds of large and small livestock, trading goods, interest on loans.

The landed property (*gzhis ka*, *chos zhing*) results in part from repeated donations, in part from the incorporation of the lands of other monasteries as a consequence of the frequent disputes, and in part from new investments. Its administration is in charge of the *spyi pa*, in other words the official responsible for the common property (*spyi*). With regard to the administration of great monasteries such as *Se ra, dGa 'ldan* and so on, applicants for the office of *spyi pa* apply to the government with an appropriate request, as a consequence of which the office is generally bestowed by the state on a particular official. There are two types of administration. In the first the *spyi pa* transfers the usufruct (*bog ma*) of specified parts of the communal property to particular families, who are called *bog bdag*. The fields are then cultivated by the monastery peasants (*mi ser*), who instead of remuneration receive a piece of land (*'tsho rten*) serving for their support, and as monastery employees need to pay no taxes. The leaseholder (*bog bdag*) has to deliver a part of the harvest to the *spyi pa* according to a previous agreement, and to pay the taxes to the government. Arrangements of this kind usually turned out to be very lucrative, and nearly all *bog bdag* belonged to the aristocracy. The other procedure is the following: the *spyi pa* delegates a representative (*sku tshab*) for the monastery domains, who is charged with the overseeing of the harvest work and the supervision of the peasants. The produce of the harvest is then delivered to the *spyi pa*. In both cases there is a substantial profit-margin.

Besides their lands, the monasteries possess considerable numbers of livestock, yak, *mdzo*, sheep, goats, which are looked after by herdsmen (*'brog pa*). The most important aspect here is the monastery's production of butter. Butter (*mar*) on the one hand serves for nutritive purposes, and on the other hand is used extensively in the liturgy (in particular for lamps, *mar me*, *chos me*). During the so-called 'butter-harvest' (*she sdud pa*) an agent of the *spyi pa* makes the rounds of the monastery property to collect the butter and to determine the number of animals born in the course of the year. On this occasion it is the normal practice to give the *spyi pa*'s agent five measures (*khal*) of butter for every *mdzo* or yak. There are two procedures used for the sheep and goats. In one case the births and deaths that have taken place in the herd are counted, and the living animals evaluated at three measures (*khal*), the dead at one measure. Verification of the number of animals which have died is made on the basis of their horns and skins, which the herdsmen have to show to the *spyi pa*'s agents. The other system of counting does not include the new-born animals in the reckoning and is therefore called *skye med*, 'without the born'. If the animals have died, the agreed quantity of butter still has to be delivered; if, however, the herd has increased the producer only needs to keep to the amount agreed, and he can deliver a smaller quantity of butter than that corresponding to his actual production.

Another source of revenue for the monastery is trade (*tshong*), primarily the buying and selling of goods from China and India, apart from barter transactions with the herdsmen (*'brog pa*). These barter exchanges are called 'buy in summer, sell in winter (or spring)'. Because of the herdsmen's pressing need in summer for barley, wheat and other products, the *spyi pa* advance all their needs to them at this period according to their agreement. When the *'brog pa* descend from their hills in the autumn or winter to trade in the markets, they first of all have to reimburse the *spyi pa*, in butter, wool, skins and so on, the value of the provisions advanced in summer. The result of this system was that the warehouses of the *spyi pa* (*spyi khang*) in the bigger cities, especially in Lhasa, were better supplied than other shops.

Loans to private individuals also represent a not inconsiderable source of revenue for the monks. These loans mostly work according to the rule of thumb 'out of four make five', in other words the interest consists of a quarter of the loan.

Not to be forgotten, finally, are the special revenues: endowments and pious gifts of believers made on the most varied occasions, as well as the gifts which the government makes, particularly to the monasteries of the Yellow Sect (the *dGe lugs pa*), for example at each new issue of coinage (*dngul lo*).

In many regions of Tibet those monks who come from the class of small landed proprietors have a dwelling belonging to their family within the monastery. In such areas one member of the family always takes up the monastic career. Such a monk can look after his own upkeep, since his family has a piece of land always set aside for this purpose, which guarantees his economic independence. In theory, however, all the private property of the monks belongs to the monastery. When the monk dies he is not able to appoint members of his family as heirs, though this does not mean that his relations cannot be provided during his life to a greater or lesser degree with an allowance from his property. In accordance with his last wishes, his property can be inherited by his favourite disciple (*sras*, spiritual son), whom he has usually chosen when the disciple was still young, in the first place to serve as his attendant. In any case the question of property is met by a peculiar piece of casuistry: private property is tolerated because it enables the monk to share in the expenses of the monastic community for his upkeep, clothes and so on, and in addition his personal means allow him to take over on his own account the hospitality provided by the monastery on occasion, at least as far as his own visitors are concerned. The monastery has no right to claim back from a monk a loan that he has made to another person, nor can it reclaim gifts to his family or to those who look after him when he is ill. Nor has the monastery any control over objects belonging to the monk which he has placed in someone else's house.

Each monastery forms a self-existent economic entity (*dgon gzhung*). All the property which it has come to possess by inheritance or any other means belongs fully and entirely to the monastic community living in it, as do donations made for the benefit of the entire community with the exception of special gifts to individual monks on the occasion of special ritual presentation (*sku 'gyed*). The great monasteries have attached to them small daughter-monasteries (*dgon lag*) of the same sect, which almost always have control over their own property, which supports their own existence. Their inmates are bound to spend a certain period of training in the mother monastery.

It can be seen that monastic life in Tibet deviates more than a little from that of the great monastic communities which once existed in India. While we are poorly informed about their organization at the time of Buddhism's adoption in Tibet, the monastic organization nevertheless, thanks to its central role in the country's life, had to take up new tasks and functions during its progressive development to its eventual gigantic proportions. This process had already begun in the time of *Khri srong lde brtsan*; when the first monastic communities, founded at that time, possessed not only special rights and freedom from taxation, but also landed property and serfs for the upkeep of the monks and as a material foundation for the ritual life they cultivated. This already gave the monastery a position independent of the lay authorities, an occasion, as we have already discussed in another section of our account (cf.p.12), for violent differences between the aristocracy and the church authorities. During the renewal of

Buddhism during its second diffusion in Tibet, and through the growth of the great monasteries (*Sa skya*, *'Bri gung*, *Tshal*, *mTshur phu* and so on) the pre-eminence of the church authorities was ever more clearly displayed. This led to the consolidation of monastic feudalism through a kind of symbiosis between a religious 'chief' and his lay patron, who was responsible for the protection of the monastery and became its 'secular arm'. A division of labour developed between the purely religious and spiritual functions of the abbot or incarnate (*sprul sku*) on the one hand and the duties of the administration on the other.

The union of political and economic power achieved in the monasteries inevitably led to the public authorities taking on a theocratic character. The Yellow Sect (*dGe lugs pa*), from the time of the Fifth Dalai Lama onwards, only brought to its conclusion a process whose foundations had already been laid further back. This evolution was the work of numerous factors, including not only the great economic power of the monasteries, through which they brought under their control in many ways the most important sources of revenue in the country, but also their undeniable aptitude for satisfying appropriately the religious desires of the Tibetan people. The monastery rapidly became the central point of the entire life of the part of the country concerned, providing the region's economy with an outlet. Above all, however, the monastic community with its church liturgy assured spiritual assistance to the laity. The monks, through knowing how to present the beneficial results of gifts given to the community in the right light with respect to the donor's whole future salvation, succeeded not only in increasing the monastic revenue but also in infusing into the multitude a feeling of confidence concerning the fate of each individual. In each situation of life, in birth, illness and death, and at harvest time, the monk was present, and always and everywhere he made the most of the basically magical outlook native to the Tibetans. Every act and achievement of the believers, in short, was under supervision of the monks, and they sought their salvation only through the monks and their ritual. Besides, Lamaism took under its protection those festivals and local rites which since time immemorial had served to banish or render favourable the spirits and demons of the depths, although it made a point of clothing the old myths and rites in Buddhist dress. In this, Lamaism took account of the Tibetan's characteristic inclination towards the spectacular; thus the monks promoted the growth of a kind of folk theatre which was certainly founded upon Indian models diffused by Buddhism, but progressively took on an individual character accessible even to the multitude. While these spectacles, through their visible character, awoke religious feelings in the spectator, at the same time they reinforced the masses' confident faith in the Buddhist doctrine of salvation and in its priests.

The sacred dances associated with these spectacles contained a guarantee of the victory of good over evil, of the coming of an age of general prosperty, of the banishing of demonic powers.

Obviously this development still contained seeds that could have dangerous consequences. The individual monasteries, as strictly organized and economically strong structures, were as little inclined as the lay aristocracy had been to renounce their self-government and independence. This promoted the continual tendency to splitting up which gradually smouldered under the unitary veneer of official faith, all the more so as the majority of the monks were scarcely able to master studies only accessible to a limited élite, and thus provided an easily swayed monastic proletariat always ready to take action on suitable occasions.

We will pass over here well-known occurrences such as the active interference of the great monasteries in the political intrigues at the time of the Sixth and Eighth Dalai Lamas, and recall only certain later events after the death of the Thirteenth Dalai Lama in 1933. The great monastery of *Se ra* intervened forcibly at that time with its monk-soldiers in the troubles which lasted in Lhasa throughout the regency of the Taktra Rimpoche. The monasteries thus formed, up to the time of Tibet's absorption into the realm of Chinese domination, an obstacle to the striving for unity attempted by each central government. The Thirteenth Dalai Lama attempted to restrict the power of the monasteries in various ways, but he was hindered in these efforts through the circumstance that he himself was only an exponent of the monastic life, to which he remained bound for better or for worse. On the other hand the great power of the monasteries was a constant source of discontent among the lay aristocracy, who saw themselves hampered at every step in their efforts and claims at domination by the monastic communities, and were never able to summon up the power to shake off this yoke.

SIX

THE FOLK RELIGION

1 General characteristics

In the preceding chapters it was emphasized that the development of Lamaism was significantly influenced by the nature of religious life in Tibet before the spread of Buddhism. This religious life was made up of, on the one hand, doctrines and cults introduced from India and other countries (discussed in the next chapter), and, on the other hand, a true 'folk religion'. The beliefs, myths and customs of this folk religion are widely known and followed among the ordinary people (*'jig rten pa*). They govern the daily life of the Tibetan, and determine his behaviour with respect to the supernatural powers which surround him.

This 'folk religion' has flourished alongside the teachings and liturgy which are the special province of the monks and which are passed on in the various religious schools; everywhere among the Tibetans one can perceive in the beliefs of the people the survival of the multifarious and all-encompassing pre-Buddhist beliefs of the land of snow. Besides, the observation that every new religion seeks to incorporate within itself the totality of beliefs which it finds already in existence is as true here as elsewhere. In Tibet the situation was particularly favourable for the admission of indigenous religious elements, because there were remarkable analogies between the local traditions and the world of Tantrism, and both were governed by a similar psychological atmosphere. Already in India Mahayana and Vajrayana Buddhism had willingly accepted the heritage of folk religion. It is enough in this connection to recall scriptures such as the *Mahamayuri* and other tendencies common in many places, e.g. in Uddiyana (Swat), or in Bengal, where an important part of the Tantric scriptures was written down. One can also think of certain doctrinal formulation such as the inclusion of folk deities (*'jig rten pa*) in Tantric 'families' and so on. This theme became once again in Tibet the object of heated debates, because the problem of the compatibility of the indigenous *numina* and *dii minores* with the deities of

Buddhist theology necessarily intruded upon the realms of theological debate. In the course of time it was decided to consider as 'gods of the everyday world' (*'jig rten pa*) those governed in only a vague and fitful way by the thought of 'Enlightenment'. These included the local gods of mountains and rocks, *'dre*, *srin*, *btsan* and so on. These were now to be explained as 'protectors' and 'defenders' of the Buddhist Law, since they had obeyed the command of great teachers such as Padmasambhava and let themselves be converted by them. They possess supernatural power, they are capable of working miracles, but not without restriction, nor exclusively in the service of salvation; if they are offended in some manner or are discontented, their violent nature wins the upper hand. Many of these *'jig rten pa* gods are, however, basically benevolent in disposition and ready to fight against evil powers. It was in this way, for example, that *gNyan chen thang lha*, one of the most widespread and popular of the divine figures of the pre-Buddhist period, became a Bodhisattva, and it was similarly that the planet Rahu became, according to some authorities, a Bodhisattva of the tenth 'earth'. The field of action of these gods is confined to the various basic magical operations of pacifying, bringing good fortune, increasing the possibilities of good karma, and destroying evil powers; to participate in bringing about the highest goal, that of salvation, is not allowed to them. This task is reserved to the supramundane gods (*'jig rten las 'das pa*). The Buddha himself expressly recommended that one should not have too much to do with the worldly deities. These lower gods are given auxiliary functions of a very subordinate kind. In connection with the *mandala* for example they act as guardians of the 'doors', and so stand at the edge of the specifically initiatory sphere. According to certain doctrinal writings these deities are no more than emanations of the god (*gtso bo*) to whom the *mandala* is dedicated, manifestations which he has freely taken on for the defence of believers. This question became in the course of time the subject of endless discussions, in these debates it was also suggested that many 'mundane' gods had the power to become 'supramundane' through spiritual purification, while others must remain irredeemably evil.

Theologians speculated upon why such evil *numina* should exist; they were not the result of some kind of 'black' creation opposed to the 'white' or good but arose exclusively from the karma of the divine beings themselves. Because of their bad actions they became *'dre* (No. 52, cf. No. 74, p.1), their mind is 'contaminated' (*sems la gdon sems*), in addition some of them have not kept the vow which they made to protect and defend Buddhism (*dam tshig nyams pa*, No. 74, p.2). Such examples make it clear that Lamaism in its folk aspect is a complex product of elements of very varied origin, age and content, containing both prehistoric traditions and more recent influences. It is in this way that the religious life of the Tibetan has acquired its extraordinary richness of forms.

To come to a just evaluation of the specific nature of Tibetan folk religion one needs to apply the concept 'folk religion' in a perhaps rather wide sense. The Buddhism understood and practised by the educated monk must of course have certain basic traits resulting from his monastic life and his function within the social structure. By contrast the Buddhism of the layman appears in forms which are substantially different, freer and above all simpler. Whether the light of the Law shines more or less brightly in the spirit of the layman, he is still, through the simple fact of existing outside monastic life, released from over-strict rules. In general it can be asserted that the religious practice of the layman is still strongly under the influence of the pre-Buddhist and folk heritage. He is familiar from his childhood with the epic deeds and marvellous happenings with which the literature and traditions deriving from this heritage are filled. The particular kind of religious feeling which gives life to them regulates all the relationships between the Tibetan people and the immense, uncertain world of the demonic and the divine. The *numina* who reside there assist him in his difficulties, they stand by his side in his incessant struggle to defend himself against obstacles and dangers, open and secret adversaries, who everywhere threaten his existence, his well-being, his property. Often enough, however, it is precisely these numinous powers who are at the root of his misfortune.

The life of the Tibetan is, as it were, enclosed in a world of multifarious divine manifestation, in which all appearances are suffused with religious significance. The numinous powers accomplish their inexhaustible epiphany, so to say, in classifiable groups and sub-groups. The Tibetan is free to respond to the invisible, but nevertheless unquestionable, presence of the powers in his own individual way and according to his personal inspiration. Monastic Lamaism rarely opposed the hardy, cleverly contrived fusion which took place between indigenous religious customs and the magical and religious concepts and experiences introduced into Tibet through the Vajrayana scriptures. Naturally the layman holds to the old heritage more tenaciously than the monk and tries to preserve it more faithfully.

But if Lamaism allowed the *numina* of the indigenous religion to continue to exist, it went to some trouble to adapt their invocations and festivities to its own ritual world. Even the *dGe lugs pa* order did not blush at accepting Cinggis Khan among their *chos skyong*,[1] when they set about sending missions among the Mongols, although in general they gave in to this tendency less willingly than the other schools. Many indigenous deities found entry into the Lamaistic pantheon through the simple pronunciation of the word *rdo rje*, diamond, (a word which, as indicated previously, enshrines a profound symbolism), or through the granting of new names to the deities which corresponded better to Tantric terminology. Thus the twelve terrible *brtan ma* (or *bstan ma*) goddesses kept their original names as 'secret names' but their new liturgical names were transformed in accordance with the new requirements. *Rong gi Jo mo kha rag*, for example, the deity of the mountain between *dBus* and *gTsang*, became *rDo rje dpal gyi yum* (Nebesky-Wojkowitz, 1956, p.183). However, the majority of the *numina* kept their old names.

Faced with the exuberant profusion of the pre-Buddhist mythological world, of its pantheon and its numerous local manifestations, a need for orientation became operative. In part use was made of the old divisions, in part new ones were devised. So there came to exist different lists of the *sa bdag* in which one finds the most important *genii loci* along with others which vary considerably according to the places of origin of the list, long lists of *dgra lha*, *dregs*, *bstan ma* or *gnyan*, and so on. None of the local communities was ready to renounce its old protective gods. Even the *srung ma* and *chos skyong* of particular monasteries are quite often local *numina* converted through various miracles to Buddhism. Admitted into the new religion as guardians of the Law, they now punish each violation of the Law or transgression of the Buddhist vow. However, even in such retributive functions their old demonic violence breaks out anew; in their duty as *defensores fidei* they know no forgiveness, they can be carried away by their inborn brutality, and reveal themselves as implacable avengers of evils committed. The demonic powers of this type appear in groups: *'bar ba spun bdun*, 'the seven *'bar ba* brothers', *phyugs lha spun bdun*, 'gods of the flocks, the seven brothers', *ma mo mched dgu*, 'the nine *ma mo* sisters'. Many of them live in a copper castle or in a lake of blood, or drink blood (*khrag thung*). *Yam shud dmar* feeds on the flesh of men and horses; assimilated to *Tshi'u dmar*, chief of the *btsan*, he was originally it seems a god of death and judge of the dead. This central trait places him alongside the *srog bdag*, 'lords of life', guardians and protectors of life but also, like the *dgra lha*, destroyers (*srog gcod*) of their enemies; or alongside the 'sixteen executioner-brothers' who seize upon the spirit of life (*dbugs len gyi shan pa bcu drug*). Many of these *numina* are of terror-inspiring appearance, such as the Cyclops (*mig gcig*) or the One-footed (*rkang gcig*) like *The'u rang rkang gcig*, or again the goddesses *Gangs dkar sha med* 'White Snow-goddess without flesh' and *Sha med* (fleshless) *g.yu sgron ma*. Certain special social groups worship their own deities, for example the *'brog pa* (nomadic pastoralists) worship a group of nine *'brog mo* (*'brog mo spun dgu*), and the farming population have the god of the fields (*zhing lha*). The *numina* of the rocks accompany the god of the mountain, who exceeds in importance almost all the other gods; practically any rock which overlooks a path, village or bridge in a threatening manner serves as the seat of a *brag lha*, whose favour must be made sure of. The attire and the mounts of these gods indicate unmistakably the pastoral and warlike nature of the corresponding social strata; the *numina* of this type ride on antelopes, yaks, wild asses (*rkyang*), wild dogs; they wear armour, often a copper helmet or a felt hat (*phying zhwa*), with bird feathers on the hat and a mirror in their hand. This latter of course belongs among the essential items of equipment of the shaman.

In accordance with the general tripartite cosmological division the realm of the *numina* is divided into three parts, that of the heavenly spaces, that of the depths of the earth and that of the intermediate world (*tshang rigs*: *lha*, *snang rigs*: *btsan*, *'og rigs*: *klu*), although there are no strict lines of separation between them. In the god-lists of theological literature the attribution of particular *numina* to one or another of these three realms is quite often indeterminate and ambiguous (e.g., concerning the *gnyan*), but greater (*che*) and less important (*phra ba*, *phra mo*) deities are distinguished; thus the enumerations proceed from the highest to the more lowly (*man chad*) and close with the lowest of all.

Attempts at other types of division seem to indicate the influence of certain aspects of the Taoist pantheon. In these cases the gods are surrounded by a court; in the manner of kings they have consorts, ministers, generals and a whole following. So infinite in number are the transcendental forces surrounding the Tibetans, so indeterminate for the most part are their characteristics that it is difficult to subject them to a fixed and intrinsically justifiable system of ordering. So it happens that the pantheon is continuously extended and regenerated out of the powers of imagination (filled with fear or joyful with hope) of its believers, for whom any thing or any process can take on sacred character in a spontaneous hierophany.

The *numina* of this type are not only ambiguous and indeterminate; at times they do not even have a name. They are then no more than a vague indication of a sacred presence. If one asks why it is better for one to keep away from a certain place, or how one should behave oneself there, then one receives an almost universal answer: 'Because there is a *lha* (god, spirit) there'. On the other hand some *numina* have kept their past glories to such a degree that they are today still invoked in the liturgy as protectors of Tibet, for example the twelve *bstan ma*, who are also called 'patrons of Tibet' (*bod khams skyong*). *A phyi lha mo* is similarly patron of Tibet (*bod skyong*). This tradition is so deeply rooted that these patron deities maintain their fixed place even in the liturgies of the *dGe lugs pa* (No. 70, p.2), and one offers *bsangs*, incense, to them so that they will take the locality, the dwelling places (*gnas gzhi*), the monastery (*gdan sa*) or the hermitage (*sgrub gnas*) under their protection. *sPu rgyal*, the mythical king, is also patron (*skyong byed*) of Tibet (No. 70).

All these indigenous *numina* acquired, as it were, rights of citizenship in Buddhism after the introduction of the new religion. Although this process of naturalization took place gradually and without interruption, it was believed that its origin could be precisely established; it was due to the acts of Padmasambhava. Padmasambhava did not merely possess magical powers (*mthu*), he commanded also another miraculous gift (*mthu stobs*), true speech which could never lie, the genuine word of the Buddha (*bden pa bslu ba med pa'i mthu*).

The description in the *Thang yig* (No. 3, p.244) of the triumphal procession of Padmasambhava, set forth in epic language, reveals very clearly a long series of sacred localities of the pre-Buddhist epoch, and also the traces of certain powers who enjoyed high reverence there. It is concerned throughout with local and mountain gods, and often also with lineage and ancestral gods. Thus the eulogy reports about the region of *Myang* (Nyang), which has its capital at Gyantse, how Padmasambhava, before making his entry there, brought about the submission of no fewer than thirteen demons, each of whom is mentioned by name (No. 4, p.8b). Many of these mountains have preserved their sacred character up to the present day, and also their names which go back to the pre-Buddhist period: *btsan*, *khyung*, *'brong* (wild, demonic yak as opposed to the white yak, *g.yag dkar po*).

The *numina* whom Padmasambhava met and overthrew on his victorious journey through Tibet eventually accepted their new role as *defensores fidei*, while retaining their fear-inspiring character. The vanquished *numina* brought the conqueror their 'heart' (*snying*), that is to say mantra which represented their secret substance; they promised to behave in future as ardent defenders of the Law. By this solemn oath (*dam bca'*) they were admitted into the Law. Their submission brought about the construction of a new world over the old, the establishment of a structure consecrated according to the scriptures and symbolizing the *novus ordo*. King *Srong btsan sgam po* could only propagate the law after the preliminary *defixio*[2] of the *Srin mo* or female demon who lay on her back under the land of Tibet, which was carried out by erecting on her shoulders, feet, hands etc. as many temples. The construction of the monastery of *bSam yas*, which was consecrated in the presence of Padmasambhava, put the seal on the final submission of the gods he had vanquished and converted; *bSam yas* is the symbol of the Buddhist world planted magically and irrevocably in Tibet, superseding what had been there before it.[3]

The legend here referred to (Tucci, 1956, p.279) thus symbolizes a significant turning-point in the history of Tibet. It ascribes the fusion between new and old which was accomplished at that time to the action of a single personality, Padmasambhava. As far as possible Tibetan Buddhism continued what was traditional in Tibet, although with those restrictions which it had to stand by if it was not to be untrue to its own basic ideas, for example, the prohibition of blood-sacrifices.

In his everyday religious life the layman should constantly repeat the formula of the triple Refuge (in the Buddha, in the Teaching, in the Community) and devoutly worship his guardian deities (*yi dam*), along with those of the most important deities of the Buddhist pantheon in which he has particular faith. For this reason there is in the house of every Tibetan who is not entirely without means a chapel (*chos khang*), on the altar of which one will find images of the gods made of wood, terracotta (*rdza sku*), bronze, as well as books and paintings (*thang ka*) representing the gods, cycles of gods or religious teachers who enjoy particular veneration in the family concerned. Great tolerance is the general rule in the choice of these representations; in the family context there is no trace of the strictness to which the monks are committed by their affiliation to particular doctrinal schools. The layman knows no partiality in his worship of monks and monasteries. In his eyes every monk possesses the sacred value which comes to him through his belonging to the Community, the third of the 'Three Jewels', and is therefore deserving of the greatest veneration, without distinction of doctrinal affiliation or sect.

In the domestic chapels one finds the most indispensable utensils for the simpler liturgical celebrations. Every morning the oldest people in the family give water (*yon chab*) to the images of the gods, while a lamp (*mar me*) is kept continually burning in front of them. It is the general practice to offer *suffimenta*,[4] incense (*bsangs*) in the early morning, through burning sweet-smelling trees and shrubs, especially juniper (*shug pa*), *ba lu*, a type of rhododendron, birch (*stag pa*), and so on. One *bsangs*, to be considered later in more detail, is consecrated to the *dgra lha* and is confined to men, though in Lhasa women may perform it, since Lhasa enjoys the protection of a female deity, *Ma gcig dpal lha mo*, who has a karmic relationship (*rten 'brel*) with women. Here it should be noticed that *bsangs*, while certainly a liturgical act (*mchod*) in its own right, is distinguished from *cho ga*, that is ritual whose practice is the responsibility of the monk, either alone or with other monks, in accordance with the prescriptions of the Buddhist liturgy. A ritual act can only be designated *cho ga* (Skt. *vidhi*) when it is performed by an initiated person, in other words by a monk consecrated in accordance with due form. Failing this, the act would not only not be able to bring about the desired end but would be bound to have harmful consequences.

As well as the recitation of the mantra dedicated to one's personal *yi dam*, the repetition of the mantra of the six sacred syllables (*om ma ni pad me hum*) is very common. It is connected with a special manifestation of Avalokitesvara, known as Sadaksara. In the morning, in addition to the formula of the triple refuge, passages are recited which are taken from certain very widely used prayer-books, for example from the *Tshig bdun gsol 'debs* (part of a text called *Le'u bdun ma* and attributed to Padmasambhava) or from the *bSam pa lhun grub*, where one can read the following:

In the time of iniquity, in the last age of the Kaliyuga
Every morning, every evening I will come for the salvation of Tibet.
I will come as a rider mounted on the crown of rays of the rising sun,
But on the tenth day in the form of the waxing moon.

It has already been explained (cf.p.146) that the Tibetan calendar is rich in festivals, which take place for the most part within the grounds of the monastery; at many of them the lay population of the region is admitted as spectators. Besides these there are festive occasions to which the monks are naturally invited, in order to give the occasion greater splendour and to assure its effectiveness, but which are essentially the affair of the lay population, for example the *ma ni dung sgrub*, the festival of the recitation of the 'hundred-million six-syllable mantras' which is celebrated in the villages in winter time. Another example is the sixteen-day long period of fast known as the 'Eight pairs of white fasting' (*bsnyen gnas dkar po cha brgyad*), during which the fasters take white foods (milk, rice, cereals) in alternation. This custom is particularly widespread in the province of *Khams*. It includes prayers (*gsol 'debs*) to the deities, and also to the great teachers of Buddhism who even if they have reached the level of *nirvana* have retained their connection with the world out of compassion for mankind. To these latter is addressed the invocation (e.g. No. 59) to direct their compassionate gaze upon those praying to them: 'From the realm of the essential identity of *samsara* and *nirvana*, look down upon me' (*'khor 'das dbyer med klong nas gzigs cig*).

Other ritual acts, varying from place to place, which are not tied to precise points of time but are generally linked with the summer period are grouped under the general concept of *lha gsol*. These are basically festive gatherings, on mountain-tops close to villages, for the purpose of offering *bsangs* to the *sa bdag*, *btsan*, *lha* living on the mountains and imploring their protection for the well-being of the community. These are survivals of very ancient cults in reverence of the sacred mountain, the spirit of the region (*bla ri*) or the seat of the ancestral spirits.

It is difficult to find a precise concept corresponding to the folk religion of Tibet. The expression *mi chos*, customarily used in this sense has, according to some authors, a considerably wider range of meanings; it covers an extremely rich cultural and spriritual domain which is only partially and indirectly connected with the religious sphere of experience (at least in the usual sense of the word religion). The entire existence of the Tibetan, his knowledge and desires, his feeling and thinking, is suffused and coloured by the experience of the sacred. His folk religion is not restricted to myth, to liturgy, or to a reverent attitude towards the *numina* we have discussed; it is also the living interplay of traditions of cosmogony and cosmology, genealogical legends of particular groups and families, rituals of magic and atonement, proverbial folk wisdom (such as is known in the *Blon po bka' thang*). It is in short, an all-embracing heritage of the centuries, which has certainly been everywhere exposed to the influence of all the religious systems which have taken root in Tibet, but which at the same time has continued to safeguard from them its diversity, its own particular nature, and even the contradictions contained within it.[5]

A folk religion of this kind could scarcely present a unified picture; it is dependent upon geographical peculiarities, on ways of life of very diverse kinds, linked to the contrasting pastoral and agricultural economies, to the nomadic and sedentary ways of life (not without a distant echo of the primitive hunting society); it is closely connected with the traditions of particular clans and lineages, which have preserved for later times the heritage of earlier strata. For reasons of space we must restrict ourselves here to indicating certain specific aspects where the symbiosis between indigenous and foreign, between lively spontaneity and systematic rigour, which is so characteristic of Lamaism, emerges with particular clarity.

2 Man face to face with divine and demonic powers

The relationships between things and events on the one hand and man on the other are in the main of two kinds: *bkra shis* and *bkra mi shis*, that is favourable and auspicious, or hostile and harmful. Whether man is favoured by fortune, or is her victim, does not depend on chance. It is rather the fruit of his karma; but there are other factors too that aid the effectiveness of karma. Every fact, every event is the result of the intervention of a conscious will or of a conscious power, that sometimes takes material and visible forms of manifestation, but at other times remains indeterminate and impossible to grasp. Many of these powers are hostile under all circumstances, evil in nature, but most behave in an ambiguous and inconstant manner. The way they act depends on the way men conduct themselves towards them. They are touchy beings, inclined to anger, demanding respect and veneration.

In a certain sense, however, they are dependent upon man, they must be nourished and worshipped by him. If he neglects to do this, he can be sure of their revenge. In the liturgy of atonement and the *bsangs* they are invoked and induced to descend from their seats; they are imagined as being present. It is for them to accept (*bzhes*) the invitation, the offering, of whatever type it might be (*'bul* or *gtad*; *'bul* for the gods, *gtad* for demons to be exorcized), or the presentation of *chang* (*phud rgod*[6]); the sacred action ends with the wish that the receiver of the offerings may be appeased, be satisfied, be happy.

There is a close connection between many of these beings and mankind. If, for example, a man through his negligence causes the illness of a *klu*,[7] then the offending man will meet the same fate himself.

In general the supernatural powers can be divided into two groups; white (*phyogs dkar*) and good, and black and evil (*phyogs nag*, *ngan*), a division according to Indian tradition, resting upon the working of karma, though also corresponding to the division into two created worlds in certain theological doctrines of Iranian origin which were taken over by the *Bon po*. The consequence of the enmity of these malefic powers, whether it is innate or provoked, is always a *gdon*, a pernicious influence against which man must protect himself in advance. The relevant rituals and magical formulae have two principal objectives in view; in the first place prosperity, well-being, good fortune (*bde legs*) in the most material sense, as well as long life (*tshe ring*), health (*nad med*), riches (*longs spyod*) (No. 12), victory over enemies etc., and then the driving out (*bzlog*) and elimination of all which stands in the way of this *bde legs*, such as poverty, illness and early death. The activity of the exorcist (*sngags pa*) thus has an infinitely wide field open before it; in case of drought he can invoke rain, he can banish hail or conjure it to inflict vengeance, he can call a halt to epidemics among men and flocks. In this immense area of ritual techniques for the furtherance of good and defence from evil the traditional heritage of Tibet and the contributions of India and China can be clearly distinguished. In the field of astrology the contribution of China (*nag rtsis*, as contrasted with *rgya rtsis*, astrology of Indian origin) is particularly noteworthy, and in fact not so much in its learned expression as in its popular, magical and exorcistic form. India's contribution primarily derives from Tantrism and its particular interest is in the magical rituals which have for their aim the pacifying (*zhi*) of hostile powers, furtherance (*rgyas*) of well-being, acquisition of power (*dbang*) or acts of a terrifying nature (*drag*). Thus there has come about an extremely complex syncretism, a symbiosis of the diverse elements which have found fertile soil in the particular psychic disposition of the Tibetan. The Tibetan lives in a permanent state of anxious uneasiness; every physical or spiritual disturbance, each illness, every uncertain or threatening situation leads him to embark upon a feverish search for the cause of the event and the appropriate means to ward it off.

According to a book ascribed to Padmasambhava (No. 20, p.77) man is inevitably condemned to unhappiness and misfortune, because, often without being fully aware of it, he has committed various acts in this life or in previous existences which must necessarily have as a consequence for him corresponding reactions by particular demonic powers. Certain female divinities, however, can come to his aid, provided that each is invoked on those particular days on which her tutelary function is operative. He who is attacked knows, then, not only the nature and original cause of his illness or his misfortune, but also the appropriate means to relieve himself from misfortune. Illness does not merely have a physical origin. In it one has to distinguish the primary cause (*rgyu*), which consists of a disturbance of the equilibrium of the three 'humours', from the contributory cause (*rkyen*), which is to be sought for in an impurity (*mi gtsang*), a shadow, a defilement (*grib*). This impurity (*mi gtsang*) or shadow can be of various kinds; it can originate in a sinful action, but also from other causes, for example from eating various impure foods (*mi gtsang pa'i zas*). Thus food offered by a widow or a murderer brings about a dangerous condition (No. 75). Burnt foods (*zas thab can*), which offend the *phug lha* (cf. below, p.188), also cause defilement, as does the pouring on the hearth of liquids (cf. No. 56) or substances producing evil smells or smoke, which anger the god of the hearth (*thab lha*). Other causes are lighting fires on mountains (*ri la me rgyab*, No. 76, *kha* p.18), and staying in neighbourhoods where *gnyan* live (*gnyan sa*). Impurity also arises through associating with men who emanate a dangerous sacredness, as for example with smiths (*mgar pa*, No. 56, p.3b) and armourers (the *'das log* treatises consign these to hell, No. 76, *ga*, p.6b, p.22b), though the prescription is not a universal one; the idea seems to have had more effect in western Tibet (including Ladakh) than in other regions. It is evidently a survival of prehistoric connections between the craft of the smith and the infernal powers, connections which in many communities give the smith great prestige, while in others, by contrast, because of the gradual progress of demythologizing, they merely cause the demonic shadow of commerce with dangerous powers to lie upon him. In the same way associating with *bandhe* and *Bon po* can cause impurity; they are accompanied and protected by particular *numina* (their *srung ma*) and so can unleash *gdon* (No. 22, p.6a).

Sacred impurity obstructs a favourable destiny and renders one receptive to all that is unfavourable. The *gdon* take advantage of such

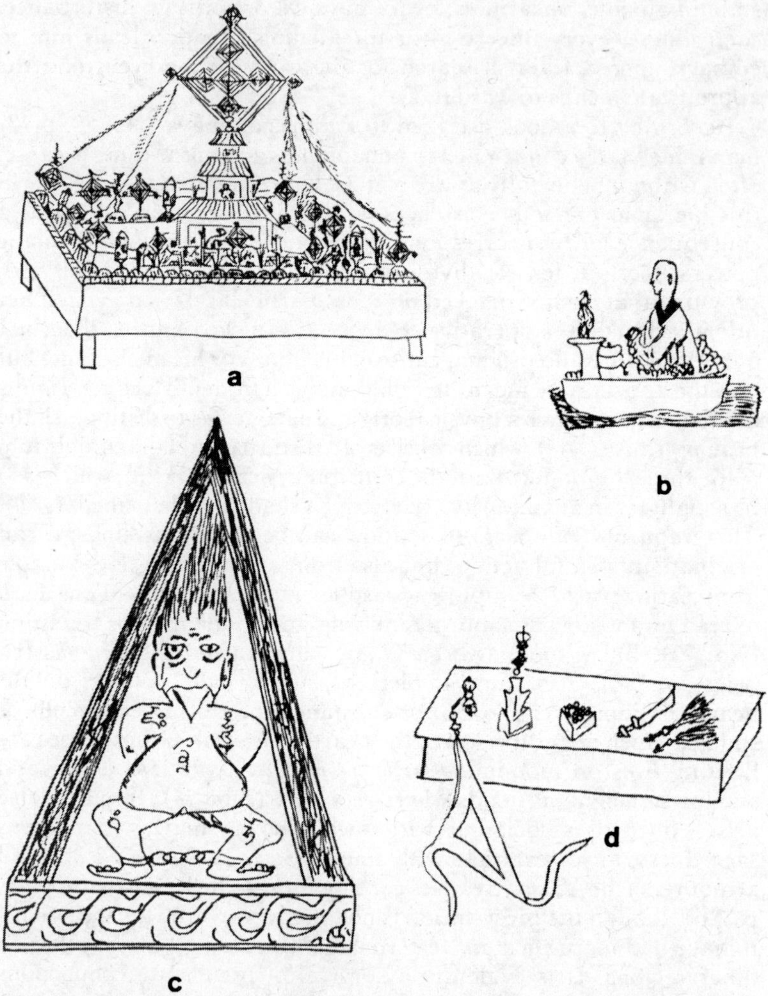

Figure 15 Accessories for the *mdos* ritual
(a) *mdos*: a miniature three-storeyed building, inside which is the *glud* (cf. p. 177) of the person for whose benefit the ceremony is being performed. In front of it is the *pho glud* or *mo glud*, *glud* for a man or for a woman (cf. Figure 16), with the eight signs of good fortune and representations of terrestrial, aquatic and domestic animals, fruits and grains all around, and also *nam mkha'*, that is threads wound around a cross (cf. Figure 18), twigs of sweet-smelling plants and lamps on the four sides. The figures are made of coloured *tsamba*.
(b) *glud*: modelled reproduction of the person concerned in the form of a *gtor ma* (of *tsamba* and butter); in front, representation of foods which are conceived

occasions. They form a very numerous class of demons who are admittedly lacking in precise features. As a general rule the powers who bring about illness are referred to as *gdon*. In the medical treatises they correspond to the Indian *graha* or *bhuta* (in the translation of the *Astangahrdaya* VI, 3 and VI, 5 *gdon* is used in the first case for *graha*, in the second for *bhuta*); for this reason they are generally called '*gdon* of illness'. *gdon* must be distinguished from other unfavourable and malefic forces (*mi mthun*). *gdon* are powers in many ways like the planetary spirits (*gza'*), with whom they are often brought into relationship. These bring about what appear to be psychic maladies and madness, rob man of the consciousness of his actions and take him fully into their possession. Thus King *gLang dar ma* was brought to apostasy and led to persecute Buddhism because a *gdon* had brought him under its power and robbed him of all sense of responsibility. Thus *gdon* is the condition which breaks out as the result of a sin or, more generally, a defilement. By performing the appropriate ritual actions,[8] for example through an ablution (*khrus*), every stain left by bad actions is cleansed, and the *gdon* lose their power over the man so purified. Essentially they are no more than the embodiment of disturbances of psychic and bodily equilibrium, primarily caused by the influence either of the planets, of the *'byung po* (= Skt. *bhuta*; the expression is ambiguous in Sanskrit and also in Tibetan, referring both to the elements and to the demons) in the world above, between heaven and earth, or of the *gnyan* in the underworld.

In describing the *gdon* it should also be mentioned that they appear in three groups, outer, inner and secret (*phyi*, *nang*, *gsang*). The outer *gdon* appear in material form as demons, planets etc.; the inner *gdon* are released as powers of destruction through the commission of evil, sin and defilement; the secret *gdon* arise from a faulty control of the vital breath of respiration (*rlüng*) during the process of yoga.

To prevent the calamitous consequences (*gnod*) of acts which provoke the *gdon* of 'king' spirits (*rgyal po*, like *Pe har*), of *btsan*, of male and female *'dre*, of *sa bdag* ('lords of the soil') and so on virtuous actions

of as provisions for the journey, and also of other gifts, thought of as a payment of accounts for debts towards the powers who are causing the misfortunes threatening the person commissioning the ritual. In front, a lamp (cf.p.183).
(c) *ling ga* (cf.p.185): triangular, with tongues of fire represented all around, in the centre an image of the supposed enemy (*dgra*) bound hand and foot with chains.
(d) *bsgral chas*: utensils for disposing of the *ling ga*: a black-coloured standard, a *phur bu* or ritual dagger, a stone for crushing the *ling ga*, an iron triangle enclosing white stones (*rdo thun*), a knife to cut the *ling ga* into pieces, two fly-whisks made of owl-feathers (*sgro g.yab*)

are the most useful defence. These actions include the reading aloud of sacred texts, chosen according to the particular case and with regard to the nature and occasion of the evil and the affliction; the restoration or redecorating of a *mchod rten*[9] fallen into disrepair; the repainting of a *lha khang* (temple) or of sacred images (*lha khang sku dkar gsol*); the votive offering of *jo dar*;[10] the incising of images (*rdo lha*) or of the *om ma ni pad me hum* formula on rocks; the setting free of animals intended for death (*tshe thar*, *srog slu*); recitation by oneself, or by others one has commissioned, of particularly efficacious books, above all the *rDo rje gcod pa*,[11] and so on. We are dealing here with the same pious actions which are recommended by those condemned to the torments of hell to persons whose fate it has been to descend to hell and to be able to return to earth (*'das log*); these actions are also the most efficacious way to influence favourably during this life the inexorable ripening of karma (No. 76). The auspicious (*bkra shis*) elements will according to Buddhist teaching be strengthened through the accumulation of virtuous deeds. Out of good works flows *dbang thang*, a psychical and material strength and security resting upon the knowledge of past karma. This is not all; faced with the unfortunate (*bkra mi shis*) events which approach realization, man has available also an inexhaustible mine of formulae and rituals, rituals of driving out (*bzlog*) of adverse forces through powerful exorcistic actions (*gto*), and rituals of ransoming (*bslu*, *glud*). The *bla*, the soul, can for example be ransomed from danger (*bla bslu*), as in cases of unconsciousness; one can also ransom from death (*'chi bslu*) at the very moment of death, and so prolong life. One can even fetch back the life-force (*srog bslu*) at the moment it leaves the body.

The *mdos*, *yas*, *glud* and *gto*, which are now to be discussed, are devices to extricate oneself from the threatening dangers of hostile powers. These powers can be of bodily and material (*gzugs can*) or immaterial and invisible (*gzugs med*) nature.

Since *yas* and *glud* are included within the concept of *mdos* and can be considered as variants of *mdos*, it is first necessary to outline the characteristics of *mdos* and *gto*. The first-named ritual gives protection, either for he who performs it or for him on whose behalf it is performed by another, against dangers, hindrances, injuries, illnesses, obstacles of any kind whose origin is attributed to the evil powers. In an application more closely connected with Buddhist doctrine, this ceremony can also be performed to overcome obstacles on the way to the achievement of the highest goal, Enlightenment. The sacred action consists of offering gifts which are particularly valued by the hostile powers, so that, contented (*mnyes*) and satiated (*tshims*), they will calm themselves (*zhi ba*) and abstain from further persecution. *mdos* is therefore a way to remove (*bzlog thabs*) the hostile powers through a kind of expiatory offering, such as when a condemned man ransoms himself by paying a fine, or when an enemy threatening war is appeased by offering tribute payments.

In the *mdos* ceremony the offerings are either real things like grain, barley, clothes, or representations made out of *tsamba* of animals, sheep, horses and so on.

The *yas* ceremony is less important, and the offerings are scantier too in this case. While the *mdos* ritual is performed by a *sngags pa*, here the person giving the offerings frequently acts on his own behalf, throwing down the offerings at a crossroads at the edge of the inhabited area with great shouts and cries.

Behind every *mdos* lies implicitly the concept of ransom (*glud*). The ritual accordingly requires an image of the person (*ngar glud*, *ngar mi*) on whose behalf the ransom is to be effected or who is to be protected (*srung bya*). In the case of the illness of an animal, its image will be made. If the image is of a man it is fitted out with clothes or shoes of rags; if it is an animal it will have hairs taken from the animal's neck or tail. Sometimes various personal objects of the sick person are also represented. Essential requisites for the ritual are pieces of *tsamba* which have special symbolic value according to the particular case, for example a hollowed-out disc with butter placed in the middle, representing food for the demons (*ting lo* or *til lo*). The shape called *chang bu* is obtained by squeezing a piece of *tsamba* in the closed fist so that it takes on the form of a small rod, out of which the points caused by the hollow spaces between the several fingers project tiny pieces of *tsamba* (*theb skyu*) which are used to symbolize gifts for the gods. The *glud* thus obtained serves as a substitute for the sick person or for the sick or endangered animal, it is offered to the demonic being causing the evil in question as a ransom.

The distinction between *glud* and *ngar mi* consists in the fact that the first expression refers to the ritual concerned in its entirety, its arrangement and all its accessories, while *ngar mi* indicates the image representing the human being seeking to be ransomed. To the right and left of this figure are placed the *chang bu*; in its folded hands it holds the *ting lo*; in front of it is put a lamp.

Sometimes the *glud* is a living scapegoat, most often a beggar who for a small payment or in exchange for a new piece of clothing agrees to take upon himself the illness afflicting another person. The *glud* (scapegoat) even has his official place in the calendar of religious festivals of the church at the time of the New Year celebrations, of which he is one of the most remarkable features. At any rate it is a question here too only of a local version of a custom found all throughout Tibet.

The *gto* by contrast is a powerful exorcistic ritual (*drag po*). He who

Figure 16 Magical ransoms (*glud*) for a man and for a woman
(a) ransom for a man: (1) *shing byang* = wooden board; (2) *pho ris stag gos can* = representation of a man dressed in a tiger skin.
(b) ransom for a woman: (1) *shing byang* = wooden board; (2) *mo ris gzig gos can* = representation of a woman dressed in a leopard skin.
(c) arrow (in the magical ransom ceremony for a man): (1) *mda' stong kha* = notch; (2) *sgro bzhi* = four pennons; (3) *tshon sna lnga dkris* = five-coloured ring; (4) *mdel* = arrow-point.
(d) board for keeping the arrow.
(e) spindle (in the magical ransom ceremony for a woman): (1) *skud pa* = thread; (2) *phang yu* = shaft; (3) *snal ma* = wool threads; (4) *phang 'khor* = ring; (5) *phang khab* = nail.
(f) board for keeping the spindle.

d e f

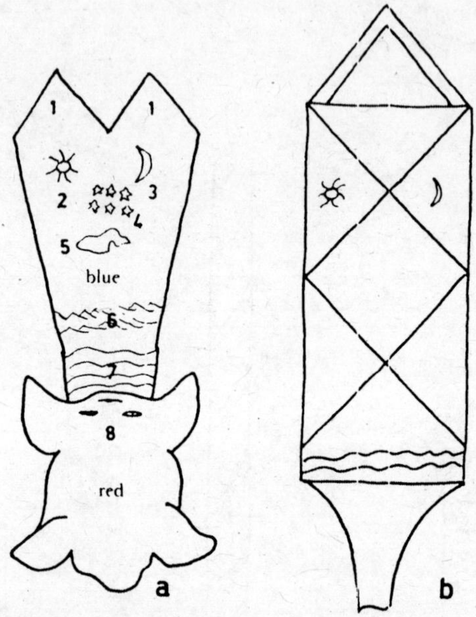

Figure 17 Ransom for misfortune striking the village or home
(a) wooden knife: (1) *ral gri rtse gnyis* = two-pointed sword; (2) *nyi ma* = sun; (3) *zla ba* = moon; (4) *skar ma* = stars; (5) *sprin* = cloud; (6) *ri bo* = mountain; (7) *mtsho* = lake; (8) *sbal mgo* = frog's head.
(b) same in a simpler form.

is to carry it out must be expert in the meditation of one of his guardian deities (*yi dam*) who is here invoked in his fierce and terrifying aspect. The offerings (*gtor ma*) consecrated in the *gto* are thrown in the direction where the powers causing the evil are believed to dwell. The gifts offered symbolize the flesh and bones of enemies, and the protective deities, *srung ma*, *chos skyong* and such, are to use them to bring about the destruction of the hostile powers. After the countless host of the *srung ma* has been set on the track of the enemies in this way, it is expected that they will fall upon the adversaries and overcome them. For this reason there are weapons among the accessories (*yan lag*) of the *gto* either made of *tsamba* again, or sometimes real, which in their separate receptacles indicate, together with the *gto* itself, the means of attack which the *srung ma* should use in their war against the hostile powers. The *gto* must always be triangular in form; it is made out of flour ground from black corn; the bloody entrails of animals are spread out around the *gto*; a hedge or fence (*ra ba*) of twigs of black, thorny shrubs (*tsher shing nag po*) represents an enclosure; at the corners of the enclosure are pieces of black wood (*rtsang*), while a human skull (*thod pa*) reigns over the whole assemblage (cf. Tucci, 1966, p.148, Figure 7).

Lan chags is the bringing to actualization and overcoming of a misfortune arising from karma acquired in the past. *Lan chags* is a kind of accumulated debt (*bu lon*), so that both expressions are frequently used side by side in the liturgy. Debts can be conceived of numerically; as many little balls or rods of *tsamba* dough illustrate the corresponding numerical quantity, for example a hundred, or one can set them out according to the years of life of the man for whose benefit the ritual action is being performed, or one can follow various other sorts of criteria. At the end of the ceremony the formula *lan chags song, bu lon sbyang* is repeated: 'the burden of debt is gone forth, the debts are settled'.

As the above description indicates, he who is celebrating the ritual acts, along with his employer, moves on two different levels; the level of ordinary reality, at which things and events are what they seem, and a magical and hallucinatory level, dominated by a special psychological state, such that representations enter in the place of things and lay claim to the same unimpeachable reality as the things themselves.

On the basis of a psychic certainty in which all partake and which is subject to doubt on no one's part, through the state of receptivity and emotion so produced, which is further strengthened by the formulae recited and the meditation associated with them, a temporary reversal of the two levels is achieved–experienced by each of those taking part with greater or lesser intensity. The hostile *numina* display themselves in the forms handed down by the iconography.The ritual, and the hopeful expectancy of those taking part, conjures up a multifarious world. In it the offerings to the *numina*, modelled with *tsamba* and butter into strange symbolic shapes, also take part, as also do the other immeasurable, inconceivable powers ('exceeding all that can be thought of', runs the formula concerning them), which cannot be made directly visible, but which are present to the interior vision; their grace overflows the universe, and can be summoned to the struggle against the hostile powers of evil. The operations performed in this ritual have for those who take part the same reality as ordinary experience. The psychic forces brought into the fight through the combined action of the factors mentioned are in no sense incompatible with everyday life, rather they lead it without break into another dimension, for they represent always the hidden, but not for that reason any less powerful or effective thread in the web of existence.

If we now return to the *mdos*,[12] we observe first that their basic scheme is always that of a cross. The arms of the cross are joined together by threads of different colours forming a diamond-shaped pattern (*nam mkha'*).[13]

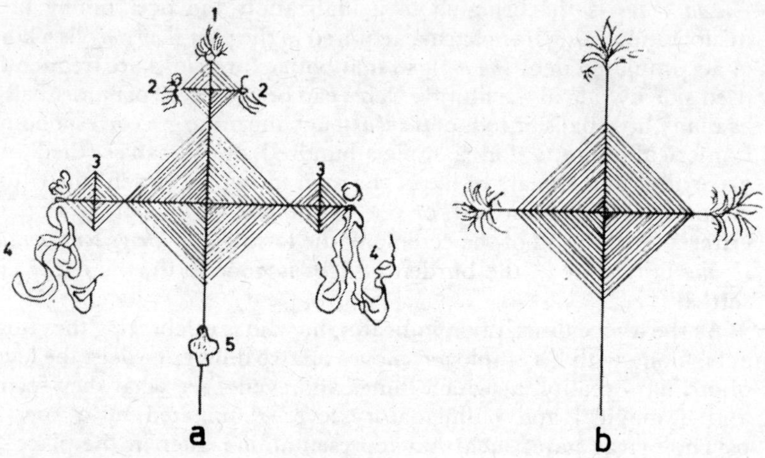

Figure 18 *Nam mkha'*
(a) in an elaborate version; (b) in a simpler form.
(1) *bya spu* or *bal tshon* = bird feathers or wool threads;
(2) *dar* or *shog bu'i dpyangs* = cloth or paper fringes;
(3) *nam mkha'i lag pa gnyis* = the two 'hands' of the *nam mkha'*;
(4) *dar gyi dpyangs* = cloth fringes;
(5) *yungs kar gyi sgang bu* = box with white mustard-seeds.

In the *mdos* rituals the world is so to say reconstructed in a magical manner in accordance with the traditional schemes; on a platform reigns Mount Meru (*ri rab*), the seven-staged (*bang rim*) axis of the world; above it is placed the vessel (*bum pa*) containing the ritual substances (*rdzas*); around it are disposed the four main continents (*gling bzhi*) and the eight subsidiary continents.

Such a magical recreation of the world is necessary because he who performs the ritual must return to the beginning of creation or to express the concept differently, he must put himself into a special situation which is brought about through a radical abolition of time. It is therefore not surprising that a ritual of this kind is quite frequently linked with recitals of the creation of the universe (*lo rgyus*), which sometimes give the impression of alien elements in the Buddhist context. One also finds elements of this kind in the writings of those authors who have taken it upon themselves to cloak pre-Buddhist or foreign cults, rituals and mythic themes with a mantle of relative orthodoxy, as for example with *Pad ma dkar po*, where at any rate such elements occur side by side with the classical cosmogonic teachings of the Abhidharma (No. 66).

It goes without saying that the strict doctrinal position would maintain, when justifying the *mdos* rituals, that they are to be seen as one of the countless modes of experience of the cosmic illusion, and that the powers (*lha*, *'dre* etc) addressed in them represent only deceptive products of our own ignorance (No. 66). At the same time this does not detract from their practical usefulness in a world where the existence of a thing is the same thing as its imagined existence.

The powers called upon in the *mdos* are ready to intervene in their quality of great helpers (*gnyer chen*) of the Doctrine (No. 66, p.9a), as subjects (*'bangs*) of the 'Three Jewels' (loc.cit.).

The evil powers to be warded off either accept the offerings and allow themselves to be appeased, in which case they tacitly reaffirm their promise of obedience to the Law, or else they disdain the gifts and prefer to persevere in evil. In the first case they are invited to continue in their obedience to the Law; this is made easier for them by showing them the way which they should follow (*lam bstan*) (No. 63, p.5a). So that they will not lose their way in the darkness of night, a lamp, made, as always, from *tsamba*, is specifically placed in front of the curative image (*ngar glud*). The retreating powers are warned not to look back (*phyi mig ma lta zhig*). If they refuse the offerings more drastic methods are required: 'If you break your promise, the king who holds the diamond in his fist (assimilated to the exorcist in the ritual) will flare into anger and you will be reduced to ashes' (No. 66, p.13).

Sometimes (No. 21) the exorcistic action is accompanied by a dialogue between the exorcist and the malignant power. After becoming one with the deity ruling over the ritual (without such an identification his actions would be useless), the exorcist is in a state of trance in which he enters into combat or discussion with the power inflicting harm upon his protégés. In this state of mind he reports on all the vicissitudes of the imagined confrontation. (This does not exclude the possibility of ceremonies where the conflict is between two people, the exorcist and the man incarnating the demon.) The image of the person afflicted by illness or misfortune, the accompanying shapes of *tsamba* dough (*chang bu*, *theb skyu*, etc.), the little *tsamba* figures of men and animals all round the main figure–these are all transformed in a magical fashion into real things and beings able to satisfy the desire of the demonic power, even though this power may only acquiesce after a long struggle. If the confrontation takes place without success, then recourse is had to threats and finally to means of magical compulsion.

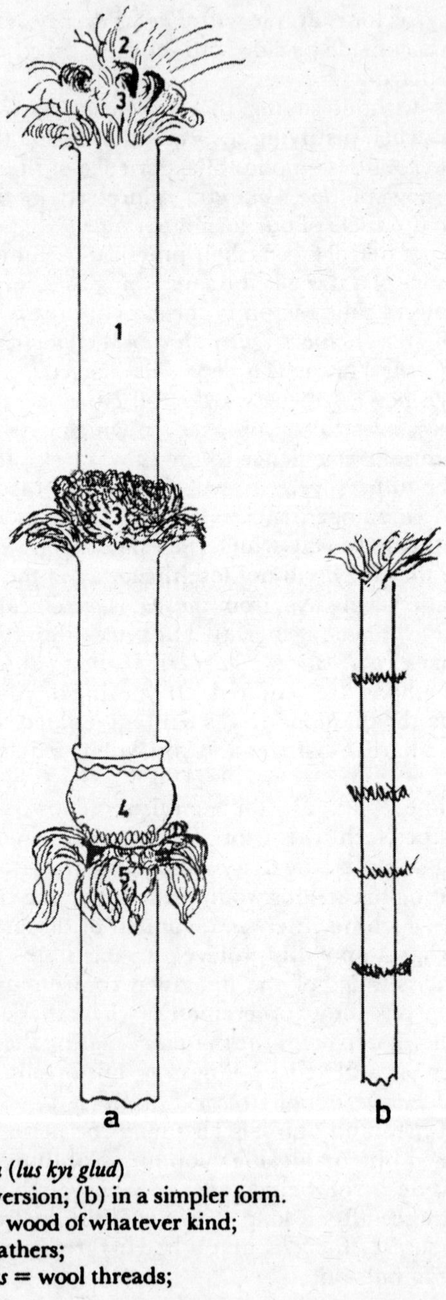

Figure 19 *rGyang bu* (*lus kyi glud*)
(a) in an elaborate version; (b) in a simpler form.
(1) *shing gang rung* = wood of whatever kind;
(2) *bya spu* = bird feathers;
(3) *bal tshon sna tshogs* = wool threads;

In certain cases exorcism (*bzlog*) aims at the effective annihilation of the evil powers or even of persons believed to have hostile intentions. In the latter circumstance the magical action brings about their death or fatal illness. The enemy to be overcome is represented by a *tsamba* figurine called *ling ga*.. It is, however, quite distinct from the *ling ga* used in the *glud*-ritual, which is also made out of *tsamba*, though in that case mixed with blood. On a piece of paper the syllable *nri* (Skt. *nr*, man) and the name of the hostile person are written and all around them the formula *maraya* ('kill') and the invocations to particular classes of demons with the injunction to them to trample on the enemy and annihilate him (*non*). After the *sngags pa* has transformed himself, along with all the assembled ingredients necessary for the ceremony, into a divine state of being, he must bring together on the twenty-ninth day of the month, at the time of the waxing moon, nine armoured warriors, nine widows, nine left yak-horns, nine little heaps of earth, nine sharp stones, nine peppercorns, nine dry branches of alpine willow (*glang ma*), and nine plants of a kind called *tsha rgog ram pa*. If he cannot manage to assemble all these accessories, the exorcist takes nine skulls of dogs or wolves or the left eye of a horse and divides everything between the eight parts of the world. In the next section of the ritual the life of the *ling ga* is evoked (*ling ga bskyed*); then comes the moment which will bring about the annihilation of the enemy and his dismemberment. At this point in the action the magician proclaims his identity with the fourteen terrible deities, headed by Heruka, under whose patronage the ritual process stands, then he recalls previous subjugations of enemies brought about through the intervention of these deities, and finally he fetters the adversaries threatening from the four celestial directions and banishes them into the left yak-horn and so on. In the further progress of the magical ritual the victories of famous figures of antiquity over the hostile powers are recalled. The deeds are laid down as a precedent; just as they succeeded, according to the old traditions, in discovering and destroying the hiding-place, receptacle or bearer of the spirit of those demons in, for example, a stone or a tree, so the actions of the present-day magician will be crowned with success. As the masters of old performed these deeds at the command of the ancient kings, so the magician of today proclaims himself, in the service of his employers, as 'the king of the terrible deities', 'the executioner of foes and demons' (*dgra* and

(4) *yungs kar kyi sgang bu* = box with white mustard-seeds;
(5) *dar sna'i dkris* = cloths of various colours.
(The *rgyang bu* are small pieces of wood forming part of the *mdos*, cf. Tucci, 1966, p.118n.–G.B.S.)

bgegs). He places all the dreaded enemies in fetters and imprisons them in the left yak-horn, or in the other objects named above. Then he secures the horn under a hearth-stone (though not one from his own hearth), at a crossroads or under a *mchod rten*. He then prepares an arrow made of metal fallen from the sky (*gnam lcags drag po = mtho rde'u*) and soaked in poisoned or impure blood, while the upper part of the bow is made of human ribs, the lower from human skin (*zhing chen lpags*). As he fires the arrow, the magician cries out to the winds that the enemy, wherever in space he might be, will meet annihilation. When he deposits the horn in which the enemy's spirit is imprisoned at a crossroads, he commands the adversary to stay in this prison and not to cause any injury for as long as he is unwilling to take the binding vow of Enlightenment; a manifest concession to the world of Buddhist concepts in the course of a magical ceremony which has little or nothing in common with Buddhism.

Although the concept of the *ling ga* in the procedure we have just described differs from that in the *glud*, and although the intended goals also differ in nature (here killing, there ransom) this kind of *ling ga* is sometimes used in the *glud*, for example in a special ritual (called *gto nag dgra zor*) where the representation can even be made life-size. In this case the *ling ga* is stuck in the mouth of the *glud*. This is meant to show that the exorcistic ritual is not merely intended to overcome the harmful influences of the adversary through the ransom, but that it is desired in addition to deal with the enemy decisively, to kill him.

How did it come about that Buddhism, at least in its Lamaistic form, could tolerate the killing of an opponent, even if only for purposes of defence? Here we meet a very subtle distinction; the assistance of the 'Protectors of the Law' is certainly invoked for the total annihilation of the demons, such that their bodies leave no more than dust behind, but this request is accompanied by the prayer that their conscious principle may be liberated in *chos dbyings*, in the realm of absolute potentiality (No. 21, p.4; *rnam shes chos dbyings su sgrol*). Besides, even Indian Buddhism permits the killing of an enemy in certain special circumstances, for example on the pretext that it will bring him spiritual gain in that he will be prevented from loading his conscience with further heavy sins.[14] Examples are not lacking to show that even famous masters of the Doctrine did not disdain to have recourse to incantations with such an intention, even in war or out of personal motives. *U rgyan pa* for example, during a pilgrimage in Swat when he met some brigands, consigned those of them who threatened his life from life to death through the use of particularly effective magical formulae (Tucci, 1967, p.183).

It is not always superhuman powers who threaten and persecute man. There are also human creatures, especially of the feminine sex, who can change themselves into demonic beings. They then become demons in human form and can cause the same misfortune as real demons. Such beings are called 'living demons' (*gson 'dre*).

Meeting such women in the evening can trigger off fever and illness. While their body lies lifeless as in sleep their spirit (*bla*) becomes at night a demon (*'dre*) which wanders around restlessly bringing misfortune and lingering illness to those with whom they come into contact. Those who see these demonic women from close up can ascertain their identity.

A dead man too can change into a demon (which is called *shi 'dre*), if at the moment of death he makes a vow of vengeance (*smon lam*) against someone, or if he dies through violence. The principle of consciousness of the murdered man is then ruled and driven on by the desire to kill his murderer; he desires to break off his vital spirit (*srog*).

3 Personal protection and protection of the house

The previous pages have been entirely concerned with apotropaic actions performed in specific cases, in accordance with the particular circumstances. However, the entire spiritual life of the Tibetan is defined by a permanent attitude of defence, by a constant effort to appease and propitiate the powers whom he fears. These powers have their residence everywhere: thus on his right shoulder there is the *dgra lha* ('enemy god', a heritage of the primeval traditions of a warrior and hunter society!), in the right armpit the *pho lha*, in the left armpit the *mo lha*, in the heart the *zhang lha*. The last three Tibetan expressions literally signify male god, female god and god of the mother's brother. These beings incorporate the continuity of the family, the paternal and maternal ancestors who watch unceasingly over the continuing existence of their lineage. Further to be mentioned in this connection are the *thab lha*, the god of the hearth, the *phug lha* or *khyim lha*, the deity of the home who dwells in the inner pillar of the house, and finally the god of the store-room, *bang mdzod lha*. These last-named *lha* and others of similar kind are not only linked to man as such, but more particularly to his dwelling-place, to that place where the Tibetan truly feels protected and secure, provided that he has not injured or offended the invisible powers living there alongside him. For this reason the tent and the house are not places like all other places; not only is the indissoluble community of life between present and past perceptible here, but besides this, the home is capable of being interpreted cosmologically as a projection of the universe into earthly existence. The house renews and represents the original act of creation; the symbolism which is thereby enshrined within it is evoked in all its details in the wedding songs (Tucci, 1966, p.105). To the parts of the door (lintel, sill, four surrounding beams) correspond specific colours (turquoise, gold, rock-crystal, the colour of a conch shell) and these colours recall the four world-eggs out of which came the entire creation (Tucci, 1949, p.722), of the four doors of heaven, likewise watched by animals of various colours (shell-coloured, gold, turquoise, iron).

The correspondence is extended to, for example, the staircase linking the ground-floor with the floor above. It has thirteen steps, as many as the layers or successive stages of heaven. The entry of the bride into her new home and her ascent into the upper storey is symbolically equated in tradition and in songs with the ascent to heaven; the bridegroom's father and mother represent the heavenly powers.

In a similar manner in the tent the opening at the apex which lets out the smoke corresponds to the highest gate at the summit of the world, which opens into the unbounded space where sun and moon describe their eternal courses.

In the house the defence system is, so to say, condensed into two parts of the building. One of them is the *pho lha mkhar*, 'castle of the *pho lha*' (also called *gsas mkhar*), which is either an extension in the middle of the ridge of the house roof or else four extensions at the four corners of the house. The great age of this custom is already apparent from the name indicating the residence of the *pho lha*, especially in *Khams*; *gsas mkhar*, an expression where the old word *gsas* used for the holy buildings of Bon (*gsas khang*) reoccurs.

The *gsas mkhar* (also called *spo se* or *pho lha mkhar*), the seat of the *pho lha*, is provided with a cavity which serves to receive the offerings of *bsangs* (*bsangs khang*).

In many houses, but especially in monasteries, the *pho lha mkhar* shares its protective function with a large cloth cylinder fixed on a wooden support, girded about with hairs from yak-tails and overlooked by a death's head and also a trident (*thug*). The whole assemblage is exclusively intended for apotropaic purposes.

A similar function to that described for the protection of the outside of the house is possessed as guardian of the interior of the house by the *phug lha* (the name itself signifies 'interior god') or 'maternal god' (*mo lha*), also called simply 'house god' (*khyim lha*). His seat is customarily found either in a pillar, or in a branch of wood in the most hidden corner of the kitchen. While the *pho lha* is considered to be the god especially of the men, the *phug lha* is the god of the women; he is entrusted with their protection and has his place in precisely that part of the house where the women's life mostly takes place. Like all *lha*, the *phug lha* is ambivalent in his behaviour. He can easily be offended; he does not like it when exorcists (*sngags pa*) or *Bon po* come too close to him, because they are accompanied by their protective deities (*srung ma*); the *phug lha* will not tolerate the interference of these rivals and adversaries. He is not even too happy to see women belonging to other families come into his proximity, because this could lead to a conflict with the *phug lha* of another family group. The presence of a stranger is also not always welcome to him. If the bride becomes restless or ill in her new home, it is presumed that the *phug lha* has no particular liking for her; he must then be made favourable through appropriate ceremonies. The *phug lha* also controls the property of the family, especially the live-stock. If the flocks are transferred to a new owner but do not appear to feel at ease in his house then it is necessary to appease the *phug lha*. He is the symbol of the house and of the property. When moving into or building a new dwelling-place and abandoning an old one the *phug lha* must, so to say, take part in the removal. A branch of the auspicious tree attached to the central pillar, generally of juniper, will then be taken along with great care and without allowing it to be damaged; it is the 'inner receptacle' (*nang rten*) in which the *phug lha* has its seat. Thus it appears that the *pho lha* and *phug lha* share in the protection of the house and of the family who lives there; the *pho lha* is concerned with their external protection, still having his combative nature as one of the *dgra lha*, the *phug lha* by contrast looks after the inside of the house and the property of the family.

As already mentioned, the *thab lha* is the god of the hearth. The hearth is the central point of the house or tent and so of the entire life of the family; it has a sacred character not only as the place where food is prepared but also as the spot where the fire of the family burns. The hearth tolerates no impurity; any defilement arouses its anger and draws one of the family members in sympathy into a state of weakness and vulnerability to evil. An impurity of this sort can however be brought about by chance, inadvertently (cf. above, p.173), as for example when the liquid contents of a cooking vessel flow over spreading around a bad smell or vapour. In order to secure oneself in advance against dangers of this kind and to give the *thab lha* no occasion for anger, one has recourse to the usual *bsangs*. The sacred character of the house, its homologizing, as reproduction or projection, with the universe, man's desire to enclose himself within the invulnerable security offered by the house,[15] and almost as it were to become a god within it—all this is reflected also in the structure of religious communities; these are conceived of after the manner of a house, and the masters of this house are described, according to their greater or lesser importance, as pillar (*ka ba*), beam (*lcam*) and so on, all this with the aim of reinforcing anew the scheme or archetype of an order beyond time ruling within such an institution.

The Tibetan experiences the house as a microcosm, as a secure enclosure, in contrast to the space outside, which is the playground and hiding-place of countless, omnipresent powers continually threatening to ambush him. So it is evident why nothing which has been in contact with these powers, which is consecrated or forfeit to them, may be kept in the interior of the house. Such objects must always be removed, be carried out into open country, particularly to crossroads–favourite places of the *numina*.

4 The soul

In a large part of popular magical ritual the word *bla* is used in the sense of 'soul'. If someone becomes unconscious it is said that his *bla* has left his body; if someone is dying this means the *bla* has become separated from the body, it is wandering around somewhere, it has been taken away. In each of these cases specific rituals are performed to call the *bla* back into the body (for example *bla khug*, *bla bslu*, *'chi bslu*, ransom of the *bla*, ransom of death; Lessing, 1951). Other rituals have the object of prolonging one's own life (*srog bslu*) or saving the life of another, as for example with the so-called golden bridge (*gser zam*) built of stones inscribed with the formula *om ma ni pad me hum*.

The ritual which has the ransom of the soul (*bla bslu*) as its purpose is too extensive for it to be described here in detail. It must suffice to indicate that care is taken to trace this custom too back to a traditional precedent, to its revelation by a god or its first performance by a particularly famous wonder-worker of the past such as Padmasambhava. Through this precedent the nature and mode of this ritual performance was established once and for all, unalterably (as in No. 51 in the case of the illness of *rgyal bu Mu khyud 'dzin*). The withdrawal of the *bla* from the body and the consequent danger can be the work of a *lha* (god) or a *'dre* (demon). Therefore it is necessary to establish first of all which of the two is responsible for the seduction of the *bla* in the case at hand, because, according to which it is, quite different kinds of rituals are employed. This basic preliminary decision is made with the aid of dice (*shwa* = *sho*), and in doing so the white die is offered (*'bul*) to the *lha*, while the black is thrown (*gtad*) for the *'dre*. High scores (*shwa chen*) are assigned to the gods, low (*shwa chung*) to the demons. If high figures are thrown, it is certain that a *lha* is the cause of the illness or the threatening death of the man for whose benefit the ritual is to be performed.

The ceremony requires all sorts of accessories; a *bla* figure modelled out of *tsamba* and resembling the endangered person, the right thigh-bone of a sheep, a piece of wood, a white stone, water, precious substances, a white die, a coral, a turquoise and so on. These are all placed in a bowl (*sder*), which is then covered with its own lid and placed on a vessel or a measure (*bre*) of barley. After this the white die is offered to the *lha*, the black is thrown to the *'dre*, while an arrow from which hangs a white cloth is brought over the previously mentioned vessel. Around the *tsamba* figure of the sick man, which is if possible smeared with his sweat or spittle, are placed his shoes, his hat and a living animal which has been specially liberated in order to free it from being killed (*tshe thar*). The magician now announces that the sacred action he is performing is a repetition of that accomplished for the first time by Padmasambhava. After having established in the manner mentioned above in whose hands, those of a *lha* or a *'dre*, the soul of the sick man has fallen, he requests the *lha*, if the die has fallen in favour of a *lha*, to accept a white lamb (*tshe thar*), while he offers the *bla* as support the right thigh-bone of the sheep and implores him to take up his abode in this (*bla rkang*) and then successively in the white die (*bla yi shwa*), in the turquoise, in the coral, in the stone (*bla rdo*), in the piece of wood (*bla shing*) and so forth.

To finish, the exorcist declares that the figure offered as ransom (*glud*) is not a lifeless or dead thing, but a living creature; then he invites the *lha* to set at liberty the soul enchained by him and to accept the *glud* in its place, while the soul is cautioned not to go astray (*yo*), not to stumble, not to disintegrate (*nub*), not to break apart (*chag*), not to wander about.

The utensils mentioned, especially the bowl (*sder* or *phor pa*), must always be kept by the actual person for whom the ceremony is effective, because all these ingredients are now very closely linked with his *bla*, having actually become its residence (*gnas*) and support. Their loss or theft would expose the person concerned to the greatest danger. The bowl particularly he must henceforth handle with care and make constant use of. The measure of grain however belongs to the exorcist.

The same ceremony, naturally *mutatis mutandis*, is used in the case of the seduction of the soul by the *'dre*; in this case the demonic powers coming into question are enumerated by classes (*ya bdud kyi sde*, *lha yi sde*, *gnod sbyin*, *klu*, *bdud kyi sde*, *rgyal po'i sde mu rje*, *skyes bu lung btsan*, *gnyan chan thang lha*, *sman kyi sde*, *the'u rang*, *rgyal chen bzhi*, *yul gzhi bdag*).

If it is a question of saving a human being whose safety is of importance for religion, on account of his learning or his holy behaviour, it can also happen that the powers who have determined upon his downfall can be directed to another goal, provided that another person is prepared to offer himself in his place; such a person is called 'substitute in flesh, substitute in bone' (*sha tshab rus tshab*).

The *bla* has a definite shape (*gzugs*); despite this it resides in various kinds of objects, in the wood, in the stone, in the die, in the coral, and so forth. If it can be extricated from the clutches of the *lha* or *'dre*, it is exposed to the danger of disintegrating or stumbling. It can also break apart. It gives out its own light, it can need food; it is almost omnipresent, because it allows itself to be localized in so many different places.

Although in Buddhism, at least as far as its doctrine is concerned, there is no place for a soul, since the decision-making centre of karmic continuity resides in *vijnana* (Tib. *rnam par shes pa*), the new religion of Tibet was not able totally to suppress older concepts such as the pluralism of souls, which as we know was particularly common among the ancient Chinese and the tribes of north-central and south-west Asia.[16] The *bla* is a kind of living double of the individual concerned; to gain control over it means to gain control over the person to whom it belongs. Certainly it is not as easy to destroy as any material body, but it can be injured, and it is also subject to wear and tear.

Alongside the *bla* exists the *srog*, that is to say the vital force identical with the duration of life (No. 9 (*Bon*) Ch.2,p.8b, *srog ni tshe ste*). It flows in the breathing (*dbugs*), has its seat in the heart and penetrates the whole body (loc.cit.). Although the concepts involved here frequently vary and can only with difficulty be reduced to a common denominator, it is at least clear that they mean the principle which is the opposite to the state of death. The disappearance of this force is equivalent to death. Thus we are concerned with a kind of life-impulse, respiration (*dbugs*, Skt. *prana*), vital spirit, that becomes weaker along with the life as such. So it is that in certain texts (No. 51) there is mention of the duration of life of the soul (*bla tshe*), of a vital duration of the *srog* and so of the respiration (*dbugs tshe*), and thus it is that the gods are invoked in specific cycles of deities to hold back 'the time of life' (*tshe khug*), since the life in this its triple aspect has become injured and damaged (*nyams pa*). The various forms of bodily incarnation, assumed one after the other, are dependent upon the *srog* (No. 10, p.14b), but here we enter into a vicious circle, for these bodily incarnations in connection with the principle of consciousness and with moral responsibility determine the causation of a greater or lesser stock of merits (*dbang thang*), and this in its turn determines the variation in the following *srog*. *Bla* is accordingly a mobile soul, which can take its residence anywhere, in a tree, a rock, an animal, but nevertheless remains linked most closely with the life of the person concerned. The soul always needs a support (*rgyab rten*). Thus the invocatory prayer aims to prevent this support from becoming ill, breaking up or being destroyed (No. 11, p.5b, and No. 51). The *srog*, which can take up its dwelling in any desired object (e.g. *ljon shing*, No. 11, p.11b) is obviously exposed to similar dangers. There is also a kind of collective soul; thus mountains are the *bla ri* of those communities who worship them as ancestral deities. Mount *Ti se* (Skt. *Kailasa*), for example, is looked on as being the *bla ri* of *Zhang zhung*.

The respiration (*dbugs*) too has the same duration as the life as such. It is always spoken of, as already mentioned, in close connection with the *srog* (the *dam sri*, demons of death, seduce away the *srog* and *dbugs* of man, so that he falls ill and dies, No. 75). We are concerned here with the double aspect of the breathing/soul found widely distributed in the beliefs of many peoples, and in which the traces of much more complicated ideas can still be perceived. Such ideas are particularly evident in the group of the *'go ba'i lha*, the 'guiding deities', and also in that of the *dgra lha*.[17] These concepts rest upon especially ancient foundations. The *lha* with which they are concerned are enumerated and classified in a quite different manner; in groups of 5, 7, 13, 21 *'go ba'i lha*.

Here we must limit ourselves to the group of five *'go ba'i lha*, who have become protective gods.[18] They are addressed in order to obtain their protection, and yet they are born immediately together with man (*lhan cig skyes*). One of them stands, as we will see, at the side of a person after his death at the moment of judgment (cf.p.194). In this group we come across *lha* already known to us. We should not overlook the circumstance, in this connection, that all these *lha* have their seat in the human body, are born together with man and accompany him throughout his entire life. In the invocations addressed to them they are requested not to allow the vital force (*srog*) of the person placed under their protection to come to harm (No. 69, p.3) and similarly with the *bla* and the *mdangs*. The last word designates the glowing appearance of a man in good health and full strength, thus corresponding to the Sanskrit concepts of *ojas* or *tejas*. It can also be supposed that in the case of this group of five *'go ba'i lha* we are concerned originally with the deifying of forces which are rather inherent within the human being, with what were protective souls, before they changed into protective gods on whom depend the bodily integrity of the individual.

5 Death

In relation with what has been said above it can be seen that, according to the Tibetan conception, death is not merely a question, as in earlier Buddhism, of the consequence of the process of maturation of karma which has effect at a particular time and in a particular manner; it is also a separation of the life-principle, *bla*, from the body, which can be traced back to factors which are fortuitous rather than karmic in a strict sense. This separation is, however, not irreparable, for there are appropriate techniques available to call the *bla* back into its bodily shell and so give life back to the body. The subversion of the basic teachings of Buddhism, already continually making progress in its Tantric expression, takes on such great proportions in Tibet that the previously mentioned indigenous conceptions persist ineradicably. Because of its representative nature the *Bar do thos grol*, the recitation of the 'Book of the Dead' by the pillow of the dying or dead man intended to awake the liberating consciousness in his consciousness principle, can here be referred to again. In its various versions (cf.pp.74-5), adapted to the doctrinal systems of each tendency, this book stands at the centre of the Lamaistic technique of liberation. The salvation practice of the *Bar do thos grol*, especially in the sense in which the *rNying ma pa* and *bKa' brgyud pa* understand it, has a remarkable peculiarity; its final goal is always to afford relief from the appointed processes of karma.

In the *Bar do thos grol* the consciousness which the lama performing the practice attempts to awake in the consciousness principle of the dead man has a purification as its object. The lama who whispers the syllables of the book in the ear of a dead man still retaining a trace of his own consciousness principle is in reality a *psychopompos*[19] who accompanies the dead person step by step on his difficult path during the forty-nine days of the intermediate state (*antarabhava*) between death and rebirth. If the recitation of the book does not succeed in awakening the consciousness of the dead man, and so in bringing about his transition into a better form of existence, then his consciousness principle will be led before the god of the dead for the last judgment. Then before him (Tucci, 1958) he sees darkness, from behind the storm assails him, and the messengers of *gShin rje* (the god of the dead) strike him. However, he does not arrive in front of his judge alone, but attended by two accompanying figures; one is the 'demon of evil works born with man', the other the god born with man. One is black, the other white; one has black pebbles in his hand, the other white, to reckon at the moment of judgment the good and bad actions committed by the dead man. These spirits, who exist and are present simultaneously in man, enter into existence together with him and grow to maturity along with him as the embodiments of the good and evil deeds he has accomplished. At the moment of his death they take on a concrete form. Here the *dgra lha*, discussed above, is faced by his counterpart; however, on this occasion we are no longer concerned with a purely material protector in the *dgra lha*, but with a kind of counsel for the defence of man before the last judgment.[20]

A new idea breaks through in these eschatological representations;

the dividing of conscience into two and accordingly its twofold embodiment in a defending god and accusing demon–a division which evidently arises from ethical preoccupations. The reckoning of good and bad works is made through the black and white pebbles mentioned above, and also with the help of a mirror and of a balance (to refute the sinner's protestations of innocence) quite apart from a register in which all the past acts are inscribed. Certain particularities seem to suggest prototypes in Iranian eschatology, where the conflict between the good and bad consciences, particularly, is a characteristic feature, a conflict which stretches on into the hereafter and upon which the fate of the individual soul depends.

Thus according to the *Dâtastân-i-Denîk*,[21] during the third night, as dawn begins to break, the guardian of good deeds comes in the form of a beautiful girl in the prime of life to meet the soul and shows to it the accumulated store of good works, while on the other side the soul is faced by its sins, embodied in a fear-inspiring old woman burdened with all the evils the soul has committed.

In the same way, in another book,[22] the guardians who watch over the good and evil deeds of men struggle with each other for possession of the soul. If the guardian of good actions wins, he then frees the dead man from the clutches of his accuser and leads him before the Great One who sits upon his throne and further into the presence of the Luminous. But if the guardian of sins turns out to be the victor, then the soul will be torn from the hands of its defender and delivered over into the realm of hunger, thirst and excruciating illnesses.

Even more marked are the correspondences with the Iranian *Cinvat* bridge, that bridge of judgment in the world beyond over which only the pure succeed in crossing, while the damned plunge into the river of hell beneath it. Ideas which correspond exactly can be found in the *'das log* writings (e.g. No. 76, *ka*, p.6a and *ga*, p.4b), where the river is called *gShin chu nag po nga ro can*, the bridge *gShin rje zam pa*, 'bridge of *gShin rje*'. In the text cited in the second place there is also mention of a passage narrow as a hair, through which only the righteous can pass, while the others fall down with fearful screams into the floods of hell.

For all this it could in no way be maintained that the theory and practice of the *Bar do*,[23] as presented among the *rNying ma pa*, are entirely the result of Iranian influences. Apart from Indian elements, one can also clearly distinguish others of a shamanistic character, as for example the mention of the terrifying noise which blocks the way of the soul of the dead man, or torments it, and also the belief well known in the shamanistic realm of a sojourn, shorter or longer (lasting up to forty days), of the soul in the neighbourhood of the grave (that is if we are not concerned here with a purely Lamaistic element), the conception of the soul being severely threatened on its journey beyond the grave, the conception of a multiplicity of vital principles or souls and so forth.

The elements of diverse origin which one comes across in the *Bar do* have naturally been adapted to the eschatological framework of Buddhism. Besides this, the *Bon* religion has a literature of its own, complete with practical applications, which has as its subject the cycle of peaceful and fear-inspiring deities (*zhi khro*) who appear in the *Bar do* state. It goes without saying that the deities in question have here other names, but in both cases we are concerned with the same principle, so that one is led to think that the parallel versions of the *Bon po* and *rNying ma pa* are derived from the same prototype.

Other rituals which Lamaism offers to its followers to free the dead person from the fate prepared for him by his own deeds seem to be less complicated. Liturgical prescriptions of this kind are included in the works of the great doctrinal masters of Buddhism; they follow the usual plans of Tantric ritualism. Although they are basically of Indian origin, they represent in their actual formulation a concession to Tibetan beliefs. This is particularly so in regard to the hope which they arouse of being able to alter the fate of the departed in some way. The Mahayana and Vajrayana had already found ways to circumvent the law of karma; it surely ought to be possible to bring about some modification of its inflexibility, in the first place through pious practices and works or through the transferral of one's own merits to another person, especially to one's own relations. Thus one finds the formula repeated, in for example the inscriptions of Ladakh and the dedications of the *sKu 'bum* in Gyantse, that the consequences arising from a meritorious act, such as the building of a *mchod rten*, a '*mani* wall' or a temple, may benefit one's deceased relations. All this implies unequivocally that quite apart from the *Bar do thos grol* liturgy there existed the belief that it was possible to have an influence in some way on the fate of the dead.

The practices of the Tantras, and the liturgical processes connected with them, set themselves the basic task of bringing about a sudden reversal of the planes of existence, from the time-bound existence of *samsara* to the extra-temporal plane of *nirvana*. This goal ought necessarily to be the most precious thing of all for the Tibetan, but all his thoughts and endeavours go to escaping from the inexorable maturation of karma or at least to mitigating its consequences. Thus ingenious liturgies were elaborated in Tibet which either aim at procuring directly the entire cleansing of karma (*sdig sgrub sbyangs*, Nos 25, 26) or else intend to bring about the transformation of bad karma into good karma and so offer, as an immediate consequence of the ritual performance, a guarantee of a rebirth (new life) opposed to that allocated by the karma which has been accumulated. This kind of process has to be achieved through the awakening of the consciousness principle of the dead man, since it is required that he respond to the ritual invocation. A powerful reversal of the planes of existence is then called forth for his benefit. One of these liturgies, composed by *Ngor bla ma*, has as its centre the cult of *Kun rig*, a special manifestation of *rNam par snang mdzad* (Vairocana).

It is unnecessary in the present account to go into the details of the introductory ritual through which is brought about the purification of all that can be thought by its identification with the void (*stong pa nyid*), and the becoming one in substance of the celebrant and the deity. There follows the evocation of the Buddhas of all directions of space, who reveal themselves through their radiance, so manifesting their apparent bodies, while they preach the doctrine of salvation. The centre of the ceremony is formed by the evocation of *khro rgyal bgegs tshogs 'dul*, the 'conqueror of *khro rgyal*,[24] the overcomer of all *bgegs*'. This leads into an invitation to the demons (*bgegs*) to depart and leave the field free.

The specially made *mandala* is now clothed with an aura of immaculate sacredness, and the deification of the celebrant achieved according to the prescribed manner (Nos 25, 26). Afterwards a piece of bone (*rus*) belonging to the dead man is placed upon the *mandala*, or else a piece of paper or wood on which his name is written (*ming byang bu*), apart from the ingredients necessary for the purificatory ritual (*sbyang ba'i yo byad*), grains of sand (*bye ma*), white mustard-seed (*yungs kar*) and so on. Now the dissolution of these things into the void is brought about through the meditation process. Behind this act lies the idea that the objects to be ritually purified (*sbyongs stegs*), among them the piece of paper or wood inscribed with the syllable *nr* (Skt. 'man') and the appropriate initial letter of the dead man's name,[25] then emerge anew from the void. In the following phase the image of the dead person, his name, his bodily appearance, in short the totality of his visible components (*phung po*, *khams*, *skye mched*, with the exception of the consciousness principle), is visualized. Now two lights shine forth from the syllable *nr* conceived of as being in the heart of the dead person and the *hūm* visualized in the meditator's heart, in order to draw to themselves the consciousness principle of the dead man, wherever it might be, and to bring it into the piece of paper or wood already mentioned. If it appears to be white in colour, that is in its original state, then a ritual circuit is made of the *mandala*, turning to the left the *rdo rje* (*rdo rje gsor*) held in the right hand, while the little bell is placed in the left, meanwhile offering *gtor ma* (*ting lo* and *chang bu*, cf. above p.177) to the *gdon* and *bgegs* as recompense (*rngan*). The *gdon* and *bgegs* are now requested to go away and to leave the consciousness principle of the deceased, since this latter has forfeited its innate purity through their entry. If the powers reject this request, they are compelled to let loose their prey by the diamond consciousness (*rdo rje ye shes*) which is identical or analogous to the spiritual nature (*thugs*) of all the Tathāgata. The sins weighing down the dead person next materialize, first as a black point, then as a scorpion; this burns in the fire to the right or dissolves in the water to the left. The sins which have become materially visible in such a way having been overcome, nine mantras are next recited before the bone of the dead man or the piece of paper or wood which bears his name, apart from other purificatory rituals, which can be passed over here.

The special role of the bone in this connection is noteworthy. It is in the ceremony just described not only the support of the dead man, but also, in accordance with ideas distributed over all Central and North Asia, the principle of life; the soul has its residence in the bone and life can arise again out of this element.

The extent of Buddhism's tolerance towards popular ideas appears clearly in the ritual described. As we have seen we are concerned here with a kind of 'summoning to judgment' of the soul (that it is referred to in this context as *rnam par shes pa*, consciousness principle, has little significance), in order that the bad karma should not merely have its efficacy limited but be directly annihilated. The sins are here conceived as something material and physical which takes possession of the soul, as a pernicious black substance that can be eliminated from the soul through the ritual action so that it attains once more its original white colour.

Ideas analogous to these are common in another genre of Tibetan literature, in the stories told of human beings who have temporarily died or who have returned from a journey in the world beyond (*'das log*)[26] into this world in order to report here what they have seen. Lamaism uses writings of this kind to impress its teachings on simple people and to spread its ethical precepts. Sometimes these ideas recall very closely the journeys of the soul common in the world of shamanistic culture, apart, naturally, from the transformations brought about by Buddhism in the basic religious conceptions.

In most cases a grave sickness (*nad drag po*) precedes the journey to the hereafter, an illness which strikes man unexpectedly and has particular symptoms; fever, burning in the throat, cold shivers. Before the journey the *'das log* has terrible visions and hallucinations, he imagines himself in the middle of frightening storms and whirlwinds, he hears a fearful noise, he believes himself attacked by mighty hailstorms, which shatter his bones and lacerate his head (No. 76, *ca*, p.2b), he feels like a shipwrecked man at the bottom of the sea or as if thrown to the heights of the sky, he believes himself to be dead, for the real world disappears from his view and he sees the world of the hereafter. Sometimes he throws himself into the air in front of his house on a horse which has suddenly appeared in front of him and he is led on his journey by the command of invisible beings serving him as guides. His reawakening too is slow and painful. These and other similar details recall many of the experiences of enrapturement that accompany the journeys through heaven and descent into the underworld of the shamans, but one cannot mistake a certain difference between such shamanistic visions and the reports of the 'return' described. While in the realm of shamanism the shaman undertakes his journey of his own free will, here the event befalls the person concerned in a quite unexpected manner, it has an expressly fortuitous character, although those particularly suited by their natures for adventures of this kind are preferred. Both realms have in common the exit from oneself and return, the journey to the hereafter and the healing of the soul, while in the Buddhist milieu such healing is synonymous with the overcoming of moral defilement and sinfulness.

While the representations of the world hereafter have changed from the older conceptions, such as those characteristic of the *Bon* tradition, one can still see today that the idea of a continuous connection between earth and the regions of paradise has not totally disappeared from the Tibetan folk imagination, and that the belief is still common that the dead person keeps in the world beyond the appearance he had while alive, that he undertakes his voyage to the heavenly fields on a cloth scarf, carried by his meritorious works, along with similar ideas. Evidently the piece of cloth here has the role of a bridge–a concept certainly different from that of the rainbow body mentioned previously (p.86, cf. Tucci, 1949, p.733), although even in this case the archetypal background remains the same.

6 The *bsangs* or *suffimen* (offering of incense)

We have already mentioned the *bsangs* above (cf.p.169) as being one of the most notable liturgical acts of Tibetan folk religion. It is a *suffimen*[27] which, accompanied by prayers, is offered every morning, more rarely in the evening, by the father of the house, or, in his absence, always by a man. In *Khams*, for example, performing *bsangs* in the evening is in fact considered to be dangerous, in that it can bring death to horses. This daily ritual act belongs to those liturgical ceremonies which are referred to in Hinduism as *nityapuja*, daily divine service, and which are distinguished from those rituals performed only for a particular reason, or on festive occasions. The *bsangs* exhibits diverse variations in its actual performance; its essential nature, however, is always that of a *suffimen*, a fumigation using aromatic and perfumed herbs (*bdud rtsi shing*) such as juniper. A purifying and atoning action is attributed to the sweet-smelling smoke of these offerings, which spreads in all directions. The fumigation is the basic element of these rituals, even though there can be attached to this *suffimen* the offering of valuable gifts or also of reproductions of animals. In the accompanying invocations and fervent prayers the world of folk religion, with its many levels looking back far into the past, is mirrored with particular clarity. Closely associated with the *bsangs* is the reward-offering (*brngan*) to the equivocal powers peopling space, who need to be rendered favourable through such donations of desirable and costly things (*'dod pa'i mchod pa*), for the most part simply represented by reproductions. The person making the offerings takes up his position at an idealized centre of space and time, so that through his *suffimen* and the gifts associated with it all conceivable powers will be purified and appeased (*zhi ba*): *chos skyong*, *dri za*, *grul bum*, powers of the ground and the earth on which the maker of offerings lives (*sa bdag*), and also the various *lha*, the deity of the house, of the herd, of the store-room (*bang mdzod lha*), the *pho lha* (with his seat in his *mkhar*), the god of the door, etc. To which are added the countless indeterminate powers who have a protective function and who can bring all sorts of misfortune on man and on his property if offended or neglected: the god of horses (*rta lha*, *rma dpon*), the god of the herds (*phyugs lha*), and also the *numina* who watch over the fields (*zhing lha*), or those of the subterranean region (the *klu*), of the region above the earth (the *sman*), then the *srung*, the twelve great *brtan ma*, the thirteen *mgur lha*, apart of course from the powers who by their nature cause nothing but ill, the *'dre* and *bgegs*.

Once these powers who surround man have been pacified and the offerings have been gracefully accepted, the invocation is addressed to the five gods born with man (cf.p.193). All the powers appeased in this way are implored for prosperity and blessing (*g.yang* and *phya*).

For such a prayer to be granted presupposes moral and ritual purity in the petitioner. As already indicated (cf.p.173), in the domain of the ritual conceptions which have control here the impurity which can bring forth anger and vengeance of the powers, and for which pardon is implored, is not to be understood merely in an ethical sense. It has rather a considerably wider range of meaning; guilt of this kind can be brought about through acts which are free of any ethical valuation. The underlying idea of guilt here does not only result from the transgression of Buddhist moral laws, since it is not limited to the plane of karma. We are not exclusively concerned here with a sin whose retribution comes to maturity according to the law of karma. Karma is individually conditioned, it is a sort of settlement of accounts, and the author of each act is well aware that this settlement must be made under all circumstances. The law of karma prepares for each one of us a continuum closed in upon itself, which from its very origin, because of the given suppositions, excludes all external influences. Things are quite different in the folk religion. Here it is a question of a pollution, an impurity, a shadow, a contamination (*grib*) which brings about in man a particular state of weakness, which opens the way for hostile and evil-wishing powers (*gdon*), the *lha*, *'dre*, *bgegs*, as was shown before in the discussion of *gdon* (cf.p.173) but is easy to illustrate through further examples. The *dregs* also are demonic beings, but *dreg* in addition means uncleanness, filth. *Grib* is not only a group of dark, evil *numina*, but also means spot, shadow, in short always a lack of lightness, a stain. Such a state causes the deities inborn with man and his protective deities to abandon him, to 'turn away their sight' from him, since he has become polluted and impure. The meaning of *bsangs* as an essential element of this liturgical action can thus be understood; *bsangs* is derived from *sangs*, to purify, and so it denotes an act of purification, by which every impurity, *dreg*, *grib*, *gdon*, is overcome. At the same time this act of purification does not only extend to he who performs the offering, and who as a result is immune to any attack by hostile powers and made worthy of the requested protection of the appeased deities; it also applies to the deities themselves whom he addresses. The ritual purifies them too and obtains for them the condition of purity. This is why we find in many formulae *bstan srung bsangs*, *gzhi bdag bsangs* 'purified are the *bstan srung*, purified are the *gzhi bdag*', (No. 70).

Two of the many occasions which provoke the ill-humour and vengeance of particular powers (in this case the *klu* ruling the underground or the *sa bdag*) are the carrying away of stones (*rdo slog*) and the digging of the earth (*sa brko*). Such actions must therefore be preceded by a ritual of propitiation based upon the *bsangs*. These actions are dangerous in themselves and for those who perform them because they represent a damaging irruption into the domain of the powers of the underworld. Since the moment when the first king, *Ye smon rgyal po*, introduced agriculture, this impurity has weighed upon man. The working of the earth by man signified the coming of a new order of things, upsetting the previous state. The *klu*, *gnyen*, *lha*, *lha mo*, *sman* and all the other countless *numina* burned in anger at this and punished man's lack of consideration with all kinds of harm. Thus man was obliged to assure himself of the assistance of the seers, those first *institutores* of a civilized common life, who instructed him in the necessary rites of atonement and defence operations. The customs related to the *bsangs* (and similarly to the *gto*, *glud* and *mdos*) which are prescribed on laying the foundation stone of a house go back to these very teachings and models. The celebrant, whether acting in his own interest or commissioned by another (the *sbyin bdag*) renews a sacred action first accomplished *in illo tempore* (*sngon gyi bskal ba'i dang po la*, No. 63, p.4), his action repeats a liturgy of atonement revealed *ab initio*. In the ritual act once becomes Now: 'I am the body which destroyed the three poisons, I am identical to all the victorious ones, I am the forefather of the triple world, I am the father of all creatures. The *lha* and *srin*, who cause harm to all the world, are all slaves awaiting my command' (No. 67, p.3).

7 Looking into the future: investigating the favourable or unfavourable omens for an action

In view of the dependence of man on the powers afflicting him from all directions and his being at the mercy of their good will it is understandable that he looks in all directions for appropriate means and ways to obtain indications of his future fate and hints on how best to conduct himself. On such preconditions rests the enormous success of astrology, which had in part already taken a firm foothold in Buddhism with the Tantric scriptures, but which now also entered at various times from China (cf. pp.142, 172). The oracular teachings of the *Yi king*, as embodied in the symbolism of the eight trigrams (*pa kua*) and five metals, penetrated to Tibet and here provided the preferred theme for the amulets or fortune-telling cards which the Tibetan carries around with him or keeps in his house. However, in the course of time these objects lost more and more their divinatory and astrological character and came to take on a more narrowly apotropaic function.

Alongside the mood of expectation, suspicion, anxiety which overshadows the entire existence of the Tibetan runs the conviction that the future of man can in some way show itself through indicatory omens (*ltas*), good or bad. It therefore becomes extraordinarily important to acquire the ability to uncover, to understand, to interpret rightly omens of this kind. In the present context we cannot go into more detail about all the modes of predictive experience, which represent a common possession of almost all cultures. Their great significance holds too in Lamaistic contexts. Here a truly initiatory role is often conferred upon dream visions, but Tibet is not alone in these matters and in this regard it has little to offer that is essentially new and individual. Besides there are other methods to discover the imminently approaching fate of an individual person, thanks to which he is put into a position to take appropriate remedies.

Procedures of this kind are prophecy and the drawing of lots, which are already indicated in certain inscriptions and documents (Tucci,

1950, p.52) of the dynastic period, and which were officially used at this period whenever there were important decisions to be made. Thus we are concerned here with a survival from pre-Buddhist times. One of the most frequent methods of inquiring into the future consists in the use of dice, *sho*, a method which is placed under the patronage of *dPal ldan lha mo*, *dMag zor ma* or some other deity; an unmistakable indication of the taking over of an old, indigenous custom by particularly popular Buddhist deities. Besides this, predictions of the future and advice at moments of uncertainty rely also on the oracular pronouncement of a *btsan* (in such a case referred to as *mo lha*) such as *btsan rje snying krung*.

This last *btsan* belongs to the circle of those *numina* with which the so-called *pra*-liturgy is concerned. In this procedure a person, usually a woman or a child, is able to uncover the future because the *btsan* has descended upon the person concerned; he is then referred to as the 'support of the *pra*' (*pra brten*). An essential utensil here is the mirror (*me long*), support of the ritual and of the revelation of the future (*sgrub rten*). Other requirements are an arrow with the usual five-coloured cloth, the offering of milk and *chang*, of flour mixed with butter (*phye mar*) and of barley. The *btsan* who is evoked and called upon to accept the offerings appears in front of the magician black as pitch; he is dressed in a jacket (*go zhu*) of black material and rides on a dark horse with black hooves; on his head he bears a black feather; his speech is resounding. He is asked to accept the gift and then to decide in favour of the good and against the bad, for good fortune against evil fortune.

But sometimes the situation is much more complicated (No. 55). The support of the *pra* is then a boy or a girl; if a boy, he must be between eight and sixteen years old, if a girl, she must be between twelve and sixteen.[28] The deity descends upon his bearer (the relationship is expressed in words as *rten-brten*; *rten* the bearer of the *pra*, *brten* what is born, the deity entering into him) in order to give signs predicting the future through the 'person taken into his possession' (who looks fixedly into a mirror where appears all the good and evil in the world, *snang srid kyi legs nyes 'char ba'i me long*). Through having been taken possession of, if only temporarily, by a *lha*, the person concerned is set off from the crowd of his equals, he becomes a *lha pa*, 'one whom the *lha* has descended', indeed in whom it has as it were incarnated. The person to be 'possessed' must be prepared and chosen for his task; among other things he must somewhere pick up, unseen, a stone, which, carefully wrapped in a black and white cloth, is hidden by the *sngags pa* conducting the ritual (*pra mkhan*) under his knee. This stone is called *bla rdo*, soul-stone—a further indication of the incorporation of shamanistic ideas in this new context. The celebrant must be clothed in white. Though the formulae used are more or less

Sanskrit in character, the entire plan of the ritual betrays a far more ancient foundation, for example in the meditation on the divine yak, in the designation of the female goddesses as *sman btsun*, turquoises (in the Buddhist context their names are preceded by *rdo rje*, Skt. *vajra*, 'diamond'). These goddesses descend from a tent which is made out of a 'heaping-up of precious clouds'; or the deity dwells beyond the heavenly spaces, beyond the sun, on the peak of a mountain which is as white as a shell. In the middle of a lake, similarly white as a shell, there is a tent of rock-crystal (*shel gur*) in which the god rests who is now called on to descend, without wearying himself, to foretell the future. The lots of destiny are of three kinds, those which concern the house (*khyim phya*), life (*srog phya*), or the birth of a son (*srid phya*). Besides using the mirror, the revelation can be brought about by staring at the finger-nails (*sen pra*).

In this whole area of folk religion the fundamental principle of Lamaistic liturgy remains valid; the celebrant is only qualified to perform the sacred action when he has transformed himself into a god (*lha bskyed*) through the appropriate meditation. It is only thanks to this deification that he can become master of the opposing powers. In this context the taking possession of a human being by the deity is not excluded, as the *pra*-ritual shows. In the latter case however the ceremony does not bring about a deification, it serves rather to put the subject of the process into a passive and receptive state; thus he becomes the support and the bearer whom the deity invoked uses for his temporary stay. The *numen* needs a human support to be able to act and speak. Here we are not concerned in any way with a mystical rapture, but with a specific state of possession.

Among the many forms of oracles and divination, for example for decisions in cases of doubt, we will cite here only the practice of scapulimancy, divination with the aid of a shoulder-blade, which is in use in Tibet as elsewhere.

8 The protection of property and of flocks

Apart from his own personal protection, man must also be concerned about the security of his possessions. The dangers which threaten him also bring into doubt the sources of his well-being. According to whether we are concerned with a nomadic pastoralist or a sedentary agriculturalist, the liturgical form which is used varies. For the agriculturalist the most important thing of all is that he be spared by bad weather, especially hail, mildew (*btsa*) and drought (*than*), and on the other hand that he be favoured by rain at the right moment (*char chu dus su rgyun mi 'chad par phebs*) so that he obtains an abundant harvest (*lo tog, lo thog, lo thog dang 'bru'i tshogs phun sum tshogs*) and so on. He also wishes to keep illness, poverty and hunger (No. 12, p.9) away from himself and his family. Thus invocations to the god of the fields, *zhing lha* (No. 60), and to a whole host of other deities, some equivalent to Indian gods (*Tshangs pa* = Skt. *Brahma*, etc.). others local, are followed by offerings to the powers who damage the harvest. Here too are inserted in a liturgical practice which is probably of Indian origin (e.g. Skt. *ghatasthapana*;[29] in India there is similarly an extremely rich magical and exorcistic literature on the protection of the fields) some names of pre-Buddhist *numina*; most of the time these are no more than names, the skeletal residue of a very ancient vanished mythology.

In the case of a bad harvest recourse is had to the 'ransom of the year' *glud* (No. 61), a *glud* which is primarily directed towards the evil powers *bse rag*, *'gong*, *dam sri* and *'byung po*, considered to be the authors of the damage suffered by the performer of the exorcism. Here the magician identifies himself with *Khrag thung* Heruka: 'I am *khrag thung* (blood-drinker) Heruka'. In the course of this process the demons, if they do not accept the offerings and will not renounce their evil purposes, are driven back by the magician with threats. He faces them, armed and armoured, a sword in his hand, and cries aloud the magic formula *gi ha*. However, before going to such extremes the demons are offered *yas* (cf.p.176) in order to pacify the *'gong po*, the 'Nine Brothers' divided according to cosmological tradition, and persuade them to change their evil disposition (*zhe sdang*) into a feeling of compassion (*byams pa'i sems*) for all creatures. In this case too we are concerned with the settling of a debt entered into with respect to the powers and arising from man's conduct (No. 61).

The nomadic part of the population (*'brog pa*), whose economy rests on pastoralism, especially on the yak and the horse, possesses a special pantheon of its own, at whose centre stand the *Phyugs lha spun bdun*, the 'Seven Brother Gods of the Herds', namely the horse-god, the god of the yak, the god of the tame domestic yak (*'bri*), the god of the *mdzo* (yak-cow cross), the god of oxen, the god of sheep and the god of goats. In the case of illnesses of horses one carries out the ransom of the horse (*rta glud*), a ceremony connected with the *gtum chen*. We must content ourselves here with these particulars and with indicating in a general manner that the religious world of the nomads presents peculiar features, along with reminiscences of ancient origins from many different levels, which would justify a special investigation.

9 Final considerations

The folk religion of which an outline has been given in the previous pages reveals a religious and magical heritage, a structure of rituals, beliefs, oral traditions and legendary accounts behind which stands centuries of past history and which has only been able to integrate itself slowly and hesitantly into the world of Buddhism. Convictions which had been widespread since ancient times flowed into the new religion through the *sngags pa* and the *bandhe*, who themselves depended upon the same beliefs, but were more easily able to unite them into a systematic liturgical system. Tantric ritual afforded a stronger and better-defined framework for the customary religious practices. Invocations of Buddhist deities had to suffice to lend a Buddhist veneer to rituals which originally had not the slightest connection with Buddhism. The divine figures introduced through Buddhism from India thus co-exist with the indigenous deities, even though they sometimes bear openly the signs of intruders (cf. for example the insertion of Heruka into the ritual described in the preceding section). Tantric liturgy with its ritual superimposition on the practice of *gtor ma*, *mdos*, *bsangs*, *glud* and so forth nowhere eliminated the ancient religious sub-stratum. Reproductions of animals made out of butter and flour, pieces of *tsamba* modelled in countless ways each having a name according to its form and destination–all this has nothing to do with the Tantric ritual of India, even if individual words correspond, as for example *gtor ma* to the Sanskrit *bali*. The nature and construction of the customs in question are basically different from those of the Indian rituals which provide a mere exterior covering for them. We are dealing here with ancient customs which cannot everywhere conceal their primitive crudity. Thus we come across clear echoes of shamanistic ideas in the plurality of souls, in the possibility of a soul being possessed or made captive, in the journey of the soul to the world beyond and so on. The liturgical instruments are often those of *Bon* and of the shamanistic world; the pole-drum (*rnga*) and the *damaru*, both essential instruments in every ceremony, are employed not so much to frighten the hostile powers as rather to help bring about a state of inner composure which will facilitate the descent of the divine powers invoked and their taking possession of the exorcist who is thereby to some degree deprived of his consciousness. The arrow[30] with its attached piece of cloth of five colours, the mirror which is an indispensable part of the *Bon po's* armoury, are of similar provenance. The celebrant must make it known that he has accomplished the return to the initial state (e.g. *sngon gyi srid pa'i dpe bzhin*, 'according to the example laid down at the beginning of existence'), in other words he identifies himself with the teacher who introduced the ritual in question (e.g. *bdag 'dra Pad ma 'byung gnas*, 'Padmasambhava who is alike to me'). In order to achieve its full efficacy the ritual must be performed by someone who has transformed himself into its first author. Only the reversibility of sacred time guarantees the success of the ceremony.

Ideas of this kind govern the Tibetans of practically all classes of society. In the context of this social structure the *'das log* literature (that of those who have died and returned to life), created for the people and among the people, in order to diffuse and deepen religious ideals among them, ascribes only a limited degree of importance to the monastic community in its own right. In these writings (No. 76, *kha*, p.35) the enumeration begins with the leaders of the citizenry, the lords (*skyong chen, mi chen*), then goes on to their counsellors or officials (*drung 'khor*) and only then names the monks, even then beginning with the 'great meditators' (*sgom chen*), the ascetics who are not necessarily tied to the monastic life. Among the members of the monastic order the *dge bshes* (Skt. *kalyanamitra*) are given a prominent place (in some lists of this kind it is however only *dge 'dun*, monks in general, who are mentioned), and further the *btsun ma* (the female religious), though in many enumerations they are preceded by those who practise *gcod* (No. 76, *ga*, p.27). There follow the exorcists (*sngags pa*), and then the *ma ni pa* (Stein, 1959, *Recherches*, pp. 324, 330), and then men, women, beggars. Particular significance is attached to the *ma ni pa* (No. 76, *kha*, p.37). They preach to the whole people (*rgyal khams pa*), they are great tellers of stories, such as the narratives, known everywhere, of Visvantara, *gZugs kyi nyi ma* and *'Gro ba bzang mo*,[31] they recite genealogies of dynasties and families (*rgyal rabs*), which are regularly preceded by myths concerning the genesis of the world, accounts of the origin of particular Tibetan clans, stories from the garland of myths which surrounds Padmasambhava, from the epic of *Ge sar*[32] and from biographies of holy persons (*rnam thar*). The *ma ni pa* thus act as guardians of a literature transmitted and recited orally, though often also preserved in writing, which has a double purpose. On the one hand it is concerned with the diffusion and inculcation of the fundamental ideas of Buddhism, in a generally accessible form, by illustrating them through famous examples (who often inspire also the religious dance-drama) in whom the supreme virtues recommended by this religion find their noblest embodiment. On the other hand this secular literature preserves and transmits a popular heritage of varied content and manifold nature, including within it also mythological ideas about the origin of the world and of the races of man, not without glorifying the divine ancestry of particular familes, while epic narratives rescue the almost disappeared hoard of ancient legends and transmit them to people of today. In this respect the activity of the *ma ni pa* does not differ fundamentally from that of the bards (*sgrung pa*), whose task is to celebrate the divine manifestations of ancient times and the glory of the ancestors. Or rather it would be better to say that this task was given to them in the past, because nowadays the *ma ni pa* have in general sunk to the level of beggars who offer their wishes for good fortune at the time of the New Year festivities. As we have already indicated, pre-Buddhist and Buddhist elements appear alongside each other in these cosmogonies. The mountain preserves undiminished its sacredness as the ancestral deity. The powers of the underground, the prehistoric cycles of myths, the deities of the atmosphere and of the storm, are directly experienced in all their feared presence, but on the other hand they appear side by side with the Buddhas of the supreme pentad and with the Bodhisattvas. Thus is confirmed for us in a continually repeating manner the indissoluble co-existence of Buddhist and non-Buddhist traditions, which through their combined action produce the religious experience lived by the Tibetan. If some elements of this whole appear at first sight to have value simply as chronicles rather than genuine religious substance, it should not be overlooked that the religious expectation of salvation infuses everything with sacredness and so integrates this apparently disunited world into a total picture. It is true that Buddhist ritual also sometimes assumes a darker aspect during this process, at least in some sects, as in the fearful description of bloody sacrifices, even if these are only meant symbolically, or with regard to the sacrificial remains of rebellious demons killed by the protective deities. We are concerned here certainly with traits which are not foreign to certain Indian schools, but which have here in Tibet prevailed to a disproportionate extent, thanks to the symbiosis achieved by Lamaism between old, indigenous traditions and the new world of religious experience. The bloody offerings, even if they are now substituted by *gtor ma* made of *tsamba*, which are however still thought of as being transformed back magically into their true nature, are an integral part of certain of the exorcistic rituals, particularly those dedicated to the *srung ma*, the *ma mo* and the *brtan ma*. To these deities the flesh and blood of certain animals are offered (e.g. the flesh of a black horse, a *rkyang mo*, a female wild ass, a black dog). The best of offerings (*rdzas mchog*) is a human heart (*mi snying*, No. 65, p.7b), but as stated, all this is in general confined to the realm of symbolism, it is no more than a linguistic survival of older rituals whose names have been taken over in Lamaism. The places where many of these *numina* stay, for example the *bdud*, are described with an abundance of grisly details; *gNya' rings khrag med* ('long neck bloodless') lives in a *bdud*-castle built of skulls of men and beasts in the middle of a sea of blood (No. 71, p.3b). It is precisely thanks to its extreme flexibility with respect to the indigenous magical and religious heritage that Buddhism succeeded on its entry into Tibet in becoming to a certain degree an integral part of the folk religion and in co-operating with it in all areas.

If victorious Buddhism had to accept a re-evaluation of many of its values, if Lamaism in adapting itself to the lay world seemed always prepared to comply with the most extraordinary requirements, it was nevertheless not willing to abandon the ritual structures it had brought from India, not even when dealing with powers entirely foreign to Buddhism, inherited from old, indigenous levels of experience. The activity of the *sngags pa* can expect success in so far as he, in accordance with the norms of Tantric liturgy, has transformed himself into a god, is born as a god (*lhar skyes*). The powers which he must invoke in order to obtain their protection and then to command them are compelled by him, summoned from their residences before his presence, drawn into the liturgical drama, thanks to the formulae he uses, thanks to the ritual he performs. Only these formulae, only the painstakingly exact performance of the ceremony guarantees the effectiveness of the ritual concerned (*sgrub*).

In this realm the soul of the shaman no longer goes on journeys to heaven, no longer does it descend to the underworld; at most the *sngags pa* or *lha pa* brings about in himself or in another (as in the case of the boy used for the *pra*) a state of possession by a particular power. Besides there always hovers over these half-friendly, half-hostile encounters with innumerable powers the incessant thought of the voidness of everything (*stong pa nyid*), in the light of which, devoid of all colour, and yet for that very reason blinding, all things dissolve and into which all finally disappears. This 'purification of all things which are empty by nature' forms the prelude to every ritual act. However, in their practical application this precondition does not prevent the presence of the powers who are invoked, the hostile or ambivalent forces, the *sa bdag*, *gnyen*, *btsan*, *klu* and so forth, from being accepted in ordinary consciousness, within the limits of daily experience, as having an absolutely solid reality which must be taken into account most seriously, since the fortunes of men depend on it.

In this connection the importance attributed to the stone in domestic ritual is remarkable, going so far that certain authors (e.g. Hummel) would even see in it genuine survivals of a megalithic culture. We have already come across the stone on many occasions as support or bearer of the soul, we have also found it in rituals to foretell the future (*pra*) where the celebrant must place a white stone, evidently again serving as support for the soul, under his knee, as a secure and not easily visible place, apparently so that when the soul of the magician leaves the body during the ritual to give place to the *lha* it can descend into it and occupy it temporarily. Heaps of stones constructed of various colours and in various ways are also regarded in many wedding ceremonies of West Tibet (Tucci, 1966, p.175) and other regions as the seat of favourable powers and are used in driving away those which are unfavourable. In the mountains stones form the preferred resting-places of local *lha* and *btsan*. Stone heaps at the summits of mountains or on mountain passes (*lha btsas*) are cult places, regularly visited; the community makes its way there each year on the days prescribed by the calendar of festivals in order to honour the deity who dwells in this locality or who sanctified it through his hierophanies and revelations in the time of the ancestors.

Through Buddhism a continuous process of demythologizing was let loose. It was at most fragments and echoes of the old indigenous world of myths which found entry into its ritual, mostly little more than the mere names or iconographical details preserved by routine at the time of the conversion to new religious ideas, as hidden allusions to the supposed seats of these deities, or as a feeble echo of the long-past contrasts and altercations between the two religions. More and more the architectonic and systematizing element, the complexity of this system of ritual unique to Tantrism and introduced with it, gained the upper hand. While doctrinal speculation remained confined to a few chosen people, the ritual system began to rule the entire Lamaistic world, whether we are concerned with its monastic expression or with the liturgical forms created for the everyday requirements of the layman, and intended to enable him to become master of his fears and find peace in his expectation of salvation. In any case one cannot fail to recognize that a new process of myth-formation began as a result of the Buddhist victory, even if it was not very deep-rooted. It appears in the cycle which has formed about Padmasambhava, who has become a symbol of the struggle between the old and new faiths and also of the peace and the compromise which followed. His historical role (*lo rgyus*) and his archetypal image (*dpe*), are constantly made present in the ritual action; a noteworthy example of the creation of a myth around a doubtless historical figure who under these circumstances has been reworked into the central figure of an epic and magical cycle. Admittedly we are here concerned only with a kind of secondary myth-formation founded on a conception primarily thaumaturgic and implicitly ritualistic, in so far as Padmasambhava's actions arise out of his magical ability (*mthu*), which is so to speak to be reactivated and made once more efficacious in the ritual, and through that ritual too whose prototype he himself created, adapted it is true to the liturgy in normal use.

Another remarkable characteristic of Tibetan religiosity is its striking lack of social compassion. Authentic Buddhism counsels love for all creatures; at its centre is the vow to strive for the good of all beings to the uttermost limits of self-sacrifice; its goal is to free all beings from suffering and to lead them to the light of final salvation. Indeed, every prayer in Tibet closes with this vow, including those recited daily by the layman, but the teachings enshrined in the vow rarely receive more than a vague theoretical assertion. Its simple enunciation brings peace to the soul of the Tibetan, along with the assurance that he has fulfilled his duty as a Buddhist. Apart from this and from the great celebrations organized with the intention of transferring to others the resulting merits, Lamaism in all its organization is oriented towards particular concrete ends; to bring benefit to this or the other person, above all to the *sbyin bdag*, the person commissioning the ritual concerned, to a particular family or a clan having a common origin, when the group in question feels itself threatened by a common danger or in its common interests. The community recreates the experience of its unity on the occasion of certain festivals, for example at the New Year celebrations, where the co-operation of all for the good of all seems to be required (cf.p.150), or in the type of popular religious festivals which are dedicated to a mountain or ancestral god. This still remains restricted however to the particular group that believes itself to be watched over and protected by the same *sa bdag*, *gnyan* or *lha*. These apart, all the daily activity of the cult turns about the well-being or misfortune of the individual or of his family, the family unit like the individual being thought of as controlled and protected by a complicated system of *lha*.

The singularly variegated and ambivalent image and function of the celebrant is thus to be understood. Even if the *sngags pa* are not in general classified into 'white' and 'black', as is usual in relation to *Bon po* and shamans, their practical activity reveals an inclination to and preference for one or another system of magical and religious operations. One exorcist specializes, so to say, in the *ling ga* ceremony with the intention of killing a man, a second in the summoning of hail to damage another's property; both belong without question to the class of 'black' magicians. However, this distinction is not in current use; the exorcist has at his disposal a technique which can bring about good or evil results, but the choice in individual cases depends upon the desire of the person commissioning him. In all these matters this folk religion is naturally anything but uniform. It is uniform to the greatest extent in its psychological presuppositions and foundations, but certainly not with reference to its content. As we have already indicated, the forms in which the religious world of a nomad appears, a pastoralist who is not tied to the earth but more exposed to the powers of nature, are essentially different from those of the agriculturalist, the warrior clans, the peace-loving caravan traders. Way of life, mode of settlement and habitation and so on give to the folk religion an almost unbounded range of variation with respect to its content, its mythical equipment, and not least with respect to the reactions to its very existence. As a complex witness of archaic forms of life and of their local expression it offers us the possibility of penetrating into the pre-Buddhist religious world of Tibet, provided that we consider it in its own proper context, beginning from the total psychic disposition of the Tibetan, for whom the presence of the sacred manifests itself everywhere, in every place, in every object or happening. The world (*snang srid*) is for him not as it is presented to him, and also to us, by ordinary experience, it is not physical and material reality, but a complex of living forces and potencies, conscious expressions of will, psychic essences, which are in a situation of constant movement and violent conflict between each other. On many of the features of this singular religious picture of the world new light will surely be thrown by study of the popular magical and exorcistic liturgies of Tibet, which has so far scarcely begun in a systematic manner.

The Tibetan, overwhelmed by the powers who everywhere lie in wait for him, threaten him and humiliate him, has found in Lamaism an effective system of defence, always ready to function. The magical force (*mthu*) radiating from the faultlessly accomplished ritual and the properly recited formula (that is, recited in full consciousness of its power and efficacy, at the prescribed moment of the total liturgical process) puts at his disposal a power thanks to which he hopes to emerge victoriously from the fight; it assures him of his superiority over the *numina*, so that these powers, rendered defenceless and harmless in the presence of the incomparable superiority of the holy word of the Buddha, must withdraw.

Against the unbounded turmoil of the forces, powers, *numina* who place in question, capriciously and unexpectedly, the existence of man, against this world of irremediable conflict, arbitrariness and disorder stands a sure, eternal standard, dominating the chaos of the world; the Law of the Buddha which determines and rules all the development and all the life of the universe.

SEVEN

THE BON RELIGION[1]

The *Bon* religion is the indigenous religion of Tibet, which despite all the influences of Buddhism has preserved itself until the present day. (*Bon* is also the name of the country, *Bod* or *Bod yul*, Tibet.[2]) *Bon* monasteries and *Bon* shrines are distributed throughout the whole country. They are especially numerous in East Tibet, and in the western border areas of the country such as *bLo* (Mustang) which belongs politically to Nepal but culturally and linguistically to Tibet; they are less frequent in the central provinces, though there is an important monastery near Shigatse. The religion we are discussing, then, is still alive today; it has its own adherents, cult places and monasteries. It has maintained itself in the midst of Lamaism, and has borrowed many of its concepts and teachings from it, without Lamaism ever being able entirely to suppress it. If we are discussing the *Bon* religion only at the end of our account, it is, among other things, because our preceding descriptions, especially of the folk religion, and of certain special aspects of Lamaism, have in some degree opened the way to understanding *Bon*.

If we can disregard some short texts found in Central Asia, we can deduce that the pre-Buddhist religion of Tibet had to undergo a vast process of evolution to become able to compete with the incomparably more solid doctrinal structure of Buddhism. We have to keep in mind also that many of the scriptures which confront us today as part of the doctrinal edifice of *Bon* were written at a comparatively late period, and under the obvious influence of Buddhism. From Buddhism too came the classification of the *Bon* scriptures into two collections, *bKa' 'gyur* (containing the revelation of *gShen rab*) and *bsTan 'gyur*. The teachings of *Bon* began to take on literary form, it seems, at about the same time that Buddhism started to penetrate into Tibet. The ritual customs, for example, which had until then been transmitted according to tradition by the exorcists and *Bon* priests underwent a process of codification. This codification took on ever greater dimensions as the interest in doctrinal and theoretical matters grew for the reasons mentioned. The original rituals had at their base the goal of assuring protection and assistance to the person of the king, the tribal chieftains and privileged families, as with the rituals of the folk religion today, still concerned with defence against the powers of evil in situations of crisis and of danger to life. Such customs provided the base on which a doctrinal super-structure could gradually be constructed. This took place under the influence not only of Buddhism, but also of other religious concepts and doctrines, knowledge of which the Tibetans owed to their Central Asian conquests, and to their contacts with China and India. The *Bon* traditions themselves preserve allusions to particular places of origin of the most famous masters and codifiers of their doctrine. Areas named include *Bru zha* (Gilgit and neighbouring regions) and *Zhang zhung*,[3] a geographical term normally used for West Tibet but which also served as the name of a very much larger region extending from the west of the country to the north and north-east (a region within which eight main languages and twenty-four less important languages were spoken). In addition masters from *Kha che* (Kashmir), from China and from the *Sum pa* are named. Gilgit (the same goes for Kashmir) indicates an area whose religion was strongly affected by Saivism, and in the immediate neighbourhood of which, in Hunza, gnostic teachings of origin both Iranian and Saivite had spread. These gnostic teachings found their expression in a famous book of the Ismaili schools, and enjoyed great popularity in this area. *Zhang zhung* also, that vast frontier land, was destined to transmit not only its indigenous religious ideas but also the echoes of foreign concepts. The *Bon po* tradition also knows a country called *sTag gzig*, a name which in Tibetan literature refers to the Iranian (or Iranian-speaking) world, or even the world of Islam. From all this we can deduce the influence of Saivism in the doctrinal field–an influence which was recognized by the Tibetan writers of treatises too (cf. e.g. No. 82).[4] Admittedly some agreements with Saivite ideas can be explained indirectly through the mediation of the *rDzogs chen* (cf.p.82); in other words they may have taken place after this sect, which had much in common with Saivism, had exerted an influence on the systematization of the *Bon po* teachings. Other, clearly older, elements indicate perceptible influences of Iranian beliefs, especially, it would seem, those of Zurvanism.[5] For example, an original god of the world is spoken of, *Yang dag rgyal po*, a *deus otiosus*, who existed when there was neither sun nor moon, nor time, nor the seasons, but only pure potentiality. Then two lights were born, one white and the other black, and these in their turn brought forth two creatures: out of the black light arose a black man, and out of the white light a white man. The black man represents the principle of negation, of Not-Being. He is armed, and is called *Myal ba nag po*, 'black grief'. From him originate the constellations and the demons, and also drought; he brings along with him pestilence and misfortune of all kinds. Thus the demons, *'dre*, *srin*, *byur*, began their sinister work, while faith in the *lha* was extinguished.

The white man, on the contrary, is the positive god, the good god of Being (cf.p.235). His name is *sNang srid sems can yod pa dga' ba'i bdag po* (also *'Od zer ldan*, the Radiant), the principle behind all that is good. After he appeared the *lha* were worshipped again and the struggle to overcome the demons began. Here we obviously move in a world of concepts which has been affected by Zurvanism.

Other works of a didactic and theoretical character (No. 10) distinguish three aspects of existence: being in itself, existing from eternity (*ye srid*), inactive (*byed mkhan la mi ltos*); being as active (*byed byas srid*); and the material causes thanks to which being unfolds itself and differentiates itself (*rgyu mtshan gyi srid*). This speculative conception is bound up with another, according to which things exist by virtue of an essential nature which is inherent in them, just as in the external world the flame according to its nature strives upwards and water seeks its course downwards, or in the same way that in the human realm the instincts are at work inside man. Thus there exists a world of potentiality which is actualized through the intervention of a creator (*byed mkhan*). In this way being manifests itself in the various aspects of the world of appearance (*snang srid*), our world of existence.

The figure of the creator, who corresponds to the Isvara of certain Saivite schools, bears various names, among them *sNang ba 'od ldan* (No. 10, p.9), *Kun snang khyab pa* and *Khri khug rgyal po*. That which he creates has two aspects, the exterior world (*phyi snod*) and that contained within it (*bcud*), a division that corresponds to that between the Indian *bhajana-loka* and *sattva-loka*. The cosmology which is attached to this is surely very old, and is throughout constructed on a dualist basis. From the breath which streamed out of the creator there emerged the two syllables *hu hu*, and, progressively, the entire universe. The creation of the contents of the world was brought about through the agency of a beneficent father (*phan yab*) and a father who created evil (*gnod yab*). One arose from a white egg, the other from a black egg; the former is lord of Being (*yod pa*), the latter is the lord of Non-Being (*med pa*) and the origin of the demonic powers (*bdud*). The name of the positive god varies in its orthography between the original form, *Shangs po yab srid*, and an alternative, *Tshangs pa* (=Skt. Brahma) which clearly betrays a contamination by religious terminology of Indian origin. The god born from the black egg is called *bsKal med 'bum nag*, though he has a beneficent mother (*phan byed yum*) at his side, born from the water and therefore called Queen-Lady of the Waters, *Chu lcam rgyal mo*.

With this an unending theogony begins to unfold. From the union of *Shangs po* and *Chu lcam*, the Water Goddess, were born the eighteen brothers and sisters (*srid pa'i ming sring*), nine male and nine female beings. The first-born of the male beings was *Srid rje 'brang dkar*, the first of the sisters was *gNam phyi gung rgyal*, Goddess of Heavenly Space. According to other texts she is called simply *A phyi gung rgyal*; she is *Srid pa'i sman* (No. 2, p.5a), resides on *Ti se*, Mt Kailasa (loc.cit.), and is also called *sman mo gNam phyi gung rgyal* (ibid., p.12a.). She belongs to the innumerable class of the *sman*, female goddesses who enjoy great popularity in the folk religion of Tibet.

The creations of the black, malevolent god produce illness, plague, famine, arms, and in brief all the forces opposing being, in the same way that Anra Mainyu (Ahriman) is opposed to Ahura Mazda (Ohrmazd) in Zoroastrian mythology, or that the nature of darkness is opposed to that of light. Each of the nine sons and each of the nine daughters is united in turn with other goddesses or gods (themselves emanations, *sprul*), and in this way various classes of divine beings are born. These beings, *lha*, are ambivalent in nature, not exclusively malevolent. In the same way the gods of the four seasons were born, and also the twelve goddesses who preside over the twelve animals over the twelve-year calendrical cycle, and other deities who have the power to rule various tribes of demons and make them submit to their will.

The malevolent creation proceeds in a similar way. It encompasses the *shi*, the *dmu*, the *gnod*, the *bgegs*, the *sri*, the *klu*, the *bdud*, the *the'u rang* and the *spun dgu*. Here we see a colourful world of gods and demons, in which opposing beings co-exist without being mutually exclusive. It is worth noting that even the tradition has preserved the memory of a layer of beliefs and rituals which were gradually modified and assimilated to each other, and of a primitive, preliterate state in which various forms of exorcism and magic co-exist. These forms, as we have seen, have survived in the folk religion, above all in the funeral rituals (as far as the placing of tombs is concerned) and in the protection of the living from the evil threatening them from the dead or from demons.

The idea of the multiplicity of souls (*bla*, *la*),[6] of which we have already spoken, goes back without doubt to this primitive sub-stratum of Tibetan folk religion, and can be placed alongside similar concepts of neighbouring peoples. Concordances and differences will emerge more clearly if one bears in mind the historical situation in which the religion treated here developed. Tibet had still not reached political unity, but was divided into various little states or tribal divisions, according to a tradition which surely reflects an actual state of affairs (e.g. No. 85, *ja*, p.4b). The twelve *Sil ma*, and later forty minor kings, fought among themselves, besides having constantly to fear invasions by neighbouring countries. Each of these local rulers had power only over a limited area, which was ethnically not entirely homogenous; he gave his name to this area, or received his name from it. In these little states affairs were directed by a number of powerful families, who traced back their family tree to a heavenly ancestor, often in the form of a mountain, and performed corresponding rituals.

The sacred places, both those of the plains and those in the mountains, were called *gsas mkhar* or *gsas khang*. During the twelve years in which *gShen rab mi bo* accomplished his work of revelation and carried out his first mission (No. 31) he visited each year a mountain which was a *gsas mkhar*. The use of the number 360 in this context is especially striking, and is surely not without reference to astrology. A well-known family of gods, the *Gi khod* or *Ge kod*, contains 360 members, and there are also 360 *gsas mkhar*. 360 is the number of languages in which *Bon* was written, and from which *gShen rab mi bo* translated them into only one language, the 'language of the *svastika*' (*g.yung drung skad*), out of which the various peoples retranslated the holy texts again into their own languages. The concept of the *gsas mkhar* has not vanished, though the name is now restricted to the special vessels or receptacles for the protective gods on houses or on mountains.

In a religious context in which mountains are held to be sacred, the motif of birth from a mountain or from a cave is found in connection with numerous localities centring about *Ti se*. For example, the King of *Zhang zhung*, *Tun yar mu khrod*, an emanation (*sprul pa*) of *Tshad med 'od ldan*, had no sons. One day a herdsman told him that, following his oxen who were at pasture, he had heard a voice coming from a rock. The king went to the place in question and had the rocks torn aside; there appeared to him an eight-year-old boy, whose form was woven from the light of the rainbow. This story has doctrinal ornamentation closely bound up with it; the child answered questions put to him by saying that his father was the void (*stong*), his mother *gSal ba ye shes* (radiant transcendent consciousness), and his radiant body the identity of light (*gsal*) and void (*stong*). He said that he came from beginning without birth (*skyed med klong*) and was going to immaterial being (*dgag med dbyings*) (cf. No. 2, p.25a). All these however are later additions, as can be seen from the terminology of Buddhist origin. To some degree it can be asserted that this *Bon* religion, like the folk religion, appears different in the various regions where it is found. Despite certain common characteristics, it expresses religious ideas of a variety that escapes any classification, although the nature of many powers remains essentially the same. The powers which survive in the folk religion, and the fragments of myths relating to them, are remnants of a religious world of the past, which have succeeded in entering either Buddhism or *Bon* through the tenacity of the belief in powers which intervene in life and in the work of men.

The theogonic conceptions are equally numerous and various in nature, though here too we are essentially concerned with the same kinds of powers in all cases. The tendency to distinguish between the profitable and the harmful, in order to regulate the relations between man and man, appears to dominate. Traces of divine couples, father–mother, heaven–earth, are not lacking. Thus we find the union between the goddess of heaven, *A phyi gung rgyal* or *gNam phyi gung rgyal*, and a god of heaven, *gNam gyi lha rgod thog pa*, and also an earth-goddess, *Sa rgyal dong gi dbal mo*, along with an earth-god, *Sa bla dog rum* or *Sa yi lha 'od*. Similarly there is a water-god, *Chu lha*, from whom serpents come, or a water-goddess (*Chu lcam*, cf.p.215), and so on. In some genealogies the sun is female. Many are the gods of the seasons and of the twelve-year calendrical cycle; then there are the gods of the arts and sciences, *Yi ge pa* ('he who can write'), *bZo lha* ('the artist,' *bzo*), *gSo byed pa* ('the master of healing'). Some of these divine figures have a bellicose nature and are enemies of the forces of evil; among these are *dgra 'dul*, *rgod 'dul* and *nad 'dul* ('defeater of illnesses'). To these can be added the ancestor gods of particular clans, *sTod*, *A zha*, *Zhang zhung*.[7] Many classes of gods are ambivalent in nature, like the *bdud*, *dmu*, *gnyan*; they oscillate between the good creation and the evil creation, where we also meet the *mKha' lding*, a legendary bird of *Bon po* mythology which is the enemy of the *Khyung* generally associated with the good creation. The most malevolent powers against which man has to defend himself are the male *sri* and female *srid mo*, who dwell in cemeteries and at gates. An evil god rules over dreams which bring misfortune. As can be seen, we are dealing with a classification into pairs of opposites, though it is indefinite in that the same powers are cited sometimes in the good column of the list, sometimes in the bad, following the psychic reactions of men. Nothing however allows one to define *Bon* as a religion characterized exclusively by the worship of heaven. Such worship only takes place in special circumstances and at particular moments, that is when there is mention of a *gNam Bon*, a '*Bon* of heaven'.

It is impossible to classify these deities in a completely logical way, partly because it is often a question of local ancestor gods, another indication that each country originally possessed a chief god of its own, particularly an ancestor-mountain. The list given in the bibliography as No. 38 (cf. Tucci, 1949) provides an indicative example, in which the equating of individual gods (*srid pa'i chags pa'i lha dgu*, cf. above, p.210) with particular mountains emerges clearly, beginning with *'O de gung rgyal*, to this day the name of a mountain in the region of *'Ol kha*. The same can be seen from the kings of Tibet. Seven of them descended onto mountains, three (beginning with *gNya' khri btsan po*) at *Lha ri gyang tho* in *rKong po*, two onto the Potala of Lhasa, and two at *Sham po la rtse* in *Yar klungs*. The mountains where the ancestor descended or on which he lived acquire special sacredness, and cosmogonic or theogonic accounts or complex philosophical attempts at interpretation become attached to them. Because of their sacred nature such mountains become in a sense the soul of the country, they assure its perpetuity, and protection for the men living at their feet. The most famous example of this kind is *Ti se*, Mt Kailasa in West Tibet. It towers under the heavenly sphere like a parasol with eight ribs (*rtsibs*) and above the earth like an eight-petalled lotus, like a spread-out carpet (No. 2, p.3a). It is the navel of the world (*'Jam bu gling lte ba*, No. 2, p.28b), seat of the sky-goddess *gNam phyi gung rgyal* or *Srid pa'i sman* (No. 2, p.5a).

Ti se is *Bon ri*, the *Bon* Mountain, or *Zhang zhung bon ri*, the *Bon* Mountain of *Zhang zhung*; it is *bla ri*, *bla ri gangs dkar Ti se* (No. 2, p.21), Soul-Mountain. The Soul-Mountain of *Zhang zhung* is a ladder which simultaneously ascends to heaven and descends from heaven (*mtho ris them skas*),[8] and it thus has the same function as the *dmu thag* or *gnam thag*, the 'heavenly cord' which links heaven and earth (No. 2, p.14b). The emanation-body of *gShen rab* descended onto this mountain.[9] The host of *Ge khod* gods has its palace there. According to a tradition followed by the *Pad ma thang yig* (No. 3, p.245) there are 360 of these gods; the identification of *Ti se* with the axis of the world, about which revolves the year with its 360 days, is obvious. The mountain is imagined as an enormous *mchod rten* made of rock-crystal, or as a palace where various families of gods reside. It has four gates: *rgya stag* (Chinese tiger), *rus sbal* (tortoise), *bya dmar* (red bird) and *g.yu 'brug* (turquoise dragon), which have the duty of guarding the four cardinal points, East, North, West and South.

Through the adoption of elementary philosophical ideas representing a middle way between *rDzogs chen* and Saivism these concepts became transformed into symbols. The 'means' (*thabs*) leading to salvation was symbolically identified with the father–mountain, while Lake Manasarovar (*Ma pham*) came to represent the mother, the symbol of transcendent consciousness (*ye shes*) (No. 2, p.17a). Here we are evidently dealing with a gnostic interpretation superimposed on previously existing mythic concepts, in other words those of the mountain–father and the lake–mother. Elsewhere the question is raised of how the apparently existent world (*snang srid*) has come about. From where has this existence (*srid*) come forth, and how? It derives from a principle existing *ab aeterno* and designated *klong* (a term used also by the *rNying ma pa*); it is born from *bon nyid*, that is from *ye nyid stong pa*. The expression *bon* in this imitation of Buddhist doctrine has the meaning of *chos* (Skt. *dharma*), so that *bon nyid* corresponds to *chos nyid* (*dharmata*), infinite potential existentiality, from which all that we ascribe reality to, or which appears to us as an object, as an element of existence (Skt. *dharma*) arises. *Bon nyid* is thus the void, *ye nyid stong pa* (cf.p.215). From this initial state or first phase there subsequently arises (second phase) a liberation, a process of actualization (*grol*) such that the possibility inherent within the 'void' frees itself and takes on form.

The third phase consists of the process of divine emanation (*sprul*) itself. In this complex of ideas the ancient indigenous cosmogonic concepts re-enter even more perceptibly. Characteristic of this moment is the apparition of light streaming out of the snow of Mt *Ti se* and the waters of Lake *Ma pham*.[10] The fourth phase is characterized by the formation of the five elements, which manifest themselves in the cosmic egg. The fifth phase is called *brdol*, springing forth, emanation, in other words each of the five elements manifests itself in accordance with its own proper nature. The sixth phase is formed by the birth (*'byung ba*) of a miraculously produced body (emanation-body, *sprul pa*), *dBal chen ge khod*, accompanied by his following, 360 gods in all. The seventh phase is that of illusion or miracle (*rdzu 'phrul*) and is characterized by the birth of *srid kyi g.yag po dkar po*, the White Yak of Existence.[11] The eighth phase is the 'fall' of the yak, in other words its descent into *Zhang zhung*, the land of *Bon*. In the ninth and last phase takes place the 'coming' (*byon*), the arrival of *Shel gyer* in the form of the *dGra bla* of *Bon*; the yak descends from heaven on to the mountain and thus goes out into the world. Thereupon he tears with his horns the mountains to right and left, and the earth becomes covered with flowers (No. 2, pp.17a ff.). With this the creation is completed.

This cosmic myth, in which a yak is given the function of making the earth habitable and suitable for the epiphany of the *dGra bla* (= *lha*), has clearly been interpolated in a specifically doctrinal context. *Ge khod* is the principle of other emanations from his heart; (a) *Ye shes lha bdud 'dul gsang ba drag chen*, God of Transcendent Consciousness, Secret, Conqueror of the *bDud* or demons, Most Violent God (with nine heads and eighteen arms), accompanied by his paredra (*yum*); he in his turn emanates (b) *Ku byi mang ske* in the form of a body of co-fruition (*longs spyod rdzogs kyi sku*, Skt. *sambhogakaya*) of green colour (one head, two arms); from him emanates (c) *A ti mu wer*, without ornaments, naked.

According to another cosmogony or theogony contained within the same text (No. 2, p.2b) existence liberates itself from the Absolute-Void, from its spontaneous cause; the great mother of potential existentiality (*dbyings*) emanated existentiality itself. *gShen lha 'od dkar* was emanated out of the light, *Shangs po bum khris* from the rays, the

Master *gShen rab* from the wind, *A ti mu wer* from the plane of mind, *Ku byi mang (s)ke* from the plane of the word, *dBal chen ge khod* from the physical plane.

The simultaneous presence of various schemes in the same text is noteworthy here; their separate elements evidently came from different localities, social groups or traditions.

These cosmogonic, theogonic and genealogical ideas, differing from place to place, have remained alive as long as they have continued to be transmitted as tradition in particular families; the claims to divine origin contained within them naturally promoted their continuance. In other cases such family traditions were taken over by other family groups linked to them by kinship or otherwise. Such reciprocal influences and fusions are clearly recognizable if these myths are submitted to a careful examination.

Various types of fusion can be observed. The most important is that officially recognized by Buddhism and already appearing in early works such as the *bKa' thang sde lnga*. Here we have works that transmit aspects of pre-Buddhist thought or of tenacious survivals within Buddhism. There are texts, for example, of the *Sa skya pa*, the *g.Yu thog pa*, the *sTag lung pa* or of the *Phag mo gru pa*, which begin from a creation of the world out of an egg and a first divine being, *Ye smon rgyal po*, and arrive progressively at the divine ancestor born on a mountain in a miraculous fashion and protected by a dragon, a tiger and a vulture.

The many-layered nature and the multiplicity of cosmogonic myths, which never fully fuse with each other into a single account, but are transmitted onwards in a literature clearly influenced by local traditions, confirms the correctness of what was said above: this mythical world is dominated by a basic cosmogonic interest (although it appears in the most varied forms), namely the question of the origin of the gods, of the clan chiefs, of the human race. These are all seen as proceeding from a primal state which is more than simply chaotic or formless; it is a primal state of void potentiality from which, directly or indirectly, the primal egg (one or several) is born, from which the world arises or rather from which is born the being who calls the world in all its aspects into existence. However, the tradition of a cosmic tree, from which four eggs of various colours originate, is also known. Alternatively the origin of the world is attributed to the fragmentation of an original being, the various parts of whose body give origin to the present world (*srid*). Another tradition places at the beginning a primal being (*Ye smon rgyal po*, *Shangs po*) equipped with demiurgic functions and given various names in different accounts (Tucci, 1949, p.712).

Often the primal state of non-being or of the pure potentiality of being consists simply of a light–an indication of the extremely ancient origin of that 'photism', that doctrine of light, which was later organized into a theoretical system through the Tantras, but which had long been an object of reflection for the Tibetans, who had populated their indigenous Olympus with numerous gods of light. In another section of the cosmology the *klu* play a significant role. These beings correspond to the Sanskrit *naga*, 'serpents', and in general indicate the powers of the earth and of the waters on which the prosperity of agriculture is believed to depend. An entire cycle of myths has grown up around these beings, forming the theme of an extensive literature. The most important book is the *klu 'bum*, the 'Hundred-thousand *klu*', which is divided into three parts: white *klu*, multicoloured *klu* (*khra klu*), black *klu*.

The burning problem of origins, which so preoccupied the Tibetans at all times, is reflected also in the social domain; it finds an echo in religious organization and its function of protecting society. How and why did the various social and civil institutions, the various customs and arts arise? Since the world took form, since it became a mode of being (*srid*), man has intervened to create the necessary ordering and to give an appropriate form to the habits of his life. This process, however, has brought a new situation into existence which often disturbs or injures those powers who hitherto called particular domains their own. The building of a house, the erecting of a tent on a particular spot, building a bridge over a river, digging in the earth—each of these are intrusions into the domains of other powers which require expiation through appropriate rituals. The *Bon po* sources account for these rituals or narrate the origins of particular customs in the appropriate contexts. Generally they narrate an event which took place *in illo tempore* and then add 'from this derives such and such a custom' (*gtan tshigs kyang de nas byung*, e.g. No. 32, p.21b), in other words this event was the origin of the custom. The bards (*sgrung*) treat of these subjects (cf.pp.207,232) and their narratives not only provide an explanation for the origin of the custom concerned, but also contain the assurance that no harmful effect can arise from it, and that its repetition will evoke once more the primal moment when after an offence had been committed against the divine and demonic powers the sure means to remedy it was found. In short, the recital expiates the offence which has taken place and provides protection against its consequences. However, the *sgrung* can also recite stories of miracles, for example the extraction of gold with the aid of the spirits of the dead, the control of the *ma sangs* demons, and so on.

The same variety appears in the genealogical trees generally accepted by the historians of later times. Thus we possess an extended list of kings, in which one king follows another until semi-historical times, culminating with *Srong btsan sgam po*. Since this order of succession was certainly not compiled until after *Srong btsan sgam po* had unified Tibet, this genealogical tree is naturally to be examined carefully rather than accepted as literally true. The first thing that strikes our attention and awakes suspicion is the equating of the remote ancestor *gNya' khri btsan po* with an Indian king. Here we are clearly concerned with a fiction established after the triumph of the Buddhist doctrine, which was intended to bring the royal family into connection with India, even (according to some sources) with the family of the Buddha.

This list of kings corresponds to the tripartite division of existence: *gnam*, heaven; *bar*, intermediate space; *sa*, earth. Two intermediate groups are however interpolated, *stod kyi steng*, the rulers 'above' (or the rulers over the high-lying part of Tibet) and *'og gi btsan*, the 'lower' kings. In reality these interpolations indicate breaks or interruptions in the sequence. The later kings (*'og gi btsan po*) begin with *Lha tho tho ri*, the king to whom is ascribed the first miraculous contact with Buddhist teachings. Without doubt we are dealing with a legend here, but we can perhaps approach a more solidly founded tradition with its help. What, however, does the list mean as a whole? We have already spoken of *gNya' khri btsan po*. *Gri gum* indicates a definite break according to most opinions; many things changed during the period of his rule. In this connection, an allusion is also made to a conflict between his *majestas* (*mnga' thang*) and magical power (*mthu*). Earlier he is placed in connection with *Myang ro* in *gTsang*; however, there is nothing to prove a special link with the family of *Srong btsan sgam po*. Then, after his death, he was given the name 'Killed by the Dagger', although other sources call him *Ge mun* (No. 35, p.15). Some traditions, which connect his heresy with the arrival of teachers from Kashmir, appear to confirm that he belongs to the western regions of Tibet.

According to *Myang chung* (No. 4, p.139a) the palace of *Gri gum* was at Tshechen near Gyantse. The uncertainty betrayed by the hesitation between two different forms, and the eventual return to the name hallowed by tradition, in which the word *gri*, knife, appears as the basic element, leads one to think of the introduction of particular sacrificial rituals. The whole context suggests the possibility of an infiltration of ideas, carried perhaps by immigrants coming from the countries to the west of Tibet; survivals in many forms of local religious traditions, here and there suffused by Saivite elements (the disposal of the dead reminds one more of the customs of the Kafirs than of strictly Hindu mortuary practices), which may nevertheless have been indigenous in the areas in contact with Indian culture.

Here one should not forget that since the most ancient times the region around Mt Kailasa and Lake Manasarovar has been a significant centre of attraction for Indian pilgrims and believers from all the adjoining regions. This is indicated even by the presence of Hindu temples and deities (Tucci, 1959).

What has been said compels us to bring up a related theme: the problem of the evolution within the *Bon* religion itself, the question of its development in the context of the transformation of the life and customs of Tibetan society, brought about through contact with other peoples or by the intrusion of religious concepts of other kinds. We find the echo of such modifications not only in the events of the time of *Gri gum*, but also in the traditions that have come down to us. Thus No. 82, for example, speaks of three consecutive phases in *Bon*: *'jol Bon* (= *mjol Bon* in Lalou, 1952, p.350), *'khyar Bon* and *'gyur Bon*. *'Jol Bon* was the first of these stages, still without literature. Here it was still simply a question of overcoming the harmful powers. The second stage of development, called *'khyar Bon*, 'deviating *Bon*', to be equated with *dur Bon*, was concerned above all with funeral rites. It began with King *Gri gum* and was the result of a collaboration of many religious masters or heads of schools of whom nothing is now known. In other words, this phase marked the beginning of a period of development in theory and organization and of contact with other religious centres, possibly including some outside Tibet. The third stage is called *'gyur Bon*, 'modified *Bon*', because in this phase the *Bon* religion felt it necessary to take on a doctrinal form, which it had previously done without, and perhaps also to change certain rituals, as well as making its own a significant part of the Buddhist teachings. This is apparently the period introduced by *gShen rab*, who is eventually portrayed in the *Bon po* literature as an explicit *Bon po* correlate to the Buddha.[12] Even conversions and defeats of the demons of localities and mountains are ascribed to him, closely resembling those which the legends centring about Padmasambhava tell of that miracle-worker (No. 33). It is difficult to say on what sources such a tradition could have been based. However, this development evidently corresponds to an inner law; from a primitive starting-point of purely magical or shamanistic character, varying from place to place, we come in the time of *Gri gum* (who doubtless indicates an especially significant factor in the development of the *Bon* religion) to the first beginnings of an organizational process probably brought about through the contrast between the royal authority and the magical power of *Bon*. As we will see, it is also possible that *Gri gum* means rather more than this; he is perhaps to be seen as the representative of the cult of chthonic deities, in opposition to the cult of heavenly gods. Earth-burial, the appearance of *dur Bon* ('*Bon* of funeral practices') and so on indicate the return of the body to the earth; a megalithic culture, resting on funeral rites and the rites of constructing tombs, breaks into another culture, in which, although the *klu* still play a significant part (they have an important and central role in the tripartite division of beings in the world into *lha*, men and *klu*), the heavenly gods, the gods of light, the gods of white light, enjoy the definite favour of believers. In any case it is well established that a significant break in funeral customs follows the death of *Gri gum*. Concerning the time before him the tradition speaks of an ascent of the king to heaven with the help of a cord connecting heaven and earth. In such a manner the dead king left no trace of himself behind; he vanished like a rainbow. At the time of King *Gri gum* however the cord broke, and the corpse was enclosed in a coffin and thrown in the river.

The memory of the cord connecting heaven and earth is also found in other family histories, though various causes are given for its breaking. The mode of disposal of the dead also varies according to the various classes or groups of kings listed in the old Tibetan classification of dynasties: in vessels, sarcophagi, rivers, as is still the custom today in many parts of Tibet. It is certain, however, that the technique and architecture of the royal tombs was determined in its fundamental traits by the time of *Srong btsan sgam po* (Hoffmann, 1950; Tucci, 1950). Concerning this king the tradition speaks of subterranean chambers, nine in number (nine and thirteen are the sacred numbers of the *Bon po*), and a central chamber. The corpse was placed in a silver coffin, while immense treasures were placed in the other rooms. Along with the funeral rites there took place sacrifices and the burial of men and horses (Lalou, 1952), though out of respect for Buddhism the appropriate chapter of the *bKa' thang sde lnga* says no more about them. Tumuli like those of the Tibetan kings at *Yar klungs* are found in other regions of Tibet as well. Very frequent also are tombs of megalithic type in the form of a circle, with or without a central stone. I saw the greatest burial place of this kind near *Seng ge rdzong*, on a mountain peak. There clearly stands behind the nine chambers of the tomb of *Srong btsan* the intention of giving the tomb the form of a magical projection of the world (Tucci, 1950, p.9); the king at the centre was to represent the axis of the world for time immemorial, while the treasures piled up in the tomb, especially gold which was conceived of as the element of life, would guarantee the good fortune and prosperity of the kingdom.

Here one can point out that the figure of King *Gri gum* corresponds to King *Glang dar ma* in the Buddhist tradition (cf.p.12). Both are described as opponents of the prevailing religion, although in many *Bon po* texts *Glang dar ma* in no way appears as a victim of his zeal for the *Bon po* faith. Just as *Glang dar ma* was killed by a monk, *dPal gyi rdo rje*, in order to put an end to the persecution of the doctrine, so *Gri gum* was murdered by one of his ministers. The explanation for *Gri gum*'s murder appears to lie in his hostile attitude to the *Bon* religion as it existed in his time, which he wished to submit to a renewal.[13] Both kings were killed by an arrow-shot, though with respect to *Gri gum* the tradition wavers between a dagger (*gri*) and an arrow. Both kings were possessed by a *gdon*. In short, a kind of model of a schismatic king has taken form. The body of *Gri gum* was laid to rest in a closed coffin of copper and thrown into the river. The dead man reached *rKong po*, where a demon took possession of him. His sons sought in vain to ransom the body, but according to other sources a king, *Mang po rje*, succeeded in overcoming the 'dagger-demon' or 'dagger-death' (*gri shi*) and brought the corpse to *Yar klungs*. When the corpse was uncovered, the sound *nga ra ra* came out of it, and the place has been called *Ngar pa thang* since that time. People went around the corpse for 360 days (the *ge khod* circle around *Ti se* conceived of as the *axis mundi* for 360 days too); then it was buried on the peak of a mountain. Since then it has been considered as the *deus loci* of the mountain.

One of *Gri gum*'s sons, *Sha khri* or *khyi* (according to other sources *Bya khyi*) is equated with *sPu de gung rgyal*; he moved to *rKong po*. The same person is also called *rKong dkar po* (No. 28, p.127) and *rKong rje dkar po* (No. 110, *ka*, p.21b). Some sources, however, connect *Sha khyi* = *sPu de gung rgyal* with *Yar klungs*. Nor is it clear how the identification of *Sha khyi* or *Bya khyi* with *sPu de gung rgyal* was arrived at. (One should note however that in some sources his name begins a new list of kings, the so-called Six *Legs*.) We can deduce that we here have to do with another family tree, which was inserted into the genealogy which had become orthodox. The most significant character trait ascribed to *sPu de gung rgyal* is his authorship of social rules aimed at creating a more secure and active existence for mankind.

The history of the first name on the list of kings, *gNya' khri*, also requires careful examination. The situation becomes particularly complex if one looks at the statements referring to his descent. While the official tradition states that his descent took place at *Sham po lha ri* in *Yar klungs*, other sources (including No. 85, *ja*, p.6b) place it at *Lha ri gyang tho* in *rKong po*. As I hope to have shown in a study at present under preparation, the entire orthodox genealogy of the Tibetan kings has an explicitly fragmentary character; we are concerned without doubt with a list revised to incorporate other dynastic and clan genealogies, originating from various centres and put together artificially. These centres include *Myang ro*, *rKong po* and *Yar klungs*. Much the same is true of *'O de gung rgyal*, who is also regarded in the Tibetan edicts as the first king, originating from heaven; he seems to have nothing to do with *sPu de gung rgyal*. As has already been indicated above, *'O de gung rgyal* is the name of a deity-mountain south of *'Ol kha*, but in this connection too there is mention of a descent from heaven, as occurs with almost all mountain-ancestors. *sPu rgyal* is not a mountain; according to one tradition he descended from heaven (No. 110, *ca*, p.18), while according to other, more usual accounts he is identical with one of the sons of *Gri gum*, though no reason is given for the new name. For this reason too we come to the conclusion already drawn above, that in Tibet numerous genealogies existed side by side (as many family trees as there were powerful families!), and that the origin attributed to *Srong btsan sgam po* is a composite of fairly early date, as emerges also from the variations of the Tun-huang texts (Bacot et al., 1940); it can certainly not be taken as an authentic genealogy. Its compilers were probably motivated by the desire to incorporate into the new genealogy the genealogies of families allied by marriage with *Srong btsan sgam po*'s family, but excluded through the play of political forces. Through this device the ruling dynasty came to form the crown and conclusion of a complex historical sequence, and became heirs to a sacredness based upon these heavenly ancestors and on the sacred ancestor-mountains. In this sense it seems probably to me that there are at least three different tribal chiefs or ancestral lords involved in this account from different regions and periods: *gNya' khri*, *sPu rgyal* and *'O de gung rgyal*. *Gri gum* appears to be an isolated figure. The details given show what an impenetrable maze we are in when considering these cosmogonies, theogonies and genealogies. The confusion is increased still further in that in all the important centres the traditions predominating locally have had attached to them new, more or less arbitrary connections with particular powers which have gradually claimed and found general recognition, and been assembled in particular groups. The *lha* of *Ngar pa thang*, for example, were connected in this way with the cycle of myths concerning *Gri gum*. In this manner local cults came to be brought more and more into connection with other myths and to be merged with them.[14]

The various kinds of *Bon* to which writers often refer, such as Heaven *Bon*, *Bon* of funeral practices and so on should also not be understood in the sense of a temporal sequence. The question is much more one of a kind of division of labour, or of an attempt to force into a unified system the multiplicity of lived religious experiences, each emphasizing one or another magical and religious motif according to the individual locality. In this way a classification into nine *gshen* was arrived at at a certain point in time. These *gshen* were classes of priests or magicians whose duties, according to some texts (No. 31, cf.p.228), had been assigned by *gShen rab mi bo* (cf. above, p.224) during the twelve-year period in which, after the fashion of the Buddha, he performed his twelve 'memorable acts' (*mdzad pa bcu gnyis*). To each of these nine groups corresponded a 'vehicle' of its own; as I have already mentioned, after the systematization of the *Bon* religion its followers speak of nine vehicles[15] or groups of scriptures, as do the *rNying ma pa*. The principal scriptures of *Bon* are divided into 'four doors' (*sgo bzhi*) and 'five treasures' (*mdzod lnga*),[16] and the nine vehicles are also divided into two groups, a first group of four called 'cause' (*rgyu*) and a second group of five called 'fruit' (*'bras bu*).

Following this classification, the first vehicle was that of the *phya gshen*. In contemporary usage, outside of *Bon* circles, *phya* means chance, omen, good fortune, prosperity (in some writings on *Bon* religion the term is erroneously given as *cha*). We find *phya* in association with another term, *g.yang*, which has a similar meaning of good fortune.[17] The duty and function of this class of magicians consisted principally in preparing *gto* (generally nine in number, cf. No. 37, p.27) (cf.p.176). Three hundred and sixty types of *gto* were known, with 84,000 magical modes of action and remedies. They were practised according to the investigation of omens (*dpyad bcos ka*) along with the offering of libations (*gser skyems*), participation in ceremonies with *chang*, meat and so on. Another function of these priests was the use of the *ju thig*[18] (No. 85, *ja*, p.8b), primarily in divination. Through the *ju thig* they were able to distinguish the profitable from the dangerous, and therefore to function as diviners or augurs.

The second vehicle was revealed to the *snang gshen*, who specialized in the four 'doors' of the ritual songs (*gyer sgo bzhi*). They possessed a small drum made of juniper wood, thanks to which they could fly through the air. Their characteristic sign was the *bal tshon sna lnga*, five-coloured ornamental threads of wool (No. 85, *ja*, p.8b however attributes these to the *'phrul gshen*). They specialized in the use of *glud* and *yas* (cf.pp.176ff.). On their heads they wore a woollen tuft (*bal thod can*, No. 85, *ja*, p.8b). They were trained in magical operations to bring about the well-being and prosperity of their clients. Rituals to create prosperity and blessing thus fell within their field of action.

The third vehicle was that of the *'phrul gshen*, miracle-workers whose job it was to drive from the world the causes of misfortunes threatening or obstructing an individual or the community, in other words to remove hindrances (*bar chad*) of all kinds. They had the power of overcoming both human enemies (*dgra*) and hostile demonic powers (*bgegs*). They bore standards ornamented with figures of tigers, and wore jackets (*stag sham thabs*) and hats made of tiger-skin; they wore tiger-paws and tiger-teeth as ornaments. In their exorcistic ceremonies they offered tiger-flesh to the gods. These bloody sacrifices secured the continuity of the clan.

The fourth vehicle was that of the *srid gshen*, who took care of the living and the dead (*gson gshin*), in the sense that they protected the life of the living (*gson po'i srog skyobs*) and could recall the spirit of the dead.

This is a custom whose survival can still be seen in the folk religion (*bla khug*, cf.p.190). They could also secure a happy existence for the departed, although this is not described in detail. In any case it was they who influenced the fate of the dead, and they could even close the door of the god of death (*gshed sgo*) or of his assistants. They were armed; burial ceremonies and the construction of tombs fell within their competence. They correspond to the *dur bon* mentioned in other texts such as the Tun-huang fragment published by Lalou (1952). This text also names the two classes of *phangs bon*, great and small, as concerned with the funeral ceremonies (op.cit, pp. 351–2).

The fifth vehicle was that of the *dge bsnyen gshen*, who aided in the accumulation of merit and the cancellation of sins. In addition they were responsible for the exact separation between winter and summer, which probably means that they were responsible for the observance of the calendrical festivals.

The sixth vehicle contained the special teachings of the sixth *Bon* group, in other words those of the *g.yung drung bon*, the '*bon* of the *svastika*'. The *svastika* of *Bon* is not identical to that widely used in Buddhism, but runs in the opposite sense (anticlockwise). The representatives of this group are also called *Bon* ascetics (*drang srong bon*); they had to follow a pure and irreproachable way of life (*ma gtsang ma spyod*).

The seventh vehicle was reserved to the *a dkar bon*, the '*bon* of the white letter A'.[19] They were trained particularly in the secret mantras (*gsang sngags*). According to the prescriptions of *gShen rab* they presided over the sacrifices offered to the divinities with nine vessels and nine *gtor ma*. Their symbol was the arrow (*mi gyur mda'*). They conferred the initiation into the secret mantras, they sang the songs called *gshen glu*, they could bring the world within their control through the power of their arts and ensure the normal course of natural events.

The eighth vehicle was in the possession of the *ye gshen bon*, who had the privilege of using the *ju thig* (cf.p.234) and thus had knowledge of past, present and future. We are concerned here with a late assimilation.

The ninth vehicle comprised the *bla na med rgyud*, the 'Tantra of the highest class' (as in Tantric Buddhism, cf.p.72) and was in the possession of the *snang srid bon*. Here we meet again the name of a class of *gshen*, which strengthens the supposition that the fifth to ninth groups of the classification should be given only secondary significance; within these groups the terminology and philosophical doctrines of Buddhism obtrude ever more perceptibly.

The whole classification evidently comes from a later period, and reveals the intention of ascribing twelve noteworthy 'acts' to *gShen rab mi bo* to correspond to those of the Buddha; each of these acts is placed in connection with a particular revelation and the event inserted into the twelve-year cycle. In this way the twelve-year cycle is simultaneously justified in terms of its origin and its form.

The same classification given in No. 31 appears, with minor changes, in No. 82. Here the divisions are:

Group I (Vehicles of the Cause): *phya gshen*, *snang gshen*, *'phrul gshen*, *srid gshen*.

Group II (Vehicles of the Effect): *dge bsnyen gshen*, *a dkar gshen*, *drang srong gshen*, *ye gshen*.

Other sources, however, mention only the first four classes of *gshen* (*gshen rigs bzhi*, e.g. No. 85, *ja*, p.8b). They can also speak simply of the four classes (*rigs bzhi*). These are *snang gshen*, *'phrul gshen*, *phya gshen* (the text has *cha gshen* by mistake), and *dur gshen*, which corresponds to the *srid gshen* in other lists. We find the same list again in the *rGyal rabs*. No. 35, p.45, however, follows No. 28 and No. 31 in enumerating nine kinds of *gshen* and nine vehicles. The functions described for the first four classes are approximately the same as those in No. 28, with the introduction of a few other details such as the name of the god specially worshipped by each group: *Gar babs btsan pa* for the *snang gshen*, *sBar gsas rngam* for the *'phrul gshen* and *rMa po* for the *srid gshen* (the *phya gshen* are not mentioned).[20]

One should not conclude, however, that these four *gshen* classes exhaust the entire multiplicity of the *Bon* religion. Although the most important role was played by the *gshen* priests (priests is admittedly not a very appropriate term; it would be more correct to speak of magicians or exorcists), there can be no doubt that there were also other practitioners in existence, *Bon po* exorcists, *snyun bon*, *smug bon*, *rlad bon* (Lalou, 1952, p.353) and *sman bon* (ibid., p.355) whose task it was to collect the medicinal plants (*sman*) or who were perhaps responsible for the cult of the goddesses called *sMan*. There were also *khri bon*, *gnyer bon*, *'o bon*, *'tshams bon*, *dmu bon* (No. 29, p.3b).

In the description of a sacrifice carried out in the time of *Khri srong lde brtsan* yet other participants entrusted with various functions are mentioned. The description is contained in a text which is not very old, but it comes from a very much earlier source in which a very ancient tradition appears to be preserved (No. 32, p.62). On the occasion of the sacrificial ceremony numerous animals were killed, even including some antelopes. Nine *bon mkhas*, learned *bon*, were present and stood in the centre of the place of sacrifice, while to their right and left nine men endowed with great magical powers (*mi mthu chen*) took their places. Before them stood their sacrificial assistants (*mchod g.yog*) who had to kill the animals with their sacrificial knives (*gri ri*). In addition the ceremony required the presence of a '*bon* of the lustration' (*khrus bon*); he had to submit the sacrificial animals to a ritual purification using a golden spoon, while the *zhu bon* were responsible for the invocation to the gods. These acts introduced the sacrificial ceremony. At its conclusion the *gshen bon* seized the animals by the horns to perform the sacrifice. Then the *bshig bon* cut the animals to pieces, while the *bse bon* were responsible for a ritually impeccable distribution of the pieces of meat. At the end the *grangs bon* had to count the pieces of meat; then he poured the blood into cups and placed these on the skins of the animals, while the meat was spread out on other skins. The ritual finished with loud cries.

Bon is a generic term; as we have seen even the *gshen* are included among the *bon*. In the text on the rites of the dead (Lalou, 1952) the *mjol bon* direct the sacrifice; the *dur bon* and the *phangs bon*, who are named in the same text, do not take part in the sacrifice. The *phangs bon*, however, invite the dead to take part in the meal (cf. note 2, p.271, on the significance of the word *bon*) and receive their souls. The *snyun bon*, *smag bon* and *'jol bon* sing. The *gshen* or *sku gshen* are the actual sacrificial priests. They are helped by assistants. The term *gshen* is probably to be connected with *gshed* which means executioner, torturer (*'tshe bar byed*). The *sku gshen*, however, is the protector of the king and is the head of the hierarchy (No. 35, p.26a); he must belong to the family (*rigs*) of the *gshen* on which the duties devolve on the king's death.

It seems certain that in the period of the dynasties there already existed a religion which had its own books such as that edited by Lalou and others which we know only as fragments or from the extracts and commentaries included in later books. These early texts were manuals for ceremonies and liturgies used by various kinds of sacrificial priests specialized in particular functions. We can deduce this from the nomenclature contained in the texts and referred to in later documents. This multiplicity both of liturgical acts and also of celebrants who perform them, as well as of genealogies and cosmologies which were recited, at least on special occasions, shows that this religion was at the time of the dynasties already very complicated. It had its own mythology, its codified rituals and a pantheon that varied from place to place and was subject to extension and mutual influences; but all this was without a doctrinal structure comparable to that of Buddhism. This circumstance led to the progressive adoption by *Bon*, perhaps through a master named *gShen rab*, of Buddhist doctrines and terminologies, within which, however, some of *Bon*'s original intuitions survived.

As can be seen, the world of *Bon* moved between theogonies, cosmogonies, genealogies and conjurations of ambivalent and hostile powers. It was dominated by funeral rituals for the protection of both the living and the dead, and it gave very great importance to divination. Evidently the preoccupation with the future overcame everything else; no action could take place until the favourable and correct way had been established. This necessity was met by *mo*, divination. This was not only, and not originally, performed with dice, but especially through the use of the *ju thig*, those little divinatory cords whose interpretation was reserved to the *phya gshen*. With their help it could be established what malevolent powers (*gdon*, cf.p.201) were to be feared in the immediate future and by what means these dangers could be eliminated. Such conjurations were performed by the *gShen gnyan*, the exorcists of *'dre* and *srin*, who stood by the king's side (No. 35, p.34).

We are here in the presence of a world which is without doubt far distant from the organization presented by Buddhism. *Bon* dominates the community in general and its leaders in particular, above all the king. In this sense it is said in some chronicles that the *bon* look after the life (*'tsho*) of the king or aid his ministers with word and deed, or that they keep in view the defence of the country's borders.

Thus it comes about that some chroniclers maintain that society (*chab srid*) is protected by three groups of people, the *bon*, the *sgrung* and the *lde'u*. The concept of *bon* here includes the entire religious system which bears that name, its priests, the *gshen* and the other exorcists just discussed. The *sgrung* were the 'bards' who sing songs and heroic epics, family genealogies and cosmogonic myths. Their present-day successors are the *sgrung pa*, the bards who sing the epic of *Ge sar*, which has been the subject of an exhaustive study by Stein (1959a).

The narratives mentioned above and the fragments uncovered in Tun-huang are poetical works in metrical form which recount the history of particular families. In essence these consist of the same material which recurs over and over as the introduction to the family histories, and was not eliminated even after the triumph of Buddhist orthodoxy, although these stories not only have nothing to do with Buddhism, but reflect an essentially older substrate, faithfully transmitted from generation to generation. These accounts give not merely genealogical outlines, but detailed histories of the origin of the family concerned, of the ancestor's descent from a mountain or from the sky (e.g. *Po ti bse ru* or the history of the *Sa skya pa*), of struggles with hostile powers, the overcoming of demons and so forth.

In these narratives cosmogonic myths also occur as introductory material. This myths usually have as their subject the transition from chaos (at first in nature, but also in society) to order and the successive social and cultural 'discoveries' which have benefited man; thus they form a mythical history from the origins onwards.

It would be interesting if we could establish at what season and on what occasions the *sgrung* came into action. Among other peoples this happens in extraordinary moments and in special circumstances. The cosmogony, or the narration of the descent of a family onto the earth, was probably not an end in itself; these events may also have been represented in ritual, and the myth thus turned into a rite able to liberate magically operative powers. This could happen at the beginning of the year or at other solemn occasions, such as when departing from the hunt, on the occasion of calendrically fixed festivals or of the harvest, in other words whenever the return of the primal event necessitated its ritual re-enactment. The song of the *sgrung*, and the portrayal of particular heroes in masked dances, for which we have sporadic evidence, had surely not only the purpose of entertaining the crowd which had gathered. In a society such as that of Tibet there was, least of all at the beginning, not a single event to which a definite religious and social meaning was not attributed. The ceremonies centred about the *sgrung* had the task of commemorating and bringing to life once again that moment of origin in which the ancestors descended to the earth, in order to call down their help and protection on the society tracing its descent from them, and thus to ensure its continuation. The recitation of a myth of origin thus has the meaning of a restoration of a primitive state; this evocation of the origins (even if it only lasted for a brief moment) gave new strength to society and to the family dominating it, through the function innate within the ritual of making a connection between the three worlds (the heavenly world, the intermediate world and the world of men). The three worlds were brought together in the ritual in a unity which in daily life continually deteriorates and which is consequently always in need of renewal.

The narrative, given magical power through the ritual, brought about the return to the origins and thus the continuity of all that happens–a goal continually present to the mind of the Tibetan. The past is for him a *dpe*, an example or model to be repeated.[21] The task of the ritual is precisely the continuous bringing of the model to mind. Thus in many songs, whose performance is accompanied by ritual dances, the repetition of events that happened in the previous year is evoked (Tucci, 1966, pp.94ff.). Sun, moon and harvest, all have been good. The ritual if fully accomplished will bring about the renewal of the same processes and natural events in the present.

That the retelling of the past has a liturgical function can also be deduced from the contents of numerous religious tractates, especially those concerned with exorcistic and magical liturgies (particularly with *mdos*). Some of the many examples given in these texts have already been mentioned in our discussion of the folk religion, which can be referred to here (cf.p.206).

These narratives are naturally particularly detailed when they are discussing the origins of magical practices or of the implements used by the magicians. An example is the collection of stories in No. 33, *cha*, pp. 210ff., where the discovery of the *ju thig*, the divinatory cord, is narrated. The story begins with the illness of a queen and the consequent summoning of a soothsayer (*mo pa*), in other words a *phya gshen*, by the king. The magician-priest prepares a kind of *mandala* out of white felt (*ling phying dkar po*) and places the necessary implements on it: the arrow with the coloured bands, lustral water, incense, roasted barley; then he invokes the *Mu wer dkar po* (who consist of three brothers and three sisters) and makes an offering to the 360 *bdud lha*. Onto the *mandala* he throws three times the *ju thig* (*bcu thig* in the MS.) *shar ba rkyen drug*, which is called the *dung gi ju thig* because it consists of an arrow to which six threads of white wool are attached. If the oracle is negative, the magician-priest counsels the king to turn to *gShen rab mi bo*; only he can recognize the cause of the illness and the *gdon* responsible and so procure a remedy. This story offers a pretext for narrating the origin of the *ju thig shar ba rkyen drug*, which is regarded as a store-house or receptacle for the soul of the world and as an indispensable tool in divinatory and magical operations. It is made of the wool which once grew on the shoulders of the great Primal Sheep. This animal is ascribed a cosmogonic significance, and is called 'Divine Sheep with the Great Wool' (*lug lha bal chen*). It brings about the growth of barley, which gives flour, and it produces milk and butter. The 360 *bdud lha* taste it and are so enthusiastic that they say *a la la*; this exclamation, which expresses general satisfaction, is traced back to this event.

In the beginning there was nothing but heaven (*gnam*); from the essence of heaven earth was born; the sheep scratched the earth, and the turquoise *g.yu* (which is placed upon the felt *mandala*) came from it. All this happened in the course of an incessant conflict between the two mighty opponents *Ye rje* (= *Ye smon rgyal po*), who ruled on the Mountain of Being (*yod ri*), and his enemy *Nyam rje* who lived in his castle of darkness. From the forge of a smith dark smoke arose, which condensed into a cloud from which rain fell; *Ye rje* was soaked through, but the sheep made him a hat out of its wool, to protect him against the downpour. His opponent shot an arrow which, however, hit not *Ye rje* but his hat. *Ye rje* laid the arrow on the felt *mandala* and decorated it with a silver mirror and a piece of white silk; he entrusted all these objects to the 360 gods.

On another occasion there was again strife between *Ye rje* and *Nyam rje*, but *lha* and *bdud* assembled in the open space between the two. The *lha* took their refuge at the Mountain of Being (*yod ri*), the *bdud* went to the black mountain, the Mountain of Coal (*sol ri*). This event inspired in the 'witness' (he who has to distinguish truth from falsehood) the phrase *lha rgyal lo*, 'the gods are victorious'. Out of this occasion too arose the separation between the world of the gods and the world of *srin*, between oath and perjury, in general. Then the art of counting with pebbles arose, and so astrology developed, along with the use of pebbles to predict the future (*dpyad*), divination by means of dice, and so on.

When *Ye rje* and *Nyam rje* were on friendly terms, trees grew in the space between them whose leaves were of silk cloth and whose buds sprouted forth like treasures. Their sap was ambrosia, their bark protected life, weapons appeared out of their thorns, their flowers were festive ornaments. Who was able to explain (*dpyad*) the meaning of these appearances? A *Phya g.yang dkar* explained them; he had come riding on a sheep, the divine arrow with white pennants in his hands. He came to the Mountain of Existence (*yod ri*) and here he divined what would happen: eternal conflict between the law of the *lha* and the law of the *bdud*, the struggle between *Ye rje* and *Nyam rje*, antagonism between the world of Being and the world of Non-Being, but in the end the victory of the god of Being. His name *Phya g.yang dkar*, 'he who is endowed with mystical foresight, he who knows', thus acquired its full meaning. Since this event it has been possible to predict the future of the world.

How was the sheep born, though? From a wish of *Ye smon rgyal po*, who was disturbed that all the riches of the world, jewels, gold, silver were being treated as stones of no use to men. Therefore he took the counsel of his consort *Chu lcam* (Water Consort) and went to the summit of the Mountain of Existence (*yod ri*). Here he thought deeply about how his wish could be fulfilled. He concentrated within himself all the saps and vital substances of heaven, earth and the elements, and wished that a being might arise able to free the creatures from hunger and thirst. After he had stayed for three days on the white peak of the Mountain of Existence the sheep, the means of nourishment and exchange for the human race, appeared to him. From the shoulder of this sheep came the wool of the *ju thig* called *shar ba rkyen drug*. It could not be held still, but began to fly and reached first the tree of heaven, then the *khyung* (a kind of eagle), then seven of the mountains surrounding the earth, and finally the tortoise which supports the world; it then returned to the Mountain of Existence and fell down again on the divine sheep. With it the god wove six threads, whose ends were called castle (*mkhar*). The *ju thig* was called *gur chen* ('great tent') and was placed on the *mandala* (*lha gzhi*). The *Phya g.yang dkar* used it for his prophecies concerning the past, the future, the present, dangers and advantages, illnesses and death, the kind of burial (*dur*) and so on. He also used it for examining and interpreting prophecies regarding the king, the ministers and the subjects in all the situations of life, and for all questions concerning them and their destiny.

The context in which these stories originated is surely of great age, even if later additions have been made to them; it is a world of pastoralism. Two themes intersect in it but remain clearly separate: divination through the *ju thig* made of wool, and the conception of the sheep, not only as the animal providing the indispensable element for preparing the divining apparatus, but also as a primal being, as one of the first-born creatures, recognized as a foundation and principle of the existence of society. Society here is divided into three principal groups: kings or chiefs, their counsellors or ministers, and subjects. The arrow mentioned (*mda' dar*) with the five-coloured silk bands attached to it is an essential element in a large part of the popular liturgy. It is the work of a smith who is in contact with the powers of evil, but the god of good things takes possession of it. Behind concepts of this kind we can perceive a pastoral society, that lives in felt tents and uses the felted skin as the prototype of the *mandala*, spreading upon it the objects held to be sacred; a society which desires to know the future in advance and to obtain the means through which it can avert the calamitous events predicted by the omens.

There is always a clear distinction between good and evil. Everywhere there is conflict between good and evil powers, helpful and harmful forces, personified as two opposing and sharply distinguished beings. They are clearly separated already through the dividing space situated between them, in which their conflicts take place, but the concluding of pacts is also possible. Pacts, oaths, obligations have at the same time sacred and social meaning.

The power or *majestas* (Tib. *mnga' thang*) of the king rests above all upon his sacredness. Originally this was to guarantee purity and immunity against defilement by the evils threatening him and the kingdom. If a king is attacked by leprosy, or if he has a son born blind, then king and queen are buried alive, and the son cannot ascend the throne until he acquires the power of sight (No. 85, *ja*, p.12 and No. 117, p.51a, b). If the king does not fulfil the requirements imposed on him then his *mnga' thang* is extinguished, the grass dries up and all goes to the bad (Bacot, 1940; Bacot et al., 1940, p.133). The king is consecrated and blessed through a purificatory ceremony (No. 35, p.18, 1) and is then the guarantor of the fertility of the earth. *gNya' khri btsan po* descended onto the earth in the form of rain (Bacot, et al., 1940, p.86), and so brought about prosperity and abundance. *sPu de gung rgyal* had the same task (ibid., p.127).

There seems to me no reason to give up the opinion which I have expressed elsewhere (Tucci, 1956, p.197), that the king renounced his power as soon as his son reached the age at which he could mount a horse, that is at thirteen years. This number expresses completeness and purity. Reliable indications are lacking concerning the further destiny of the old king. His ascent to heaven by means of the *dmu thag*, the rope of *dmu*, may indicate that he was removed by violence or exiled. In any case the power went into the hands of the son, whose minister stood at his side. This is confirmed indirectly by Chinese sources, from which it emerges that among the Tibetans the old were objects of contempt, the mother had to greet the son and the son had pre-eminence over the father; when entering or leaving the young went first and the old followed (Pelliot, 1961, p.3). In the same sources it is said that King *Srong btsan sgam po* ascended the throne as soon as he was given a man's hat (the Tibetans say as soon as he could mount a horse). Numerous similar examples could be cited from Tibetan history. Each new king completely transformed everything. He had his own magician-priest, *sku gshen*, whose place was at his right, while his minister sat at his left, an indication of the pre-eminence of the priest over the minister. The list of ministers has been preserved in the chronicles. No king resided in his father's palace;[22] the new king lived in his own castle. In short, when a king ascended the throne a *novus ordo* came about. The sacred character of the kingdom emerges too from the ritual dances which introduced the new year. On this occasion a costume was worn which recalls vividly the dress of the shamans. It was white, the hair of the head was rolled up and held together by silver bands, protected by a turban bearing the image of a *khyung*, that eagle-like mythical bird which represents the good creation, and is the traditional adversary of the *mkha' lding*, the Tibetan equivalent of the Indian *Garuda* and the enemy of serpents; a natural consequence of the veneration of *klu* in the autochthonous Tibetan religion.

The helmet, *dbu rmog*, was the symbol of royalty. The efficacy of the royal power is referred to by the expression 'supreme helmet', which recurs frequently both in the inscriptions (including those in Ladakh) and in the texts.

There was a close connection between kingdom and helmet. Certain texts give lists of the eighteen family trees of the kings ruling in the eighteen districts (*khri sde*) of *Zhang zhung*. The lists mention not only the kings, but along with each king the religious teacher (here referred to as *drang srong*) who acted as protector of the *Bon* doctrine during his reign, and also the name of his palace and of his helmet. In fact, in some cases instead of a helmet horns, *bya ru* (= *rwa co*) are mentioned, which these kings wore above their head-covering. Some kings are even distinguished according to the (generally valuable) material out of which these horns were made. The list begins (No. 2, pp.90ff) with *Zhang zhung srid pa'i rgyal po Khri wer la rje*, who bore gold horns. Then follow others: kings with *bya ru* made from coral (*bye ru* = *byi ru*), from the radiance of *gar ljang 'od* (in other words from a special green turquoise, *g.yu gar ljang*, No. 5, p.3, I.4), from iron, from *vaidurya*, from *candrakanta* (moon-stone), from *suryakanta* (sun-stone), from *gnam lcags* (meteoric iron?), in the form of a *khyung* and so on. It seems that each individual king had a special crown or horned headdress, as was the case with the Sassanid kings, where each king was also recognizable by his particular crown. We are certainly dealing here with mythical kings, but this is unimportant, for there are surely real usages at the base of the tradition, especially considering the Iranian parallels.

It is more difficult to explain how the *lde'u* came to have such importance that they were inserted into the triad on whom the fate of the king and of his realm depended. As far as I know, there no longer exist any *lde'u* priests, although the custom itself with which they were connected is still alive. Today it is a question of a pastime, a game of riddles, with which educated people too occupy themselves at festive gatherings:

> It is no tiger, yet it has stripes (on its skin);
> It is no leopard, yet it has spots;
> It is no *mdzo*, yet it sucks.
> (Solution: the bee.)

Riddles of this kind are current in distinguished families. We can deduce that the *lde'u* were probably diviner-priests to whom one had recourse at critical moments, for example before military campaigns or other perilous undertakings.

The sacred character of the *lde'u*[23] is made clearer by the statement that they are different from other men because they are descended from *lde'u* (Bacot et al., 1940, p.123).

Further clarification of this whole series of questions is made possible by, for example, the wedding-songs. In these customs riddles have a special significance, as do homophones (words sounding the same but with different meanings) which can lead to misunderstandings, or ambiguous questions to which correspond ambiguous answers. In the wedding songs are preserved numerous customs and traditions, fragments of cosmogonies and mythological concepts of varied origin and diverse ages. One should not be surprised then to find in such passages of ambiguous speech, in such sequences of questions and answers an echo of the mantic function of the ancient *lde'u*. Only under this assumption can we understand the protective role (*skyong*) ascribed to them in relation to the state.

Concerning this characteristic of the *lde'u*, it is not without interest that (among the extremely numerous emanations spoken of in the *Bon po* literature) a light emanated out of the right hand of *rGyal ba gShen rab* from which was born *gShen chen po*, *lde bo gsung chen* ('the *lde bo*, the great word', No. 2, p.18b).

Our reconstruction of the *Bon* religion, mostly undertaken *a posteriori* and relying in general on later texts, is fully confirmed in a number of places by the Chinese sources (Pelliot, 1961, p.92), which date from the period of the first Chinese-Tibetan relations. In these sources repeated sacrificial offerings are mentioned on the occasion of taking oaths towards the king. Every three years, in fact, there took place a great taking of oaths, on the occasion of which dogs and horses were sacrificed. As already mentioned, these animals possessed a special sacred character and were buried, along with cattle and asses and even men, together with the king (ibid., p.82). The yak on the other hand was not a sacrificial animal, but was killed in the course of hunts and ritual feasts.[24]

At the sacrifices the bones of the animals were broken and their entrails torn out. As we have already mentioned, in rituals in honour of the terrifying deities the entrails (real or made from coloured *tsamba*) are still today coiled together around the ritual offerings (*gtor ma*) made of *tsamba*. The same Chinese sources witness the striking veneration of the entrails by the magician-priests and the diviners (ibid., p.3).

The taking of oaths also occurred in connection with other events, for example at the conclusion of a peace treaty (in the year 822, ibid., p.114). This ceremony was sufficiently tenacious that it continued even after the introduction of Buddhism. The *cella* consecrated to the Buddha was separated from the altar where the ritual took place, at which sacrificial animals were offered in clear violation of Buddhist doctrine even at the time of *Ral pa can*, although this king is regarded as a faithful protector of Buddhism and of its commandments.

According to a tradition which is generally accepted, *gShen rab mi bo* was the creator of the systematic doctrinal structure of the *Bon* religion. In other words, he arranged together in an organic whole a varied and contradictory mass of ritual practices, exorcistic formulae, celebrations and customs–it would not so much have been a question of literary texts, since these existed only in small numbers before his time. He came from *'Ol mo lung rings* in *sTag zig*; we will return to this place name later in another context (cf.p.242), but it could also be of Tibetan origin.[25]

gShen rab has assumed the same position within the literature of *Bon* as Sakyamuni has within Buddhism. He is *rNam mkhyen rgyal ba gShen rab mchog*, 'the Omniscient Victor, the Supreme *gShen*'; his seat is in the *'Og min* paradise; his rank is that of a fully-accomplished Buddha (*mngon par sangs rgyas*). Moved by compassion for living beings, however, he descended to this world as representative (*rgyal tshab*) of the *gShen lha*, the 'divine *gShen*'. According to some sources (No. 2, p.19a), he first of all went to the paradise *'Od gsal lha*, where he was born as the son of *dMu rgyal*. His *katabasis* was, however, not yet finished. As soon as the demons (*bdud*) of the various regions of Tibet heard about these events, they set out to do battle with him under the leadership of the *bdud* of East Tibet (*mDo khams*). At this he descended in *Zhang zhung*, as the son of *dMu rgyal*, amid earthquakes and flashes of lighting. Rage seized the gods (*lha rigs*) of *Zhang zhung* under their leader *Ti se*, the *rma rigs* of *Bod khams* under *Thang lha*, the 999,000 *srid pa'i sman*, and the twelve *brtan ma*, guardians of the world. However, *gShen rab* subdued them all, and to confirm their submission for all time they offered him the secret syllables enclosing the essence of their power (*srog snying yig 'bru sa bon*). In this way they became guardians of the teachings of *rGyal ba gShen rab*, they drank the consecrated water (*dam btags snying po dam chu kha ra btung*) and bore the symbol of the *Bon* teachings, the *svastika* (*g.yung drung*) on their heads. From then on they were called *dam can ye shes spyan ldan*, 'those who have taken the vow and who possess the eye of transcendent consciousness'.

This narrative is worthy of note in that it clearly echoes the story of the subduing of the *Bon po* gods by Padmasambhava. The testimony which it provides for the existence of local groups of gods (among them *Ti se*) who are indubitably older than the systematization of *Bon* attributed to *gShen rab* is equally instructive.

In all other respects *gShen rab*'s biography follows faithfully that of the Buddha, although here and there traits indigenous to the world of *Bon* can certainly be found. These, however, are not sufficient to give a clearer picture of his personality.

Entry into the *Bon po* community was bound up with a special ritual which imposed reciprocal obligations whose breach involved severe punishment. The details of this ritual are unknown to us, but we know that its principal part consisted in invoking on those guilty of a breach of their word the most terrifying threats, with whose actualization special gods were entrusted. Such gods have survived until this day, and belong precisely to the class of *dam can* ('those who have taken the vow'). They form part of the general class of *chos skyong*; within the Buddhist domain too they watch over the keeping of vows and are at the same time, however, regarded as protective deities. All those who had taken the vow and belonged to the community were called *mched*, brothers. They were dressed in white and formed a kind of *Männerbund*, although this expression is inappropriate in that women too took part. This community consecrated by the ritual is somewhat more than the *ganacakra* of the Buddhists; the latter is rather a congregation for the performance of a particular ritual, while the religious act in which *Bon po* of both sexes took part was by contrast a kind of sacrament bringing about the state of brotherhood which continued to exist after the end of the ceremony. Those taking part were bound to a promise (*dam bca'*), breaking which excludes those guilty from the community, as does participating in impurity of spirit or body. In *Bon* purity is not only a spiritual property but also a physical one; the body must guard itself against any contact with things regarded as impure.

The liturgical action was preceded (cf. e.g. No. 37) by a bath in a consecrated receptacle filled with consecrated water. (Bathing with pure water, *gtsang khrus*, lustration, was an essential component also of the royal consecration ceremony, No. 35, p. 18b.) The *suffimen*, the burning of incense, followed, in the form in which it has survived to this day in the exorcistic liturgy (*bsangs*), with the use of juniper wood. The smoke was an offering (*dud mchod*) which was valid for both the peaceful and the terrifying gods (such as the 360 *Ge khod* or *Gi khod*). The entire community of brothers and sisters (*bsgrub bon mched lcam*) took part in this ritual. The acts of purification extended to impurities of all kinds, including not only moral defilements (the elimination of the five 'poisons' or vices) but also physical impurities: incest, war, trade, contact with persons in a state of mourning or those who have broken their vows, contact with people with leprosy or incurable illnesses, wearing impure clothes and so on. The 2,400 sacred places (*gdan gsas*) were also submitted to purification.

Essential elements of the *Bon* liturgy were the three-step dance, three-part songs and the word of three levels (*ngag tshigs gsum*). The ritual and sacred character of these dances, songs and recitations can be deduced from the fact that they are always preceded by the word *gshen* (No. 2, p.19b). The king could not undertake anything if the *gshen* had not spoken the three words and performed the songs (*glu*) three times (No. 35, p.266). Only after this could the king and ministers begin to sing and dance.

The *Bon po* rituals were certainly accompanied by some kind of beating of a drum (*gshan*,e.g. No. 85, *ja*, p.8b). In their course the magician-priests mounted on a deer (*sha ba*) made of clay, on which they could rise into space, or rode on a drum called *rnga*. Their drum-beats could make water spring forth and juniper grow (No. 35, p.62).

In our description the word shaman has occasionally been used. There can surely be no doubt of the existence of certain similarities between the old Tibetan religion and shamanism; the ride through the air, the magical use of the drum, the calling back of the souls of the dead or dying—all these were duties of particular classes of *gshen*. One could be born a *gshen* (cf. *gshen rigs*, lineage of *gshen*, Lalou, 1952, p.353), in other words one could belong to a *gshen* family, as often happens with the shamans. This does not exclude later possession by a demon. This is what happened, as I understand the legend, to the youth spoken of in No. 85, *ja*, p.8b. He came from a *gshen* family in *'On mo lung ring* (cf.p.239) in the land of *'On*, and had asses' ears (evidently an allusion to a particular form of hat). At the age of twelve he was stolen away by a *'dre*. He was returned after another twelve years and introduced the use of a woollen hat (*bal thod*, cf.p.228) with broad side-sections to cover his asses' ears. All the same one can scarcely find here definite traces of those ecstatic aspects of shamanism so well portrayed by Mircea Eliade.

The penetration of Buddhism, especially that of the *rDzogs chen* school, took place gradually, and *Bon* received from Buddhism a doctrinal structure of its own.

After the prohibition of *Bon* its teachings were written down in *gter ma* form in accordance with the prediction of *Dran pa Nam mkha'*, as happened in the *rNying ma pa* school too (cf.p.38). The texts were written with 'divine', *lan dza*,[26] *zhang zhung* or other letters, on white-coloured heaven-paper (*lha shog*), red Indian (or Chinese?) paper (*rgya*), yellow Tibetan paper or blue *Mon* paper. Then the *gter ma* were enclosed in rectangular chests (*ga'u*) of *vaidurya* (No. 2, p.33a). After this the *gter ma* were divided into five principal groups, which were confided to the five eternal elements and placed under the protection and guard of the goddesses watching over the magical operations: *zhi*, *rgyas*, *dbang*,*drag* and*ye shes dbal mo*. The less important *gter ma*, deposited in cemeteries and other places, were entrusted to various classes of guardians (*gter srung*).

The classification of the masters who actualized the truth is also borrowed from the Buddhists, although the content is in part different (cf.p.110). The *Bon po* too know the eighty *siddha* (Buddhism has eighty-four) and the *vidyadhara* (Tib. *rig 'dzin*), the 'possessors of magical knowledge'. They were divided into various categories or groups according to the kind of knowledge they possessed; those who were in possession of the *phyag rgya chen po* (Skt. *mahamudra*) belonged to the physical plane, and could at will be born or appear within a tree, a rock, an egg, a womb and so on. Those of the verbal plane could change themselves at will into women or men; those of the mental plane (*thugs*) could take on a rainbow body (*'ja' lus*). Those who had cultivated the principle of perfect equality (*kun snyoms*) were able to go at lightning speed to any point of heaven and of earth, without hindrance from material objects. Finally those of action (*phrin las*) had the power to direct all living beings.

Even one of the characteristic precepts of the *Bon* religion, the anticlockwise circumambulation (which was in any case not unknown to the Buddhists; it was practised with respect to Samvara) could be transformed into its opposite; at a later period the *Bon po* too took over the clockwise movement (*g.yas skor*), and in this case they also clearly took into account the doctrinal principles with which it was connected.

The clockwise circling was regarded as the circle of the means (*thabs skor*) and the anticlockwise as the circle of transcendent consciousness (*ye shes skor*). Another principle of division was also used, and in some rituals the clockwise circumambulation was reserved for men and called 'sun-circling', while the anticlockwise or 'moon-circling' was reserved for women (No. 2, p.45a).

Just as the Buddhists distinguished three or four bodies, or three, four or five phases of illusory being in its manifestation and revelation, *Bon po* philosophy too makes use of the same schematizations. The *Bon po* accept five such bodies, which are given as follows (No. 6, p.204): *bon sku* (= *chos sku*, Skt. *dharmakaya* of the Buddhists); *longs sku* (*sambhogakaya*); *sprul sku* (*nirmanakaya*); *ngo bo nyid* (*svabhavikakaya*); *mngon byang* (body of Enlightenment).

This classification can be considered as fixed by the doctrine, although it is amplified through further triadic and pentadic divisions, which evidently serve to give a special position to various secondary local deities (No. 2, p.15a). Thus *A ti mu wer* becomes great god (Skt. *mahadeva*) of transcendent cognition, *ye shes lha chen*; *Ku byi mang (s)ke* becomes great god of magical emanation, *rdzu 'phrul lha chen*; *dBal chen ge khod* becomes great god of manifestation, or of the miracle, *sprul pa'i lha chen*.

These three gods presuppose a higher being, *gShen lha 'od dkar*, 'divine *gShen*, White Light', who is expressed by the name and symbol of *Kun tu bzang po*.[27]

These gods also correspond to an iconographic scheme. Thus, for example, *rDzu 'phrul gyi lha* (*Ku byi mang ske*) is represented as turquoise in colour, in the mudra or posture called *brda ston*, 'interpreting signs'. His right hand holds a golden club or golden sceptre (*gser chag shing*) (No. 2, p.16b) and his left hand bears a book, with the palm of the hand turned upwards.

The *Lha chen po* ('Great God', a title recalling that of Siva Mahadeva) *dBal ge khod* by contrast is represented with nine heads and eighteen yellow-coloured arms. On his head he bears a flying *khyung* (*khyung chen*); like kings he is enclosed in golden armour (ibid., p.18a) with the sign of the *svastika* on his breast; he is clothed with the skins of demons, antelopes and men (*bdud g.yang gzhi mi lpags*). His lower body is covered with the skin of *bdud* and of the eight kinds of *dregs*. His girdle is made up of five kinds of poisonous snakes. His head is decorated with a diadem of eight *Lha chen*. He is seated upon eight great serpents. His symbols (*phyag cha*) are the eight great planets, his ornaments the stars (*rgya skar*) and his followers are the eight *Lha chen* (*mahadeva*). He subjugates the envoys of the kings of the four cardinal points (*rgyal chen* and *gnod sbyin*), he rules and directs the whole of existence (*snang srid*) and the three worlds.

Here too we are evidently concerned with a conception formed of various elements of obviously different origins. The eagle, *khyung chen*, certainly was of central significance in the old Tibetan religion, but (as mentioned before) it is also possible that such a head-ornament might have been influenced by the diadem of the Sassanid kings. The name of this deity, *Lha chen* (corresponding to Sanskrit Mahadeva), his seat on eight great serpents, his girdle of five kinds of poisonous snakes and so forth lead one to think of Saivite models.

Testimonies and monuments of pre-Buddhist or non-Buddhist religion are only rarely to be found. *dNgul mkhar* (cf.p.273), the 'Silver Castle' of West Tibet, *Khyung lung*, is today only a ruin. The royal tombs may be regarded as the most famous example of constructions erected in the spirit of *Bon* ritual, above all the tomb of *Srong btsan sgam po*, of which the plan and disposition are well known, although this royal tomb, like all the other burial places of Tibetan kings, suffered great damage during the confusion which followed on the collapse of the dynasty. We know the funeral ritual from several sources; that which was observed at the burial of King *Srong btsan sgam po* is given in particular detail. A sacred meaning was surely attached to the columns erected over the graves of these kings (cf. Tucci, 1950, p.9). Moon and sun were also invoked in the treaties with China. The two columns represent imitations of Chinese models.

Further tombs of uncertain date were discovered by Aufschnaiter (1956) not far from Lhasa. They provide no definite chronological data, since the ceramics accompanying them are notably atypical in character and the other objects found also do not permit even an approximate dating.

Another group of burial places which can be mentioned here was indeed uncovered in a region of Tibetan culture and religion, but the indigenous ethnic foundation of the area cannot be designated Tibetan. These are the tombs at Leh, which as far as their ceramics are concerned appear to stand in clear relation to those which have been uncovered by the Italian Archaeological mission in Swat, Pakistan, in the Indus Valley,[28] burial places which must doubtless be ascribed to Dardic tribes. At any rate a positive decision concerning this question will only be possible when research results are available covering the whole of the Indus Valley and adjoining regions. Non-Buddhist cult and burial sites certainly exist, but more definite conclusions concerning them must await further scientific excavations. These sites consist of circular areas enclosed by great stones piled upon each other and with one or more monoliths at the centre (Tucci, 1966, p.115). We are evidently concerned here with genuine cult places. Examples of such sites are those discovered by Francke in his time, and those which I have examined myself more recently. I have established the presence of an installation of this type near Doptradzong and of others near Sengedzong. In other cases the limited dimensions of the stone enclosures lead one to think of tombs. Megalithic monuments also exist on many mountain passes, though at these places, as already mentioned, simple piles of stones (*lha btsas*, *lha tho*) are more usual. Heaps of stones are also erected in some wedding ceremonies; they are intended to keep away hostile powers and summon benevolent deities. There are numerous objects that without doubt go back to pre-Buddhist or non-Buddhist cultures. For example, there are the so-called 'heaven stones' (*thog rde'u*) which are found in the earth when working in the fields. Some of these are eagle-shaped (*khyung*), others round, some represent other animals (such as monkeys). They are made of bronze. The Tibetans believe that anyone who finds nine of them together is guaranteed to become prosperous. It is worth noting that many of these objects show a surprising similarity to those of Luristan.[29] This suggests the existence of very ancient relationships between the culture of Tibet and that of peoples under Iranian influence. Such contacts may have come about as a result of pastoral nomadism and trade connections through Badakshan, Gilgit, Ladakh and West Tibet (Tucci, 1966). The so-called necklace-pearls (*gzigs*) made of glass paste belong to the same realm; they are for the most part of white glass with dark brown or black colouring. Those which are decorated with round black patterns, usually called 'eyes' (*mig*), are especially valued. Above all beads with nine 'eyes' are held to be extremely powerful talismans and are given a correspondingly high value. The Western origin of such beads is beyond doubt, although we cannot say whether they were originally used as talismans or merely as ornaments.

If we now attempt to bring this material together and draw some conclusions, it must first be said that there are many difficulties in the way of formulating a clear definition of the *Bon* religion. The derived term *Bon po* refers to the adherents of this faith, and also in a narrower sense to its class of exorcists and priests. Certainly there has been great regional diversity in this religion since the most ancient times; this can be seen already from the fact that different clans and localities had their own *Bon* and transmitted it as such. In the course of time the distinctions between *Bon* and Buddhism (especially in the *rDzogs chen* form) became ever more attenuated. This occurred not only in the field of magical and exorcistic religious practice, in which area the activity of the exorcists (*sngags pa*) of the two religions for the good of society or of the individual are often virtually identical (cf.p.211), but also in the field of doctrine.[30]

We have already seen, however, that the doctrinal formulation represents a late phase of development, specifically aimed at matching the rival religion, while the older texts give a primarily ritual and magical picture of the *Bon* religion. In these older sources *Bon* is to a large part directed at the overthrow of hostile or ambivalent powers, or at least keeping them in check or appeasing them, and also at ensuring that the dead do no harm to the living in the course of death and burial rites and so on. Many of these rites and practices were able to survive in the folk religion, often even in Buddhist clothing. One scarcely does justice to the old *Bon* religion if one affirms (as is often done) that it is a religion of the sky, though certain *Bon* concepts (e.g. *gnam bon*) could justify this name. In fact we find here not merely a heavenly space but a whole series of circles of heaven piled up on top of each other, above which there is an infinite space in which the sun and moon circle; we even come across a goddess of the centre of heaven. Sun, moon and stars, are, however, also considered outside of this context, and this is particularly true for the earth as we have said above (p.218). However, all these concepts have no systematic connection with each other; while in many cosmogonies the heavens and the gods of the heavens stand at the centre, in others the gods of the soil and of the earth, including the interior of the earth, play the principal role. The soil here is equated in a certain sense with the mountain ancestor, as the holy place where the descent of the ancestors from heaven occurred. This element is also present in the liturgy for the dead: when the kings were buried, grain was buried with them (Lalou, 1952, p.354). Other texts (No. 110, *kha*, p.42a,b) indicate that the dead man secured fortune, abundance of food and drink, and a good harvest to the people. At the end of the burial special dances were performed; a man dressed as a ram united himself with a woman (Lalou, op.cit., p.359). On the other hand, kings who died young had no tomb (No. 35, p.126), evidently because they had not had time to accumulate the *mnga' thang*, magical power or *majestas*, which constituted their essence. It had to be 'collected' on the orders of the successor during the ceremony (Lalou, op. cit., p.353).

It seems that two traditions, and thus two religions, existed simultaneously, and later flowed together. They have been united since the time of *Gri gum*, as said above (p.224). *Gri gum* in my opinion personifies the memory of a transition of great significance in the history of Tibetan culture, and this transition deserves to be studied carefully.

The summit of the sacred mountain is also the place of contact between earth and heaven. The connection between heaven and earth is a primeval article of faith for the Tibetan; in this connection one must recall the rope (*dmu thag*) which linked heaven and earth, but which was later cut, through the fault of man or as a result of a violation of the liturgical rules. As a result the two worlds have remained for ever parted. The mountain was, and is until the present day, the midpoint of settled space. Some consorts of the first kings bore names which refer to various aspects of the mountain (Stein, 1962a, p.29). On the mountains even today the seasonal rituals and festivals are celebrated, and it is there too that the dead were once buried, and are now exposed. Many details lead us to think of a superimposition or co-existence of two diverse concepts, one concerned with the cults of heaven and of the ancestors, the other being of earthly and chthonic character (Tucci, 1955). The group of goddesses who are equated with particular mountains (*brtan ma*, cf. Skt. *dhrti-prthivi*) has a notably terrifying character, the singular ambivalence, fluctuating between life and death, which we found in concepts relating to the Magna Mater. A similar abundance of diverse aspects, partly contemporaneous and partly belonging to successive phases, can be seen in the funeral rites. Here we find disappearance into heaven (placing on the peak of a high mountain?), placing on rocky mountain slopes, the throwing of corpses into rivers (still practised), burial in the earth, which was used by the Buddhists as well in historical times (in many places the corpse was buried or placed on a mountain, and its image, or preferably its clothes stretched on a wooden frame, was thrown into the water), and cremation.

The multitude of powers who inhabited this world, and still today survive in the folk religion, were divided into various groups: *gnyan*, *btsan*, *sa bdag*, *klu* and so on. With each of these groups a domain of the world was associated: air, under the earth, water. Thus four or eight divisions were arrived at (*lha srin sde brgyad*). They remained vague, however, just as the ideas relating to these powers were vague, endowed with names but scarcely with definite forms. Only at a later time was an attempt made to assign precise forms to these schemes, and *Bon* iconography was born. Since then we possess many-armed and many-headed gods like those of Tantrism, above all terrifying gods, who are without doubt the more ancient.

The functions of the various classes of exorcists were more clearly delineated, though from the enumerations given above it can be seen that here too reciprocal influences and displacements of boundaries took place in the course of time. The common denominator of all these groups, however, remained their magical power (*mthu*), which was opposed to the *majestas* (*mnga' thang*) of the kings, although that too acquired a sacred character. The magical power of the exorcists was either acquired, possessed through belonging to a privileged family, transmitted by a demon who possesses the subject (*lha pa*), or awakened by initiatory practices (among other things by special trials to which the candidates were subjected). Notwithstanding this indigenous nucleus, which is very closely linked to the place of settlement and the lineage organization of the groups living there, there can be no doubt about the external influences on the *Bon* religion. These already emerge from the fact that *Bon* itself indicates such connections in various places. Beyond this, however, there are importations that can be unambiguously traced from Iran, Central Asia, India, and China, as well as more than one might suppose from the north-west of modern Pakistan through to Badakshan. Thus our description can give only an approximate, schematic idea of the profusely interwoven nature of *Bon*. It is impossible, however, to give a more complete picture until scientific investigations have supplied us with further, as yet inaccessible, material upon which to work.

CHRONOLOGICAL TABLE

620(?)–49 *Srong btsan sgam po**
Foundation of Tibetan power
641 Marriage with Princess Wen-ch'eng
Conquest of *Zhang zhung*
Thon mi sam bho ta sent to India; he creates the Tibetan alphabet

649–76 *Mang srong mang brtsan*
Conquest of T'u-yü-hun (*A zha*)
Acquisition of Chinese territories in Central Asia

676–704 *Khri 'du srong brtsan*
Expansion of Central Asian possessions
692–4 Their partial reconquest by the Chinese

704–55 *Khri lde gtsug brtsan*
710 His marriage with the Chinese princess Chin-ch'eng (originally intended for his father)

755–97(?) *Khri srong lde brtsan*
Reconquest of Central Asian possessions
Santaraksita, Kamalasila and Padmasambhava in Tibet
775(?) Foundation of the monastery of *bSam yas*
779 Buddhism recognized as the state religion
783 Peace treaty with China
792–4 Council of *bSam yas*
Beginning of political decline and of loss of some Central Asian possessions

797(?)–9 *Mu ne btsan po* (chronology and descendants uncertain)

799–815 *Khri lde srong brtsan Sad na legs*
Important political influence of *Myang Ting nge 'dzin* and *Bran ka Yon tan dpal*

* His date of birth is much disputed. I shall return to this question in an article to be published shortly.

815–38	*Khri gtsug lde brtsan*, better known under the name *Ral pa can* Intense activity of translation of Buddhist literature 822 Peace treaty with China; the Tibetans retain possession of most of their Central Asian possessions
838–42	*Khri bdu dum brtsan*, better known under the name *Glang dar ma* Persecution of Buddhism. End of the period called the 'First Diffusion of the Doctrine' (*snga dar*) by Tibetan scholars
842	Murder of *Glang dar ma* Struggle for power between *Khri lde* (known as *Yum brten*) and *gNam lde* (known as *'Od srungs*)
866	*Khong bzher*, who had proclaimed himself prime minister, falls in battle with the Chinese Loss of the Central Asian possessions; the descendants of *Yum brtan* remain in possession of the principalities of *gTsang* and *dBus* (especially *bSam yas*) Descendants of *'Od srungs* in *Yar klungs* Another descendant of the same family, *sKyid lde Nyi ma mgon*, founds a dynasty in West Tibet (*Gu ge* and Ladakh)
9th-10th centuries	'Second Diffusion of the Doctrine' (*spyi dar*), introduced by the activity of *dGongs pa rab gsal* (832–915? or 892–975?) and his disciple *Klu mes* (around 950–1025) *Rin chen bzang po* (958–1055) is sent to Kashmir around 970 by the king of West Tibet, *Ye shes 'od*, to deepen his knowledge of Buddhist doctrine and bring teachers and artists back with him to Tibet; founding of the first temples in West Tibet, Tabo, Tholing, Nako etc. *Byang chub 'od*, King of West Tibet, sends *Nag tsho lotsava* to Vikramasila in India to convey an invitation to Atisa
1042	Arrival in Tibet of Atisa Dipamkara Srijnana (died 1054), his meeting with *Rin chen bzang po* Atisa continues his missionary activity in Central Tibet and dies in 1054 in *sNye thang* near to Lhasa; founding of the monastery of *Rwa sgrengs* (Reting) (1057), centre of diffusion for the so-called *bKa' gdams pa* school
1055	Birth of *Ma gcig Lab sgron ma*, female student and collaborator of the founder of the monastery of *Ding ri* and head of the *gCod* sect, *Dam pa sangs rgyas* (died 1117)
1073	Foundation of the head monastery of the *Sa skya pa* school by *'Khon dKon mchog rgyal po* (1034–1102), a student of *'Brog mi* (died 1074)
1076	Great council at the monastery of Tabo, summoned by the king of West Tibet, *rTse lde*

1079	Birth of *sGam po pa* (*Dwags po lha rje*), disciple of *Mi la ras pa*
1098	Death of *Mar pa*, translator and mystic, to whom the tradition of the *bKa' brgyud pa* school goes back; teacher of the great mystic and poet *Mi la ras pa* (1040–1123)
1136	Birth of *Nyang ral Nyi ma 'od zer* (died 1203), the discoverer of 'hidden treasures' (*gter ma*) and founder of the *rDzogs chen* school
1158	*'Gro mgon Phag mo gru pa* founds the monastery of *mThil* (or *Thel*)
1175	*Zhang rin po che* founds the monastery of *Tshal*
1179	Definitive foundation of *'Bri gung* (Digung) by *'Bri gung rin po che* (1143–1217) (first founding by *Mi nyag sGom rin*)
1182	Birth of *Kun dga' rgyal mtshan* (died 1251), better known as 'the learned *Sa skya* scholar', *Sa skya pandita* (*Sa pan*). Ögedei recognizes him as representative of the Great Mongolian Empire in Tibet and effective ruler of Tibet, assisted by Mongolian officials
1189	Founding of the monastery of *mTshur phu* (Tsurphu) by *Kar ma pa Dus gsum mkhyen pa* (1110–93)
1204	Birth of the second teacher of the *Kar ma pa* sect, *Kar ma pa kshi* (died 1283); he later visited China at the invitation of Khubilai
1206	Cinggis Khan wishes to set foot on Tibetan soil and receives the submission of some chiefs
1244	*Sa skya pandita*'s meeting with the Mongolian king Godan
1252–3	Mongol invasion
1260(?)	The thirteen districts of West Tibet are formally placed under the control of *'Phags pa Blo gros rgyal mtshan* (1235–80) of the *Sa skya* school; around 1270 he is appointed 'imperial preceptor' (*ti-shih*) Opposition of the *'Bri gung pa* (so called after the monastery of *'Bri gung*)
1290	Destruction of the monastery of *'Bri gung* by the *Sa skya pa* generals
1290	Birth of *Bu ston* (died 1364) who is responsible for the final form of the already translated Buddhist texts (*bKa' 'gyur*, 'word of the master', and *bsTan 'gyur*, commentaries, glosses and secondary works)
1302	Birth of *Byang chub rgyal mtshan* (died 1373) of the *rLangs* family

	This family is also known as that of the *Phag mo gru pa*, after the monastery of *gDan sa Thel* or *mThil* founded by *Phag mo gru pa* which later became the centre of their power
1354	Fighting with the *Sa skya pa*, who are defeated; various members of the family are appointed *rdzong dpon*, prefect; reorganization of the state End of *Sa skya pa* power and beginning of the power of the *Phag mo gru pa*
1357	Birth of *Tsong kha pa Blo gros grags pa* (died 1419), the founder of the *dGe lugs pa* school (also called the 'Yellow Sect')
1391	Birth of *dGe 'dun grub* (died 1475), pupil of *Tsong kha pa* and supreme head of the *dGe lugs pa* sect. After his death the principle of incarnation was affirmed; *sPyan ras gzigs* (Skt. *Avalokitesvara*) is incarnated in the supreme head of the sect (*rGyal ba*)
1409	Founding of *dGa' ldan* (Ganden), *dGe lugs pa* monastery
1416	Founding of *'Bras spungs* (Drepung), *dGe lugs pa* monastery
1419	Founding of *Se ra*, *dGe lugs pa* monastery
1437	Founding of *Chab mdo* (Chamdo), *dGe lugs pa* monastery in *Khams*
1447	Founding of *bKra shis lhun po* (Trashilhunpo), *dGe lugs pa* monastery in *gTsang* The *Rin spungs pa* oppose themselves to the *Phag mo gru pa*, taking advantage of their weakening power and allying with the *Kar ma pa*. After the first half of the fifteenth century their most important town is *bSam grub rtse* near Shigatse
1475	Birth of the second *rGyal ba*, *dGe 'dun rgya mtsho*. Conflicts with the *Rin spungs pa* and *gTsang*, becoming progressively more violent In Central Tibet the *dGe lugs pa* are supported by the *Phag mo gru pa*
1537	The fifth *Zhwa dmar Kar ma pa* allies himself with the princes of *gTsang* against the *dGe lugs pa*
1543	Birth of the third *rGyal ba*, *bSod nams rgya mtsho* (died 1588) In view of the weakening of the *Phag mo gru pa* through internal conflicts he seeks help outside Tibet; in 1578 he visits Mongolia, where Altan Khan confers on him the title of Dalai Lama; he dies in Mongolia during a second visit
1589	Birth of the fourth *rGyal ba* or Dalai Lama, *Yon tan rgya mtsho* (died 1617), whose incarnation is found for political motives in the family of Altan Khan

1617	Birth of the fifth Dalai Lama, *Ngag dbang blo bzang rgya mtsho* (died 1682). Collapse of *Phag mo gru pa* power, further growth of the influence of *gTsang* and of the *Kar ma pa* Gusri Khan of the Qosot Mongols comes to the Dalai Lama's aid
1624–36	Jesuit missionaries in West Tibet
1626–32	Other missionaries in *gTsang*
1641	Gusri Khan defeats the king of *Be ri* in *Khams*, an adherent of the *Bon* religion
1641–2	Gusri Khan overthrows the king of *gTsang* and takes him prisoner; his territory is handed over to the Dalai Lama
1642–59	Consolidation of the Tibetan theocracy; civil and military power is given to a regent (*sDe srid*) appointed by the Dalai Lama Gusri Khan becomes a kind of Protector of Tibet (died 1655) Many monasteries of the 'Red Sect' (the non-*dGe lugs pa* schools) are confiscated by the *dGe lugs pa* The abbot of *bKra shis lhun po*, *Blo bzang chos kyi rgyal mtshan*, is given the title *Pan chen rin po che* by the Dalai Lama
1651–3	The fifth Dalai Lama, *Blo bzang rgya mtsho*, visits China
1679	*Blo bzang rgya mtsho* names *Sangs rgyas rgya mtsho* as regent
1682	Death of the fifth Dalai Lama. The fact is kept hidden, and the regent carries on the government in his name
1683	Birth of the sixth Dalai Lama, *Tshangs dbyangs rgya mtsho* (1683–1706)
1683	Peace with Ladakh, and definitive inclusion of *Gu ge* and the neighbouring regions in the Dalai Lama's realm
1697	After the death of the fifth Dalai Lama is made public, the sixth is enthroned
1705	Lhajang Khan (*Lha bzang klu dbang*), the Khan of the Qosots, invades Tibet and conquers Lhasa. Murder of the regent *Sangs rgyas rgya mtsho*
1706	Lhajang Khan announces the deposition of the sixth Dalai Lama and sends him to China, but he dies on the way His successor is a monk, allegedly an illegitimate son of Lhajang Khan
1707	Italian Capuchin monks in Tibet

1716	The Jesuit father Ippolito Desideri, author of a confutation of *Tsong kha pa*'s *Lam rim chen mo*, arrives at Lhasa Another reincarnation of the sixth Dalai Lama is opposed to the claimant appointed by Lhajang Khan; for reasons of security the new claimant takes refuge in the monastery of Kumbum (*sKu 'bum*) and is educated there
1717–27	The Dzungars occupy and sack Lhasa. The Manchu announce the deposition of the Dalai Lama appointed by Lhajang Khan and proclaim that the claimant from Kumbum, *bsKal bzang rgya mtsho* (1708–57) is the Dalai Lama; however, he does not exercise effective secular power; this remains in the hands of a council presided over by *Khang chen nas*, who is killed in 1727
1733–47	The Capuchins leave Lhasa. *Pho lha nas bSod nams stobs rgyas* (1689–1747) manages to bring the internal struggles to an end and becomes the effective ruler of Tibet
1740	*Pho lha nas* receives the title of *wang* from the Chinese, and rules with their support
1741	Return of Capuchins
1745	Banishment of Capuchins
1747	Death of *Pho lha nas*
1750	His son, *'Gyur med rnam rgyal* is killed by the Chinese resident (*amban*) after being involved in an anti-Chinese plot together with the Dzungars
1751	After the Dalai Lama's attempted revolt against the Chinese garrison, Emperor Ch'ien-lung recognizes the Dalai Lama as ruler of Tibet, but he is deprived of all effective political power; this is entrusted to a council (*bKa' shag*) under the supervision of the two Chinese residents (*amban*)
1758	Birth of the eighth Dalai Lama, *'Jam dpal rgya mtsho* (died 1804)
1774–5	Mission led by George Bogle in Tibet; establishment of relations with the third *Pan chen rin po che, Blo bzang dpal ldan ye shes* (1738–80)
1783–92	Mission led by Samuel Turner Numerous incursions of the Gurkha into Tibet following their conquest of Nepal. The Chinese send troops under the command of Fu K'ang-an; victory over the Gurkha. The Chinese army crosses the Himalayas and forces the peace of Kathmandu

CHRONOLOGICAL TABLE

1806–15	The ninth Dalai Lama, *Lung rtogs rgya mtsho*
1816–37	The tenth Dalai Lama, *Tshul khrims rgya mtsho*
1838–56	The eleventh Dalai Lama, *mKhas grub rgya mtsho*
1835–42	Raja Gulab Singh of Jammu attacks Ladakh and conquers it Zorawar Singh, general of the king of Jammu, attempts to invade Central Tibet, but is defeated and killed
1854–6	Conflict with Nepal
1856–75	The twelfth Dalai Lama, *'Phrin las rgya mtsho*
1876	Birth of the thirteenth Dalai Lama, *Thub bstan rgya mtsho* (died 1933) Diplomatic conflict between Britain and Russia, each attempting to secure direct contacts with Tibet and to exclude privileges from the other
1890	British protectorate over Sikkim
1904	Lord Curzon's efforts to establish commercial relations with Lhasa remain unsuccessful. The British military expedition under the direction of Colonel Younghusband forces its way into Tibet and reaches Lhasa. Flight of the Dalai Lama. Conclusion of an agreement with the abbot of the monastery of *dGa' ldan*
1909	The Dalai Lama, who had fled to Mongolia, returns to Lhasa after a short stay in China
1910	Full restoration of Chinese control over East Tibet, followed by the dispatch of troops to Lhasa under the control of Chao Erh-feng. Flight of the Dalai Lama to India
1911	Outbreak of revolution in China. Tibetan uprising against the Chinese
1912	After his return to Lhasa, the Dalai Lama rules without allowing any Chinese influence
1913–14	Conference at Simla attended by British, Chinese and Tibetan plenipotentiaries. The Chinese refuse to ratify the agreement
1920–21	Mission of Sir Charles Bell in Tibet. The authority of the Dalai Lama is growing, but there is opposition to his policies by the *Pan chen* of *bKra shis lhun po*, *dGe legs rnam rgyal* (1883–1937). The *Pan chen* flees to China.

CHRONOLOGICAL TABLE

1933	Death of the thirteenth Dalai Lama
1934	Appointment of the Regent (the abbot of Reting) The fourteenth Dalai Lama, *bsTan 'dzin rgya mtsho* (born 1935), is enthroned as Dalai Lama in 1940
1941	The Regent is forced to resign and is replaced by a new Regent, the abbot of *sTag brag* (Taktra)
1947	Indian declaration of independence; end of the British Tibet policy
1949	Occupation and annexation of Tibet by the People's Republic of China
1950	Flight of the Dalai Lama to Yatung on the border with Sikkim
1954	Return of the Dalai Lama to Lhasa. His visit to Peking. The new *Pan chen*, *Chos kyi rgyal mtshan* (born 1938), brought up in China, is placed opposite the Dalai Lama and considered as a spokesman for the Chinese
1959	Attempted uprising suppressed by the Chinese. The Dalai Lama flees to India. The *Pan chen* emerges in his place, but is later forced to undergo 'self-criticism' Tibet becomes an autonomous province of the People's Republic of China

NOTES

Chapter 1 The first diffusion of Buddhism in Tibet

1 Or *Srong brtsan sgam po*.
2 Tucci, 1962.
3 Cf. A. Macdonald, 1966, p.479, for the legends about the first statues brought to Lhasa in the time of *Srong btsan sgam po*.
4 Tucci, 1950, pp.47, 51.
5 Tucci, 1958, pp.20ff.
6 Ibid., p.12, n.III.
7 Ibid., p.31.
8 Demiéville, 1952, pp.187, 188, 226–8.
9 Tucci, 1958, p.9.
10 Zen in Japanese.
11 Tucci, 1958, pp.20, 150.
12 He was a *bandhe*, Tucci, 1958, p.28. Cf. Richardson, 1952, p.133, and 1953, p.1.
13 Cf. Tucci, 1958, pp.30, 41, 52f.
14 Richardson, 1952, p.1.
15 Demiéville, 1952, p.177.
16 Tucci, 1958, p.43.
17 Cf. p.3.
18 Tucci, 1958, p.11.
19 Tucci, 1950, p.49.
20 The numbers refer to the list of Tibetan sources on pp.275–9.
21 Tucci, 1950, p.45. Sravaka, 'hearers', and Pratyekabuddha are those who attain to Enlightenment but do not reveal it. The Bodhisattva (in the Mahayana), following their Enlightenment, remain in the world to benefit others with their preaching and activity.
22 Tucci, 1958, p.56. Another example in Richardson, 1952–3.
23 Tucci, 1958, p.56, note 2.
24 Also, more often, *mChims phu*, 'the high part of *mChims*'.
25 The texts which contain the Buddha's revelation.
26 Toussaint, 1933, p.341. This may well relate to later conditions, since the *Thang yig* was first written down only in a more recent period.
27 Thomas, 1935–55, part III, pp.78, 104, 317, 330 (*lha 'bangs*).
28 Ibid., part II, p.330.

29 Prajnaparamita ('perfection of higher cognition') is the name of a series of texts, and of numerous commentaries, which are concerned with the doctrine of the 'void' and teach the gradual nature of mystical experience.
30 According to some traditions all beings are Buddha (*sangs rgyas*), and there is no other greater Buddha; the Buddha is in the hearts of men and is identified with pure unarticulated sound. This is why one reads in certain texts that even a being in hell can save himself in the moment in which he hears one of the formulae (*gzungs*, Skt. *dharani*) which encapsulate truth in a series of sounds. In other words, an instant of awakening, however it is brought about, is sufficient to produce the liberating *excessus mentis*.
31 Demiéville, 1952; Tucci, 1958, p.65.
32 Before he left the country, the *Hwa shang* founded a chapel.
33 Tucci, 1958, pp.65ff.
34 Ibid., p.52; Richardson, 1952, p.134.
35 Tucci, 1958, pp.65ff.; Lalou, 1939.
36 Tucci, 1958, p.67.
37 Richardson, 1952, p.72; Pelliot, 1961, pp.130ff.

Chapter 2 The second diffusion of Buddhism

1 These five *ma* are evidently to be understood according to the original significance, of an essentially magical character, which they have in the Tantric texts. They can, however, also be taken in an esoteric sense; thus *mudra* was originally the name of a plant or seed with aphrodisiac properties, then with the growth of esotericism it took on the meaning of female companion or Paredra of the god, or, in the Siddha school (cf.p.12), of the Tantric master. Finally it came to mean 'position of the hands' (in Tantric ritual), and also 'seal'.

In this book I use the Greek term *paredra* to designate the female companion who is associated with various gods, or who may be united with the celebrant in various rituals, in order to distinguish this concept from the idea of *sakti*, 'power', as it is used in the Saivite schools.
2 Tucci, 1949, pp.7–8.
3 Hoffmann, 1950, p.190.
4 The dating is uncertain. There is almost certainly an error of sixty years (i.e. one whole cycle). Thus it could be the year 915 which is in question, or 975, or even 1035. Cf. L. Petech, 'Il sistema cronologico del *Deb ther sngon po*', in Tucci, 1941, p.281; Roerich, 1949, p.xvii; H. E. Richardson, 1957, pp.60ff. The one securely dated point is *Grun Ye shes rgyal mtshan*, contemporary of Chao Hsüan-ti (905–7) of the T'ang dynasty, and disciple of *dGongs pa rab gsal*. In any case it is established that the revival of Buddhism, after beginning in *Khams*, reached both Central and Western Tibet, and then returned from the West to Central Tibet (*dBus*) along with Atisa.
5 The region of Tibet to the west of Lhasa, centred on Shigatse.
6 The community was viewed as a house. I give one example from many: the religious descendants of *Klu mes* were divided into four pilasters, two beams and two door frames (cf. No.108, p.105b).

7 According to the *sBa bzhad* they had no need of a mule to carry the load of books which they took with them; *mNgon mdzod, 'Dul ba 'od ldan* and *Las skar ma sha stam*.
8 Tucci, 1956c, pp.42ff.
9 Tucci, 1933.
10 The *bKa' 'gyur* contains the texts revealed by the Buddha, including texts on discipline, metaphysics, various teachings, the Tantras, etc. The *bsTan 'gyur* contains the treatises and the various commentaries of the leading teachers of the Indian philosophical schools, etc.
11 Sacred structures, containing relics of all kinds, and constructed according to a design of which the various elements are symbolic; a psychocosmogram like the *mandala*.
12 Offering, free gift.

Chapter 3 General characteristics of Lamaism

1 That is, that everything is only *sems*, thought, consciousness, or spirit.
2 'Essential voidness': pure emptiness, thought which is the potentiality for individual thoughts, but which does not think, because thinking is no longer the essential Void Consciousness, beyond every logical category.
3 Many *chos 'byung*, histories of the diffusion of the doctrine, even if they are primarily treating the Tibetan schools, also give information on Indian Buddhism. Examples are the histories of *Bu ston* (No.113), *Pad ma dkar po* (No.108), Taranatha (No.90), *dPa'o gtsug 'phreng ba* (No.85), etc.
4 Although attempts have not been lacking to divide the Tibetan doctrinal schools into 18 groups, as for example following *Blo bde zhabs dkar*: A:1. *brgyud, bka'*; 2. *snyan brgyud, gter ma*; 3. *zab mo, dag snang*; B. *gsar ma bka' brgyud*: 4. *kar ma pa*; 5. *'brug pa*; 6. *'bri khung*; 7. *stag lung*; C. *bka' gdams*: 8. *bka' gdams, gzhung*; 9. *man ngag*; D. *bka' gdams gsar ma* (*dge lugs*): 10. *gzhung*, 11. *snyan brgyud*; E. *sa skya pa*: 12. *sa skya pa*; 13. *ngor*; F. *pha dam pa*: 14. *zhi byed*; 15. *ma gcig lab*; G. 16. *shangs pa*; H. 17. *jo nang pa*; I. 18. *bo dong*.
5 On which see G. Tucci, *The Theory and Practice of the Mandala*, London, 1961.
6 Tucci, 1949, p.107.
7 *Zhwa nag* ('black hat') was the name which was given to *Dus gsum mkhyen pa*, because he made himself a crown or a diadem (*cod pan*) out of the hair of a *mkha' 'gro ma* ('Flier through the air'; a class of female deities generally much feared) (No.85, p.3a). On the division into *zhwa nag* and *zhwa dmar* cf. No.108, pp.162b ff.; Richardson, 1958, p.139; 1959, p.1.
8 He was a disciple of *Yu mo Mi bskyod rdo rje*, a student of *Zla ba mgon po* (Candranatha), a *pandita* from Kashmir. The monastery of *Jo nang* was founded by *Phyogs las rnam rgyal* (born 1306) (cf. No.82, p.91a).
9 In other words the *rNying ma pa* claim that the Tantras which were in circulation in India do not represent all of the Tantric literature. They cite the words ascribed to Atisa on the occasion of his visit to the library at *bSam yas*, when he remarked that there were books there unknown in India; the revelation of such texts would be ascribed to the divine *mkha' 'gro ma* (Skt.

dakini), to the *klu* etc. In this connection the *rNying ma pa* also affirm the superiority of the old tradition and of the old translators by various arguments, which are summarized under six principal reasons (No.122, pp.25ff.).

10 When *Pha dam pa* arrived in Tibet he was not at first considered to be a Buddhist (No.1, p.11b); in other words he was taken for a Saivite *sadhu* such as would often be met in, for example, the region around Kailasa. The first teachings which he proclaimed were the following (ibid., p.12b): 'You must not take hold of what appears outside of you, thus giving it rights of domicile within you. You must not project on to the outside what appears within you. The *sems* must not grow fond of the body. The body must not grow fond of the *sems*. Guard the liberty of body and *sems*, so that each can rest in itself.'

11 The two schools *zhi byed* and *gcod* are in origin branches of the same school. While the theories of *zhi byed* were followed in their basic lines by other schools as well, *gcod* preserved a greater individuality; it too, however, was adopted by various schools, with appropriate modifications.

12 Individuals (No.121, pp.3a, b) can be divided into three classes: the lowest, who desire the goods or joys of the samsaric world; the middle, who care for their own salvation; and the highest, who are preoccupied with the welfare of others.

13 So they are accustomed to say in the mystical tradition, as I myself was able to learn in India.

Chapter 4 The doctrines of the most important schools

1 Some scholars give interpretations of the suffering of which the Buddha speaks which seem to me eccentric. One only needs, however, to look at the *Abhidharma-sammuccaya* of the famous Asanga (or the *Abhidharmakosa* of Vasubandhu, or the texts of the Hinayana) to be convinced that *duhkha* is nothing other than the experience of suffering.

2 Skt. *Sambhogakaya*; the form of the Buddha preaching in various paradises to choruses of the blessed who ascend there during the process of meditation or after having conquered space and time.

3 The four consecrations mentioned are those belonging to the *bla na med rgyud*, but there are other consecrations in use too. These include the garland consecration, the water and diadem consecrations (*bya rgyud*), to which are added in the *spyod rgyud* the *vajra* consecration, the bell and name consecrations. The *rnal 'byor rgyud* introduces yet another consecration, that of the Diamond Master (*rdo rje slob dpon*, Skt. *vajracarya*). Thus one reaches a total of fourteen consecrations, since some schools (e.g. those based on the Guhyasamaja Tantra) count eleven different types of consecration within the consecration through the 'vessel'.

4 Cf. No.95, p.209, where three human states are mentioned: birth, duration (*gnas*) and death, to which *bar do* can be added. However, it is a matter here only of manifestations, of illusory states, caused by the vibratory capacity or respiration (*rlung*) and by the *sems*.

5 If, following the premises of the doctrinal schools of Indian Buddhism, Lamaism both denies the existence of a soul and rejects the concept of a soul, it has all the same succeeded through the adoption of Tantric procedures in being in a position to admit ideas that could be attached to indigenous religous concepts. According to the folk religion, people have within them a soul or several souls or soul-like entities, independent of the body, and which survive the body and can leave it during life in order to carry out particular tasks (cf.p.190).

6 The body has a double aspect: (a) physical body (*rag lus*), which is the house or container; (b) *gnyug ma'i lus*, consisting of vibratory capacity or breath (*rlung*) and *sems* (No.95, pp.209b–210a). To these two bodies can be added the subtle mental body (*yid lus*) and the *sgyu lus*, the *maya*-body, which can be transformed into *ye shes sku* and *rdo rje sku*, 'diamond body'. The vibratory capacity is breathing, individual and cosmic (Skt. *prana*), which is defined precisely as *spanda-sakti*, force, vibratory capacity.

7 For *sems* it is preferable to use the Tibetan term wherever possible; one should however keep in mind its various meanings.

8 This process is preceded by three 'isolations': isolation of the psycho-physical complex (*lus dben*), of the spoken word (*ngag dben*) and of the *sems* in its normal, unpurified state (*sems dben*). These three isolations lead to the adamantine state (*rdo rje*), i.e. to the essential state of the three corresponding planes (*sku rdo rje*, *gsung rdo rje*, *thugs rdo rje*). Cf. No.99, p.8; No.95, pp.204–5. According to the latter text the body appears after the first isolation as an accumulation of atoms, spoken word as an echo, *sems* as the intuition of the illusory nature of all things. The definitions and descriptions of this process vary from school to school but remain the same in essence.

9 The word 'reach' is really inappropriate, since there is nothing to reach; one can only accomplish an experience within oneself.

10 On this point we refer to, e.g., No.105, a much more important source than No.82 as far as the differences between the major schools are concerned.

11 *Nyams len* is here translated by 'experience', for in Buddhism every precept and every instruction must be lived within one in such a way that it leads to the desired reversal of the planes. The original meaning of *nyams len* is actually to live according to the precepts of the doctrine. This refers to all the essential moments: to desire the transcendence of the normal plane, to express the vow to attain illumination and to follow the correct view that can lead to this goal. Higher cognition (*shes rab*) must first of all examine closely the revealed truths, especially those referring to the meditation on voidness, the thought of Enlightenment and the way to achieve omniscience. The insights acquired in this way must suffuse and transform every act of life, including the whole psychic continuum and the *sems*.

Instead of *nyams len* the expression *phyag len* (*lag len*) can also be used. By this is to be understood that every act we perform, every word we speak must correspond to the teaching and be purified into an act capable of fulfilling its proper function in the process of salvation. This expression, however, is used principally, if not exclusively, with reference to Tantric ceremonies, i.e. the ritual of the *mandala*, the offerings and recitations of hymns to the deities which the officiant visualizes as before him, etc.

Nyams len comprises the entire initiatory curriculum of the devotee. According to the *dGe lugs pa* teaching the following are obligatory: (1) To turn with supreme trust to the person who acts as spiritual guide (*dge bshes*, Skt. *kalyanamitra*); (2) to meditate on the rare good fortune of being born as a human being and therefore having the necessary requisites and foundations for salvation, which are granted only to human beings, and enable them to transcend the plane of temporality and suffering; (3) to dwell in meditation on the frailness of all things and beings, an indispensable method for progressive mental purification, as also for liberation from the received preconceptions of the masses and from becoming entangled in a world dominated inevitably by transitoriness; (4) to continue to progress on the way of purification through the meditation on the sufferings of existence and the punishments threatening after death for those who have not followed the right path; (5) to seek refuge in the three 'Jewels', the Buddha, the Teaching, the religious community, in order to find protection with them from suffering and punishment; (6) to recognize the inevitability of moral causality and the irrevocable connection between cause and effect; (7) to win insight into the necessity of unbroken practice and concentrated attentiveness, which alone can offer a way out of this world of temporality; (8) to meditate on the interweaving of cause and effect (*rten 'brel*, Skt. *pratitya-samutpada*) through which existence is carried on from birth to birth; (9) to make the vow to strive for Enlightenment according to the precepts of the Mahayana, and to live within oneself the experience of the path of meditation.

12 According to some, the concept is implicit in the Hinayana too. Cf. K. Bhattacharya, *L'Atman-Brahman dans le Bouddhisme ancien*, Paris, 1973.

13 Cf. Ruegg, 1963.

14 As mentioned above (p.259), the teacher of the founder of this school was a Pandit from Kashmir.

15 This division of the Tantras into four classes, which became generally recognized in the course of time, is the result of elaboration on the part of scholiasts, and it is by no means the only division; other classifications speak of five or six groups (as with the *rNying ma pa*, cf.pp.77ff.).

16 As was noted above, we render *rlung* by 'vibratory capacity' or 'vibratory power'. The literal meaning is breath or 'wind'. The term corresponds to the Skt. *prana* = respiration, breathing, vital breath in its multiple aspects and effects. It signifies mobility, the force which represents the 'vehicle' of the *sems* and is also at the same time a universal principle penetrating everything. The so-called 'channels' (Skt. *nadi*) also do not correspond to any physiological reality. They refer rather to an ideal physiology by virtue of which the mechanism of the meditation process takes place. *Nadi* is the void, an artery, the empty branch of a plant. *Thig le* means 'drop', 'point', Skt. *bindu*, an invisible point; however, in Tantric symbolism it stands for 'semen', the origin and precondition of the unfolding of creation and reproduction. No.72, p.17a, defines the *thig le* as consciousness of Being *ab initio*, not determined by the duality of appearance and voidness. If the two syllables are separated, *thig* means absolute truth, the unalterable, the void, point, while *le* is appearance, relative truth. Hence the expression *thig*

le signifies the coincidence or non-duality of the two concepts. This multiplicity of meaning present from the beginning has to be constantly born in mind, because it is thanks to this plurality of meanings that the expression can be adapted to the polyvalent nature of mystical terminology.

17 On this question *Tsong kha pa* took a viewpoint opposed to that of the *Sa skya pa*, as is shown by No.95, pp.3, 8ff, and also by No.101, p.11a.

18 The three 'bodies' form the basis of doctrine and soteriology. Naturally the term 'body' (which corresponds exactly to the Tibetan word *sku*) is not to be understood in its ordinary sense. It is a question here of three modes of existing of consciousness of Being, concerning both its revelation and its attainment. The bodies are of the same essence (*ro gcig*, No.84, p.42b). The body of infinite spiritual potentiality is the coincidence or identity of Being and of Consciousness devoid of any emanation or vibration. The body of co-fruition or body of enjoyment is a mode of being and manifesting of the same Consciousness of Being. The apparent body is its manifestation again in this world as Buddha (ibid., pp.44a, b). The apparent body, which functions as the spiritual 'master', could neither appear nor fulfil its task if the body of infinite spiritual potentiality was not immanent within it. These three modes of being are integrated in that supreme state of existence which forms their foundation and the precondition of their existence (*ngo bo nyid sku*, the 'body *in se*'). In the process of meditation it is therefore not a question of living through phases separate from each other but rather of achieving aspects of a single, indivisible and atemporal unity, once the dichotomy which imprisons us in a net of empty appearances and relationships has been overcome.

The body of infinite spiritual potentiality, a fundamental element in the Buddhist system of salvation, is consequently to be distinguished clearly from the *chos dbyings* (Skt. *dharmadhatu*), for which concept I might propose the translation 'infinite potential existentiality'. In fact *chos dbyings* designates voidness transcending all qualification, the overcoming of every dichotomy, and simultaneously also the precondition of the dichotomy. Dichotomy and voidness, in fact, become one and the same, since one cannot exist without the other and both actually represent a succession of oppositions which cease in the supreme silence. This is a very concise presentation of a subject on which the doctrinal opinions of the different schools (and especially that of the *Jo nang pa*, cf.p.68) frequently diverge.

19 The *Sa skya pa* and *dGe lugs pa* recognize a fivefold division of the 'method of achievement' (cf.p.56) (although they hold other groupings to be also possible): after the preliminary isolation of the body (*lus dben*) follows (1) isolation of the word (*ngag dben*); (2) isolation of the mind (*sems dben*) (cf.p.108) through concentration of the mind on three points or drops (*thig le*) in the nose, the heart and the genitals; (3) isolation of the *maya*-body (divided into pure and impure); (4) isolation of the light, which is also divided into two kinds (*dpe*, exemplary, reflected in the moment of experience in which it is received, and later real, *don*, in the moment of actualization); (5) coincidence (*zung 'jug*) of the moment of experience with that which is beyond experience (Buddhahood). Cf. Ruegg, 1966, pp.101ff, note 1.

20 The other schools generally speak of three vehicles only, that of the Sravakas and Pratyekabuddhas (the Hinayana, or Lesser Vehicle); that of the Bodhisattvas (Mahayana, or Great Vehicle, also called vehicle of the Paramitas); and Vajrayana, the Vehicle of Tantra. Cf. above, p.257, n.21.
21 Or better, as Mircea Eliade proposes, 'entasy', or, as I would suggest, 'synentasy'.
22 The five Buddhas (Vairocana, Aksobhya, Ratnasambhava, Amitabha, Amoghasiddhi), either alone or together with their various paredras.
23 These phonemes (*mantra*) are syllables which each correspond to a divine plane represented symbolically by a deity. The syllable, which is filled with evocatory power, contains the essence of the god, which can be expressed by a pure sound. *Man-tra* is besides a series of norms which must be observed and followed according to their strict meaning. They protect (*tra*) the mental processes (*man*) from the seductions of the world and thus aid the process of liberation.
24 On the term paredra cf. Chapter 2, note 1 (p.258).
25 I.e., the wish to attain Enlightenment.
26 Skt. *stupa*; tomb of a saint, reliquary, etc.
27 In other words, the *libido* reintegrated into unity with consciousness of Being.
28 *Rig pa* is present in us as inner intelligence (*nang rig*) and has the capacity to transform itself into *sems*, the dichotomizing principle. The process of reintegration consists in the quiescence of *sems* and of its activity through the reattainment of *rig pa* and of the light of Being. Thus the transcendence of all that can be thought in the world of illusory objects is brought about, and the radiant *rig pa* returned to its indefinable purity.
29 Each of these five rays has its own colour: white, red, green, yellow and dark blue.
30 The five Buddhas, cf. note 22 above.
31 The progressive actualization of the vision is accomplished through four 'looks' (*gzigs*) which gradually illuminate the various aspects of the apparent world (*snang ba*). These looks are also symbolically called lamps. They are the lamp of water, the far-reaching (*rgyang zhags*), i.e. the manifestation of objects through the vision of the eye, in that the apparent world is the inner light which has gone out of itself; the lamp of flesh, i.e. of thought (Skt. *citta* = *sems*) which is the light as subject (*sha'i sgron ma* or *shes rab sgron ma*); the lamp of emptiness, which illuminates the 'drop', 'point', potentiality of all things (*thig le*) situated in the heart; and finally the 'pure lamp', the vision of existentiality in its pure state (No.103, pp.24–5, and No.155, pp.77ff.). If thus the 'karmic vibratory capacity' is recognized in the vision of the 'lamp of the existential sphere', its pure part evokes the vision ('lamp') of the void, which is situated in the point, in potentiality (*thig le*). This point appears as round and surrounded by five lights. If it is contemplated through the 'far-reaching lamp', the experience of the object-free inner intelligence (*nang rig*) which is within us takes place. This experience is the lamp of spontaneous cognition (No.103, p.31).

According to other sources:

1 Lamp 'of flesh': the five lights are seen not as projected outwards, but as

situated inside, like a lamp contained within a vessel.

2 Lamp 'of the artery' (*rtsa*, Skt. *nadi*, cf. note 16 above), as the path that leads to the manifestation of the five lights.

3 Lamp 'of the water', as the door through which the five lights shine.

4 Lamp 'of existentiality' (*dbyings*), when the five lights appear as objects.

5 Lamp 'of the void', revelation of the five lights.

6 Lamp 'of supreme consciousness', i.e. of the transcendent consciousness which represents the essence of *rig pa* in its own being.

Such experiences take place at the moment of death or during ascetic practices.

32 So too with the *bKa' brgyud pa*; taking up a motive that often recurs in the Saivite schools of India *bSod nams rgyal mtshan pa* praises the human body as a means of salvation: There is nothing higher than the human body (No.118, p.18).

33 Other methods are known too (No.72, pp.12ff.).
(a) to fix one's gaze on the heaven as on a white surface (*dkar khrid*).
(b) to fix one's gaze on the rising and setting sun (*dmar khrid*).
(c) to fix one's gaze on the moon (*ser khrid*).
(d) to fix one's gaze on the sun through a thin cotton cloth (*seng ras khra khrid*).
(e) to fix one's gaze on three lamps (*me khrid*).
A rock crystal or a silver mirror can also be used.

34 *Tsamba* is the name of the everyday Tibetan food made of barley flour mixed with tea and butter. This paste is also used for the preparation of *gtor ma* during ceremonies.

35 *Bum* here = *mandala* = paradise.

36 Besides the division into the five families of the pentad other groupings also exist; for example, that into six families, the standard five plus Vajradhara. This division is accepted by the authors of the *bya rgyud* treatises.

In a further division into five families, also from the *bya rgyud*, the names are different: *Tathagata*, *Ratna*, *Padma*, *Karma*, *Vajra* (i.e. Vairocana, Ratnasambhava, Amitayuh, Amoghasiddhi, Aksobhya).

37 Here we are dealing with an extremely complicated meditation process, which, although it has its roots in the teaching of Naropa, makes use of different methods for its actualization in the different schools, The indications I give above are to be understood therefore as a summary account of those points held in common. The *sgyu lus*, the *maya*-body, is interpreted in very different ways by the various schools. Some authors, going back to a fundamental idea of the Mahayana, that all the apparent world is at base *maya*, take the *sgyu lus* to be simply *sgyu ma*, Skt. *maya*. I am writing a work on this subject which will appear shortly, and in which I will discuss the various interpretations of the six 'principles' of Naropa.

38 I.e. maya-body, cf.above, p.58.

39 I.e. the body of the intermediate existence between death and rebirth.

40 I.e. the incorporeal mental body.

41 White = male, red = female.

42 In the images of paradise, of the heavenly worlds and of the *mandala* which are evoked in the course of the meditation process, each of our individual elements is drawn into a particular sphere of radiation: the components of our illusory personality (*phung po*) into the pentad, the four or five spheres of the senses (*khams*) to their four or five paredras, the arteries and muscular fibres into the lesser deities (*dPa bo, mKha' 'gro ma*, etc.). These emanations can either emerge from the light radiated from the *sems* and from the very subtle respiration, which are situated in the heart, or from the light awakened by the complicated yogic exercise.

43 The eight kinds of danger from which *sGrol ma* saves are lions, elephants, fire, snakes, thieves, water, epidemics, enemies (Tucci, 1949, p.390).

44 In ordinary people, that is.

Chapter 5 Monkhood, monastery life, religious calendar and festivals

1 Upper and lower, that is, with respect to the localities where they evolved.

2 *gTsang* (West-Central Tibet) is the province where *bKra shis lhun po*, Gyantse, Shigatse etc. are situated; *dBus* is Central Tibet where Lhasa is situated. Many monks from the two Tantric colleges were among the refugees who came to India in and after 1959, and the schools have been formed again in India, where they continue to operate (G.B.S.).

3 The *rdo rje*, literally 'diamond' but also 'lightning' is an instrument which is held during the ceremonies. From a central nucleus three or five rays emerge which join again at the ends. Cf. Figure 2.

4 A slightly alcoholic beverage produced by the fermentation of barley.

5 The items used for the offerings or as ritual implements are called *nye bar spyod pa*. Twelve or sixteen of these are listed, of which the most important are listed in the text below (beginning with the objects symbolizing the five senses). However, the individual rituals vary very much, depending on whether the deities invoked are peaceful (*zhi*) or terrifying (*drag po*), and also depending on the mode of performance, which follows a particular Tantra. This is especially true for the musical instruments. In many liturgies, for example, only the *sil snyan* are used (reserved to *Kye rdo rje* in the *Sa skya pa* and *Ngor* schools). In the rituals concerned with the confession of sins (*ltung bshags*) only *ting shag* are used, etc. In addition, in liturgies addressed to the terrifying deities the *mchod pa* begins from the right and proceeds anticlockwise, while for peaceful deities it starts at the left and goes clockwise. *mChod* are divided into four groups, each higher than the preceding one: outer, i.e. the offerings; inner, i.e. mental; secret, accompanied by the practices acquired in the course of the initiation, without any intention of obtaining any kind of return; pure meditation on the 'void'.

6 These are, more precisely, the five 'great kinds of flesh' (*sha chen*): flesh of cattle, of dog, of horse, of elephant, of man. The five 'ambrosias' mentioned are excrement, blood, sperm, juice of the five 'great kinds of flesh', urine. In general though the *gtor ma* whose names appear to indicate the use of animal or even human remains are made out of moulded and coloured

butter and flour in such a way that the moulded forms are shaped according to the organs, entrails, heart etc. mentioned.

7 Among the *Sa skya pa*, for example, there are the following disciplines: (i) *rgyud sde spyi rnam bshad*; (ii) *ljon shing chen mo;* (iii) *rtags pa gnyis pa*. Among the *rNying ma pa*, there are the works of *kLong chen pa*, etc.

8 In the *rNying ma pa* school there are special mantras for bringing about a reincarnation.

9 The following religious acts were performed: recitation (*kha bton*), meditation (*bsam gtan sgom*), ceremonies accompanied by the corresponding hand gestures (*phyag skor*) and by liturgical action (*mchod phul*) (G.T.).

As a consequence of the Chinese takeover, these four great monasteries, and the many smaller monasteries which were dependent on them, no longer exist as functioning entities. According to recent reports only a few old monks remain in *Se ra*, *dGa' ldan* and *'Bras spungs* in place of the many thousands before 1959. What is described in the text, although mostly given in the present tense, therefore refers to a past situation. The principal monasteries of the other schools, which were also for the most part in Central and East Tibet, also appear to have been closed down or reduced to only a nominal existence.

Tibetan monasticism, however, continues to flourish, at the time of writing (1977), both among the refugees and in certain regions around the borders of Tibet. The *rNying ma pa* and *bKa' brgyud pa* have long been the dominant sects in Sikkim, Bhutan and parts of Nepal, and they still have numerous monasteries among the culturally Tibetan peoples of these areas. Further West, in Lahul, Spiti and Ladakh, now under Indian control, there are some monasteries of the *dGe lugs pa* and other schools. The monastic life of these regions was not directly threatened by the Chinese takeover of Tibet proper, and indeed the influx of refugee lamas has led to something of a religious revival among some of these populations, in the short term at least.

The refugees themselves, now settled in India, Nepal and elsewhere, have established many small monasteries and temples. Monks from the great *dGe lugs pa* monasteries described in the text, and from major monasteries of the other sects, have reconstituted their monastic communities in exile. Many aspects of the organization described by Professor Tucci (e.g. the monastic training, the debates, the *dge bshes* examinations) thus continue to exist among the refugees, if on a reduced scale (G.B.S.).

10 Religious education is divided into two clearly separate but converging aspects; first the study of the sacred texts, using the interpretations of the master as a basis (*thos*), and then reflection on the object of study (*bsam*).

11 One can also speak of a division into four groups of *dge bshes*, since besides those mentioned there are also the *dge bshes rdo ram(s) pa* and the *dge bshes gling se ba (gseb)*. These, however, do not have to follow the heavy curriculum of the first two groups, and often they are merely titles conferred in recognition of special merits.

12 The spring teaching period, for example, begins with *dpyid chos dang po* and ends with *dpyid chos chen mo*.

13 The studies in the *chos grwa* are divided into four periods: (a) morning study-period (*zhogs chos*) during which recitation of sacred texts predominates, and discussions and debates on theological and logical questions play only a secondary role; (b) day period (*nyin chos*), in which the reverse is true; (c) evening period (*dgong(s) chos*, also called *sku rim*) in which recitation predominates; (d) night period (*mtshan chos*, also called *dam bca'*), reserved exclusively for debates, and confined to those monks who are well-versed in the sacred scriptures.
14 During the seventh month two gatherings each day (called *rig grwa*, wisdom courses) are organized for fifteen days. In these learned monks expound the sacred scriptures or dispute on questions of logic. On this occasion the *spyi gso* presents the monks with *tsamba* and a bread baked of flour and barley, which is of a longish shape in *Se ra* and round in *bKra shis lhun po* (these are called *kha zes*, at *bKra shis lhun po* they are also known as *khur ra*). This custom also takes place at the other main festivals (*dus chen*).
15 Though there exist other classifications of the Buddha's life, both into twelve acts and also into sixteen.
16 Magical instrument; also name of a deity invoked in exorcistic ceremonies.
17 The *sMon lam* festival lasts for twenty-one days, from the fourth to the twenty-fifth of the first month. During its course six solemn monastic gatherings take place; three are 'dry' (*skam tshogs*) and three 'wet' (*rlon tshogs*), with the two types alternating (dry-wet, wet-dry, etc.). During the 'dry' assemblies liturgical ceremonies take place during the day and the scriptures are read at night, without the monks receiving tea, soup and money (*sku 'gyed*) as they do at the 'wet' ceremonies, which consist exclusively of the reading of liturgical texts.
18 Various liturgies are used for this ritual, e.g. *dPal mgon phyag drug*, *dMag zor rgyal mo*, *gDugs dkar mo*, *Seng ge gdong ma*. The *Sa skya pa* use *dPal mgon gur zhal bzhi pa*, and the *rNying ma pa* employ *bKa' brgyad*, *gDugs dkar mo*, *mGon po ber nag*.
19 *dbyu gu drug cu* (*rtsa*) *bzhi*, the sixty-four deities of the mandala of *gShin rje* (= Skt. Yama).
20 The deer also plays an important role in the *Bon po* rituals and was sacrificed in their New Year ceremonies (cf.pp.273, note 24).
21 Protective deities, opposed to the powers of evil.
22 For another ritual cf. in the *Rin chen gter mdzod* VII,ll,*ba*; XV,8.

Chapter 6 The folk religion

1 Protectors of the Law.
2 Binding down through magic (Latin).
3 *Rin chen bzang po* too had to bring about the submission of a local demon (a *Bon* divinity) before he could build his temples: *sKar rgyal*, No. 113, p.214.
4 Burnt offerings of incense or scented herbs (Latin); singular, *suffimen*.
5 I prefer not to designate this folk religion by the term *mi chos*, because *mi chos* can have a much wider range of meaning. That is to say, this expression is often used for the complex of moral laws and customs which Buddhism

prescribed uniformly for all believers at the time of its adoption. Cf.No.98. This, however, is the learned tradition; in the folk songs of Spiti, for example, one finds *lha chos* (Buddhism), *bon chos* and *mi chos*. Cf. Tucci, 1966, p.92.

6 *Phud* alone refers to the offering of milk and barley. *gSol phud* is an offering which is common in, for example, the *sgrub grwa* or Tantric schools: on a silver dish (*pad sder*) the vessel for the *phud* (*phud phor*) is placed, containing the drink-offering (*skyems*); the offering consists of grains of various kinds mixed with tea, *chang* and milk. Alternatively various offerings (*phud*) mixed with milk, *chang* and tea are prepared in a special vessel called *mchod thib*.

7 Serpents, subterranean powers who live, in particular, close to sources of water.

8 For one who is pure a *gdon* can cause no danger even if it does arise, since he can defend himself through Tantric formulae (*gsang sngags*), meditations on the void or on compassion, through worship of his *bla ma*, through exorcisms of some powers (*klu*, etc.).

9 = Skt. *stupa*, cf. Chapter 4, note 26 (p.264).

10 Tucci, 1966, p.193.

11 The *Vajracchedika* or 'Diamond Sutra'.

12 There are many types of *mdos*; those for the prevention of dangers threatening one in the physical realm (*lus*), in the spiritual realm (*sems*), dangers threatening the land (*yul*), those threatening a man, a woman, property, herds, etc. The most appropriate places to perform the *mdos* ritual are three-peaked mountains, junctions of paths and crossroads, places near waterfalls or those where neither sunlight nor moonlight can fall.

13 These *nam mkha'* are an essential part of the *mdos*. They are mentioned in the treatise on funeral rites edited by Lalou (1953, p.351). Cf. Figure 18.

14 Cf. the murder of *Glang dar ma* (above, p.19), and also the Chinese version of the *Mahaparinirvana Sutra*.

15 Stein, 1957 ('Architecture' and 'L'habitat'); Tucci, 1961.

16 Cf. I. Paulson, *Die primitiven Seelenvorstellungen der nordeurasiatischen Völker*, Stockholm, 1958; E. Porée-Maspero, 'La ceremonie de l'appel des esprits vitaux chez les Cambodgiens', *BEFEO*, vol.45, 1951, pp.145–269; I. Paulson, 'Seelenvorstellungen und Totenglaube der permischen und wolga-finnischen Völker', *Numen*, vol.11, 1964, pp.212–42.

17 Cf. in this connection the illuminating investigation of R. A. Stein in *Sino-Indian Studies* (1957c).

18 They consist of (1) *srog lha*, god of the *srog*, the vital strength concentrated in the heart (cf. above); (2) *dgra lha*, whose duty is the destruction of the enemy in battle (*dmag dpung bkyes la dgra dpung thul*, No.69); (3) *pho lha*, god of the father's lineage or paternal ancestors (*pha mes*); (4) *mo lha*; (5) *yul lha*, with its seat on the crown of the head etc. Many accounts put the deified mother's brother (*zhang lha*), the god of the mother's lineage, in the place of the *pho lha*. In this group of *lha* we find incorporated to a certain degree the continuity and defence of the kin-group and its property, if with certain variations which can be explained as the result of differences in epoch and of social organization (matriarchy and therefore greater importance of the

maternal kin). On the soul according to Tibetan conceptions cf. Stein, 1957c.

19 Guide of the soul after death (Greek).

20 Although there is as far as I know no analogous tradition in India, there are, however, two books, the *Bhaisajyaguru* (Taishō No.449, p.403) and the *Avatamsaka Sutra* (*Hua yen king*, translated by Buddhabhadra, Taishō No.278, p.680) in which two gods are spoken of who accompany man and have the same origin and same name as him. In other books, which are certainly apocryphal, these become gods who are born together with man and who observe what good and evil he does. On the development of this doctrine in China (including the Taoist schools as well) cf. M. Soymié, 1966.

21 Cf. Pavry, 1929, pp.86, 87.

22 Ibid., p.87.

23 The *Tibetan Book of the Dead*, as we know it in its various present-day versions, which vary very much from each other, is composed of diverse elements. A very much simplified version was found at Tun-huang (cf. Lalou, 1949).

24 The king of anger. The *bgegs* are demons.

25 Only the initial letter, not the prefix; if the name is *blo* (pronounced *lo*) the letter *l* is written, if the name is *ngag* (as in *Ngag dbang*) the letter *ng*.

26 Literally = died, returned.

27 Cf. note 4 above.

28 In the *gtor ma* ritual one is instructed to use a support in the form of the divine yak (*lha g.yag*); the kind of stone which lies under the knee of the celebrant of the *pra* ritual is also prescribed. The signs appear in the mirror and are divided into good and bad; they act as predictions of the future: *khyim phya, srid phya, gdon phya, chos phya, lam phya* etc.

The many-sided Tibetan scholar *'Jam mgon Mi pham rgya mtsho* wrote a book on omens and their interpretation which is very widely distributed in Tibet (*brTag pa sna tshogs pa'i skor nor bu me long*; vol.*nga* of his collected works).

29 Propitiatory or apotropaic ceremony which involves the use of a consecrated vessel (*ghata*).

30 According to Chinese sources the arrow was also used by other 'barbarians' for the transmission of messages. Cf. P. Demiéville, 'Quelques traits de moeurs barbares dans une chantefable chinoise des T'ang', *Acta Orientalia Academiae Scientiarum Hungaricae*, vol.15, 1962, no.1–2, p.74.

31 These are some of the best-known edifying dramas or narratives of Tibet.

32 On which cf. Stein, 1959a.

Chapter 7 The *Bon* Religion

1 Since the publication of this book many *Bon po* texts have been published in India. This chapter is necessarily based only on the material available at the time of writing (i.e. before 1970).

2 d and n are often interchanged in Tibetan. No.35, p.6 also affirms that *Bon* = *Bod.*

The word *bon* is to be related to the verb *bon*, which is used in the sense of *zlo*, 'pray', 'murmur' (of formulae; Skt. *japa*), 'invite', to invoke or ask a higher being, king or god, and also in the sense of *gsol*, 'present, offer something' (cf. Uray, 1964). However, it is clear that these meanings make up only a small part of the area of signification acquired by the word *bon* in the course of its development. Cf. also Snellgrove, 1967.

3 Concerning *Zhang zhung* I remain of the opinion which I have already expressed (Tucci, 1956); cf. Petech, 1967, p.252.

4 According to some sources (e.g. the *La dwags rgyal rabs*), *Glang dar ma* was led into heresy not by the *Bon po* but by four Indian Brahmins. Richardson's suggestion (1957, p.76), that *Glang dar ma* fell under the influence of Saivite schools, although only a hypothesis at present, deserves to be taken into account in future research. In any case one must note that Saivite schools and cults flourished in the regions bordering on West Tibet (Kashmir, Gilgit, Swat), cf. Tucci, 1958, pp.297ff.; 1963, p.70. Of course when one speaks of Saivite influences on the *Bon* religion it is primarily the form of *Bon* which the Tibetans called 'modified *Bon*' (cf.p.224) which is meant, the stage which first began to be organized systematically. The *Bon po* invited by *Gri gum* (cf.p.224) came from the land of Gurnavartta between India and *sTag gzig*, they performed rituals (No.85, *ja*, p.7a) and behaved like certain extreme sects of Saivism such as the Kapalika. Gurnavartta is unknown to me; in the geographical lists of the *Purana* the only name of similar sound which I can find is Urna: *Urna darvas tathaiva ca*. Cf. D. C. Sircar, *Studies in the Geography of Ancient and Medieval India*, Varanasi, 1960; W. Kirfel, *Das Purana vom Weltgebäude*, Bonn, 1954, p.118 v.56 (Sircar, op.cit., p.37 reads *huna* here). These people are called mountain-dwellers (*parvatasrayina*).

5 These came about either through contacts with Central Asiatic peoples, through the intermediary of Manichaeism, which was widespread in these regions, or, later on, through the influence of the Uighurs (Gabain, 1961).

6 It can be deduced from the description of the king's funeral rituals, in which at a particular stage the soul is 'gathered together', that the soul was understood as something of material nature, if extremely subtle.

7 According to No.35, p.22, the *Bon* books too would have been translated from books of other countries (*Sum pa*, *sTag gzig*, *Zhang zhung*, India, China, *Khrom*).

8 Though a peak of the same group of mountains also bears this name (No.2, p.14).

9 *Ti se* is Mount Kailasa, on which according to Saivite tradition Siva resides together with Parvati.

10 We are confining ourselves here to the tradition as it has taken form in West Tibet. In East Tibet a similar cycle of myths is centred around the mountain *sPom A myes rma chen.*

11 This white yak is opposed to the black, demonic yak; the yak is tamed like the horse. Many legends have arisen on this theme; they are connected with the hunt which, as mentioned above, itself had a ritual character.

(Several fragments of these legends have come down to us, Thomas, 1957, ch.1A, pp.20ff.) The legends were probably recited before the hunt in order to assure success.

12 The name under which he is known is *gShen rab mi bo*, 'the man, the supreme *gShen*'. Some understand *rab* as *rabs*, meaning 'origin', so that *gShen rab* would represent 'the man who is descended from the *gShen*'. This interpretation seems unacceptable to me; *gShen rab* corresponds to the Indian *paramaguru*, 'supreme master', and indicates that even if there had been and were many *gShen*, he surpassed them all. He is the great master (though cf. also note 25, below).

13 As also the *Bon po* (No.35). He was possessed by a demon and was a bitter enemy of the *Bon* teaching.

14 I have gone into detail with these genealogies, which certainly go back to very ancient times, in order to make it clear that when we speak about the pre-Buddhist religion in Tibet (even if we wish to call it *Bon* after the name of some of its priests) we should remember that it consists of many different layers, as the genealogies themselves bear witness. The genealogies are closely linked with the cosmogonies and the recitation at the New Year's Festival, and so to the religious life of a particular group.

Naturally all these religious forms have something in common, which is why we can speak of *Se Bon*, *Bon A zha*, *Bon Suṁ pa*, the *Bon* of *Zhang zhung* and so on. There were analogies and points of contact. However, we cannot deduce that the pre-Buddhist religion was unified in nature either in a spatial or a temporal sense.

The name *Bon* itself, which was borne by the priests, could be transferred by analogy to the exorcists of other countries where almost identical cult-forms and exorcisms could be found. This is still true today; the folk religion as it is practised in West Tibet at the present time certainly differs with regard to its myths and the divine and demonic presences recognized in it from the folk religion of the East or South-East. This results from the facts that the ethnic basis in these areas differs, their contacts with other cultures have been different, and finally the resistance which Buddhism encountered from the local tradition was not the same everywhere.

15 According to some sources (No.42, p.41) the names of the nine classes given above are apparently the Tibetan ones; the corresponding names in the language of *Zhang zhung* (*zhang zhung theg pa*) are *tho tho*, *yang tho*, *spyi tho*, *snang ldan*, *rang ldan*, *bzhed ldan*, *lha rtsi*, *yang rtsi*, *bla na med*.

16 Or perhaps 'four doors' and 'a treasure as fifth', as Snellgrove (1967) translates. Unfortunately I received Snellgrove's work only after finishing my own. In this case we would have the plan of a *mandala*, a square with four doors and the treasure at the centre.

17 However, *phya* (which is also written *phywa*) also designates a class of gods who determine the course of events.

18 Little cords of various colours.

19 'A' as the symbol of pure sound, as in the Saivite and Buddhist Tantric texts, and as origin and source of all sounds.

20 No.31 also knows only four *Bon* groups (p.267 of Francke's edition), namely *sna tshogs pa'i bon po*, *g.yang ldon pa'i bon po*, *dmu thag 'dogs pa'i bon po*

and *zhal srod pa'i bon po*. Despite the differences in the terminology we can recognize in the third group, the *Bon po* who bind the rope of the *dmu*, the *phya gshen* who predict the future through the *ju thig*. The *g.yang ldon pa'i bon po* who procure good omens and circumstances (*g.yang*) are very similar to the *snang gshen*. Similarly the *dur bon* can be seen in the *zhal srod pa*, those 'with a sombre appearance' (*srod = mun pa*, darkness). The *sna tshogs gshen*, the '*gshen* of all things', are probably the priest-magicians with miraculous powers, the *'phrul gshen*. The terminology is evidently different because the book edited by Francke comes from another region where the designations varied although the ritual functions remained the same. In late lists one also finds five *gshen*, namely *phya* (trained in *gdon* and *yas*), *snang* (control over *lha* and *'dre*), *srid* (control over *bla*, soul, and over mind and body), *'phrul* (control of *dgra* and *gnyen*) and *ye* (capable of understanding the non-duality of existentiality and of the transcendent mind) (No.42, p.7a). In late texts the *gshen* are also summarily reduced to three, corresponding to the three planes, those of body, speech and mind, which we referred to so often in discussing Buddhism: *sku gshen*, '*gshen* body', without birth; *gsung gshen*, 'word *gshen*' without interruption; *thugs gshen*, 'mind *gshen*', not subject to error (No.40, p.47,a,b).

21 This is the same also among the Gurung of Nepal (cf. Pignède, 1966).

22 Therefore the palace was also called 'house of the souls'.

23 The name *lde'u* also appears as an essential element of the names of many Tibetan kings, some mythical, others historical.

24 Special sacrifices in which a deer with great antlers was the sacrificial victim were of particular importance (No.3, pp.318, 19). With the victory of Buddhism a change took place, and a deer-skull was used for the offering of the ritual gifts (the sacrifices of yaks and rams were similarly substituted by images of these animals made out of *tsamba* and butter, loc.cit.). This custom of using a deer-skull (*gtsod thod*) still exists today in the offerings for *rTa khyung 'bar ba* (one can also use an iron vessel in its place). The various offerings are placed within it, along with goat's or dog's blood. The ceremony has the purpose of driving away hostile beings (*bgegs*, *'byung*, *nad gdon* etc.). *rTa khyung 'bar ba* is represented iconographically with a horse's head and the face of a *khyung*. During the meditation accompanying the ritual one imagines that the neighing of the horse makes the triple world shake, while flames leap forth from the *khyung*. In this deity *rTa mgrin* (Skt. *Hayagriva*) and the *khyung* converge into a terrifying synthesis.

25 No.85, p.8b, places *'On mo lung* (called 'land of the *gshen*') in *'On*, while No.35, p.27, situates *'Ol mo lung* in *sMan yul*, which is named together with *Phan yul* and *Yar mo thang* (ibid., p.5) and in *sTag zig*. A biography of *gShen rab* (No.31, pp.313, 331) has him originally come from *Sogs kha*; elsewhere *Sogs kha* is the name of Tibet at the time of *sPu rgyal gnyan po* and indicates a locality near the mountain *Sham po lha rtse*, where the descent of *gNya' khri* took place. More worthy of trust is the general affirmation that he was born in *Zhang zhung*, more precisely in *dNgul mkhar*, the Silver Castle. This tradition is supported by the fact that this sacred place is constantly referred to in *Bon po* litanies and prayers.

From a passage in No.35, p.23, it can be concluded that the tradition distinguishes between *gShen rab mi bo*, who descended from heaven and revealed the *Bon* doctrine, and *gShen rab* who came from the region of Lake Mànasarovar. Of this latter figure it is reported that he resided in *Khyung lung* and was the author of the part of the *Bon* scriptures which is regarded as *'bras bon* ('*Bon* Fruit') in distinction to *rgyu bon* ('*Bon* Cause') (cf.p.228). Elsewhere the parts of the *Bon* scriptures are said to have been dropped onto various places in the world by various animals; for example the scriptures were dropped in *Zhang zhung* by a *khyung*, an eagle-like bird (No.35, p.24a). In any case *gShen rab mi bo* is a master like the Buddha.

The Moso or Na-khi, whose religion was the subject of important investigations by Rock, and who moved from *A mdo* to Li-chiang, trace the origin of their religion to Dto-mba Shi-lo. This name is identified by Rock (and also by Bacot) with *sTon pa* (master) *gShen rab*. Róna Tas has now advanced another opinion (1964, p.16).

26 Name of an alphabet used in Nepal.

27 In another place (No.7, p.2a) a different principle of classification is used: *bon sku* = *Kun tu bzang po*, *longs sku* = *Srid pa rgyal mo*, *sprul sku* = *bDe 'gro gsang yum*. In other texts (No.8, p.26a) *bon sku* = *Kun tu bzang po*, *longs sku* = *gShen lha 'od dkar*, and *sprul sku* = *Ye gshen gtugs phud*.

28 Francke, 1914, p.71.

29 Goldman, 1961; Tucci, 1963, p.156.

30 In the last analysis the essence of *Bon* is the mind, *sems* (No.41, p.4b). In the later doctrine however the world of manifestation (*snang ba*) and the '*Bon* body' (*bon sku*) are identical (No.42, p.6b).

BIBLIOGRAPHY

1 Tibetan sources

1 *gCod kyi tshogs las yon tan kun 'byung* (by *Si tu'i ming can bstan pa'i nyin byed*)
2 *'Dzam gling gangs ti se'i dkar chag tshangs dbyangs yid 'phrog dgos 'dod*
3 *Pad ma thang yig*
Translated by G. Th. Ţoussaint, *Le dict de Padma*, Paris, 1933.
4 *Myang chung*
5 *dBal gsas las rim gyi bsdus don nyams len snying po* (by *Khyung po rje btsun Tha yud wer ya tshul me*)
6 *'Dus pa rin po che'i rgyud dri ma med pa*
7 *dGongs gsal*
8 *dGongs rgyud drug gi klad don*
9 *rGyud 'grel*
10 *sNang srid mdzod phugs kyi gzhung dang 'grel pa 'phrul gyi sgron me*
11 *rGya nag skag zlog ces bya ba'i gzungs*
12 *Lha srung spyi'i gser skyems dang 'phrin bcol nyung bsdus*
13 *bSang mchod yid bzhin nor bu*
14 *Gangs ti se'i gsol 'debs*
15 *bZang spyod 'chi bslu thar lam gsal byed*
16 *dGra lha'i gtor 'bul*
17 *Chos skyong mgon po dgra lha bcu gsum gyi bsangs mchod legs pa*
18 *Seng ge'i gdong pa can gyi mdo*
19 *Sri bzlog tsa kra bcu gsum pa*
20 *U rgyan pad mas mdzad pa'i lha mo brgyad kyi tshes grangs rtags pa*
21 *U rgyan pad ma 'byung gnas kyis mdzad pa'i dam sri g.yag ru dgra 'jom*
22 *bDud kyi zhal sgyur*
23 *lTo nag mtshan ma'i dgra zor*
24 *Zab don gcod kyi man ngag bsdus don len chags nyer gcig pa nyi zla kha sbyor*
25 *rGyal bas dri med lung gis bsngags pa'i rdo rje 'chang kun dga' bzang po'i zhabs kyi gsung rab glegs bam bzhi pa las dpal kun rig gi dkyil 'khor yongs rdzogs kyi sgrub thabs sgrib pa rnam sel*
26 *bCom ldan 'das mi 'khrugs pa'i sgo nas gshin po rjes su gzung pa'i cho ga*
27 *gSol 'debs le'u bdun ma'i lo rgyus rim pa phan yon*
28 *sNang srid mdzod phugs kyi gzhung dang 'grel pa 'phrul gyi sgron me*
29 *sTon pas lha klu mi gsum gyi slob ma la dpe bu tse rnam pa gsum gyis bon btsan pa'i mdo*

30 *sTon pas 'od zer spro ba'i mdo*

31 *gZer myig*
Edited and translated by A. H. Francke, 'gZer myig, a book of the Tibetan Bonpos', *Asia Major*, vol.1, 1924; vol.3, 1926; vol.4, 1927; vol.7, 1930; vol.1 (n.s.), 1949.

32 *Bod kyi jo mo ye shes mtscho rgyal gyi rnam thar mdzad tshul gab pa mngon du byung ba*

33 *sTon pas 'gro ba sems can gyi nyon mongs pa'i sgrib pa sbyong zhing thar par drong ba'i kun rig sgron ma'i cho ga bstan pa'i mdo (cha)*

34 *bDe bar gshegs pa'i bstan pa thams cad kyi snying po rig pa 'dzin pa'i sde snod rdo rje theg pa snga 'gyur rin po che'i rtogs pa brjod pa lha'i rnga bo che lta bu'i gtam*

35 *Gling bzhi bstan pa'i 'byung gnas* (manuscript of another version of *rGyal rabs Bon gyi 'byung gnas*)

36 *Vaidūrya dkar po* (by *Sangs rgyas rgya mtsho*)

37 *Phya rgya ltar gsang sngags spyi spungs 'gro lugs bris bskang*

38 *bsTan srung ma dam can rgya mtsho'i ming grangs*

39 *Bla ma ston pa pha bu bkra ba gnyis rnam thar*

40 *Lung drug gi 'grel pa*

41 *lTa ba seng ge sgra bsgrags pa*

42 *Man ngag 'khor ba dong sprug*

43 *sGrub thabs nor bu'i phreng ba'i lo rgyus dang po'i myu gu*

44 *rTa khyung 'bar ba'i me mchod me rlung 'khyil ba'i zhal shes gnad yig*

45 *Bla ma drag po rta khyung 'bar ba'i me mchod me rlung 'khyil ba*

46 *sNga 'gyur rnying ma la rgol ngan log rtog bzlog pa'i bstan bcos* (by *Kun mkhyen ngag gi dbang po*)

47 *Bla ma drag po rta khyung 'bar ba'i las byang bklags chog tu bsdebs*

48 *Gag pa gso ba'i thig bdud btsan 'phrang sel*

49 *Chos nyid nam mkha'i klong mdzod las, dus bzang yar ngo tshes bcu'i dus kyi mdzod pa dran pa'i gsol 'debs mthong ba rang gsol gyi gdams pa*

50 *rDo rje phur pa'i mo sgrub pa'i zin bris gsal ba'i me long*

51 *Bla bslu 'chi bdag gi g.yul las rgyal ba slob dpon chen pos gnang ba*

52 *Shi 'dre'i glud*

53 *gSang bdag dregs pa 'dul byed las tshogs dam sri'i glud mdos*

54 *Gag pa gso ba'i zin thig bdud bcom 'phrang sel*

55 *Srid pa gsal byed pra sen dbab pa'i man ngag gzhung gsal byed lag len dang bcas pa'i skor rnams*

56 *gDon khrol dang glud kyi cho ga kha skong sogs dang bcas*

57 *Bla ma rgyang 'bod kyi gsol 'debs mos gus snying gi gzeng 'debs*

58 *g.Yang 'gugs me tog char sil*

59 *Srog bskyed pa bzhi ldan gyi gto cho ga*

60 *Zhing lha bstod pa'i mchod chog gsol 'dod dgu'i sprin phung lo rtog 'phel byed*

61 *Lo glud 'gong po bkar las lan chags tshun byed*

62 *Zhing lha tshangs pa'i mchod chog g.yang skyabs dang 'brel ba gzhan phan mtha' yas dngos grub 'dod pa 'jo ba'i bum bzang*

63 *Ma mo'i 'khrugs bskong bya tshul nyes brgya'i tsha gdung sel ba chu shel dbang po* (by *Ngag dbang tshul khrims rnam rgyal*)

64 *Srog bdag yam shud dmar po'i thugs sprul bstan srung A khu btsan po dgra lha'i sgrub thabs gtor chog gi rim pa cha tshang ma*

65 *O rgyan bka' nan rab brjid don grub*
66 *mDos chog nam mkha'i mdzod* (by *Pad ma dkar po*, vol. *nya*)
67 *Bla ma rig 'dzin rgya mtsho mkha' 'gro chos skyong srung ma rnams dang phas kyi lha lngas skyob pa'i man ngag gdam*
68 *rTa glud*
69 *sDe brgyad kyi sgos mdos kyi gyer mchod* (by *Pad ma dkar po*, vol. *nya*)
70 *bSangs kyi cho ga dngos grub char 'bebs* (by *Ngag gi dbang phyug bstan 'dzin dpal*)
71 *Mi phyugs gang yin gyi rim gro'i glud rdzongs bya tshul*
72 *rTa phag yid bzhin nor bu las mun khrid 'od gsal khor yug*
73 *Theg chen gyi mngon pa'i sde snod las byung ba'i dbu ma'i skor gyi ming gi rnam grangs* (by *Klong rdol bla ma*)
74 *gNam sa snang brgyad ces bya ba theg pa chen po'i mdo*
75 *Lha mo brgyad rtsis gza' 'bras dang bcas*
76 Collection of *'Das log*
77 *sDom gsum rab tu dbye ba'i bstan bcos* (by *Sa skya pandita Kun dga' rgyal mtshan dpal bzang po*)
78 *bKa' gdams kyi skyes bu dam pa rnams kyi gsung bgros thor bu ba rnams*
79 *bKa' gdams kyi man ngag be'u bum mngon po'i 'grel ba* (Commentary by *Dol po pa* on the *bKa' gdams kyi man ngag be'u bum* by *Po to pa*)
80 *Jo bo yab sras kyi gsung 'gros pha chos rin po che'i gter mdzod byang chub sems dpa'i nor bu'i 'phreng ba rtsa 'grel*
81 *dPag bsam ljon bzang*
Edited by S. C. Das, Calcutta, 1908.
82 *Grub mtha' thams cad kyi khungs dang 'dod tshul ston pa legs bshad gsal ba'i me long*
83 *Zhi byed dang gcod yul gyi chos 'byung rin po che'i phreng ba thar pa'i rgyan*
84 *rGyud sde spyi'i rnam par bzhag pa* (by *Sa skya pa bSod nams rtse mo*)
85 *Chos 'byung* (by *dPa'o gtsug lag phreng ba*)
86 *Klu 'bum*
87 Chronicles of the Fifth Dalai Lama
88 *rLangs kyi gdung rgyud Po ti bse ru*
89 *Vaiḍūrya g.ya' sel* (by *Sangs rgyas rgya mtsho*)
90 *Chos 'byung* (by *Tāranātha*)
Edited by A. Schiefner, St Petersburg, 1868.
91 *Deb ther dmar po*
Edited as *The Red Annals, Part One*. Part I, Tibetan text. Gangtok 1961.
92 *Bar do thos grol*
93 *Lam rim chen mo* (by *Tsong kha pa*)
94 *sNgags rim* (by *Tsong kha pa*)
95 *rGyud kyi rgyal po dpal gsang ba 'dus pa'i man ngag rim pa lnga rab tu gsal ba'i sgron me* (by *Tsong kha pa*)
96 *gTor ma'i bshad khrid legs bshad don bsdus gzhan phan rab gsal* (by *dGe slong spong ba rdo rje*, vol. *kha*)
97 *dPal stag lung gzi'i gdung rabs zam ma chad par byon pa'i rnam thar ngo mtshar nor bu'i do shal skye dgu'i yid 'phrog*
98 *Lha chos dang mi chos 'bul ba'i bslab bya nor bu'i 'phreng ba* (by *sLob dpon sPong ba pa rDo rje ming can*)

99 *dPal gsang 'dus rten gyi dkyil 'khor phyin ci ma log pa'i gsal byed dngos grub kun byung* (by *Blo bzang don grub*)
100 *rDzogs pa chen po klong chen snying thig gi gdod ma'i mgon po'i lam gyi rim pa'i khrid yig ye shes bla ma* (by *Rang 'byung rdo rje 'jig med gling pa*)
101 *rGyud sde bzhi'i don rnam par bzhag pa sngags la 'jug pa'i sgo* (by *dKon mchog rgyal mtshan*)
102 *Grub pa'i mtha' rnam par bzhag pa'i thub bstan lhun po'i mdzes rgyan* (by *lCang skya Rol pa'i rdo rje*)
103 *Yon tan rin po che'i mdzod las 'bras bu'i theg pa'i rgya cher 'grel rnam mkhyen shing rta* (by *Rang byung rDo rje mkhyen brtse'i lha*)
104 *gSang ba sngags kyi rig pa 'dzin pa rnams la nye bar mkho ba'i dam tshig gi rdzas dang yo byad kyi rnam bzhag dngos grub gter mdzod* (by *bKra shis rdo rje*)
105 *Sa rnying bka' rgyud sogs kyi khyad par mgo smos tsam mu to'i rgyang 'bod kyi tshul du bya gtong snyan sgron bdud rtsi'i bkang gtor* (by *'Jam dbyangs bzhad pa*)
106 *rDzogs chen yang ti nag po'i mun khrid kyi zhal shes snyan khungs brgyud pa'i man ngag zhag bdun gyis sgrub thabs*
107 *rDzogs chen yang ti'i mun khrid bklags pas don grub*
108 *Chos 'byung bstan pa'i pad ma rgyas pa'i nyin byed* (by *Pad ma dkar po*)
109 *rGyal rabs 'phrul gyi lde mig gam deb ther dmar po 'm deb gsar ma*
110 *bKa' thang sde lnga*
111 *sBa bzhed*
Edited by R. A. Stein, Paris. 1961.
112 *Ma ni bka' 'bum*
113 *Chos 'byung* (by *Bu ston*)
Translated by E. Obermiller, *History of Buddhism (Chos-hbyung) by Bu-ston*, 2 volumes, Heidelberg, 1931 and 1932.
114 *Dam pa'i chos byung tshul bstan pa'i rgya mtshor 'jug pa'i gru chen*
115 *Deb ther sngon po* (by *gZhon nu dpal*)
Translated by G. N. Roerich, *The Blue Annals*, Royal Asiatic Society of Bengal Monograph Series, Vol.7, 2 volumes, Calcutta, 1949 and 1953.
116 *Dam chos yid bzhin gyi nor bu thar pa rin po che'i rgyan zhes bya ba theg pa chen po'i lam rim gyi bshad pa* (by *sGam po pa Dwags po lha rje*)
Translated by H. V. Guenther, *sGam-po-pa: The Jewel Ornament of Liberation*, London, 1959.
117 *rGyal rabs gsal ba'i me long*
Edited by B. I. Kuznetsov, Leiden, 1966.
118 *dPal na ro'i chos drug gi khrid yig bde chen gsal ba'i 'od zer stong ldan* (by *bTsun pa bSod nams rgyal mtshan dpal bzang po*)
119 *sTon pas gdul dka' btul nas bstan pa spel ba'i mdo ('Dus pa rin po che'i rgyud, nga)*
120 *Byams ma rtsa ba'i dkyil 'khor gyi cho ga bstan pa'i mdo* (*'Dus pa rin po che'i rgyud, tha*)
121 *bKa' gdams gsar rnying gi chos 'byung yid kyi mdzes rgyan* (by *bSod nams grags pa*)
122 *rNying ma rgyud 'bum dkar cag*
123 *gZi brjid rab tu 'bar ba'i mdo* (*'Dus pa rin po che'i rgyud dri ma med, ya*)
124 *rGyud sde spyi'i rnam par gzhag pa rgyas par brjod pa*
125 *bKa' gdams kyi rnam thar bka' gdams chos 'byung gsal ba'i sgron me*

126 *Be'u bum sngon po'i ming brda go dka' ba 'ga zhig bshad pa som nyid mun sel* (by *dByangs can dga' ba'i blo gros*)
127 *gSung 'bum* (Collected Works) of *Tsong kha pa*
gSung 'bum of *lCang skya rin po che Ngag dbang chos ldan*
128 *gSung 'bum* of *mKhas grub dge legs bzang po*
129 *gSung 'bum* of the first five *Sa skya* masters
130 *Grub mtha'i rnam bshad rang gzhan grub mtha' kun dang zab don mchog tu gsal ba kun bzang zhing gi nyi ma lung rigs rgya mtsho skye dgu'i re ba kun skong*
131 *'Dus pa rin po che'i rgyud dri ma med pa gzi brjid rab tu 'bar ba'i mdo*
132 *Sa bdag bshags 'bum*
133 *rGyal rabs rnams kyi byung tshul gsal ba'i me long* (Derge edition)
134 *gSung 'bum* of *Bu ston rin po che*
135 *gSung 'bum* of *mKhas grub rje* (*dGe legs dpal bzang po*)
136 *gSung 'bum* of *Klong rdol bla ma*
137 *gZhan stong khas len seng ge'i nga ro*
138 *Theg chen bsdus pa'i snying po mchan bcas*
139 *bKa' gdams glegs bam pha chos le tshan lnga*
140 *bKa' gdams bu chos le tsan gnyis dpe chos rin chen spungs pa*
141 *Man ngag rin chen spungs pa*
142 *gTam rgyud rin chen sgron ma'am rin chen phreng mdzes*
143 *gSung 'bum* of *Shes rab rgya mtsho*
144 *Kun mkhyen chos kyi rgyal po rig 'dzin 'Jigs med gling pa*
145 *gSung 'bum* of *Tāranātha*
146 *Lha rgyal bdud 'dul mthu bo che*
147 *sLob dpon chen po pad ma 'byung gnas kyis mdzad pa'i man ngag lta ba'i phreng ba'i mchan 'grel nor bu'i bang mdzod* (by *'Jam dbyangs blo gros rgya mtsho*)
148 *gCod yul kyi tshogs las yon tan kun ldan gyi dmigs rin bla ma'i gsung rgyun gyi zin bris shel dkar me long* (by *Ye shes dbang ldan*)
149 *Klong chen snying thig*
150 *dPag bsam ljon bzang*, Part III, *Re'u mig* (Chronological tables)
Edited by Lokesh Chandra, New Delhi, 1959.
151 *gSung 'bum* of *Pad ma dkar po*
152 *gSung 'bum* of *dGe 'dun grub*
153 *dGe ba'i bshes gnyen zhang sha ra ba yon tan grags kyis mdzad pa'i lam rim*
154 *rGyal ba'i bstan pa la 'jug pa'i rim pa skyes bu gsum gyi man ngag yid bzhin bdud rtsi nyin khu* (by *Tāranātha*)
155 *gSang ba bla med 'od gsal rdo rje snyin po'i gnas gsum gsal bar byed po'i tshig don* (by *Klong chen rab 'byams pa*)
156 *rDzogs pa chen po sems nyid rang grol* (by *Klong chen rab 'byams pa*)
157 *bsTan 'gro yongs la phan pa'i O rgyan sprul pa'i glegs bam* (by *Blo bde zhabs dkar*)
158 *rNam par 'dren pa mchog rnams kyi sku gam la mchod pa bya ba'i cho ga tshogs gnyis rin chen chu 'dzin*
159 *rMi lam bzang ngan brda brtags kyi rim pa*
160 *sTon pas theg pa bzhi pa srid gshen gyi bon gtan la phab pa'i mdo*
161 *bKa' zab mo shes rab pha rol tu phyin pa theg pa chen po yum gyi dkyil 'khor don bstan pa'i mdo*
162 *Dra ba nag po'i sgrub thabs drag po gnam lcags thog 'bebs*
163 *Dam can rgya mtsho mkha' la rang bzhin gyi mnga' gsol*

2 Books and articles

Aufschnaiter, P. (1956), 'Prehistoric sites discovered in inhabited regions of Tibet', *East and West*, vol.7, pp.74–88.

Bacot, J. (1921), *Trois Mystères tibétains*, Paris. (Translated into English as *Three Tibetan Mysteries*, London, 1924.)

(1925), *Le poète tibétain Milarepa*, Paris.

(1934–5), 'Le mariage chinois du roi tibétain Sroṅ bcan sgam po', *Mélanges chinoises et bouddhiques*, vol.3, pp.1–60.

(1937), *La vie de Marpa le 'traducteur'*, Paris.

Bacot, J., Thomas, F.W., Toussaint, G. C. (1940–6), *Documents de Touen-houang relatifs à l'histoire du Tibet*, Paris.

Bareau, A. (1961), 'Indian and ancient Chinese Buddhism: institutions analogous to the Jisa', *Comparative Studies in Society and History*, vol.3, no.4, pp.443–51.

Bell, C. A. (1924), *Tibet, Past and Present*, Oxford.

(1928), *The People of Tibet*, Oxford.

(1931), *The Religion of Tibet*, Oxford.

Blechsteiner, R. (1937), *Die gelbe Kirche*, Vienna.

Bogoslovskii, V. A. (1958a), 'K voprosu o nekotorykh terminakh v tibetskikh dokumentakh VII-IX' vv. *Filiologiya i istoriya mongol'skikh narodov*, Moscow, pp.323–32.

(1958b), *Nekotorye voprosy sotsialno-ekonomicheskikh i politicheskikh otnoshenii v Tibete VII-IX vv.*, Moscow.

(1961a), 'Nekotorye voprosy istorii Tibeta v osveshchenii bonskogo gyerapa,' *Kratkiye soobshcheniya Instituta Narodov Azii*, vol.57, pp.5–9.

(1961b), 'O nalagovykh terminakh v tibetskikh dokumentakh VII-IX' vv. *Kitai, Yaponiya, Istoria i filologiya.* K semidesyatiletiyu akademika N. I. Konrada. (Mélanges offerts a N. I. Konrad a l'occasion de son 70ᵉ anniversaire.), pp.58–65. Moscow.

(1962a), *Ocherk istorii tibetskogo naroda: stanovlenie klassogo obshchestva*, Moscow. (Translated into French as *Essai sur l'histoire du peuple tibétaine, ou, La naissance d'une société de classes*, Paris, 1972.)

(1962b), 'Dva otryvka iz tibetskogo apokrifa "Pyat' skazanii"', *Kratkiye soobshcheniya Instituta Narodov Azii*, vol.53, pp.56–64.

Campbell, W. L. (1919), *She-rab Dong-bu or Prajnya Danda by Lu-trub (Nagarjuna)*, Calcutta.

Carrasco, P. (1959), *Land and Polity in Tibet*, Seattle.

Chapman, F. S. (1938), *Lhasa, the Holy City*, London.

Combe, G. A. (1926), *A Tibetan on Tibet*, London.

Conze, E. (1957), 'Buddhism and Gnosis: Studies in the History of Religions', Supplements to *Numen*, Leiden, p.651.

Csoma de Körös, A. (1912), *Tibetan Studies. A Collection of his Contributions to the Journal of the Asiatic Society of Bengal*, edited by E. Denison Ross, Calcutta.

Das, S. C. (1881–2), 'Contributions on the religion, history, etc. of Tibet: I. The Bon (Pon) Religion', *Journal of the Asiatic Society of Bengal*, vol.50, no.2, pp.187–251, and vol.51, no.1, pp.1–75, 87–128.

(1891), 'Life of Atisa', *Journal of the Asiatic Society of Bengal*, vol.60, nos.1–3.

(1893a), 'The marriage customs of Tibet', *Journal of the Asiatic Society of Bengal*, vol.62, no.3.
(1893b), *Indian Pandits in the Land of Snow*, Calcutta.
(1902), *Journey to Lhasa and Central Tibet*, edited by W. W. Rockhill, London.
Dasgupta, S. B. (1958), *An Introduction to Tāntric Buddhism*, Calcutta.
David-Neel, A. (1929), *Mystiques et magiciens au Tibet*, Paris. (Translated into English as *With Magicians and Mystics in Tibet*, London, 1931, later editions retitled *Magic and Mystery in Tibet*.)
(1930), *Initiations lamaïques, des théories, des practiques, des hommes*, Paris. (Translated into English as *Initiations and Initiates in Tibet*, London, 1931.)
(1931), *La Vie surhumaine de Guésar de Ling*, Paris. (Translated into English as *The Superhuman Life of Gesar of Ling*, London, 1933, revised edition 1959.)
(1952), *Textes tibétains inédits*, Paris.
Demiéville, P. (1952), *Le Concile de Lhasa*, I, Paris.
(1962), 'Quelques traits de moeurs barbares dans une chantefable chinoise des T'ang', *Acta Orientalia Academiae Scientarum Hungaricae*, vol.15, pp.71–85.
Duncan, M. H. (1955), *Harvest Festival Dramas of Tibet*, Hong Kong.
(1964), *Customs and Superstitions of Tibetans*, London.
Eberhard, W. (1942), *Kultur und Siedlung der Randvölker Chinas*, Leiden.
Ekvall, R. B. (1939), *Cultural Relations on the Kansu-Tibetan Border*, Chicago.
(1952), *Tibetan Skylines*, London.
(1954a), 'Some differences in Tibetan land tenure and utilization', *Sinologica*, vol.4, no.1, pp.39–48.
(1954b), *Tentes contre le ciel*, Paris. (Also appeared in English as *Tents Against the Sky*, London, 1954.)
(1960), 'Three categories of inmates within Tibetan monasteries: status and function', *Central Asiatic Journal*, vol.5, no.3, pp.206–20.
(1964), *Religious Observances in Tibet; Patterns and Function*, Chicago.
Evans-Wentz, W. Y. (1951), *Tibet's Great Yogi Milarepa*, London.
(1954), *The Tibetan Book of the Great Liberation*, London.
(1957), *The Tibetan Book of the Dead*, London.
Ferrari, A. (1958), *Mk'yen Brtse's Guide to the Holy Places of Central Tibet*, Rome.
Festugière, A. M. J. (1965), *Enquête sur les moines d'Égypte* (Historia monachorum in Aegypto; Les Moines d'Orient, vol.4, part 1), Paris.
Filchner, W. (1933), *Kumbum Dschamba Ling, das Kloster der hunderttausend Bilder Maitreyas*, Leipzig.
Francke, A. H. (1901), 'A Ladakh Bon po Hymnal', *Indian Antiquary*, vol.30.
(1905), 'The eighteen songs of the Bono-na festival', *Indian Antiquary*, vol.34.
(1907), *A History of Western Tibet*, London.
(1909), 'The ancient historical songs of Western Tibet', *Indian Antiquary*, vol.28.
(1914), *Antiquities of Indian Tibet*, part 1, Calcutta.
(1923), *Tibetische Hochzeitslieder*, Hagen und Darmstadt.
Francke, A. H., Ribbach, S., Shave, F. (1902), 'Ladakhi songs', *Indian Antiquary*, vol.31.
Gabain, A. von (1961), *Das uigurische Königreich von Chotscho 850–1250 (Sitzungsberichte Dtsch. AdW zu Berlin, Kl.f.Sprachen, Literatur u. Kunst, Jg. 1961 Nr.5, Berlin)*.

Getty, A. (1928), *The Gods of Northern Buddhism*, Oxford, 2nd edn.
Goldman, B. (1961), 'Some aspects of the animal deity: Luristan, Tibet and Italy', *Ars Orientalis*, vol.4, pp.287ff.
Gordon, A. K. (1959), *The Iconography of Tibetan Lamaism*, Rutland and Tokyo, 2nd edn.
(1963), *Tibetan Religious Art*, New York, 2nd edn.
Govinda, A. (1959), *Foundations of Tibetan Mysticism*, London. (2nd, revised and enlarged edition of the work first published in German as *Grundlagen tibetischen Mystik*, Zürich and Stuttgart, 1956.)
Grünwedel, A. (1900), *Mythologie des Buddhismus in Tibet und der Mongolei*, Leipzig.
(1915), *Der Weg nach Sambhala*, Munich (Abh.Kgl.Bayer.Ak.d.Wiss.).
(1919), *Die Tempel von Lhasa*, Heidelberg.
Guenther, H. V. (1959), *sGam-po-pa's Jewel Ornament of Liberation*, London.
(1963), *The Life and Teaching of Nāropa*, Oxford.
(1966), *Tibetan Buddhism without Mystification*. The Buddhist Way from Original Tibetan Sources. Leiden. (US edition, without Tibetan texts, entitled *Treasures on the Tibetan Middle Way*, Berkeley, 1971.)
Hackin, J. (1928), *Mythologie du lamaïsme*. (Tibet, Mythologie Asiatique illustrée.) Paris.
Haenisch, E. (1940), *Steuergerechtsame der chinesischen Klöster unter der Mongolenherrschaft*, Leipzig. (Berichte über die Verhandlungen der Sächsischen Akademie der Wissenschaften zu Leipzig, Philologisch-historische Klasse, 92 Bd.)
Hermanns, M. (1946–9), 'Schöpfungs- und Abstammungsmythen der Tibeter', *Anthropos*, vol.41–4, pp.275–98, 817–47.
(1948), 'Überlieferungen der Tibeter', *Monumenta Serica*, vol.13, pp.161–208.
(1949), *Die Nomaden von Tibet*, Vienna.
(1956), *Mythen und Mysterien der Tibeter*, Cologne.
Hoffmann, H. (1950a), 'Die Gräber der tibetischer Könige', *Nachrichten d.Akad.d. Wissenschaften in Göttingen*, vol.1.
(1950b), *Quellen zur geschichte der tibetischen Bon-Religion*, Wiesbaden.
(1950c), 'Die Qarlug in der tibetischen Literatur', *Oriens*, vol.3, p.190.
(1956), *Die Religionen Tibets*, Freiburg i.Br. (Translated into English as *The Religions of Tibet*, London, 1961.)
(1960), 'Manichaeism and Islam in the Buddhist Kâlacakra system', Proceedings of the IXth International Congress for the History of Religions, Tokyo and Kyoto 1958, Tokyo, pp.96–9.
(1964), 'Das Kalacakra, die letzte Phase des Buddhismus in Indien', *Saeculum*, vol.15, no.2, pp.125–31.
(1967), 'Žaṅ-žuṅ: the holy language of the Tibetan Bon-po', *Zeitschrift der Deutschen Morgenländischen Gesellschaft*, vol.117, pp.376–81.
Hummel, S. (1949), *Elemente der tibetischen Kunst*, Leipzig.
(1953), *Geschichte der tibetischen Kunst*, Leipzig.
(1957a), 'Die heilige Höhle in Tibet', *Anthropos*, vol.52, pp.623–31.
(1957b), 'Eine Jenseits-Darstellung aus Tibet', *Acta Ethnographica Academiae Scientiarum Hungaricae*, vol.6, nos.1–2, p.233.

(1958), 'Der Hund in der religiösen Vorstellungswelt des Tibeters', *Paideuma*, vol.6, no.8, pp.500–9.

(1959), 'Eurasiatische Traditionen in der tibetischen Bon-Religion', *Opuscula Ethnologica Memoriae Ludovici Biro Sacra*, pp.165–212.

(1960), 'Der magische Stein in Tibet', *International Archives of Ethnology*, vol.49, pp.224–40.

(1961), 'Die Leichenbestattung in Tibet', *Monumenta Serica*, vol.20, pp.266–81.

(1963), 'Günstige und ungünstige Zeiten und Zeichen nach dem Tibetischen des Chags-med-rin-po-che', *Asian Folklore Studies*, vol.22, pp.89–132.

(1963–64), 'Tibetische Architektur', *Bulletin der Schweizerischen Gesellschaft für Anthropologie und Ethnologie*, vol.40, pp.62–95.

(1964), 'Kosmische Strukturpläne der Tibeter', *Geographica Helvetica*, vol.19, pp.34–41.

(1965a), 'Die Kathedrale von Lhasa, Imago Mundi und Heilsburg', *Antaios*, vol.7, no.3, pp.280–90.

(1965b), 'Die Steinreihen des tibetischen Megalithikums und die Ge-sar-Sage', *Anthropos*, vol.60, pp.833–8.

Iwai, H. (1955), 'The word Pieh-ch'i *Beki* and Mongol Shamans', *Memoirs of the Research Department of the Toyo Bunko*, No.14.

Jackson, A. (1965), 'Mo-so magical texts', *Bulletin of the John Rylands Library*, Manchester, vol.48, pp.141–74.

Kawaguchi, E. (1909), *Three Years in Tibet*, Madras.

Kolmaš, J. (1967), *Tibet and Imperial China*, Canberra. (Australian National University, Centre of Oriental Studies. Occasional Papers, No.7.)

Lalou, M. (1949), 'Les chemins du mort dans les croyances de Haute Asie', *Revue de l'Histoire des Religions*, vol.135, no.1, pp.42–8.

(1952), 'Rituel Bon-po des funérailles Royales', *Journal Asiatique*, vol.240, no.3, pp.339–62.

(1953), 'Tibétain ancien Bod/Bon', *Journal Asiatique*, vol.241, no.2, pp.275–6.

(1957), *Les religions du Tibet*, Paris.

(1958), 'Fiefs, poisons et guérisseurs', *Journal Asiatique*, vol.246, pp.157–268.

(1939–61), *Inventaire des manuscrits tibétains de Touen-houang conservés à la Bibliothèque Nationale* (Fonds Pelliot tibétain), vols 1–3, Paris.

Laufer, B. (1901), 'Über ein tibetisches Geschichtswerk der Bon po', *T'oung Pao*, vol.2, no.1, pp.24–44.

(1908), 'Die Bru-ža-Sprache und die historische Stellung des Padmasambhava,' *T'oung Pao*, vol.9, pp.1–46.

(1911), *Der Roman einer tibetischen Königin* (bTsun-mo bka'-thang), Leipzig.

(1914), 'Bird divination among the Tibetans, with a study of the phonology of the ninth century', *T'oung Pao*, vol.15, pp.1–110.

(1923), *Use of Human Skulls and Bones in Tibet*, Chicago. (Field Museum of Natural History, Anthropology Leaflet No.10.)

Lessing, F. (1935), 'Wesen und Sinn des lamaistischen Rituals', *Hyllningsskrift tillägnad Sven Hedin*, Stockholm.

(1942), *Yung-ho-kung; An Iconography of the Lamaist Cathedral in Peking with Notes on Lamaist Mythology and Cult*. Vol.1. (Sino-Swedish Expedition, vol.8, part 1.) Stockholm.

(1951), 'Calling the soul: a lamaist ritual', *Semitic and Oriental Studies*, vol.11, pp.263–84.

(1954), *The Eighteen Worthies Crossing the Sea* (Report from the Scientific Expedition to the North-Western Provinces of China under the leadership of Dr Sven Hedin), Stockholm.

Lessing, F. and Wayman, A. (1968), *mKhas grub rje's Fundamentals of the Buddhist Tantras* (translated from the Tibetan), The Hague.

Li An-che (1945), 'The Sakya sect of Lamaism', *Journal of the West China Border Research Society*, vol.16, pp.72–86 (Series A).

(1948a), 'Rñinmapa, the early form of Lamaism', *Journal of the Royal Asiatic Society*, pp.142–63.

(1948b), 'Bon: the magico-religious belief of the Tibetan-speaking peoples', *South-Western Journal of Anthropology*, vol.4, pp.31–42.

(1949), 'The Bkaḥ-Brgyud sect of Lamaism', *Journal of the American Oriental Society*, vol.69, no.2, pp.51–9.

Li Fang-kuei (1956), 'The inscription of the Sino-Tibetan treaty of 821–822', *T'oung Pao*, vol.44, pp.1–99.

Macdonald, A. D. (1962), 'Note sur la diffusion de la théorie des quatre fils du ciel au Tibet', *Journal Asiatique* vol.250, pp.231–48.

(1966), 'Histoire et philologie Tibétaines'. École pratique des Hautes Études IVe Section: Sciences historiques et philologiques, p.479.

Macdonald, A. W. (1952), 'Une note sur les mégalithes tibétains', *Journal Asiatique*. vol.241, pp.63–76.

(1966), 'Les Tamang vus par l'un d'eux', *L'Homme*, vol.6, no.1, pp.27–58.

(1967), *Matériaux pour l'étude de la littérature populaire Tibétaine*, vol.1. (Annales du Musée Guimet, Bibliographie d'Études vol.72), Paris.

Macdonald, D. (1929), *The Land of the Lama*, London.

(1930), *Moeurs et Coutumes des Tibétains*, Paris.

Migot, A. (1955), *Tibetan Marches*, New York.

Nagao, G. (1954), *Chibetto Bukkyō Kenkyū*, Tokyo.

Nebesky-Wojkowitz, R. (1947), 'Die tibetische Bön-Religion', *Archiv für Völkerkunde*, vol.2, pp.26–68.

(1956), *Oracles and Demons of Tibet*, The Hague.

Neumaier, E. (1966), *Mātarah und ma-mo, Studien zur Mythologie des Lamaismus* (Inaugural-Dissertation), Munich.

Obermiller, E. (1931, 1932), *History of Buddhism (Chos-hbyung) by Bu-ston*, 2 vols, Heidelberg.

Pavry, J. D. C. (1929), *The Zoroastrian Doctrine of a Future Life*, 2nd edn, New York.

Pelliot, P. (1961), *Histoire ancienne du Tibet*, Paris.

Petech, L. (1939), *A Study on the Chronicles of Ladakh*, Calcutta.

(1952–56), *I missionari italiani nel Tibet e nel Nepal*, 7 vols, Rome.

(1967), 'Glosse agli Annali di Tun-Huang', *Rivista degli Studi Orientali*, vol.42, pp.241–79.

Pignède, B. (1966), *Les Gurungs, une population himalayenne du Nepal*, The Hague. (École pratique des Hautes Études, 1966.)

Ratchnewsky, P. (1954), 'Die mongolischen Grosskhane und die buddhistische Kirche', *Asiatica* (Festschrift Weller), Leipzig, pp.489–504.

Ribbach, S. H. (1940), *Drogpa Namgyal. Ein Tibeterleben*, Munich.

Richardson, H. E. (1949), 'Three ancient inscriptions from Tibet', *Journal of the Royal Asiatic Society of Bengal*, Letters, vol.15, no.1, pp.45–64.

(1952), *Ancient Historical Edicts at Lhasa*, London.

(1952–53), 'Tibetan inscriptions at Žva-ḥi Lha khaṇ', *Journal of the Royal Asiatic Society*, 1952, pp.133–154 and 1953, pp.1–12.

(1957), 'A Tibetan inscription from Rgyal Lha-khaṇ; and a note on Tibetan chronology from A.D.841 to A.D.1042', *Journal of the Royal Asiatic Society*, pp.57–78.

(1958–9), 'The Karmapa sect, a historical note', *Journal of the Royal Asiatic Society*, 1958, pp.139–64 and 1959, pp.1–18.

(1964), 'A new inscription of Khri Srong Lde Brtsan', *Journal of the Royal Asiatic Society*, 1964, pp.1–13.

Rock, J. F. (1937), 'The birth and origin of Dto-mba Shi-lo the founder of the Mo-so shamanism', *Artibus Asiae*, vol.7, pp.5–85.

(1952a), *The Na-khi Nāga Cult and Related Ceremonies*, Rome.

(1952b), 'The [2]Muan [1]Bpö ceremony, or the sacrifice to heaven as practised by the [1]Na-[2]khi', *Annali Lateranensi*, vol.16 (previously published in *Monumenta Serica*, vol.13, 1948).

(1955), 'The [1]D'a [2]No funeral ceremony with special reference to the origin of the [1]Na-[2]khi weapons', *Anthropos*, vol.50, pp.1–31.

(1956), *The Amnye Ma-Chhen Range and Adjacent Regions*, Rome.

(1959), 'Contributions to the Shamanism of the Tibetan-Chinese borderland', *Anthropos*, vol.54, pp.796–818.

(1963), *A Na-khi-English Encyclopedic Dictionary*, Part 1, Rome.

Rockhill, W. W. (1891), *Land of the Lamas*, New York.

(1895), 'Notes on the ethnology of Tibet', Smithsonian Institution, Washington, Annual Report for 1893, pp.665–747.

(1910), 'The Dalai Lama of Lhasa and their relations with the Mandchu emperors of China 1644–1908', *T'oung Pao*, vol.11, pp.1–104.

Roerich, G. (1930), 'The animal style among the nomad tribes of Northern Tibet', *Skythika*, Prague, vol.13, pp.27–44.

(1933), *Sur les Pistes de l'Asie Centrale*, Paris.

(1949, 1953), *The Blue Annals*, 2 vols, Calcutta. (Royal Asiatic Society of Bengal Monograph Series, No.7.)

Róna Tas, A. (1955), 'Social terms in the list of grants of the Tibetan Tunhuang Chronicle', *Acta Orientalia Academiae Scientiarum Hungaricae*, vol.5, no.3, pp.249–70.

(1956), 'Tally-stick and divination-dice in the iconography of Lhamo', *Acta Orientalia Academiae Scientiarum Hungaricae*, vol.6, pp.163–79.

Ruegg, D. S. (1962), 'A propos of a recent contribution to Tibetan and Buddhist studies', *Journal of the American Oriental Society*, vol.82, no.3, pp.320–31.

(1963), 'The Jo naṇ pas, a school of Buddhist Ontologists, according to the Grub mtha' šel gyi me loṇ', *Journal of the American Oriental Society*, vol.83, no.1, pp.73–91.

(1964), 'Sur les rapports entre le Bouddhisme et le "substrat religieux" indien et tibétain', *Journal Asiatique*, vol.252, pp.77–95.

(1966), *The Life of Bu ston Rin po che with the Tibetan text of the Bu ston rNam thar*, Rome.

Sakai, S. (1956), *Chibetto Mikkyō Kyorino Kenkyū*, Kōyasan.

Schmid, T. (1952), *The Cotton-clad Mila: The Tibetan Poet-Saint's Life in Picture*, Stockholm.

(1958), *The Eighty-Five Siddhas*, Stockholm.

Schröder, D. (1942–45), 'Das Herbst-Dankopfer der T'ujen im Sining-Gebiet, Nordwest-China', *Anthropos*, vol.37–40, pp.867–73.

(1952), 'Zur Religion der T'ujen des Siningebietes', *Anthropos*, vol.47, pp.1–79, 620–658, 822–870.

Schulemann, G. (1958), *Geschichte des Dalai-Lamas*, 2nd edn, Leipzig.

Shelton, A. L. (1925), *Tibetan Folk-Tales*, St Louis.

Siiger, H. (1951), 'Dancing pilgrims from Tibet', *Geografisk Tidskrift*, vol.51.

Simon, W. (1955), 'A note on Tibetan Bon', *Asia Major*, vol.5 (n.s.), pp.6–8.

Snellgrove, D. L. (1957), *Buddhist Himalaya*, Oxford.

(1967), *The Nine Ways of Bon*, London.

Snellgrove, D. L., and Richardson, H. E. (1968), *A Cultural History of Tibet*, New York.

Soymié, M. (1966), 'Notes d'iconographie chinoise: les acolytes de Ti-tsang', *Arts Asiatiques*, vol.14, pp.45–78.

Stein, R. A. (1956), *L'Épopée tibétaine de Gesar dans sa version lamaïque de Ling*, Paris.

(1957a), 'Architecture et pensée religieuse en Extrême-Orient', *Arts Asiatiques*, vol.4, no.3, pp.163–86.

(1957b), 'L'habitat, le monde et le corps humain en Extrême-Orient et en Haute-Asie', *Journal Asiatique*, vol.245, no.1, pp.37–74.

(1957c), 'Le liṅga des danses masquées lamaïques et la théorie des âmes', *Sino-Indian Studies*, vol.5, nos 3–4, pp.200–34.

(1957d), 'Les K'iang des marches sino-tibétaines, example de continuité de la tradition', *Annuaire 1957–1958 de l'Ecole Pratique des Hautes Etudes*, Section Sciences Religieuses, Paris.

(1958), 'Peintures tibétaines de la vie de Gesar', *Arts Asiatiques*, vol.5, pp.243–71.

(1959a), *Recherches sur l'épopée et la barde au Tibet*, Paris.

(1959b), *Les Tribus anciennes des marches sino-tibétaines*, Paris.

(1961), *Une Chronique ancienne de bSam yas*, Paris.

(1962a), *La Civilisation tibétaine*, Paris. (Translated into English as *Tibetan Civilization*, London, 1972.)

(1962b), 'Une source ancienne pour l'histoire de l'épopée tibetaine; le Rlaṇs Po-ti bse-ru', *Journal Asiatique*, vol.250, pp.77–106.

(1963), 'Deux notules d'histoire ancienne du Tibet', *Journal Asiatique*, vol.251, pp.327–35.

Stubel, H. (1958), *The Mewu Fantzu. A Tibetan Tribe of Kansu*, New Haven.

Tafel, A. (1914), *Meine Tibetreise*, Stuttgart.

Thomas, F. W. (1935–55), *Tibetan Literary Texts and Documents concerning Chinese Turkestan*, Parts I to III, London.

Toussaint, G. C. (1933), *Le Dict de Padma*, Paris.

Tucci, G. (1932–1941), *Indo-Tibetica*, 7 vols, Rome.

(1947), 'The validity of Tibetan historical tradition', *India Antiqua*, Leiden, pp.309–22.
(1949), *Tibetan Painted Scrolls*, 3 vols, Rome.
(1950), *The Tombs of the Tibetan Kings*, Rome.
(1955), 'The sacred character of the kings of ancient Tibet', *East and West*, vol.6, no.3, pp.197–205.
(1956a), 'The symbolism of the temples of bSam-yas', *East and West*, vol.6, no.4, pp.279–81.
(1956b), *To Lhasa and Beyond*, Rome.
(1956c), *Preliminary Report on Two Scientific Expeditions in Nepal*, Rome.
(1958), *Minor Buddhist Texts*, Part II, Rome.
(1959), 'A Hindu image in the Himalayas', *Asia Major*, vol.7 (n.s.), pp. 170–5.
(1961), *The Theory and Practice of the Mandala*, London.
(1962), 'The wives of Sroṅ btsan sgam po', *Oriens Extremus*, vol.9, pp.121–130.
(1963), 'Oriental notes, II', *East and West*, vol.14, pp.146–82.
(1966), *Tibetan Folk Songs*, 2nd edn. Ascona.
(1967), *Tibet Land of Snows*, London.
Uray, G. (1960), 'The four horns of Tibet according to the Royal Annals', *Acta Orientalia Academiae Scientarium Hungaricae*, vol.10, no.1, pp.31–57.
(1964), 'The Old Tibetan verb Bon', *Acta Orientalia Academiae Scientarium Hungaricae*, vol.17, no.3, pp.323–34.
Waddell, L. A. (1895), *The Buddhism of Tibet, or Lamaism*, London.
(1905), *Lhasa and its Mysteries: With a Record of the Expedition of 1903–04*, London.
Wayman, A. (1962), 'Female energy and symbolism in the Buddhist Tantras', *History of Religions*, vol.2, pp.73–111.
Wylie, T. V. (1962), *The Geography of Tibet according to the 'Dzam-gling rgyas-bshad*, Rome.
(1963), ''O-lde-spu-rgyal and the introduction of Bon to Tibet', *Central Asiatic Journal*, vol.8, no.2, pp.93–103.
(1964a), 'Mar-pa's tower: notes on local hegemons in Tibet', *History of Religions*, vol.3, no.2, pp.278–91.
(1964b), 'Ro-langs: the Tibetan zombie', *History of Religions*, vol.4, no.1, pp.69–80.
(1965), 'Mortuary customs at Sa-skya, Tibet', *Harvard Journal of Asiatic Studies*, vol.25, pp.229–35.
Yu Dawchyuan (1930), *Love Songs of the Sixth Dalai Lama*, Peiping (Academica Sinica).

Index

Note

Entries are alphabetized as in English, including Tibetan prefix letters; *brgyud* comes under B, not G. Tibetan ' and Sanskrit diacritic marks are ignored in this respect. While this procedure will probably seem inelegant to Tibetanists, the object is to make the index usable to non-specialists, who are otherwise unlikely to know whether to look for *brgyud* under B, R, G or Y. The brief definitions of terms, and the extensive cross-referencing, are also supplied to help the non-Tibetanist find his or her way around a complex technical vocabulary. In particular, a number of terms are referred to in more than one form in the text (e.g. *longs sku, longs spyod sku* and *saṃbhogakāya* all represent the same thing) and I have tried to cross-reference fully in all these cases, and also to distinguish between different meanings of the same term where these occur. The definitions are taken, as far as possible, from the text, and in any case refer to the meanings of terms as they are used in the book; some terms have other meanings also. Pronunciations (preceded by pr.) are given for Tibetan proper names, and some important technical terms; they follow the system used in R. A. Stein's *Tibetan Civilization* (London, 1972). In these pronunciations the final *h* represents aspiration in *kh, ph, th, chh* and *tsh* (i.e. *tsh* is pronounced as in ca*t's-h*air not as in ha*t-sh*elf, and *th* as in pi*t-h*ead not as in *th*ank). *sh* and *ch* are however pronounced as in English *sh*ore, *ch*urch. S = Sanskrit, T = Tibetan, n = name or note. An asterisk * indicates a place shown on one of the maps.

G.B.S.